Educating the Prince

Educating the Prince

Essays in Honor of Harvey Mansfield

Edited by
Mark Blitz and William Kristol

ROWMAN & LITTLEFIELD PUBLISHERS, INC.
Lanham • Boulder • New York • Oxford

ROWMAN & LITTLEFIELD PUBLISHERS, INC.

Published in the United States of America
by Rowman & Littlefield Publishers, Inc.
4720 Boston Way, Lanham, Maryland 20706
http://www.rowmanlittlefield.com

12 Hid's Copse Road
Cumnor Hill, Oxford OX2 9JJ, England

British Library Cataloguing in Publication Information Available

Library of Congress Cataloging-in-Publication Data

Machiavellianism and its alternatives : essays in honor of Harvey Mansfield / edited by
Mark Blitz and William Kristol.
    p. cm.
  Includes bibliographical references and index.
  ISBN 0-7425-0827-7 (alk. paper)
    1. Political science—History. 2. Liberalism. 3. United States—Politics and government.
  4. Political science—United States. 5. Political ethics. I. Mansfield, Harvey Claflin,
  1932- II. Blitz, Mark. III. Kristol, William.

JA83 .M245 2000
320.1—dc21

                                         00-037283

Printed in the United States of America

♾™ The paper used in this publication meets the minimum requirements of
American National Standard for Information Sciences—Permanence of Paper
for Printed Library Materials, ANSI/NISO Z39.48-1992.

To Harvey Mansfield
teacher and friend.

Contents

Part II: The Liberal Regime

Part III: America, Constitutionalism, and Statesmanship

Introduction

William Kristol

If justice is giving to each his due, this volume is an injustice. I am confident I speak for all the contributors to this volume when I assert that these efforts of his students fall short of what Harvey Mansfield deserves. Does this make Harvey Mansfield a teacher of injustice?

We rather hope not. We hope, instead, that the essays collected here will give some sense of the breadth and depth of Mansfield's achievement. Even more, we hope that they will send the reader back to Mansfield's own work, to which we provide a bibliography, and to his distinctive contributions as a political philosopher, a political scientist, and as an American.

While Mansfield has taught and written widely in the field of political philosophy, his most extensive work has been on Machiavelli. That Mansfield has become our pre-eminent interpreter of one of the pre-eminent political philosophers is no small thing, and his translations, commentaries, and essays on Machiavelli are an extraordinary achievement. But Mansfield has not just thought *about* Machiavelli. He has thought *along with* Machiavelli. That means thinking along with the great alternatives to Machiavelli. Mansfield's work, centered or apparently centered on Machiavelli, is a major contribution to political philosophy simply.

One of the fundamental alternatives to Machiavelli is of course Aristotle, the founder of political science. In addition to being a political philosopher, Mansfield is a political scientist—perhaps the leading Aristotelian political scientist of our time, perhaps therefore the leading political scientist of our time. Mansfield's genuinely original contribution in political science is to have laid bare many of the fundamental structures of the modern liberal regime, from indirect government to representation to political parties to the executive power. Mansfield has uncovered in the history of political theory the grounds of these forms of liberal democracy that we now take for granted, and he has done so in a way that does full justice to the complexities of history and political practice. He has demonstrated what is distinctively modern about the modern liberal regime, but also has shown how the liberal regime can be understood as a kind of mixed regime in an Aristotelian sense. In doing so he has greatly deepened our understanding of our history, our institutions, and our current situation.

Nor has Mansfield shied away from directly addressing our current American situation. Mansfield's occasional essays, commenting on various elections, the media, Clinton's impeachment, and the like, are of more than occasional interest. Mansfield has uncovered the deeper issues implicated in the events and arguments of the day, and has done so without distorting the contingent particularity of political events. But Mansfield has approached America as a citizen, albeit as one informed by his political science. He has made the case for constitutionalism, self-government, and deliberation in an age of informality, entitlement, and liberation, in ways both bracing and illuminating. He has sought to help his fellow Americans to succeed in our honorable effort to vindicate the capacity of mankind for self-government.

A word about Mansfield the man. That word is courage. Courage is the first of the virtues. Mansfield has it in spades. Of course he has had the intellectual courage to think things through to their conclusion, and to resist the temptation of being merely provocative or edifying. But it is Mansfield's moral courage that has emboldened him to fight unpopular and principled battles against the degradation of his beloved Harvard, which he attended and where he has taught for virtually his entire academic career.

All the contributors to this volume worked with Harvey Mansfield on their Ph.D. dissertations at Harvard. Several also studied with him as undergraduates. Mark Blitz and I would like to thank them for contributing such fine essays for this volume, and to express our regret that considerations of space prevented us from soliciting contributions from yet more of the many beneficiaries of Mansfield's gentle but powerful intellectual guidance. We would also like to thank Delba Winthrop (Mrs. Harvey Mansfield) for her help and encouragement; Steven Lenzner, a graduate student at Harvard, for his assistance on the indexes and the bibliography; and Jed Lyons, Steve Wrinn, Mary Carpenter, and Dawn Stoltzfus, all of Rowman & Littlefield, for being exemplary editors and publishers. Above all, we thank Harvey Mansfield, our teacher and friend, and hope he will overcome his customary modesty and relax his usual standards to take pride in this tribute.

PART I

MACHIAVELLIANISM
AND ITS ALTERNATIVES

1

Virtue, Modern and Ancient

Mark Blitz

Are there distinctly modern virtues? Or were all the true virtues sufficiently uncovered by the ancients? This question is important as such, and as part of the issue of the differences between the ancients and the moderns. Indeed, if modernity is rooted in, or visibly shaped by, a change in political philosophy, the problem of virtue would be the heart of this issue.

Clearly, several qualities that we moderns think are good were not praised or discussed by the ancients, at least in so many words. "Niceness," tolerance, industry, and responsibility come more or less immediately to mind. Yet, almost anyone who reads Aristotle's *Ethics* or Plato's dialogues is struck by how little has changed. The question, then, is whether the moderns simply add to, subtract from, or rename what Aristotle uncovers, without changing it fundamentally, or whether they grasp things differently at root. If the modern discussion of virtue is genuinely new, is this because the ancients failed to discover or account for phenomena that then form the ground of "modern" virtues; or is it because modern thought and opinion simply choose to emphasize the worth of things that the ancients understood but evaluated differently? What I will do is to analyze briefly the four virtues I mentioned, concentrating on responsibility.[1] I will then try to point out their distinctly unifying modern qualities. This will set the stage for the broader questions, which I will again raise, but upon which I will merely touch.

I

Let us begin with "niceness." When someone, normally a child, is told to be "nice" it is usually after he has done something rotten such as destroying his sister's elaborate sandcastle or dollhouse, often cackling with pleasure at his handiwork. Not to be nice is to pay little or no attention to others' happiness and desires while one is pursuing one's own interest, however fleeting and casual. In the more extreme case it is occasionally to enjoy causing someone else's unhappiness; in the still more extreme sense it is to be a habitually malicious bully. For tamed adults, the equivalent is to be nice by not being sarcastic, ironic, or as is sometimes now said, "hurtful." To be nice means to not be "bad" in the sense of not being selfish, "mean," or spiteful, or to be good in the sense of being helpful or "kind."

Occasionally, we tell a child to be nice after she has done something intrusively annoying, such as incessantly whining or complaining. "Please be nice, and leave me alone for a minute." Here, to be nice means not to be thoughtless and "inconsiderate." It is not merely that someone nice pays attention to others' interests, but primarily that one pays attention to them, or to their feelings, as one pursues one's own interests. Sometimes, indeed, we prospectively enjoin or beg a child to be nice when his grandparents are about to visit, for example, and his parents are afraid that he will be his usual rude, distant, and selfish self. Here, to be nice is to go a bit out of one's way in order to be considerate. It means to attend, at least a little, directly to others. So to begin with, to be nice is to be helpful or considerate, or more often not to be inconsiderate or mean. Nice people are well mannered and well behaved ("civil," not rude), though not, as such, outstandingly courteous.

The case in which a child willfully spills his milk nicely combines the nuances of this meaning: the child is not "nice" because he intentionally makes someone unhappy by inconsiderately forcing her to attend to him. (This is early training for the characteristic adolescent nastiness of purposely ruining one's parents' pleasant evening by forcing them to bail you out of trouble.) Perhaps the best example is the evil mother beloved of stage and screen who chooses the moment of her spinster daughter's first important date to think that she has become, or merely to pretend to think that she has become, deathly ill. The nice person does not "impose" herself on others; the mean person inconsiderately imposes herself on others; the truly mean, or malicious, person imposes herself on others primarily in order to make them miserable.

We can approach the second major sense of being "nice" if we consider what we mean when we speak of a "nice" teacher or boss. The nice employer or professor is one who is not demanding. He forgives mistakes easily. He listens to excuses and allows himself to be swayed by them. He is willing to accept late papers and to let people leave fifteen minutes early on Friday afternoon. He is not a rigid stickler for bureaucratic rules and standards or for the set forms by which tasks are supposed to be carried out. To be nice in this sense is a variant of being merciful: to be nice is to be flexible, to be willing to bend, to not always force students or employees to live up to standards, principles, and practices that they may find alien, difficult, or unfair. The nice professor is also approachable, even gentle, because one senses that he is willing to listen and to compromise or even to give in: he is soft, not hard; he is "reasonable," not prickly; he is pliant, not "tough"; he does not always demand his own way.

In addition to flexible, considerate helpfulness, niceness also refers to a third characteristic, general friendliness or, more precisely, general pleasantness. As we suggested, the nice child or man is as much (or more) someone who is not harmful or inconsiderate as he is one who is actively helpful or evenhanded. "Pleasantness" is the positive portrayal or display of this withdrawal or restraint. Similarly, a "nice" time or event is a generally pleasant time, or a merely innocuous time, but it is not an outstanding, noteworthy, or demanding time. "That was a nice symphony (game, meal, book, stretch of weather)." In this sense "nice" also serves as a broad synonym for "good," with the emphasis on the pleasant and undemanding, but without always being limited in this way. In short, then, to be nice is to be flexible, helpful, pleasant, and considerate, or at least not rigid, harmful, inconsiderate, and nasty. We might say that the chief characteristic of being nice is not always to demand one's own way, whether that way is proper behavior according to some principle or standard, or one's own malicious or even reasonable desires. The nice person is considerate of the wishes, possessions, and feelings of others.

About what is one flexible and considerate? Potentially, about anything. There is no set of goods toward which niceness is the proper disposition, because one can be nice or nasty, helpful or harmful, considerate or inconsiderate, flexible or rigid about nearly anything and anyone. Nonetheless, one is usually nice or nasty toward other people (or animals), and when one destroys their things the nastiness is toward the owner, rather than toward the things themselves.

A further sense is the one involved when we say that someone has made a nice distinction, point, or argument. Here "nice" means small or narrow, usually in the favorable sense of subtle, precise, graceful, and refined, or at the least, careful and not trivially obvious. We find an echo of this in "nice" manners where nice means "good" in the sense of careful, though not quite superb. Nice—as in "Nice!" after a particularly good move in sports—also means apt, precise, appropriate, or even special. Nice as good, therefore, means not merely pleasant, but also a not too taxing, if not quite egalitarian, sense of beautiful or refined.

In summary, then, someone who is nice does not always demand his own way, and considers, and often gives in to, others' interests and feelings. He is pleasant and not a bully. One can be nice about anything and toward any-one, and almost anything can be called nice.

We can explain the fact that "nice" can be synonymous with good, and even that nice in the sense of appropriate and refined is not merely homonymous with nice as pleasant, by reflecting on the equality and universality characteristic of modern countries. Niceness is a virtue more akin to the moderation and, especially, justice of which nearly all men and women seem capable than to the courage and, especially, pride of a few. Unlike moderation, however, it is not restricted to pleasures, but can cover nearly everything. Niceness is at one with the equal respect that according to modern political thought we all deserve, and it presupposes the lack of hierarchy among goods and, indeed, the lack of definition of what they are other than the fact that they happen to meet our desires and become our interests. Niceness is connected to "kindness," where to be kind is to be mild and gentle, that is, to treat what defines our human "kind" as what we share equally, easily, rather than as a set of characteristics that differentiate us and need tutoring and education. In fact, when we understand being nice as a virtue, it can become the enemy of the rigorous standards that we otherwise claim to admire, for to demand of others that they live up to standards is to be seen as inflexible, unfeeling, or, indeed, selfish and arbitrary. One is imposing one's own way, even if it is a way that we claim is generally correct.

All this is not to say that we moderns believe that to be nice is an unmixed blessing. One can be "too nice," and there is always the lingering sense that whoever is nice isn't tough enough, i.e., that to be nice is always in some sense to be too nice. Nice guys finish last, as the saying goes. This does not just mean that they obtain less of what interests them than do rigid, inflexible bullies, but that they obtain less of what they deserve. (What one "deserves" in modern life is, in a sense, an equal share of citizenship, of rights and opportunity: what one deserves is not some proper share as defined by a principle of distribution tied to substantive goods such as honor or even wealth. In practice this means with regard to such goods that one deserves whatever one is strong and lucky enough to obtain in a regime where all goods are equal opportunities, i.e., where everyone by nature has an equal right to everything. Nice guys obtain less than they "deserve" because they are not tough enough to take as much as their talents would normally obtain for them, given, or making, some luck.) One wants one's business partner, or commanding officer, to be nice to oneself but not to the enemy. One even recognizes that common success might demand that the boss be tough to subordinates. So although being nice is a seemingly unprecedented general virtue that applies to almost all goods, its sway has not destroyed all understanding of its limits.

The virtue of being nice (and of kindness) is similar to the modern virtue of compassion, but not identical to it. The likeness is in the mildness and gentleness and in the breadth of men (and animals) toward whom one feels compassion. But compassion normally is felt for those who are suffering; it is empathy with the miserable and sad, not philosophic understanding of all things, large and small. Nice men, on the other hand, let others have their way not only because they feel for those on whom they would be imposing but because they think it unfair to demand too much. Indeed, while compassion is a feeling for one's kind, human or animal, niceness is not merely a feeling but a disposition. To be nice sometimes requires a bit of consideration and discrimination about the appropriate and deserving, while to be compassionate is simply to feel. One feels compassion, but one *is* nice. Niceness is a disposition that may be supported by feelings of compassion, empathy, and gentleness ("a loving disposition") rather than by anger and indignation, but especially as a synonym for fairness it is a training of these passions. Finally, although "nice" can be a synonym for good things as well as men, "compassionate" cannot be: the senses in which something nice is something pleasant, refined, and fitting are not duplicated for compassion.

II

Tolerance is a second virtue for which we cannot find an exact classical equivalent. It is apparently a species of moderation, but moderation is about pleasure, not belief; it defines proper behavior toward those of other faiths, but it does not as such replace pious reverence for the god in whom one believes, and his commands. As is true of niceness, tolerance is a disposition, not a passion: it is a habit that must be learned, and it takes training, though not terribly much, to exercise it intelligently. As is also true of niceness, although it is not itself primarily a feeling it may be supported by passions or moods such as calm, gentleness, and mildness rather than by indignation, energy, or desire. In fact, it is the trained control of spirited self-assertion or indignation, which training is then supported by milder passions.

To be tolerant is to permit or allow others to do things in their own way. One does not interfere with them, although one need not help them. Nowadays, toleration covers more than religion. Indeed, that tolerance is primarily for those of different faiths is almost forgotten: one is more often asked to be, or fails to be, tolerant of spendthriftness, cowardice, stupidity, or pleasure-seeking. Normally we are enjoined to be tolerant of ingrained customs and habits, but this is not always the case: we can also be asked to tolerate unexpected delays or an unexpected display of temper.

To be tolerant is not necessarily to approve of what one tolerates. In fact, the tolerant man traditionally permits or allows what he does not approve. These days, however, people said to be tolerant or very tolerant seem not to disapprove at all. At least, they keep their disapproval so much to themselves it is as if they do not disapprove. Indeed, the difference in sense between tolerating and approving is (in some quarters) fast disappearing; tolerant men are often asked to support and not merely to permit.

Tolerance began as what some believed to be the proper individual and legislative disposition toward believers in religions other than the reigning Protestantism. Its effect, in fact, is to neutralize (or Protestantize) all religions by neutering their most excessive political claims. When we expand the use of "tolerance" beyond religion per se, it is quite close to niceness. One shade of difference is that while we are asked to be nice to those over whom we would ride roughshod, to the physically weak, and to those to whom we are indifferent as well as to those who fail to live up to our standards, we normally are asked to be tolerant of others' faults, difficulties, and weaknesses, not of those to whom we would thoughtlessly pay no account. "He doesn't tolerate mistakes." This retains the sense that we are tolerant of action and behavior of which we disapprove or are expected to disapprove. A second shade of difference is that while "selfish" is one apt opposite of "nice," it is not a terribly apt opposite of "tolerant." "Rigid" or "tough," which can also be opposites of "nice," are more apt. To be tolerant of foibles is to accept what one disapproves; to be nice toward the weak is to not force them to obey you. To be tolerant is not so much about unselfishly (nicely) failing to impose one's own status, will, and desires; rather it is to not completely impose one's own way of life and standards. A third difference, of course, is that while "nice" is a synonym for "good," usually, as we said, in the sense of pleasurable, "tolerable" is not such a synonym but stands for what barely passes muster. This is connected to the fact that while we tolerate what we disapprove, niceness qua niceness treats others as equal to us. In this sense niceness is a broader virtue than tolerance, because it is a form of seemingly just treatment of others and affirmatively covers good things, while tolerance covers others' foolishness or beliefs, that is, something about them but not them. Though anything, from food to philosophy textbooks can be thought and said to be tolerable, it is not very good when this is all it is. This is not to deny, as we said, that "tolerant" and "nice" are sometimes close to synonymous, that to call someone a tolerant man is often to call him a nice man or to single out an aspect of his niceness. This resemblance is caused by niceness's greater breadth as something that comes close to treating someone fairly in general, when fairly means equally in all respects. In another sense, however, this breadth of niceness itself belongs to the decline of modernity from legal respect for others' equality in rights—in interests and spirit—with faith being a central characteristic, to a bland equality in which all goods and people are equal.

Niceness, from this point of view, is a decline from tolerance, where tolerance speaks less to bland equality. Tolerance retains some sense that it is about important things—about grudgingly permitting others' freedom, but not dominance, in religion, customs, and ways of life. To the extent that being tolerant is not simply one version of being nice, as it largely is today, tolerance is nobler than—because it requires restraint that is less visibly good—and is certainly about something higher than the nice man's overcoming of selfishness. Of course, to the degree that being nice is a true echo of the original modern equality in rights, we might think of even tolerance as merely a part of this broader sense of modern justice. Tolerance too, for all the height of its primary object, is, as a kind of motion, neither the awful shuddering within which one's own self-enclosed dignity and pride comes to light and is protected, nor is it worshipful, uplifting love. As is true of being nice, it is a kind of flexibility, a lack of defensiveness or angry, spirited protectiveness. At its extreme, to permit all is cowardly flaccidity. Tolerance is a kind of steady, indifferent movement, whose effect is to equalize in blandness the religious heights that were its original object, and the compelling secular concerns that are its contemporary field.

III

We moderns also think of hard work or industriousness as a virtue. It is better to work hard than to be lazy. This is not to say that playful ease, grace, good manners, and charm are not also virtues, or that they are simply opposed to hard work. One can be both industrious and graceful or even charming. Yet there is a seriousness or earnestness in hard work and, especially, in the display and appearance of industry that rest uneasy with playful grace and charm. Even the graceful covering over of earnestness is no longer seen to be unambiguously good because we often believe one ought to appear to work hard.

Although one can be said to work too hard, this usually means that one is working too hard for one's own good, i.e., that one needs a rest so that one will be able to work more effectively in the future. Working too hard is largely a mistake only in terms of work itself, with the notion that one should nonetheless sometimes stop to smell the roses an occasional reminder that playful grace or moderate enjoyment of pleasure are virtues too.

What is industriousness? To be industrious is to work hard, sometimes with great energy but as often with mere dogged determination. To be industrious is to persevere in one's assignment. The responsible man, whom we will discuss more completely soon, also may persevere, but he is more properly understood as one who sees to it that the job is done correctly, that the intention behind the effort actually is satisfied, not merely that the effort is diligently pursued. The responsible man, therefore, has in view the purpose of the task and its place in the larger whole; indeed, he sometimes exercises his responsibility as a commander or supervisor with a bit of distance, seeing to it that things are going right, without himself moving the machine. The industrious man works diligently at his task and as such need not have in mind the larger task at all: there is something dull-witted and dronelike about mere industry. Obviously, for someone who truly works hard actually to complete his task well, and not merely to work at it diligently, he needs something of the responsible man's view of the whole. Moreover, although responsibility tends toward the noble, the comprehensive and even de-tached view that guides the completion of what is being done and pro-duced—the responsible man, as we said, sees to it that the job is done right—we initially think of being responsible as getting the job done through one's own "hands-on" efforts. Industriousness in the full sense and respon-sibility in one common sense tend toward each other.

The industrious man perseveres in his assignments—but what are they? One can be industrious about anything under the sun. As is true of the other modern virtues, there is no special good toward which the virtue is the proper disposition, as moderation is to pleasure, courage to fear, liberality to wealth, or pride to honor. We are more often said to be industrious about things or activities than about people, but we are also enjoined to be indus-trious about, to "work hard at," our "relationships." Moreover, we can be in-dustrious about plotting murders and stealing funds as well as about catch-ing criminals and investing savings. We might not be enjoined to be hardworking criminals, but the diligence as such, its quality and range qua diligence, does not seem to be affected by its purpose—at least, we do not talk as if it is.

Industriousness is diligent perseverance in carrying out or working through assignments. As a form of motion (and all virtues are some kind or combina-tion of attraction, repulsion, inclusion, and separation), it is a gathering of oneself, but not for moderate redirection of longing and being uplifted that spends itself pleasantly in enjoyment or exhaustion. Rather, it is a gathering of oneself simply for subsequent motion to and from one thing after another, with the ending or cessation not being fulfilling or exhausting but instead of such quality that the movement can be picked up, as it were, precisely where it has been left off, and where the job is not done in the sense of being com-pletely realized as much as it is done in the sense of being over: the last file has been filed, but when another file is found it too will be filed, with no loss or gain to a whole with defined parts.

Naturally, we sometimes will talk of industriousness in ways that connect it to working on something beautiful or refined, a work of fine or manual art. But the model of industriousness is more the movement of one thing after an-other, linking links in a chain that stops from time to time but is not going anywhere. In this sense, the fact that we can be said to be industrious about anything—beautiful productions and magnificent acts of military defense and protection as well as work in an office—means that all goods are seen in flat similarity when we see them as subjects of industrious activity. Hard work is the activity of producing and accumulating the interests that are the material that satisfies the flat desires of modern man. It is no accident that industriousness is the obvious virtue that defines modern (bourgeois) man for whom desire can be for anything with equal legitimacy and for whom satisfaction is a momentary resting, not a grand embracing. The industrious pursuit of satisfaction, the hardworking accumulation and securing of the resources (the interests) that allow this satisfaction, and the (near) identity of moving through one's tasks, accumulating interests (goods), and satisfying desires make industriousness equally a means and the end itself in modern life.

IV

A fourth distinctively modern virtue, one indeed that is first named around the time of the *Federalist Papers* and is now discussed incessantly by politicians of the left and right, is responsibility. What is responsibility? When we call someone responsible we mean, first, to hold him to account. From early in our childhood we are asked who is responsible for making a mess or leaving a chore undone. Later, we seek to find the person responsible for a patient's untimely death or a poorly constructed house. That is, we look for someone who is at fault, someone we can blame. It is in this sense that to feel responsibility means to feel "guilt," to feel worthy of blame and punishment. But when are we deservedly accountable, and not just blamed arbitrarily? We are accountable when we are the cause of the mistake or the wrong rather than, say, because we have been ritually selected as a sacrifice to redress it, or because an ancestor's misdeed makes us blameworthy. Our second meaning of responsibility is to be something's cause, the reason it happened. Most academic discussions of responsibility concentrate on this notion, or on the link between blame and causality, because their focus is on the conundrum of "free will" and determinism.

Accountability and guilt make us think of intention and sin, qualities and vices of the head and the heart. Responsibility's third main meaning, however, indicates something different, for to call a man responsible suggests that he concerns himself with results, and sees to it that the results are correct. A responsible physician or builder sees his work through to its end and takes care that it is done well. He is reliable and dependable: good intentions are insufficient; indeed, we will often look away from motives if the job is always done right. (While responsibility in the sense of accountability often has a negative ring—we look for the "responsible" official when we wish to complain, and we hold people to account when they make mistakes—when we call someone responsible in the sense of reliable, we mean to praise him.)

We can gather these meanings together and say that to be responsible is to be accountable for results, for outcomes, because we have effected them. To whom are we accountable? Most obviously and immediately, we are accountable to the ones for whom we are working. It is in this sense that we often ask those who are responsible to be "responsive," by which we mean that they should dance more quickly to our tunes. It is also in this sense that we speak of responsibilities as our "obligations," especially when we think of obligation simply as what we owe others, and do not have a fancy theory of it. From a somewhat more reflective point of view, however, when we encourage people to be responsible we are encouraging them to be accountable to themselves for their own effectiveness: we are encouraging them to bring about and practice the traits and skills that enable them to be successful today and in the future. Responsibility is the disposition not just to be effective, but to secure one's effectiveness. When we call politicians who worry about budget deficits responsible, or ask people to use alcohol responsibly, we have in mind the prudence and care that looks to the future.

Responsibility, however, means more than doing one's own job effectively. For we also think of responsible men as ones who take charge of tasks that seem to belong to nobody in particular, situations in which no one is obviously accountable and circumstances that no one seems to have caused. To be responsible is to take charge after a flood when nobody else knows what to do, or to work to make a successful request to a local government for more neighborhood police officers. Responsibility in this sense means taking on common tasks and seeing them through: a responsible man's actions go beyond doing and being accountable for his job, because he *makes* things his job. The responsible man holds himself accountable when he need not, although soon enough everyone expects him always to act responsibly. Responsible men and women are often the ones urged to enter politics because they effectively bring results that are commonly good, good for others as well as themselves.

This final meaning of responsibility might lead us to believe that it is an ancient virtue, newly named. Although it is clearly connected to nobility, however, it is at root modern. For responsibility fits with liberal self-interest rather than being contrary to it, as it might seem. It is not alien as is altruism, or preliberal as is the classic virtue of pride or religious duty, although it is related to them. It is their analogue, transformed to be consistent with the accumulating nature of the modern liberal self and the always voluntary nature of its attachments. In this sense, it is part of the same general understanding of goodness, satisfaction, and their breadth that we noticed with the other virtues.

We can see this better if we consider more carefully what we are seeking when we attempt to be responsible for ourselves. If I habitually spend lavishly, waste my time, or do not study, I am properly accused of being irresponsible. This means that what I am doing now will make it hard to satisfy my desires effectively in the future. Being responsible about oneself is a disposition of character through which I treat myself as a possibility for continued accumulation. Self-interested behavior, that is to say, is not ultimately for the sake of any particular narrow attachment but for the sake of self-perpetuation. Because this is the end, one begins to develop habits of steadiness, foresight, and expansiveness, and a self defined by these characteristics: these habits, indeed, are the conditions for successfully exercising economic and other rights.

This attachment to self-perpetuation can, on reflection, lead some of us quite naturally to take an ever greater long-term and common point of view. For there is good reason to think that perpetuating one's own cool, measured, calculated, ongoing attachment and accumulation will be more successful on the broad field of serving or shaping others than in the small domains of petty interest. In fact: given full competition, a long-range, expansive, and one might say imperialist perspective is needed even to stand still.

So, as some of us piece by piece make the growth and effectiveness of this responsible self our actual goal, we do increasingly responsible things such as serving common institutions, even though the equal and interchangeable nature of participation in these institutions at first makes it unclear why anyone should give time to them. There is a continuum, resting on responsibility for oneself, that leads from responsibility seen as doing one's job well to responsibility experienced as making one's own the common tasks such as political service that need to be done but belong to no one.

In saying this, I have more in mind than what we call enlightened self-interest. Rather, what happens on our progression is that we understand the self and our disposition to be responsible to it in broader ways. It becomes a matter of character, not only of calculation, i.e., responsibility becomes a virtue. I also am not suggesting that everyone will be equally responsible but rather that the steadier the responsibility, the firmer the self-interest, and the fuller the exercise of rights, the wider will be the grasp of the true requirements of common tasks.

The fully responsible man clearly opens in the direction of pride and nobility and needs more than ordinary fairness. Although responsibility points or belongs to a natural virtue, however, it more obviously indicates the transformation of classic virtue in the modern world, just as, say, the public "interest" is similar to the common "good," but is not identical with it because it belongs to a different way of seeking, finding, and holding. Our responsible men usually operate for smaller, i.e., more economic, stakes than do men of great pride, do what they do less because they are attracted to honorable independence and beautiful completion and more because they concentrate on accumulation and satisfying themselves, and typically act in situations where the common benefit is also a more or less identical individual benefit to them, rather than acting because ruling a common enterprise is their own characteristic natural field and place.

V

We may now gather together and summarize the salient points of our descriptions in order to touch upon what is distinctive in modern virtue. First, modern virtues deal with all goods without discrimination. There is nothing about which one cannot in some regard be tolerant, responsible, industrious, or nice. Second, modern virtues allow equal access, in the sense that very little equipment is needed for them (the rich can be as virtuous as the poor), and in the sense that one man's exercising the virtue does not detract from another's exercising it. The exception here is the fullest meaning of responsibility.

Third, each of these virtues displays lack of driving motion, or lack of uplifting passion, especially when it is compared to the classic virtue that it resembles or supplants. The nice man or the compassionate one is neither a spirited guardian of justice nor a cauldron of desire who seeks to moderate his passions lest they overwhelm him. The industrious man is neither the ambitious man who directs and redirects a driving wish for honor nor the steely protector of home and fatherland against strikingly present enemies and threats. His industry (and energy) lack direction as such. Tolerance is less the careful containment of passionately spirited protection of what is honorable, right, and true than it is the easy exercise of mild forbearance. And the responsible man does not hunger for pride of place nor for the beautiful completion of a noble enterprise so much as he does what he must. In general, modern virtue does not so much control yearning or fierceness as it smoothes out and restrains what is rough in order to keep things moving along.

Fourth, just as they require little equipment, the distinctive modern virtues do not require much by way of prudence or practical reason. To be nice or tolerant requires some judgment and thoughtful balance, but not terribly much; nor do they require much experience. This is why these virtues come so close to seeming to be only the visible expression of mild native dispositions rather than the habitual and prudential direction of passions, however mild these modern passions have been made by custom and legislation in the first place and however much the virtues make them gentler still. Industriousness as such requires neither prudence nor much calculation, although useful industriousness may need the rational calculation or the prudence of the artisan or owner who sets things in motion. Responsibility, the virtue with the most obvious echoes of ruling and nobility, is also the virtue with the closest tie to prudence. This is most clear when we think of the responsible man as taking on the job that is no one's in particular. But as we have said, responsibility means, more broadly if less significantly, getting one's job done. It therefore requires merely that one recognize one's job and has or acquires the tools to do it. The degree of required practical wisdom, or of deliberative judgment and skill, may be minimal, or it may be great: this depends upon the job and its author. (See *Federalist Papers,* numbers 23, 63, 70, 77, 79.)

The fifth distinctive characteristic of the modern virtues that we have discussed is that none of them, again with the partial exception of responsibility, is so desirable in itself that it seems to be a necessary part of human excellence. Indeed, it is strange to think of them as excellent at all. Taken together, niceness (compassion), tolerance, industriousness, and responsibility (as accountability) lack splendor. That "virtue" should describe the well-formed character that is the goal of education would hardly be obvious were the modern virtues all that there is to virtue. This debility is not caused simply by the fact that we have separated moral from intellectual virtue, for the classical splendor of the statesman or gentleman was not fully tarnished by this separation, nor is it altogether caused by the fact that the political and spirited virtues have been so displaced, for the modern virtues (as a group) also lack the luster of the "Christian" virtues of service, faith, and humility.

The fact that none of the modern virtues quite presents itself as a necessary part of human excellence does not appear so surprising once we recall their other characteristics—the equality and generality of the goods with which they deal and people who can hold them, the flatness of motion that impels them and that they direct and redirect, and the absence of necessarily accompanying practical wisdom and deliberation. The modern virtues are means as much as they are ends, and indeed much more means than ends for individuals and for the institutions that serve them. They belong to and help to perpetuate and secure the restless motion, the accumulation of goods (interests) with which to continue this motion, and the occasional resting (or "satisfaction") that renews energy for the uneasy flight that is the heart of modern happiness. No modern virtue is above being used well or ill: all display their Machiavellian origin.

VI

The characteristically modern virtues do not exhaust everything that moderns believe to be virtuous, for we also by and large find the classical virtues to be good. This goodness allows us to understand and pursue the classic virtues, at least partially, and ultimately allows us to seek to understand the nobility of, say, wisdom and justice on their own terms. Moreover, the (almost) independent attractiveness of a virtue such as full responsibility shades into classic virtue simply (while at the same time showing its modern origin by replacing pride, the ancient virtue whose full desirability remains ambiguous in modernity). Furthermore, virtues such as niceness and tolerance, as well as (energetic) industriousness and responsibility, shade into concepts and descriptions such as gentleness, moderation, and mildness, and quickness, courage, and venturesomeness that the classics use to divide virtue as a whole. (See Plato's *Statesman*, 305E1–309B8.)

This suggests that while modern virtue is Lockean or Machiavellian, it is nonetheless finally explicable and understandable in classic terms. Let me briefly indicate the directions of inquiry that would better establish this suggestion. A typical kind of motion of the soul, we have claimed, is integral to modern virtue. Examination reveals, however, that the directness that characterizes the motion of the modern soul is a declension from the richness and complexity of motions of classic spirit and eros, not a different impulse. One characteristically issues in ends seen in advance as a series of cumulative satisfactory results, the other as subtly completed and independent forms. This flatness of modern goods is not a new nature of things but precisely a flattening, a narrowing of the fullness of classic goods and challenges. Similarly, the freedom of liberal rights and pursuits is not altogether different from the freedom inherent in the choices of classic virtue. If we analyzed what we mean by "freedom" we would discover that to be free always means to be unrestrained and uncontrolled. But we can properly understand "control" and "restraint," i.e., we can properly understand freedom only in conjunction with the richness and complexity of the goods toward which we are poised and ready to move. To describe freedom is implicitly to posit in advance a sense of the desirability, manipulability, and approachability of goods without which there would be no experience of control or restraint. The nature of freedom and the goods with which it deals, that is to say, belong together. As is true of modern goods, so too modern freedom constricts and narrows the substance of classic freedom while increasing its extent. One is "free" or not for equal opportunities rather than, say, for noble common efforts. So, modern freedom is in one sense radically different from but in a deeper sense not incommensurable with the classic freedom that it narrows but does not eliminate. For this reason the two freedoms are sometimes surprisingly close.

The way the free play of reason is inherent in moral choice also belongs together with how the goods that reason judges and measures are conceived and first approach our possible enjoyment. My reasonable understanding of how an action I am contemplating stems from, fits within, and helps shape a classically moderate disposition to pleasure, for example, is the source of my freely causing this action precisely by forming it in the light of the wholeness and independence of my soul and the goods it can enjoy. Such a link between freedom, causality, and reason is more important for moral choice than is any calculating of how to push myself along mechanically as an industrious worker or considerate compromiser, even if we have in mind the universal push of Kantian self-determination. What seems new in the dilemmas of "free will," and perhaps even especially perplexing about them, reflects a one-sided constricting of causality, choice, reason, action, and goodness, not a set of altogether new problems. The questions of "free will" and voluntary choice are hardly identical, but they are commensurable, and one narrows the other.

On the whole, therefore, there seem to be a distinctive and coherent shape but no newly discovered phenomena at the heart of modern virtue. To explore this point fully, and to explore sufficiently the relation between modern virtue, modern political institutions, modern commerce, and modern technological rationality, would, of course, take us beyond our limits here.

NOTES

1. In addition to the *Ethics*, the most directly relevant texts for this chapter are Rousseau's *Second Discourse;* Locke's *A Letter Concerning Toleration;* Locke's *Second Treatise*, chapter 5, and especially paragraph 34; *The Federalist* 23, 63, 70, 77, 79; and Plato's *Statesman* 305E1–309B8. Consider also Harvey C. Mansfield, Jr., *Taming the Prince* (New York: Free Press, 1987), 267, and Harvey C. Mansfield, Jr., *America's Constitutional Soul* (Baltimore: Johns Hopkins University Press, 1991), 128–34, 216–19.

2

How a Liberal Picks a Fight: Marsilius of Padua and the Singular Cause of Strife

John P. Gibbons

Within the confines of the history of political thought, Marsilius of Padua, author of *Defender of the Peace,* is widely known as a great anticipator. By this it is generally meant that he raises or employs arguments that would become thematic or fundamental in later modern and specifically liberal political thought. Among these themes are the elevation of will, consent, and freedom and the consequent depreciation of virtue and the regime. Marsilius teaches that the fundamental political authority is the people, or the "whole of the citizens or its preponderant part," but that this fundamental political authority is distinct from the ruler or government. The government rules not in its own name but is an executive government, ruling in the name of the people (I.12.3, I.14.8).[1] By calling Marsilius an anticipator, rather than, say, a founder, we express the general sense that his teaching is less decisive or his thinking less clear and his break with classical political science more grudging than is true of his illustrious successors.

Harvey Mansfield has opposed this approach to Marsilius and has demonstrated that it is far more instructive to treat Marsilius as a political scientist, to learn from his hesitations as much as (or perhaps even more than) from his innovations.[2] What we now regard as Marsilius's innovations or anticipations are likely to be what is familiar to us, what we take for granted, while his hesitations are more likely to be inhibitions long since lost or possibilities long since abandoned. We cannot properly understand or judge what is familiar to us without understanding whether it was prudent to lose those inhibitions or abandon those possibilities.

I do not regard this as a matter of merely historical or even theoretical interest. Liberalism was long characterized by a kind of assertive spirit that

18

contributed not a little to its success. Mansfield has shown that this spiritedness has at least a portion of its origins in the spirit of anticlericalism.[3] And
Marsilius has yet to be outdone in the arena of spirited anticlericalism; no
one, I believe, has suggested that in this regard he was less decisive or less
resolute than his successors.

While liberalism in opposition was able to maintain its spirit, liberalism in
triumph has lost its nerve, has lost its fight, and has lost its ability to distinguish friends from enemies. Those who regard thinkers such as Mansfield as
the real enemies of liberalism only show that they are their own worst enemies. Freedom is the principle of liberalism, but it is difficult or impossible
to maintain this principle if you cannot explain why freedom is good. It becomes increasingly difficult to recognize, let alone oppose, tyranny if you
think freedom does not require some support in the proper order of the soul.

It is my intention in this brief essay only to suggest that Marsilius's *Defender* is consciously designed to lead the reader to an articulation of the relations among reason, freedom, and spiritedness.

Marsilius's description of his intention is inseparable from his explanation
of the design of his book (I.1.8). He has divided his book into three discourses; in the first, he will demonstrate what he intends through certain
methods discovered by the human mind; in the second, he will confirm what
he believes he has demonstrated by testimonies of the eternal truth and certain sacred writings; and in the third, he will present some very useful teachings to be observed by citizens, both rulers and subjects. The division of his
book is, so to speak, dictated by the human situation, by the distinction between the human mind and the divine or eternal and the consequent fact
that man as citizen is both ruler and subject. But within the order that is given
to him, Marsilius is free to further divide and order his material with a view
to an intention of his own, and so he says that he has divided each discourse
into (numbered) chapters and paragraphs. It will be easy for readers to find
what they are looking for when they are referred from what comes later to
the discourse and chapter of what had come earlier, and since the author will
not have to repeat himself, this will also produce a shortening or abbrevia-
tion of his book.

Marsilius thus communicates his expectation for his readers. They will be
a sedulous, if somewhat forgetful, group, following his cross-references,
conscientiously looking them up when they forget what had been said,
needing some guidance on where to look, but also sufficiently busy or impatient that they want the book to be as short as possible. Having indicated
his concern for brevity, Marsilius then (apparently) repeats himself. When he
assumes some truth in what comes later that had been sufficiently handled
in what comes earlier, without bothering with the proof he will refer the
reader to the discourse, chapter, and paragraph in which it had been handled
so that the reader can easily discover its certainty (I.1.8).

Marsilius frequently sets tests or exercises for his readers, and learning from the *Defender* requires the reader to recognize and work through the exercise (cf. I.6.3). Having suggested that his audience is forgetful but intent on learning and conscientious, Marsilius seems to repeat his statement on the purpose of the division of his book. He invites the reader to compare the two statements. On reflection or rereading, there are at least three noteworthy differences. First and most visibly, in the first statement Marsilius spoke of references to discourse and chapter, while in the second he speaks of references to discourse, chapter, and paragraph. Second, in the first statement, Marsilius refers to "readers," while in the second he refers to "the reader." Third, the first statement speaks of ease in discovering what is sought while the second statement speaks of ease in discovering the certainty of the thing sought. I assume that these three differences reflect a single distinction and that the many readers are called "readers" by reason of their resemblance to the single "reader," that care in finding what had been said is a reflection of care in seeking the certainty of what had been said, and I conclude that we should be especially careful to follow what I will call Marsilius's complete cross-references, that is, references to discourse, chapter, and paragraph.[4] In this essay, I will briefly discuss the first two of these complete cross-references.

Before doing so, however, I would like to touch briefly on the very short chapter (I.2) that immediately follows Marsilius's discussion of the design of his book. The topic of that chapter is the "first things sought" in the book, and Marsilius suggests that there is a natural order of inquiry supplied by raising the question "What is the city?" He also asserts that he wants to follow this order. But this natural order of inquiry seems to be interrupted by the fact that the author he had quoted at the very beginning of his book spoke not of the "city" but of the "*regnum*" or kingdom. Marsilius therefore deviates from his intended order to distinguish the meanings of "*regnum.*" From this distinction, it emerges that Aristotle had used this term to refer to a specific regime, while Marsilius (and the author he had quoted) use it to refer to "something common to every temperate regime" (I.2.2).

Marsilius's thinking would seem to be as follows: while the causes of strife that Aristotle had dealt with threaten particular regimes, the "singular" cause of strife with which he must deal threatens every regime by introducing two governments into every city. Hence what desires tranquillity must also be common to every regime. From the perspective of classical political science, what is "common" to every regime is curiously subpolitical; it stops short of what is decisive about the regime, its claim that the way of life associated with that regime is the best way of life.

Marsilius as much as indicates that this beginning is an intentional false step by his abrupt transition from what he "wants" to what he "ought" to do, quickly adopting an analogy between city and animal from Aristotle,[5] and asserting that the "faith" we can have in this analogy can be had by what "all say about each" (I.2.3). He reports what all say about health and about tranquillity and what the "more expert of the students of nature" say, but there is nothing in what is said that sounds like what men say about politics. Marsilius must rediscover the political before he can treat the cause of strife; the solution will be not something common to regimes, but a specific regime, and that not the best regime, but informed by thought about the best order of soul.

Marsilius's first complete cross-reference occurs in the course of his enumeration and description of the parts of the city following Aristotle. One of the parts of the city is the "warrior" part, the part whose end or purpose is freedom (I.6.9). The warrior part is needed both against external enemies and against internal rebels (I.5.8). Marsilius quotes Aristotle in establishing the need for this warrior part against external enemies: "nothing is more truly impossible than for that to be worthy to be called a city that is by nature a slave." By introducing this unphilosophic-sounding assertion, Marsilius reminds us of the "warrior" or spirited part of the soul and the philosophic use of that part in politics. But he does no more than remind us; he goes on to say that the need for this warrior part against internal rebels can be had from Aristotle, but he will not quote the passage for the sake of brevity and because he will introduce it in I.14.8.

The reader may find it striking but not entirely surprising that this first complete cross-reference is a forward reference. Given the deliberately inauspicious beginning of Marsilius's discussion of the parts of the city, a reference to what is prior is a reference to what comes later. Despite its demonstrative appearance, the thirteen chapters from Marsilius's description of the design of his book to his discussion of the perfect prince have the character of an ascent to what is first.

The chapter (I.14) to which Marsilius refers us is a description of the qualities of the perfect prince. The perfect prince is characterized by moral virtue, especially justice, and prudence. Moreover, prudence and moral virtue are, as Aristotle taught, one and inseparable (I.14.2,10). Only after establishing the qualities of the perfect prince does Marsilius introduce his passage on the need for the "warrior" part against internal rebels (I.14.8). Aristotle's statement is brief and typically laconic, but Marsilius treats this passage (*Politics* 1328b7) as very difficult and obscure, requiring three Marsilian interpolations, an argument, a reconciliation with another passage from Aristotle, and an etymology to clarify. Those without the benefit of Marsilius's clarification (which is almost the same as to say those *with* the benefit) might believe that Aristotle had said that for those sharing in common (perhaps those sharing in the most perfect community of thought) it is necessary to have arms for the sake of disobedience to the ruler.[6] However that may be, Marsilius is determined to avoid two possible misunderstandings: the first, that the power of the warrior or spirited part should be greater than that of the citizens, and the second, that this power should be the prince's own.

   Marsilius appears to deploy Aristotelian passages the way a skilled general deploys his troops. Why does Marsilius displace this passage from Aristotle from the discussion of the parts of the city in I.5 to his discussion of the perfect prince in I.14? I would suggest that the reason is twofold: first, to place that passage at a safe distance from his reference to the need for the warrior part against external enemies and the Aristotelian reference to slavery in I.5.8 (for if the warrior part is needed against external oppressors, what sense does it make to limit its power or to prohibit the use of the prince's own arms?); and second, to indicate that this consideration (which has the character of a deliberation) of the perfect prince, including the limitation on his spirited part, is prior to many of those Marsilian teachings generally taken as anticipations, including his elevation of consent over the common benefit in treating of regimes (I.8) and his placing fundamental political authority in "the whole of the citizens or its preponderant part" (I.12).

Before elaborating on the suggestions, I would like to make an assumption explicit. In treating of the parts of the city, Marsilius, like his teacher Aristotle, is also treating of the parts of the soul.[7] The warrior or spirited part is the part by which we assert our freedom, including our resistance to rule, especially by external oppressors. But Marsilius treats the warrior part primarily as the part through which the prince punishes. It is this that makes the prince executive in the sense that rule is understood primarily as executing laws. Marsilius's interpretation of Aristotle, which acts as an explicit limitation of the warrior part (that it not be greater than that of the citizens and that it not be the prince's own), also makes the prince executive in the sense that the prince in punishing rules on behalf of or in the name of others.
   Marsilius, of course, is not particularly interested in the punishment of common criminals, except as those criminals claim exemption from rule by reason of their clerical status. The punishment characteristic of Marsilius's prince is punishment of those who would overturn the regime (I.5.7), and his intent is to deal only with a "singular cause of strife," which is a consequence of the Christian revelation (I.1.7). Consequently, we should understand Marsilius's political teaching of prince as executive to mean that in punishing priests, the prince should limit himself to what popular anticlericalism permits or requires. More particularly, the treatment of priests should not go so far as to reflect the prince's own spiritedness or anticlericalism. It thus appears that, for Marsilius at least, the need for executive government is a result of the Christian revelation and not a general teaching.
   To return then to our provisional answer regarding why Marsilius displaced the treatment of the warrior part to the treatment of the perfect prince, we note that almost casually and by way of summary Marsilius concludes that chapter by reporting that Aristotle "is witness" to what he had taught, saying that "future princes" in the "principal offices" must have some three things: an

attachment to the existing regime, power (or capability) for the greatest works of the office, and virtue and justice (I.14.10). In reporting this, Marsilius calls attention to the fact that his teaching deviates from that of Aristotle. For Aristotle had said that the prince requires some power or capability that is clearly his own, while Marsilius in I.14 is completely silent on any such power. We might say that Marsilius substitutes the power of the warrior part for any discussion of the prince's own power. Marsilius's deviation, however, is more apparent than real. In order to show this, it will be necessary briefly to depart from the *Defender* and return to Aristotle's *Politics*.

In the course of his discussion of the causes of strife, Aristotle had said, as Marsilius reports, that those who are going to rule in the "sovereign offices" need some attachment to the established regime, power or capability for the greatest works of the office, and virtue and justice. Aristotle continues, however, that there is a perplexity (*aporia*) when all these do not coincide in the same one. This perplexity concerns "how it is necessary to make the division." Aristotle does not make clear what he means by the division; he may mean the division between human and nonhuman rule. In order to clarify this obscurity, Aristotle uses an example: "For instance, if someone is skilled in the art of war (*strategikos*) but wicked and no friend to the regime, but someone else is just and a friend, how is it necessary to make the choice."[8] Aristotle's phrase "make the choice" is striking; it cannot mean "choose" but rather means "construct the choice." Men in politics may choose, but in order that they choose well, wisdom or prudence may be required to construct the choice they make. Aristotle then proceeds to resolve the perplexity he had constructed: "It looks like it is necessary to look into two things, in what all share more and in what less." The apparent rule that Aristotle gives is that men should choose what is rare, but that this is only apparent or provisional is evident from examining his example. He continues: "For instance in generalship, look more to experience than to virtue, for they share less in generalship and more in equity, but in guardianship and the treasury, the opposites, for it requires more virtue than the many have, but the knowledge (*episteme*) is common to all." The qualifications for rule in the "sovereign offices" seem to be reduced from three to two and these two to be virtue and knowledge. Wisdom would construct the choice by determining whether the office more resembles generalship or guardianship.[9] If there is a single or predominant sovereign office, wisdom would be needed to determine whether that office more resembles generalship or guardianship. This wisdom would be inseparable from the understanding of nonhuman rule or nature or the divine. For if what is not human is unintelligible or hostile, it would seem inevitable that human rule would have the characteristics of generalship, the qualification to rule would be the art of war (invisible to the many), and the common virtue would be equity (or, as we say, compassion). But if what is not human is intelligible or otherwise friendly to man, human rule would be more like guardianship, the qualification to rule would be moral virtue, and the perfect prince would have no power or capability that is distinctly his own.

Returning to Marsilius's *Defender,* we reiterate that for Marsilius, the perfect prince is characterized by moral virtue and prudence and not characterized by any art or capability that is his own. Further, even with regard to the "power" that is represented by the warrior part of the city or soul, Marsilius teaches that the prince's power should not be greater than that of the citizens and should not be his own.

The parts of the city as they first come to light in the *Defender* are the various arts that men discover and perfect (I.5.5, I.6.9). These arts have as arts a certain order; the various mechanical arts are ordered, for example, to the art of medicine (I.5.6). It might seem reasonable to think of the order of the city as given by the order of the arts. Marsilius's answer, which is identical to Aristotle's answer, is that the arts are not ordered to an architectonic art, but that the arts are ordered to prudence and prudence is fused with moral virtue.[10] To say that the perfect prince is characterized by prudence and moral virtue is to say that within the realm of politics no one can make the prudent man's decisions better than he can make them himself, or that there is no art or science that is superior to prudence in its claim to rule a city. This is not to say that the life of moral virtue and prudence is the highest way of life; the life of contemplation, of the "speculative soul" is superior to the practical life (I.4.1). Nor is it to deny that the theoretical life can somehow provide guidance to practical life. It is only to say that the theoretical life guides practical life in a way that is fundamentally different from ruling. It was confusion on this point that characterized the papal claim to plenitude of power. As Marsilius puts it, it was the claim of the papacy that the election of a ruler could depend on the will of "one alone." Marsilius claims that by asserting this, the pope shows that he is ignorant of the "virtue and reason of choice" (II.26.5). Choice is the beginning of human government, and such choice has both a virtue and a reason, and these do not necessarily coincide.

How then might the theoretical life guide practical life? We return once again to Marsilius's discussion of the warrior part in the course of his discussion of the perfect prince. Marsilius insists that the power of the warrior part not be greater than that of the citizens and that it not be the prince's own. Why is this not something that the prince of prudence and moral virtue can decide for himself, how far to assert his spiritedness in punishing fractious clergy? Why should he exercise this spiritedness in the name of "the whole of the citizens" rather than in his own name and based on his own claim to rule? We can begin to get a sense of the answer when we recall Marsilius's description of Ludwig of Bavaria's "love of extirpating heresies" (I.1.6). Perhaps Marsilius had a premonition that the assertion of the prince's own spiritedness was bound to lead to a denial of the superiority of the theoretical life to practical life and that this could be disastrous for reason, for revelation, and for politics.[11]

Marsilius's discussion of the perfect prince is an articulation of the relationship of wisdom, prudence, and spiritedness, which finds expression in his construction of executive government. I shall try to outline briefly how that relation informs Marsilius's political science and why his executive government is only a provisional solution.

Marsilius's second complete cross-reference occurs at the very beginning of his discussion of law (I.11.1). "Demonstrating," as is his fashion, the need for law, Marsilius proposes a major premise: "It is necessary to establish in the polity that without which civil judgments cannot be made rightly, through which they are made appropriately and are preserved from defect as far as is possible for human acts." Concerning this major premise, Marsilius observes that it is "quasi-self-evident and almost indemonstrable," but he adds that its certainty "can and ought to be had" from *Defender* I.5.7.

This form of cross-reference is almost exactly what we had been led to expect from Marsilius's initial description of the design of his book (I.1.8). It is a reference to a prior passage, and the reader is told that he can discover the "certainty" of what is said here from that passage. But Marsilius also makes a small but significant addition. Not only *can* the reader discover that certainty but he *ought* to discover it. Marsilius adds this obligation because the reader or student is himself capable of being the major premise or the originating cause. To be certain that it is necessary to establish something in the "polity" is to become a founder or lawgiver.

At first glance, it is not evident what the source of this certainty is. *Defender* I.5.7 is Marsilius's description of the need for a "ruling part" in the city (and is the paragraph that immediately precedes his first complete cross-reference in I.5.8). We can begin to understand Marsilius's intention by reflecting on the major premise he supplies. Here, he speaks of establishment "in the polity" (I.11.1) whereas earlier he had sought to understand politics through the "*regnum*" (I.2.2). The *regnum* is one thing common to every temperate regime but is itself not a regime. It is impossible to found or govern a *regnum* because every regime is this or that regime. "Polity" is also the general name for regimes, but it is also the name of a particular regime, the regime in which each citizen participates appropriately in rule (I.8.3). The *regnum* points to what is one or common in politics but is itself subpolitical, while the polity points to multiplicity and the need to mix a variety of claims. At the beginning of his discussion of law and the legislator, Marsilius turns decisively to the polity.

Returning to I.5.7, the paragraph to which the reader is referred to understand the certainty of this need to establish, we note that the ruling part is necessary to moderate the excesses of civil acts and to reduce them to "equality or due proportion." The ruler requires something to measure the "due proportion" of a variety of claims. This measure will come to light as law, established by the "whole of the citizens or the preponderant part," but through that law will be evident the soul in which a variety of claims are measured and mixed to establish the polity (I.15.6).

Marsilius speaks of the need to "establish" or "institute." Marsilius's political science is a decidedly institutional political science. What is established has greater durability and more lasting power than the judgment of an individual judge. In establishing, a legislator has to choose something to rely on to provide this durability. Marsilius chooses will or willfulness. His provisional measure of a good law is one that is obeyed, and he observes that that law is best obeyed which each "seems" to have imposed on himself (I.12.6). Modern liberalism also begins with will or willfulness as the source of law, but its emphasis is different. Modern liberalism seems to take willfulness for granted or, indeed, to assume that nature assures us that men will be willful. Marsilius needs to establish a regime which encourages and sustains willfulness while educating or refining willfulness to choice. What modern liberalism assumes that nature will provide, Marsilius believes must be the work of a wise legislator.

In describing the necessity of the ruling part, Marsilius says that in the absence of a measure of justice or "due proportion" there would arise "fighting and hence the separation of the citizens, and finally the corruption of the city and the loss of the sufficient life" (I.5.7; cf. I.3.4, I.4.4). He does not envisage a "war of all against all" as showing the need for rule, but rather "the separation of the citizens and the corruption of the city." Certainly, Marsilius is more concerned with the submissive parts of the soul than is modern liberalism.[12] But by "separation of the citizens and corruption of the city" Marsilius means separation into subpolitical parts or not participating in rule. It is certainly likely that he would have regarded a war of all against all that led men to relinquish the claim to rule and consent to be ruled as tantamount to a separation of the citizens requiring the work of a legislator and political philosophy.

Marsilius's challenge is to establish a polity or regime that encourages and supports willfulness, where there is broad participation in the regime through legislation and election, and where election is of men of prudence and moral virtue. Only in such a regime is executive government as Marsilius intended it possible. In such a regime, the prince may be expected to dissemble his own spiritedness and assert the "warrior part" or spiritedness that is given to him by election (I.14.8). Willfulness as the support for law and as expressed in law is a distinctly human beginning of rule. In relying on the "warrior part" of the citizens, the prince asserts the distinctiveness of the human while dissembling the special claim to freedom of the morally virtuous. This regime resembles many modern regimes and is the regime that reflects Marsilius's intention. He clearly judges that it is the best regime possible under the circumstances he faced. He nowhere claims that it is the best regime.

But what is the support for or dignity of willfulness if not moral virtue? In a brief essay, we can only suggest the outlines of Marsilius's answer.

In the "Second Discourse" of the *Defender*, Marsilius gives an account of human perfection or of the perfect way of life that is parallel to his discussion of law and the perfect prince in the "First Discourse"[13] (II.11–14). The perfect way of life is the life of poverty. But what is meritorious in poverty is not the mere lacking of things; it is voluntary poverty that is the perfect way of life. Voluntary poverty is not suicide, it is only the will to lack more than is sufficient (and, in addition, the unwillingness to claim ownership as a matter of legal right). The perfect way of life, then, is based on the will and is the ultimate support for will. But within this voluntary poverty we can see two different strands based on different understandings of what is sufficient. There is evangelical poverty, which is incompatible with ruling, based on radical contempt for the world and which is known to be perfect only through revelation. But there is also the poverty that consists in the understanding that there is a limit to acquisition and the willingness to have only what is sufficient for the present. This form of voluntary poverty is consistent with ruling, inconsistent with evangelical poverty, and can be known to be perfect by reason. Marsilius makes no attempt to reconcile these two strands. It appears that there are two incompatible peaks of human perfection.

Marsilius could claim that the papal assertion of plenitude of power was tyrannical and he could encourage princes and other citizens to resistance in the name of human freedom. In this, he is a liberal. But his liberalism differs entirely from modern liberalism. The claim to rule based on revelation is tyrannical but so is the claim to rule based on the reason of the wisest man. The ground of freedom is human will, but the dignity of the will reflects the fact, not that we can know nothing about what is good, but that we can know that there are two great alternatives, the perfection of reason and the perfection of revelation, and that neither of these can dispose of the claim of the other.

NOTES

1. References to the *Defender* will be to discourse, chapter, and paragraph and will be included in the text. All translations from Marsilius's *Defender* and from Aristotle's *Politics* are my own.

2. Harvey C. Mansfield, Jr., *Taming the Prince* (New York: Free Press, 1989), 100–18.

3. Harvey C. Mansfield, Jr., *The Spirit of Liberalism* (Cambridge, Mass.: Harvard University Press, 1978), 11 and passim.

4. The first complete cross-reference is at I.5.8. It is curious that this paragraph is the first paragraph eight after Marsilius's initial statement at I.1.8 and refers the reader to I.14.8, that is, to the eighth paragraph eight of the *Defender*. This could be coincidence, or it could be related to Marsilius's conceit that he is treating one cause of strife in addition to those treated by Aristotle. Cf. *Politics* 1302b34–37. There are altogether 104 complete cross-references in the *Defender*, most occurring in the very and visibly curious discourse III.2.

5. Marsilian scholarship in this century has been blessed with careful translators and editors who can be counted on to check the references in the *Defender* but who sometimes go further and silently correct the reference when they conclude that our author has dozed. Some future editor or translator would do the reader a service by recognizing that, not to put too fine a point on it, Marsilius sometimes tells jokes and by concluding that it may be better to leave these jokes uncorrected. The reference to Aristotle in I.2.3 is, I suggest with trepidation, just such a joke. It is tedious or worse to explain a joke, but I will offer a comment. Having described the division of his book (a division that reflects the distinction between reason and revelation) and the consequent ease readers will have in finding what is sought, Marsilius's first reference to Aristotle is to "First and Fifth of his *Politics,* chapters 2 and 3." As a reference, this is incomprehensible: the reader simply does not know where to look. Why would Marsilius provide an incomprehensible reference? Perhaps in order to indicate why his situation requires or permits him to deviate from Aristotle. In the *Politics,* enumerating what the city will need to be self-sufficient, Aristotle counts "fifth, and first, care for the divine, which they call the priesthood" (*Politics* VII 1328b11-12). Marsilius's reference to "First and Fifth of the *Politics,* chapters 2 and 3" is incomprehensible as a reference to a specific passage or passages in the *Politics* but unmistakable as a reference to concern for the divine and what is called the priesthood.

6. Indeed, given Marsilius's careful deployment of this passage, it is impossible to avoid this interpretation. The passage to which Marsilius reconciles Aristotle's statement on the need for the warrior part is Aristotle's characterization of the guard of the *pambasileus,* or king over all. For the significance of this passage, v. Mansfield, *Taming the Prince*, 41.

7. Marsilius indeed is forced at one point to separate the parts as habits of soul from parts as parts established in the city (I.6.9, second paragraph), but even as he makes this separation he says that it must be understood to be "about this chapter and the one immediately following it," that is, elsewhere the distinction must not be made. The separation of the parts of the city from habits of soul requires that someone of an unimaginably beneficent nature do the work of the prince (I.7.1).

8. *Politics* 1309a32ff.

9. It goes without saying that the one who would be chosen can "make the choice" in this way. Closer to home, Lincoln's "House Divided" speech is an outstanding example. Lincoln establishes the choice as one between fidelity to republican principles and unscrupulous capability. In choosing Lincoln, voters not only choose a candidate but also choose a certain order of the soul in which capability is subordinate to virtue. This is the connection between the city and soul.

10. See Leo Strauss, *The City and Man* (Chicago: Rand McNally, 1964), 23–25.

11. See Leo Strauss, "Marsilius of Padua," in Strauss and Cropsey, eds., *History of Political Philosophy* (Chicago: Rand McNally, 1963).

12. See Mansfield, *Taming the Prince*, 109–10.

13. The connection between the two discussions is provided by Marsilius's assertion in I.14.8 that Aristotle "wanted" or "willed" that serious poor men should be able to rule as his proof that the "warrior part" of the city should not be the prince's own.

3

Machiavelli and the Foundations of Modernity: A Reading of Chapter 3 of *The Prince*

Nathan Tarcov

Everyone knows that Machiavelli declares his originality in chapter 15 of *The Prince*, where he says he departs from the orders of others, goes directly to the effectual truth, and rejects the imaginary republics and principalities of the writers. But before he can lay the foundations of *our* modernity he must overturn the foundations of *his* modernity, the theology, morality, and politics of his at least nominally Christian world. He begins that task most revealingly in chapter 3, "Of Mixed Principalities." Before he can praise the new prince in chapter 6 over the hereditary prince of chapter 2,[1] he must deal with the mixed prince.[2]

Machiavelli bestows the name "mixed" upon principalities in which a new state is added to the hereditary state of its prince. The text, unlike the title, says "almost mixed," perhaps because this term traditionally belonged rather to the mixture of monarchy, aristocracy, and democracy.[3] The crucial mixture in *The Prince* is between different modes of acquisition, not between different forms of government with different ends.

The chapter opens not specifically with the mixed principality of its title but more generally with the new principality, "in which consist the difficulties." The guiding principle, as in chapter 2, remains that of difficulty, presumably in maintaining one's state. Machiavelli then narrows the topic to mixed principalities only to broaden it again immediately by considering their "variations" as arising from "a natural difficulty that is in all new principalities." That difficulty is that the belief that they will do better makes men take up arms against their lords only to find by experience that they have done worse owing to "another natural and ordinary necessity," that a new prince must always offend his subjects with infinite injuries. Whereas in

30

chapter 2 the hereditary prince enjoying the goodwill of his subjects and having less necessity to offend them was called "natural," here in chapter 3 Machiavelli calls "natural" both that necessity to offend experienced most by new princes and a difficulty introduced at first as if it only affected holding new principalities but which also explains why men are dissatisfied with and willingly take up arms against hereditary princes. This opinion or belief in a "future good" is (to anticipate a phrase used later in the chapter) not a miracle but part of a necessity as natural and ordinary as the offenses of a new prince. Machiavelli now looks at these phenomena from a perspective that sees both the hopes and disappointments of peoples and the offenses and difficulties of princes as natural and ordinary necessity. Natural and ordinary necessity is not limited to easily measured forces but emphatically includes the beliefs and opinions of men.

The result of this natural and ordinary necessity is that you[4] have as enemies those whom you offended in seizing the principality and that you cannot keep as friends those who supported you because you can neither satisfy them nor "use strong medicines" against them since you are obligated to them. Machiavelli illustrates this difficulty by the example of the king of France, Louis XII, who seized Milan from Ludovico (Sforza) in 1499 but quickly lost it again in 1500 to Ludovico's forces. But when countries that have rebelled are acquired for the second time, they are "lost with more difficulty" because the returning prince takes the opportunity to secure himself by punishing delinquents, exposing suspects, and strengthening his weak points. Ludovico's reacquisition of Milan is equivalent to the duke of Ferrara's reacquisition of his principality cited in chapter 2, but Machiavelli does not identify Ludovico here as a sort of hereditary prince, the son of Francesco Sforza, the exemplary new prince of chapter 1.[5] Machiavelli's perspective has shifted from that of chapter 2's hereditary prince, who may lose and reacquire his principality, to that of the new prince who displaces him. The parallel shift in focus from maintaining with less difficulty in chapter 2 to losing with more difficulty here suggests that losing what one has acquired is practically inevitable, as would follow from the natural tendency of peoples to turn against their rulers in the vain hope of doing better. But the practical suggestion seems to be that a new prince need not wait until he acquires a country for the second time to secure himself by using strong medicines. Machiavelli does not make this suggestion but rather tempts his reader to arrive at it. The only obstacle is the belief in one's obligation to those who have supported one.

The greater difficulty of losing a country a second time is illustrated by the fact that when Louis lost Milan again in 1512 he did so facing not one Duke Ludovico but "the whole world," the Holy League organized by Julius II with Venice, Ferdinand of Spain, and officially the Emperor Maximilian I and Henry VIII of England. Machiavelli does not mention that this loss resulted in the restoration of Milan to Sforza rule under Ludovico's son Massimiliano; he is no longer interested as he was in chapter 2 in showing the resiliency of hereditary principalities.[6]

Machiavelli shifts now from "the universal causes" of Louis's first loss of Milan (the natural difficulty common to all new principalities) to the particular causes of his second loss and the remedies available to someone in his situation to maintain himself better (not necessarily "with less difficulty"). Even losing when facing the whole world is not therefore inevitable. Machiavelli adopts the position of an adviser to someone in the situation of France trying to maintain his acquisitions in Italy. This might seem an odd position for someone offering himself as an adviser to an Italian prince like Lorenzo de' Medici, whose accession to power resulted from the expulsion of France from Italy (let alone for an Italian patriot). But knowing the causes of French failure in Italy and the remedies available to France should help an Italian prince to ensure future French failure.[7] It would also help him to make conquests of his own.

Machiavelli proceeds indirectly to the causes of Louis's second loss by first showing the remedies available to him and then considering his failures to avail himself of those remedies as his errors and the causes of his loss. The "universal causes" of the first loss, in contrast, were not errors or failures to avail himself of available remedies but a natural difficulty and a natural and ordinary necessity. Louis's errors in the second case are not natural and ordinary in the same way.

Additions of the same province[8] and language as the prince's ancient state may be held "with great ease" (the opposite of difficulty), especially if they are not used to "living free," that is, if they were previously principalities rather than republics, and if there is no disparity of customs. Machiavelli illustrates this with the example of the incorporation of the provinces "which have been with France for so long a time."[9] All that needs to be done is eliminate their princely bloodlines and not alter their laws or taxes. If eliminating princely bloodlines is so easy, then the reacquisition of principalities by their hereditary princes or princely families is not as easy as chapter 2 made it seem. Machiavelli neither mentions an obligation not to murder innocent children (as he did with the obligation not to use strong medicines against one's friends) nor explains why it should not be regarded as a difficulty. This is the first clear manifestation of his view of morality, all the more chilling for being so offhand. Peoples seem to care more about the continuity of their laws and taxes than about that of the bloodlines of their princely rulers. Lorenzo's state is of the same province and language as the rest of his family's dominions, but Florence used to be free. He will have to wait a couple of chapters for advice about holding such additions. The advice given here would come in handy, however, if he acquired other principalities.[10] It would also be useful to any attempt to make Italy as unified as France.[11]

Machiavelli offers five remedies for the difficulties of holding acquisitions of different language, customs, and orders, which requires "great fortune and great industry," in contrast to the ordinary industry of hereditary princes. The greater difficulty of holding an acquisition of differing language and customs would seem to suggest a nationalist position advocating that princes acquire only territories of the same language and customs as their old state, leading to the formation of nation-states. But Machiavelli is not simply interested in minimizing difficulties. He offers Lorenzo much more advice about the difficult task of holding foreign conquests than about the easy ones of holding local conquests or his own inherited state. The advice to eliminate the princely bloodlines and keep the ancient laws and taxes in conquests within one's own nation may be insufficient: a native prince may face some of the same difficulties as a foreign conqueror. The five remedies are:

1. to inhabit the acquired state personally;
2. to send colonies;
3. to make oneself head and defender of the less powerful;
4. to weaken the powerful; and
5. to prevent another powerful foreigner from entering.

The example given of the first remedy, "the Turk in Greece" (Sultan Mahomet II's moving his capital to Constantinople after conquering it in 1453[12]), shows that observing orders (whether one's own or one's ancestors') is not sufficient to hold foreign conquests, as it was said to be for hereditary states in chapter 2. You need to be present to see and remedy disorders before they become great: disorders cannot be foreseen and prevented by orders. This example also shows that differences in religion are among the differences in customs and orders that may be overcome by mixed principalities. Machiavelli does not identify "the other orders" that Mahomet II observed to hold Greece, but we may note that he encouraged the Greeks and Italians to return to the former Constantinople by returning their houses and guaranteeing their safety; forcibly resettled both Christians and Muslims from elsewhere in his empire in the city; and restored the Greek Orthodox patriarchate and established a grand rabbi and an Armenian patriarch there. Among the other advantages of this first remedy of inhabiting the place oneself are that subjects have more cause to love the prince "if they want to be good" and more cause to fear him "if they want to be otherwise." Unlike the hereditary prince of the previous chapter, the mixed prince depends on fear as well as love and does not count on the goodness or goodwill of his subjects. The shift from maintaining with less difficulty in chapter 2 to losing with more difficulty in chapter 3 is extended in the conclusion that by employing the first remedy the prince can lose his acquired state "with the greatest difficulty."

Machiavelli says that sending colonies, the second remedy, is the better remedy,[13] but he shows its advantages only over sending garrisons, not over the first remedy of inhabiting the place personally, the advantages of which he has just stressed. The superiority of colonies over garrisons is measured by a political–economic calculus of two variables: the balance of income over expenditure and the efficient commission of offenses.[14] The economic side of this calculus reveals that not every acquisition is beneficial; some may turn into losses. This result only apparently modifies the primacy of acquisition: economic acquisition takes priority over territorial expansion.[15] The political side calculates not only how many people are offended and whether they can do harm in return, but also the effect on those not offended. Whereas garrisons offend everyone, colonies offend only the few they displace, who are left poor, dispersed, and harmless, leaving the rest unoffended yet afraid the same will happen to them. Conquerors need to offend a few to intimidate without offending the many. Machiavelli's conclusion of the side of the ledger pertaining to colonies adds another criterion: "colonies are not costly, *are more faithful,* and less offensive" (emphasis added). This central criterion seems to come out of the blue, unlike the other two, which were preceded by down-to-earth calculations. It is not obvious why colonists, who possess their own fields and houses in the newly acquired state, should be more faithful to the prince who sent them than would garrisons, who possess nothing in the new state and expect to go home.[16] (Perhaps the contrast is with mercenary garrisons.[17]) Their fidelity might depend on their being more satisfied, and it may be owed not to the old state but to the new whole body that the old state and the disparate new state have formed together, or it may be owed to the prince alone.

The less offensive character of colonies derives in part from the claim that the people they displace, being poor and dispersed, can do no harm. This particular claim is accompanied by a universal rule: that "men should either be caressed or eliminated, because they avenge themselves for slight offenses but cannot do so for grave ones; so the offense one does to a man should be such that one does not fear revenge for it."[18] There is some discrepancy between the particular claim and the universal rule, since the displaced persons are not literally eliminated. Either Machiavelli's frequent talk of elimination may not always be meant literally (it certainly seemed to be in the case of princely bloodlines), or his recommended policy of sending colonies may need to be made more violent. He may at this point be more willing to recommend the elimination of princely bloodlines than of a very small part of the population. In any case, there is no further talk of obligation: one may have to caress those one might be considered to be obliged to offend in a small way; and one may have to offend in a grave way those one might be considered to be obliged to offend only slightly or not at all.

The remaining remedies (numbers three through five) shift the focus from a single acquired state (such as Milan) to the balance of power of a whole province (such as Italy). Whereas the hereditary prince was advised to temporize with accidents, the mixed prince is to prevent the entrance of a powerful foreigner through any accident. Machiavelli proceeds to discuss the causes and effects of the entrance of a powerful foreigner into a province in such a way that the reader cannot tell whether he is discussing the entrance of the foreigner he is advising or that of a potential competitor; they are in the same situation, and the same logic applies to both. They are brought in by malcontents either from too much ambition or from fear. Machiavelli offers the example of the Aetolians' bringing the Romans into Greece (the first manifestation in the book of Machiavelli's continual reading of ancient things), without making clear whether they did so from excessive ambition or from fear;[19] the Venetians' bringing Louis into Italy to help them acquire half of Lombardy will shortly exemplify bringing in a foreigner from excessive ambition. Machiavelli shows that the ambition of the Venetians proved foolishly self-defeating, but there is no such condemnation of bringing a foreigner in from fear. A foreigner following Machiavelli's advice can be counted on to defend the weaker powers who bring him in from fear, but he will eventually weaken the powers who bring him in to help them satisfy their ambition. Machiavelli invokes here "the order of things" as the predictable interaction of such human passions as ambition, fear, and envy with the relative balance of power. This fundamental order, which Machiavelli brings to light in discussing mixed principalities, lies beneath the orders followed by hereditary princes laid down by their ancestors.

This tripartite policy (remedies three through five) is not only a matter of the balance of forces in the narrow sense. The weak must be prevented from getting too much force or *authority;* the powerful must be put down by both force and *favor;* and other powerful foreigners must be prevented from gaining either state or *reputation*. Machiavelli's presentation of this tripartite policy expands the ambition of would-be mixed princes. Whoever does not manage this policy well will hold his acquisition with "infinite difficulties" and soon lose it, whereas he who does will not only hold the state he has acquired but become the arbiter of the whole province in all things.

Machiavelli now turns to the example of the Romans, who observed these policies well in the provinces they took and did "what all wise princes should do." They are said to have followed remedies two through five, but nothing is said about their having observed remedy one. Even though Machiavelli has just spoken of how the Turkish sultan moved to Greece and now emphatically takes Greece as his example of Roman policy, he says nothing here about the Roman emperor the Sultan imitated, who moved the capital of the empire to Constantinople. Whereas Mahomet II (who declared himself Roman emperor upon his conquest of Constantinople) ended the rule of Christianity in that empire, it was Constantine who began that rule.

The use of Roman policy in Greece in the time of Philip V of Macedon and Antiochus III of Syria[20] to exemplify remedies three through five and the omission of Constantine's conspicuous exemplification of remedy one make clear that "the Romans" whom Machiavelli praises here are not any Christian Roman emperors but the leaders of the pagan Roman republic. Machiavelli began chapter 2 by saying he would leave out reasoning about republics; there he gave the modern Venetian republic as an example of a force resisted by a hereditary principality, but now he offers the ancient Roman republic as the model of "wise princes." The example of the Romans also explains why sending colonies is a better remedy than personally inhabiting a new acquisition. The latter is impossible for those who make multiple far-flung conquests that they cannot personally inhabit simultaneously, and for republics it is in effect identical with sending colonies.[21] The significance of the omission of the example of Constantine here is clarified by the opening of Machiavelli's *Florentine Histories,* which explains that the emperors' abandoning Rome to inhabit Constantinople left the western empire weakened, being less watched by them and more exposed to pillage by their ministers, and gave the northern peoples the opportunity to destroy the Roman empire.[22] The first remedy's advantages spelled out in this chapter are accompanied by corresponding disadvantages.

As model wise princes, the leaders of the Roman republic used all their industry (presumably greater therefore than the "ordinary industry" of hereditary princes) to remedy not only present but future troubles. In affairs of state, as in medicine, evils are easy to cure early when they are difficult to know about (which is possible only for one who is prudent), but difficult to cure later when they are easy for everyone to know about. Difficulty is therefore unavoidable and pure ease impossible; wisdom or prudence consists in embracing the difficulty of knowing to attain ease in remedying. The superiority of a "prudent one" over "everyone" would be at odds with the praise of a republic unless the Roman republic was so ordered as to have everyone follow the leadership of prudent ones.

The Romans remedied evils in advance since they knew war is deferred only to the advantage of others: they fought Philip and Antiochus in Greece so as not to have to fight them later in Italy.[23] Unlike "the wise of our times" and the temporizing hereditary princes of chapter 2, they sought to enjoy the benefit not of time but of their own virtue and prudence. Instead of believing in future good, they looked out for future evils. They recognized that the best defense is a good offense, and this policy, if taken to its logical conclusion, leads to world conquest, as their example shows. Machiavelli tempts attentive would-be mixed princes to extend their ambitions in proportion to the potentially "infinite difficulties," from retaining a single acquisition to dominating a whole province to indefinite expansion. The contrast between the Romans and the wise of our times clarifies the need for knowledge of both ancient and modern things indicated in the dedication to *The Prince.* The ancients provide a model of reliance on virtue and prudence and willingness to wage war in contrast to modern hopefulness and aversion to war.

Machiavelli now returns to the causes of Louis's second loss in the light of the available remedies and the Romans' wise application of them. The causes are his errors or his having done the opposite of what should be done to hold a state in a disparate province, his not observing what are now called "the rules written above." Machiavelli begins surprisingly, however, by defending Louis's sharing Lombardy with the Venetians, an apparent violation of the rule to weaken rather than strengthen the powerful (rule number four), which should not be blamed since it was necessary so as to enter Italy. Unlike the ancient Romans, the modern Venetian republic can be safely strengthened by another prince. The division of Lombardy was an error on the part of the Venetians, not Louis. Readers see that one cannot simply follow Machiavelli's "rules"—they are literally made to be broken. He gives his readers practice in breaking his own rules to prepare them for breaking other rules when necessary. The prudence Machiavelli praises is not the following of rules, even his own.

The necessity that excuses the violation of the rule is the "very natural and ordinary" human desire to acquire. Though that desire is not to be blamed, it does not excuse every violation it motivates. Men are praised if they acquire but blamed if they try to acquire when they cannot. This enables one to distinguish Louis's division of Lombardy with the already powerful Venetians from his bringing Spain into Italy to divide Naples, which makes clear that men are blamed also when they acquire at the cost of later losing both their new and old acquisitions. The desire to acquire is limited not by a moderation that allows only what is truly good for one or by a justice that recognizes the claims of others,[24] but by a prudence that recognizes distant threats to one's acquisitions. The necessity of this natural and ordinary desire to acquire is at the bottom of the new prince's natural and ordinary necessity to offend. Acquisition would not have the force of necessity if princes could be content with their inheritances, but prudence dictates that one fight one's enemies abroad so as not to have to fight them at home.

Louis could easily have maintained the reputation in Italy that he had gained through his acquisition of Lombardy if he had followed these rules, especially by defending the numerous, weak, and fearful friends whom he could have used to secure himself. But instead he committed his first error in aiding Pope Alexander VI to seize the Romagna, and thereby lost those friends and added temporal greatness to the spiritual greatness that gives the church so much authority. The balance of power is in great part one of reputation (won, for example, by defending one's friends) and even of spiritual greatness and authority. (Machiavelli would not ask only how many divisions a pope has, as Stalin is supposed to have done.[25])

Louis committed "five errors" in violating all five rules, but Machiavelli continues, surprisingly again, by saying they could not have hurt ("offended") Louis, while he lived, if he had not committed "the sixth." Along with the Emperor Maximilian and Ferdinand of Spain, he joined the League of Cambrai organized by Pope Julius II in 1508 that succeeded the next year in dividing among its members the mainland territory of Venice. Weakening the powerful Venetians would seem to be dictated by rule four. In other words, Louis could have safely violated all five of Machiavelli's rules if he had not made the fatal sixth error of then following one of them! Weakening the Venetians in accordance with rule four would have been "reasonable and necessary" if Louis had not already broken rule four by making the church great and rule five by bringing Spain into Italy. Once one has broken one rule it may become necessary to break it again. What is reasonable and necessary in one circumstance is not so in another.[26] Prudence consists in knowing when it is necessary to follow or break even prudential rules.

The significance of the qualification that Louis's five errors could not have hurt him "while he lived" is unclear.[27] It could mean that if he had lived longer (he died in 1515) they might have caught up with him, or quite the contrary that even if he had lived longer they would not have done so. It raises the question whether one can be harmed after one's death, either in this world by events affecting the enterprise and reputation one leaves behind or in another world by punishment brought on by breaking rules in this one. In any case, the result of Louis's sixth error was his second loss of Milan when Pope Julius was able to unite "the whole world" to drive the French out of Italy. Upon Louis's death in 1515, his successor, Francis I, recaptured Milan only to lose it again in 1521, and finally mounted an even more disastrous invasion of Italy in 1524 that resulted in his defeat and capture at the battle of Pavia in 1525, the abandonment of his claims to Italy, the surrender of his two eldest sons as hostages, and the near dismemberment of his own kingdom.

Machiavelli for the first time in the book introduces and replies to hypothetical objections, fulfilling his promise in chapter 2 to debate or dispute. He makes the first objector say that Louis ceded the Romagna to Pope Alexander and Naples to Spain to avoid a war (he hoped to avoid war with the Emperor Maximilian by preventing the pope and Spain from allying with him). Machiavelli replies by referring back to the reasons he gave before in discussing the Romans, that allowing a disorder to continue never avoids a war but defers it to your disadvantage. The objector seems so attached to the views of the wise of our times that he either does not think that the Roman example can apply today or does not see that deferring a war to the advantage of others is to defer it to your own disadvantage, if he has not simply forgotten what Machiavelli said so shortly before. Machiavelli puts the second objection in the mouths of some others, who bring up the faith Louis owed to the pope, his promise to aid Alexander in return for dissolving his marriage (to Charles VIII's sister, the saintly but barren and deformed Jeanne de Valois, so as to marry Charles's widow, Anne of Brittany) and appointing his minister, Georges d'Amboise, cardinal of Rouen. To these objectors Machiavelli replies by referring forward to what he says on the faith of princes and how it should be observed (in chapter 18). Machiavelli presents himself as attacked by two parties: one that puts its faith in time as certain to bring a future good (like the men who willingly change their lords in the mistaken belief that they will do better), and another, perhaps larger, that puts its faith in faith itself, especially that owed to the pope or the church, that believes in the continuing obligation of past promises. He does not answer either objection directly but instead refers those who believe in future good backward and those who believe in past promises forward. The former need to study the past (both the evil that time has brought along with good, and the Roman example), and the latter need to think about the future (what you can do for me next, not what I promised you before).

These objections explicitly defend Louis's first errors of helping Alexander to seize the Romagna and bringing Spain into Italy to divide Naples, rather than his sixth error of joining Julius and Spain in dividing the Venetian state, though they might be extended to extenuate the latter as well. They thereby bring the focus back to those first errors. Machiavelli concludes that Louis lost Lombardy (the second time) from not having observed any of the conditions observed by others who wished to hold provinces they took, and that this is "not any miracle, but very ordinary and reasonable." It is not any accident, I believe, that this denial of the miraculous in favor of the "very ordinary and reasonable" is made in a chapter where its author has affirmed the "natural difficulty" found in all new principalities, the "natural and ordinary necessity" for new princes to offend their subjects, the "universal causes" of the losses of new acquisitions, "the order of things" manifest in the interaction of relative power and human passions, the "very natural and ordinary" desire to acquire, and the shifting character of the "reasonable and necessary." Machiavelli's emphatic explanation of political success and failure on the rational basis of natural and ordinary necessity is meant to rule out the need for any other explanation, above all by any divine suspension of universal causes and of natural necessity. Machiavelli may understand the denial of miracles not as the premise of his explanation of politics on the basis of natural necessity but as its conclusion. His rational explanation of the ruinous political effects of putting one's faith in the church may count for him, however mistakenly, as the decisive evidence that the world is not governed by miracles.

Machiavelli nearly concludes the chapter with one of only two anecdotes in the book in which he appears as a character (the other is his conversation with Cesare Borgia reported in chapter 7), a dialogue between himself and Louis's cardinal of Rouen that continues the dialogue between Machiavelli and the hypothetical objectors. When the cardinal said the Italians do not understand war, Machiavelli replied that the French do not understand the state or they would not have let the church come to such greatness (the conversation took place when Cesare Borgia, the son of Pope Alexander VI, was seizing the Romagna). If the reply was meant to outdo the cardinal's remark, then understanding the *state* would be more fundamental than understanding *war*, knowing *when* to wage war would be more fundamental than knowing *how* to do so. The story clearly implies that at least one Italian understands the state. From this case Machiavelli draws "a general rule that never or rarely fails: whoever is the cause of someone's becoming powerful is ruined." One instance of when it fails would be Louis's initial strengthening of the Venetians by dividing Lombardy with them, which made his position more secure by deterring other powers from attacking Lombardy.

Although experience shows that Louis's ruin was caused by his allowing the greatness of both the church and Spain in Italy, and these errors could not have hurt him if he had not then weakened the Venetians, Machiavelli tells a story in which he singles out allowing the greatness of the church (his conversation with the cardinal in late October or early November 1500 preceded Louis's secret treaty of Granada with Spain, concluded on November 11, to divide Naples and his joining the League of Cambrai to attack Venice in 1508). This "first error" may have been the fundamental one. The spiritual authority of the church makes strengthening it much more dangerous than strengthening Venice or even Spain.

Louis's many errors illustrate a variety of faults, including a desire to flee from war that might be called cowardice; a blind belief in future good; a fidelity especially toward the pope or the church; an inability to limit the desire for acquisition to what can be securely acquired, which might be called immoderation; a belief that one can make others powerful without their suspecting or harming you; and above all an imprudence or lack of wisdom and understanding that contrasts with Roman or Machiavellian prudence or wisdom. The character and unity of Louis's faults may be clarified by reconsideration of the concluding sequence of the chapter. The denial that Louis's loss was a miracle, and the drawing of a general rule that never or rarely fails, which punctuate Machiavelli's dialogues with the hypothetical objectors and the cardinal, together raise the question of how the world is governed, a question that underlies but transcends the errors of a human prince in a foreign country. Machiavelli's answer to that question is that the world is governed not by miracles or by universal rules but by natural and ordinary necessity or universal causes. The man exemplified by the hereditary prince of chapter 2 who wants to avoid difficulty flees not only the difficulty of waging war but also that of rationally understanding the nature and order of things, the fundamental reliance on one's own virtue and prudence; instead he puts his faith in a future good, miracles, and rules that never fail, whether divine commandments or natural laws.

All these errors are of a piece, reflecting a kind of laziness most fully developed in Christianity. It was a greater mistake to strengthen the church than the Venetians because the church teaches that we should rely on miracles and rules more than virtue and prudence, that there is a future good for the sake of which we should willingly take up arms against our earthly princes, that we should keep faith (especially with the pope or the church), that kings need church approval to dissolve their marriages and appoint their prelates. These teachings blind us to the natural necessity to acquire and to offend. It is above all Christianity that distinguishes modern failures like Louis from ancient successes like the Romans.

While it was a mistake for Louis to strengthen the church, Lorenzo's family heads that institution and seems well positioned to benefit from its strength. Its teachings may weaken other princes who put their faith in them, but might work well for the Medici so long as they do not deceive themselves.[28]

If God does not rule the world by miracles or by rules the observance of which infallibly brings reward, perhaps he does so by the means Machiavelli suggests here for human princes trying to rule foreign countries. He tried coming to live here but was put to death by the Romans. He sent a colony occupying a very small part of the earth, but they were dispersed into exile by the Romans. Now he rules by garrisons (centered in the Rome abandoned by Constantine), who are faithful to his kingdom as their true home, and by their means he defends the weak, puts down the strong,[29] and excludes other powerful foreigners. His rule on earth would be a most important case of a "mixed principality," understood by Machiavelli on the same natural basis as other cases. Whether God is understood as having caused the greatness of the church or vice versa, this might also be another instance of the failure of the general rule that whoever causes the greatness of another is ruined.

If Machiavelli does not give rules that never fail, how then does he "regulate" or give rules for the governments of princes in *The Prince?* It would not be enough for a prince to know the rules set forth here; given the variations produced by the order of things, he has to know when to follow and when to break them. He has to understand natural necessity, especially the necessity to acquire and to offend. We are not given all we need by ancestors, God, or nature, but need to acquire. Sometimes it is reasonable and necessary to make others great, sometimes to pull them down; success results not from miracles or observing rules that never fail, but from prudent flexibility. The nature and order to be followed are no longer "the order of one's ancestors" of chapter 2, which went along with the ordinary industry of the hereditary prince and which succumbs to extraordinary force, but the order of things, the natural and ordinary desire to acquire responsible for both order and disorder, for both rules and exceptions.[30]

As Harvey Mansfield has written, in Machiavelli's view "the only practical alternative to depending on oneself is depending on God, which means the pope and the Church."[31] The analysis of mixed princes in chapter 3 of *The Prince* is Machiavelli's confrontation and conjunction of those two alternatives, which opens the way for his laying the foundations of our modernity in human self-reliance.

NOTES

1. Harvey C. Mansfield, *Machiavelli's Virtue* (Chicago: University of Chicago Press, 1996), 260.

2. Since chapter 3 is the second longest and perhaps the most complicated in the book, an outline may help to make this reading easier to follow (paragraphs from the Mansfield translation are indicated in parentheses):

    I. Difficulties
        A. The natural difficulty of holding all new principalities, e.g., Louis's first loss of Milan (1)
        B. The difficulty of losing reacquired conquests a second time, though Louis lost Milan a second time (2)
    II. Remedies
        A. Remedies for the difficulties of holding conquests of a similar province (3)
        B. Remedies for the difficulties of holding conquests of a different province:
            1. Inhabiting it oneself (4)
            2. Sending colonies a better remedy than garrisons (5)
            3. Defending the less powerful (6)
            4. Weakening the powerful
            5. Preventing another powerful foreigner from entering
    III. The Romans' Wisdom
        A. The Romans observed these policies well (7)
        B. They never deferred war or temporized (8)
    IV. Louis's Errors
        A. He did the contrary of these things (9)
        B. Don't blame his sharing Lombardy with the Venetians (10)
        C. He eliminated his friends, strengthened the church, and brought in Spain (11)
        D. Praise acquisition but blame failed attempts (12)
        E. His sixth error (putting down the Venetians); Machiavelli's responses to objections and dialogue with the cardinal (13)

3. See Machiavelli, *Discourses on Livy,* trans. Harvey C. Mansfield and Nathan Tarcov (Chicago: University of Chicago Press, 1996) I.2.7 (references to the *Discourses* are by book, chapter, and paragraph number in this edition); Plato, *Laws*

693de, 712de; Aristotle, *Politics* book II chapter 6 and book IV chapters 8–9 and 11; Polybius, *Histories* book VI chapter 10.

4. Machiavelli shifts to the informal second person he did not use in the previous chapter, as if his reader were a new rather than a hereditary prince.

5. Ludovico was not strictly a hereditary prince: he usurped the rule from Gian Galeazzo, the young son of his assassinated older brother Galeazzo; see Machiavelli, *Florentine Histories,* trans. Laura F. Banfield and Harvey C. Mansfield, Jr. (Princeton, N.J.: Princeton University Press, 1988) book VIII chapter 18. Louis XII himself made a hereditary claim to Milan through the marriage of his grandfather to the sister of Filippo Maria, the last Visconti duke of Milan.

6. Machiavelli instead discusses the weaknesses of the Sforza family that led to their repeated losses of Milan to the French in *The Prince* chapters 14 and 20 and in *Discourses* II.24.2. Massimiliano Sforza lost Milan to the French again in 1516, but his brother Francesco Maria regained the duchy through the victory of the Emperor Charles V over the French in 1522.

7. Mansfield, *Machiavelli's Virtue* 178; Leo Strauss, *Thoughts on Machiavelli* (Glencoe, Ill.: The Free Press, 1958), 65–67.

8. Machiavelli sometimes uses *provincia* much as we would use "nation."

9. Brittany had been joined to France only in 1491 by the marriage of Charles VIII to Anne of Brittany. This is alluded to later in the chapter when Machiavelli mentions the dissolution of Louis XII's marriage to Jeanne de Valois, which he arranged so as to marry his predecessor's widow and solidify the union of her duchy with France. When Louis later affianced Claude, Anne's daughter by Charles and heir to the duchy, to the Emperor Maximilian's grandson, the future Emperor Charles V, and in the Treaty of Blois of 1504 promised them both Milan and Burgundy, the enraged estates prevented the dismemberment of his kingdom by insisting that Claude be wed instead to Louis's heir, the future Francis I. Burgundy had been incorporated only as a result of the death of the last duke, Charles the Bold, in his defeat by Louis XI at the battle of Nancy in 1477. The marriage of Charles's daughter Mary to Maximilian had given him a claim to the duchy, but in 1482 it was included in the dowry of their daughter, Margaret of Austria, on her betrothal to the infant future Charles VIII of France. The incorporation of Brittany and Burgundy into France was therefore not so longstanding or irreversible.

10. When his uncle Pope Leo X acquired the duchy of Urbino for Lorenzo in 1516, the previous duke, Francesco Maria della Rovere, was deposed and excommunicated but not killed, and briefly recaptured Urbino from Lorenzo in 1517. After the death of Lorenzo in 1519, Leo ruled Urbino as part of the papal state in the name of Lorenzo's infant daughter Catherine, the future famous queen of France, but Francesco Maria once again reconquered Urbino during the papal interregnum in 1521 and got Leo's successor, Adrian VI, in 1522 to recognize his title and rescind his excommunication.

11. See *The Prince* chapter 26; Strauss, *Thoughts on Machiavelli* 66.

12. Mahomet II is praised by name and compared as a conqueror to King David in *Discourses* I.19.2.

13. The Italian is ambiguous: it is not clear what sending colonies is better than.

14. On the advantages of colonies, see also *Discourses* I.1.3, II.6–7, II.19.1.

15. For other ways in which territorial acquisitions may be harmful, see *Discourses* I.6.4, II.19.

16. For an example of an unfaithful colony, see *Discourses* II.13.2; for faithful colonies see II.30.4; for an unfaithful garrison, see II.20, III.6.20.

17. See chapter 12.

18. See *Discourses* II.23, III.6.11.

19. According to Livy book XXVI chapter 24, the Aetolians were moved most by the hope of being put into possession of Acarnania by the Romans rather than by fear of Philip V of Macedon.

20. 217 to 189 B.C.; see Livy books XXVI–XL.

21. A stricter equivalent for a republic would be if half or more of the population were freely to move to the new acquisition, as the Roman people were tempted to do to Veii (*Discourses* I.53.1, 54, 57), or if they were all compelled to move to a new acquisition as in the barbarian invasions of ancient Italy or the Hebrews' acquisition of Judea (I.1.4, II.8).

22. Machiavelli, *Florentine Histories* I.1; see also I.9.

23. On the danger of having to fight Philip in Italy, see Livy book XXIII chapter 33; book XXIV chapters 10, 13, 40.

24. Cf. Plato, *Republic* 421d–423c; Aristotle, *Politics* 1256b23–39, 1333b5–1334a1.

25. Valentin M. Berezhkov, *At Stalin's Side: His Interpreter's Memoirs from the October Revolution to the Fall of the Dictator's Empire*, trans. Sergei V. Mikheyev (New York: Birch Lane Press, 1994), 309–10. I owe this reference to Svetozar Minkov.

26. In this spirit, the commentary on *The Prince* attributed to Napoleon remarks on this passage that eliminating the lesser powers, listed as one of Louis's five errors, "would not even have been an error if he had not committed the others." *Niccolò Machiavelli, Il Principe con il commento di Napoleone Bonaparte* (Vimercate: Meravigli, 1994).

27. The participial phrase *vivendo lui* (literally "him living") is rendered variously "if he had lived" (Adams, Mansfield, and Musa), "so long as he lived" (Gilbert), "while he was still living" (de Alvarez), and "with him alive" (Codevilla). Robert M. Adams, trans., *The Prince* (New York: Norton, 1977); Harvey C. Mansfield, trans., *The Prince,* 2d ed. (Chicago: University of Chicago Press, 1998); Mark Musa, trans., *The Prince* (New York: St. Martin's, 1964); Allan H. Gilbert, trans., *The Prince and Other Works* (New York: Hendricks House, 1964); Leo Paul S. de Alvarez, trans.*, The Prince* (Irving, Tex.: University of Dallas Press, 1980); Angelo M. Codevilla, trans., *The Prince* (New Haven, Conn.: Yale University Press, 1997).

28. Strauss, *Thoughts on Machiavelli*, 68.

29. See the verse quoted from the Magnificat in *Discourses* I.26.

30. Strauss, *Thoughts on Machiavelli*, 57.

31. Mansfield, *Machiavelli's Virtue*, 48.

4

Necessity, Morality, Christianity

Ralph C. Hancock

". . . Machiavelli had not reflected on what made his soul less dear to him than his fatherland. . . . Strauss was indicating how the ascent from Machiavellism to Machiavelli must continue as an ascent from Machiavelli." (Mansfield 1996, 230)

My intention is to pursue the insights and hints regarding the question of Christianity and political philosophy that Harvey Mansfield provides in his published studies of Machiavelli. Unable here to undertake a general discussion of Mansfield's subtle, discreet, and often indirect treatment of this issue,[1] I will take my bearings from various remarks on religion in the essays collected in *Machiavelli's Virtue*.

CHRISTIANITY'S APPROPRIATION

For Mansfield's Machiavelli, the essence of religion is the need of most people to have their cake and eat it too: to believe in goodness—their own, and, ultimately, the world's—yet without sacrificing the human necessity of acquisition. "Goodness refuses to accept that necessity and takes refuge in religion, where it uncomprehendingly comes to terms with necessity" (Mansfield 1996, 27). It is through the notion of a mysteriously providential God that the believer embraces the "successful" outcome of immoral means within what he must continue to believe is a moral universe. The prince who understands this readiness of the people to be persuaded of the morality of successful wickedness can play the role of "God" while invoking his name in reconciling the moral appearance and the acquisitive reality of humanity, thus answering the people's necessities while serving his own. "The prince can therefore secure himself and his regime with both the recommendation and the fear of God" (77). The Christian "sect," in particular, provides at once a partial model for and the immediate obstacle to the establishment of new modes and orders: a model because "the Christian sect, unlike other less universal and less competent religions, has shown men how to unify mankind and capture the world for their own benefit" (111); but an obstacle because "Christianity is strong enough to defeat the strong, but not strong enough, because of its dependence on arms in an otherworldly sense, to be strong on its own" (120).

The ultimate cause of the weakness of Christianity in answering human necessities, according to Mansfield's Machiavelli, "is in the principles of classical political science, perhaps especially in the classical notion of the soul" (Mansfield 1996, 276). The classical understanding of the soul attempted to anchor human dignity and freedom by combining "two essentials: the soul as the beginning of motion and the soul as intellect" (277). In order to liberate humanity from the claims of otherworldliness, Machiavelli rejected the understanding of the soul as impartial intellect and thus was led to deny "the possibility of detachment in the human soul," even if this meant "denying that men are capable of voluntary action" (277). The traditional idea of human freedom is thus sacrificed to the project of the liberation of human necessities from the claims of another world.

But what can be the meaning of this sacrifice? How can Machiavelli's own activity as author be understood in relation to his reduction of freedom to the "anticipation of necessity" (Mansfield 1996, 277)? Mansfield, following Leo Strauss, seems to put the question of Machiavelli's self-understanding front and center by keeping ever in mind the Florentine's "strange suggestion that he was a prince" (ix). But what is the nature of the necessity Machiavelli himself embraces in teaching others to embrace necessity? Is this a material necessity—"because one's own body is the only common thing that can be benefited" (280)? Such a reading would seem most clearly to establish Machiavelli's decisive contribution to the prehistory of the modern (and in particular the Hobbesian-Lockean) idea of "the individual." According to Strauss, this would seem to be the decisive contribution, since "the quarrel between the ancients and the moderns concerns eventually, and perhaps even from the beginning, the status of individuality."[2]

This Machiavellian-materialist genealogy, however, does not so much illuminate the modern notion of individuality as it confronts us with the darkness surrounding this notion. For, clearly, Machiavelli's authorship cannot be understood as instrumental to some straightforwardly egoistic, material purpose of Machiavelli's: the prince of princes did not found new modes and orders in order to put a roof over his head, or secure a pension, or even, presumably, to win favor with the ladies. It is more plausible, certainly, to refer Machiavelli's authorship to the motive of "glory," but then one still has to reckon with his reduction of all glory to bodily necessity, as well as with the puzzle of the strange fame of a project that, however effective in transforming the world, would only be fully appreciated by a handful of captains, at least before the ultimately deconstructive appreciation of Leo Strauss.

There seems, then, to be something irreducible in Machiavelli's will to "acquire the world" (Mansfield 1996, xiv) by making himself "a patriot on behalf of humanity" (Mansfield 1996, 278). To master his natural concern for his own soul, Machiavelli must embrace without reserve the cause of this world. To attach himself to this world, he must renounce all claims of soulful detachment; but this renunciation itself implies a detachment from all consideration of his own "good," on behalf of a humanity itself stripped of all idea of purpose. Thus, since the idea of a free choice is inseparable from the possibility of a rational and therefore in some way "detached" understanding of the way things are, humanity's liberation from detachment must be at bottom a liberation from freedom itself,[3] a renunciation of purposive action and therefore of a meaningful orientation toward the world in the common, natural sense. Does modern individualism not then presuppose a detachment from nature more radical than that of classical rationalism, or indeed of traditional Christianity? What Strauss called the "low but solid ground" of liberalism appears to dissolve into this mysterious resolution of the abstractly humanitarian self.

To point up the mystery at the heart of Machiavelli's "realism" does not invalidate his insight into the temptation of religion to reconcile necessity with morality "uncomprehendingly," a temptation to which Christianity would appear to have succumbed more competently and universally than ancient religions. But to confront the difficulty of comprehending the spirit informing or impelling Machiavelli's own project for the management of the relationship between deeds and beliefs is to reopen the question of whether Machiavelli appropriates more than a certain strategy from Christianity. For one cannot say, finally, which party is more "comprehending" than the other, and therefore who might be better said to be appropriating whom, without undertaking a fresh reflection on the underlying problem itself, that is, the problem of the relationship between intellect and action in the human soul.

PHILOSOPHY AND PREPHILOSOPHIC NOBILITY

"Now this is what every soul pursues and for the sake of which it does everything."

—Plato, *Republic* VI

Let me attempt to outline one possible path to such a reflection through an engagement with certain texts of Leo Strauss. The duality necessity/goodness addressed in one way by Christianity and in another by the modern propaganda conceived by Machiavelli might both be understood in relation to the original philosophical question of the relation of nature, or the way things are always and of necessity, to convention, or the way things are understood to be for the purposes of human (moral, political, religious) existence. The simplest way of construing this relationship would be to understand it as an absolute dichotomy, thus keeping the categories as clear and distinct as possible, at the cost of accepting the groundlessness of ordinary human concerns. But since these are categories of human understanding, the notions of nature and convention will always touch at at least one point: namely, at the point or perhaps, rather, in the region that used to be called the soul. Thus, as Mansfield has pointed out, the soul as intellect must somehow be understood in relation to the soul as actor, or as beginning point of motion or change in the world. The tidy separation between intellect and action thus requires a separation in the soul of the philosopher between knower and human being.

According to some statements of Strauss, classical political philosophy would appear to rest upon such a clean and radical separation. Consider, for example, this passage from Strauss's "Restatement on Xenophon's *Hiero*": "As he looks up in search for the eternal order, all human things and all human concerns reveal themselves to him in all clarity as paltry and ephemeral, and no one can find solid happiness in what he knows to be paltry and ephemeral" (Strauss 1991, 198).[4] In responding here to Alexandre Kojève's neo-Hegelian argument that the deepest motive of all human activity and therefore of philosophy is the desire for recognition, which culminates in the desire to rule, Strauss argues that philosophers as such, in their desire to know the "eternal order," are indifferent to such political charms.

To defend this traditionally "detached" view of philosophy, Strauss must address Kojève's argument that the insuperable limitations of the human mind, the defect of "subjective certainty," implies the philosopher's inevitable dependence on other human beings. Strauss concedes the existence of such limitations, and goes on to consider the political implications for philosophy that proceed from the impossibility of subjective certainty (Strauss 1991, 194). More than once the argument seems to affirm the detached self-sufficiency of the philosophic life, its "divine" independence from the common life of ordinary human beings, only to be drawn back to a consideration of the ties that bind philosophers to friends or to fellow citizens.

Philosophers, Strauss concedes, do not enjoy such a hold on eternity as would transcend the need for friends. If philosophers enjoy some relation to eternal truth, their grasp of truth is not sufficient to bring them enjoyment in absolute solitude. Strauss observes, moreover, that friendship presupposes some conscious agreement. However, philosophy cannot provide a demonstrable basis for the substance of such an agreement. The agreement on the basis of which philosophers become friends must, therefore, be nonphilosophical, a matter of opinion and prejudice. For this reason, Strauss argues, philosophy is inseparable from the tendency to sectarianism (Strauss 1991, 194–95).[5] This academic party is clearly inferior to the philosophical sect, and both are to be preferred to ideology: "Much as we loathe the snobbish silence or whispering of the sect, we loathe even more the savage noise of the loudspeakers of the mass party" (195).

The love of wisdom can never rest satisfied with the opinions and prejudices shared by friends. Thus the philosopher must leave his "charmed circle" in order to seek out other opinions to disrupt and put in question what he shares with his friends. It is not accidental but necessary, then, that the philosopher go down to the marketplace of ideas, the arena of political men. If there is a way beyond the city, it would appear, it must lead through the city.

By perpetually unsettling the beliefs he shares with philosophical friends, is it not then possible for the philosopher, despite the defect of absolute subjective certainty, to declare independence from all opinions, including those of philosophical "sects"? According to this possibility, philosophy would be understood as a way of life independent of all substantive views and thus as a "knowledge of ignorance," a "genuine awareness of the problems." This understanding of philosophy is attractive, but it raises a new difficulty: "It is impossible to think about these problems without becoming inclined toward a solution, towards one or the other of the very few typical solutions." The risk of sectarianism is therefore permanent, insuperable, because it is internal to philosophy itself. "The danger of succumbing to the attraction of solutions is essential to philosophy which, without incurring this danger, would degenerate into playing with the problems" (Strauss 1991, 196).

The possibility of philosophy thus seems to be suspended somewhere between the risk of taking political opinions too seriously and that of not taking them seriously enough. Still, the nature of this suspension is far from clear. It is here, following a review of Xenophon's and Kojève's views on the motivations of love and honor, that Strauss states the difference between the philosopher and the political man as "a difference with respect to happiness. . . . The philosopher's dominating passion is a desire . . . for knowledge of the eternal order" (Strauss 1991, 197–98). As noted above, he is therefore supposed to care little for the ordinary human concerns that grip the souls of political men.

But what, then, is Socrates doing in the marketplace? Why and in what way is philosophy engaged with political concerns? Strauss first offers what one might call a reductionist explanation in terms of the needs of the body and the economic division of labor (Strauss 1991, 199). Immediately, though, Strauss extends the implications of the philosopher's shared mortality to a natural human attachment prior to any consideration of mutual benefit (199–200). The philosopher, moreover, is not a threat to harm his fellows, since his desire for truth eclipses all unjust desires. Indeed, he will be inclined to use his knowledge to try to help his fellows, without indulging the illusion that political action can bring some complete and final remedy to the evils of the human condition. So the philosopher becomes a *political* philosopher (200).

But neither the philosopher's limited material needs nor his social solidarity with his fellow citizens explains his descent *as a philosopher* into the marketplace. Strauss thus returns to the original formulation of the problem of philosophic self-sufficiency, that is, the "deficiency of 'subjective certainty'":

> The philosopher's attempt to grasp the eternal order is necessarily an ascent from the perishable things which as such reflect the eternal order. Of all perishable things known to us, those which reflect that order most, or which are most akin to that order, are the souls of men. But the souls of men reflect the eternal order in different degrees.
>
> A soul that is in good order or healthy reflects it to a higher degree than a soul that is chaotic or diseased. A philosopher who as such has had a glimpse of the eternal order is therefore particularly sensitive to the difference among human souls (Strauss 1991, 200–1).

The philosopher's interest in the virtue of nonphilosophers is not, then, merely instrumental or affective; it is intrinsic to his interest in the truth of the "eternal order." To be sure, Strauss soon observes that he has not proven the kinship—denied by reputable philosophers, both ancient and modern— between the order of virtues and the order of the whole. But this observation may point up rather than detract from the philosopher's philosophical interest in prephilosophical virtue. For if philosophy necessarily proceeds as an "ascent," then the philosopher's "glimpse" of the eternal order cannot be prior to his appreciation of healthy souls. This is not to deny that only the philosopher's soul is truly healthy or well-ordered, since only by knowledge of ignorance is it possible to escape the deformity of boasting (Strauss 1991, 210). But philosophic virtue, according to Strauss's analysis, would appear to be not so much a separate and distinct alternative to moral virtue as an interrupted, self-aware enjoyment of virtue, delicately poised between self-affirmation and self-doubt, somehow at once ironic and edifying.

Thus, although Strauss concedes the title of "philosopher" to "Democritus and other pre-Socratics, to say nothing of the moderns" who deny a kinship between virtue and the eternal order, he gives us two strong reasons for questioning that concession (Strauss 1991, 201). First, without the assumption of this kinship, philosophy can only explain the philosopher's desire to communicate his thoughts by his "desire for recognition or by his human kindness" (202). One cannot, therefore, explain it as intrinsic to the philo-

sophic interest in truth itself. But to explain a characteristic activity of philosophy as motivated by something other than the interest in truth would
seem to put in question the possibility of philosophy. Second, Strauss
doubts whether, without glimpsing a kinship between the order of the soul
and the order of the whole, it is possible to explain "the immediate pleasure which the philosopher experiences when he sees a well-ordered soul
or the immediate pleasure which we experience when we observe signs of
human nobility" (202).

Strauss believes that only by showing a certain respect to the intimations
of common morality regarding the order of soul or to conventional opinions
regarding the character of justice can the philosopher gain a foothold by
which to ascend toward what he styles "the eternal order." In other words,
the soul as mirror of an "eternal order" can never detach itself completely
from the soul as the beginning of motion.

REASON, REVELATION, AND THE ANCESTRAL GOOD

Leo Strauss is aware, however, that to understand the imperfect goodness of
morality in the light of the idea of philosophic contemplation is to follow
only one possible interpretation of the phenomenon. The great alternative to
this interpretation is represented, at least in the West, by biblical religion.
What is at stake in these alternative understandings of morality in relation to
what is higher than morality? To pursue this question, I now turn to some
pages from Strauss's essay "Progress or Return?"[6] on the relationship between philosophy and revealed religion.

It is well known that Strauss, impatient with the triviality or obfuscatory
quality of pretended syntheses of Athens and Jerusalem, is concerned especially to underline the apparently unbridgeable gulf between the life of philosophy and the life of piety. Let us briefly review some key features of the
landscape on either side of this gulf. Philosophy is characterized by autonomous understanding; biblical piety by obedient love (Strauss 1989, 273).
The Bible requires humble obedience to the demands of justice; Aristotle
makes room for magnanimity or noble pride beside the demands of justice
(276). The Bible associates poverty with piety; the Greeks believed a moderate level of wealth was necessary to virtue (277). The Bible requires man to
consider his guiltiness and impurity of heart in God's sight; the philosophers
do not imagine that God cares for purity of heart and seek rather to clarify
opinions and to understand the place of mankind in general in the universe
than to search their hearts (278–79). The Bible binds man to a community of
the faithful; the Greek quest for asocial perfection presupposes the human hierarchy and enlightenment of the city, the political community (279). The
Bible counsels fear of and hope in God; the philosopher, moved by a sense

of wonder, lives beyond fear and hope (280). The Bible teaches creation out
of nothing and divine omnipotence; philosophy teaches the eternity of the
world (281). The Bible reveals a mysterious, omnipotent, personal God essentially concerned with man, but with whom man can only relate through a
covenant by which God binds himself; the philosopher's highest principle is
an intelligible, impersonal necessity (281, 287, 293). Revelation reveals the sa-
credness of certain particular and contingent events, and the one right way;
philosophy is concerned only with the universal and necessary, and discovers the idea of nature above all conventions or ways (290, 282–84).

The gulf is indeed wide. And yet Strauss knows that in order to discuss it
he must in a sense bridge it: "every disagreement . . . presupposes some
agreement" (Strauss 1989, 273). We might say that, in order to disagree, philosophy and revealed religion must be about the same thing. What they are
both about, according to Strauss, may be roughly described as what we now
call "morality." "We observe first a broad agreement between the bible and
Greek philosophy regarding both morality and the insufficiency of morality."
What they disagree about is how this insufficiency might be overcome: the
Greeks understanding philosophical contemplation as that completion, and
the believers so understanding obedient love (291).

The unity from which revealed religion and philosophy diverge may be
defined more precisely as the "primeval . . . equation of the good with the
ancestral." "The good [or] the true . . . can be known only as the old because
prior to the emergence of wisdom memory occupied the place of wisdom"
(Strauss 1989, 294). The order of the soul, which, as we have seen above,
serves as the philosopher's means of ascent toward the eternal order, originally understands itself as obedience to laws that embody the presumed
unity of the good and the ancestral. This unity generally finds an anchor in
the identification of the ancestors with "the gods, sons of gods, or pupils of
gods" (284). But the multiplicity of comprehensive laws, each referring to its
own ancestors and gods, subverts the unity of the ancestral and the good.
Revealed religion and philosophy are the two classic means of addressing
this subversion.

Since the Bible and philosophy share a common origin, since they address
a common problem, they can be truly and altogether distinct, it would seem,
only if at least one of them actually and finally solves the problem of the mutual conditioning of the good and the ancestral. However, on close inspection, Strauss gives us plenty of reasons for doubting that this is the case.
Clearly Strauss's rhetoric throughout this discussion relies heavily on an assumption of the possibility of philosophic self-sufficiency and completeness
that is rendered quite problematic by the "Restatement" examined above.
One might well get the impression, reading these pages of Strauss, that nature is simply intelligible and that the philosopher finally and decisively transcends all human concerns in contemplating its order.[7] Strauss would have

the reader believe that the divine law, though "the absolutely essential starting point," is only a starting point that is "abandoned in the process" of philosophy itself (Strauss 1989, 286). But how can the starting point simply be "abandoned" if no alternative beginning point or origin unconditioned by the ancestral good is established with certainty? And is it not an implication of Strauss's own argument that philosophy must keep beginning by returning to the opinions of the marketplace, opinions the articulation of which, Strauss has taught us, can never be fully disentangled from implicit references to divine law?

PARTS AND WHOLES

To approach the question from another angle: Strauss argues that "philosophers transcend the dimension of divine codes altogether. . . . Instead they embark on a free quest for the beginnings, for the first things, for the principles." This quest proceeds through a kind of reasoning and awareness that may be distinguished from biblical or mystical awareness in that it "is never divorced from sense perception and reasoning based on sense perception. In other words, philosophy never becomes oblivious of its kinship with the arts and crafts, with the knowledge used by the artisan . . ." (Strauss 1989, 292). Now, Strauss has elsewhere[8] associated knowledge related to "the productive arts and crafts" with mathematical knowledge, or "knowledge of homogeneity" (Strauss, 38). However, far from simply identifying philosophy with the ambitions of such knowledge, he contrasts this "knowledge of homogeneity" with a "superior" form of knowledge, the "knowledge of heterogeneity, and in particular of heterogeneous ends" (38). Most strikingly, he associates homogeneity with the "charm of competence" and heterogeneity with "the charm of *humble* awe" (39; my emphasis). This is not to say that Strauss equates philosophy with either kind of knowledge. "Philosophy," he writes, "is characterized by the gentle, if firm, refusal to succumb to either charm" (39).

True philosophy—that is, political philosophy—would thus seem to involve a kind of equilibrium or mean between the prideful "charm of competence" of homogeneous (mathematical-technical) knowledge and the "humble awe" associated with the knowledge of heterogeneous human ends. On closer inspection, though, the picture is more complicated, since heterogeneity is at once more humble and more prideful than homogeneity. This can be seen by pursuing the discussion of the meaning of philosophy in relation to the problem of heterogeneity and homogeneity in the consideration of Plato's *Statesman* that we find in the central section (between a discussion of the *Republic* and one of the *Laws*) of Strauss's chapter "Plato" in the *History of Political Philosophy*.[9] Here Strauss explicitly associates "all

arts, and especially the kingly art" not with mathematical homogeneity, or
the "art of measurement . . . which considers the greater and the less . . . in
relation to one another," but with "measurements with a view to the right
mean or the fitting" (Strauss and Cropsey 1987, 73). Thus it appears possible
to preserve the sense of philosophy's kinship with the arts, in that the arts are
here considered not from the standpoint of production (recall Strauss's
phrase: "the *productive* arts or crafts"; my emphasis), but from the statesman's standpoint of their use in relation to the whole of human life. Strauss's
discussion of the problem of this wholeness suggests in fact that philosophy
itself may be seen as the highest appearance of a certain equilibrium or "right
mean" as a figure of the best life.

Strauss acknowledges in this article on Plato that the impossibility of
founding knowledge on an "absolute beginning" threatens philosophy and
therefore human life with "Sisyphean" absurdity (Strauss 1987, 73). What can
philosophy mean if "we are condemned to rest satisfied with partial knowledge of parts of the whole and hence never truly to transcend the sphere of
opinion?" (73). If there is an answer to this question or challenge, Strauss
suggests, it would seem to involve a linking or weaving together of the highest aspirations of knowledge—a pure and serene pursuit of cosmic truth,
which would appear to reduce common human pretensions to insignifi-
cance—with the necessarily opinion-laden affirmation of human freedom or
distinctiveness. Thus, whereas the "pride" by which human beings "divide
the genus 'animal' into the species 'brutes' and 'men'" and which underlies
the political claims of human freedom at first appears as simply opposed to
the "modesty or moderation" of the art of dialectics, Strauss finally suggests
instead that "the whole is not whole without man, without his own effort,
and this effort presupposes . . . knowledge which is not contemplative or
theoretical but prescriptive or commanding or practical" (71, 77). This participation of our pretheoretical humanity in any possible philosophic meaning of "the whole" underlies the deep coprimordiality of theory and practice
as it emerges from Strauss's highly compressed discussion of the relation of
the *Statesman* to the *Republic*.[10] Whether considering the rule of reason from
the standpoint of the political claims of philosophy (the *Republic*) or from
that of the philosophic status of the art of ruling (the *Statesman*), one arrives
at the mutual inextricability of reason and ruling: as all action implicitly involves a theoretical orientation toward a reality beyond human power, so all
reflection involves a practical affirmation of its own worth. Or, to recall
Mansfield's vocabulary, the detachment of philosophy is attached to the detachment of practical freedom.[11]

"Attachment" does not at all imply fusion; rather, it is precisely the repudi-
ation of this coprimordiality of theory and practice, the denial of a natural
link between the soul as the beginning of motion and the soul as knower,
that yields the modern construction of reason as *mastery*, or the absorption

of theory by practice, or vice versa. Strauss clearly signals his rejection of this modern fusion of radical detachment and radical homogeneity: "The whole human race, and not any part of it, is self-sufficient as a part of the whole, and not as the master or conqueror of the whole" (Strauss and Cropsey 1987, 77).

Considering Strauss's discussion of the *Statesman* in connection with the passages on which we have commented in "What Is Political Philosophy?" the reader is thus led to understand the extremes of mastery and debasement at work in the modern understanding of reason (the limitless mastery of a homogeneous, objectified "nature") as the result of an abandonment or for-getting of a classical equilibrium most fully explored in Plato's dialogues. The classical claim of philosophic self-sufficiency is there brought to terms with its dependence on the meaningfulness of humanity as that most het-erogeneous part which grounds the search for an articulate whole. At the same time, humanity's prideful sense of distinctive significance is moderated by its philosophic subordination to the question of a larger meaning that sur-passes and humbles all human pretensions. The kinship and otherness of the philosopher and the nonphilosopher thus provides perhaps the most funda-mental manifestation of the problem of homogeneity and heterogeneity; the philosopher secures his detachment from opinion only by returning perpet-ually to the opinion of detachment.

To be sure, Strauss's dominant rhetoric—a position honed in response to the modern fusion of theory and practice, and to the new tyranny it produced or facilitated—emphasizes the heterogeneity of philosophy in relation to the realm of "opinion," or of the ordinary concerns of humanity. Thus, in the orig-inal concluding paragraph of his "Restatement on Xenophon's *Hiero*," Strauss proceeds, contrary to his reading of the *Statesman*, precisely as if the whole could be understood as a whole without human "effort" or free activity: "Phi-losophy . . . presupposes that there is an eternal and unchangeable order within which history takes place and which is not in any way affected by History. It presupposes, in other words, that any 'realm of freedom' is not more than a de-pendent province within the 'realm of necessity'" (Strauss 1997, 471).[12]

Perhaps by admitting that "this hypothesis is not self-evident" Strauss means to acknowledge the legitimacy (as well as the dangers) of the Judeo-Christian and modern interest in understanding the meaning of human free-dom as somehow intrinsic to the meaning of the whole, that is, as more than a simple "province" of the "realm of necessity." Still, impelled by his domi-nant concern to resist the facile and ultimately dangerous identification of reason and revelation, or the philosophic appropriation of religious hopes, Strauss (and here we return to "Progress or Return?") seems in some texts to give himself over to the "charm of competence" of mathematical and pro-ductive knowledge, and thus to proceed as if knowledge of the whole, or discovery of a "beginning" necessity from which all things, including human things, could be explained, were simply possible—as if, that is, knowledge could be homogenized in relation to the principle of the whole, as if philosophic detachment were not attached to practical detachment. But if knowledge of ends must remain as much a form of "humble awe" as an expression of "competence," this is because the philosopher's dependence for knowledge of ends on political virtue and therefore ultimately on divine law is never simply overcome. Human ends are not knowable in the way that mathematical objects and products of art may be grasped and mastered; the linkage in tension between the soul as intellect and the soul as the beginning of motion can never be overcome altogether. The quest to understand human things as "natural" never entirely absolves itself from dependence on "memory," or the "right way" (Strauss 1989, 284) understood as divine law. Strauss can write that "the ancestral and the good are two fundamentally different things" (285), but they could be two absolutely different things only if reason were competent to produce its own ends, if theory could become wholly its own practice, or practice its own theory.

To overcome this tension between intellect and action, nature and convention, necessity and goodness, by asserting that all law and morality is simply conventional and thus ultimately the result of acquisition or violence would be to follow Machiavelli's incomprehensible or uncomprehending detachment. We can say rather that what is natural in law—what is good by nature—can never be fully extricated from what is simply inherited, from the ancestral or traditional. But this is not so much to depreciate the competence of reason as it is to acknowledge the images of the good as distilled (and distorted, of course) in memory or tradition. And does not Strauss himself invite us along this path when he describes the human soul as that singular part of the whole which is open to the whole? If this were not true already of the soul under ancestral-divine law, it could never become true of philosophers. If philosophy is "graced by nature's grace" (Strauss 1959, 39), then it is not itself identical to that grace. The philosopher can only transcend the city because the city in some sense already transcends itself.

REVELATION OR IDOLATRY

If philosophy must preserve the tension between the charms of homogeneity and those of heterogeneity, then it must in a sense preserve the memory of the divine-ancestral good from which the knowledge of heterogeneous ends is never absolved. But what of philosophy's relation to the other possible alternative to the divine-ancestral good, namely, revealed religion? Here Strauss again argues as if it were possible to break radically with the authority of the ancestral good. The revelation of a true divine law as distinct from merely ancestral divine laws seems to dispense entirely with the problem of the good, as if the soul understood as the beginning of action, the soul confronted with the choice between righteous obedience and evil rebellion, could be insulated altogether from the soul understood as intellect, with its interest in the nature or necessity of the whole.

Strauss indeed proceeds, in accordance with a distinctive and rigorous understanding of his Jewish heritage, as if the natural though imperfect openness to the whole already implicit in the ancestral good were simply obliterated by the biblical revelation of divine law. This rigorous acosmism appears to be grounded in Strauss's understanding of the radical transcendence at the heart of Jewish faith. The core of this understanding perhaps appears more clearly in the talk "Why We Remain Jews" than in Strauss's more guarded scholarly writings. Here he explains why he regards as a compliment the pagan Romans' accusing the Jews (and also the Christians) of hatred of humanity:

> A nation is a nation by virtue of what it looks up to. In antiquity, a nation was a nation by virtue of its looking up to its gods. . . . And now, our ancestors asserted a priori . . . that these gods were nothings and abominations. In the light of the purity which Isaiah understood when he said of himself, "I am a man of unclean lips," the very Parthenon is impure. (Strauss 1997, 327)

From the point of view, or rather the non–point of view, of this inconceivable purity, the highest goods by which the lives of all other peoples are ordered are revealed to be idols. This includes Christianity, which is ordered by a belief in the God-man, or in the redeemer who has already come (322). Judaism alone is defined by the "suffering stemming from the heroic act of self-dedication of a whole nation to something which it regarded as infinitely higher than itself" (323). The Jewish people stand alone as "the living witness for the absence of redemption" (327).

To any soul in the least responsive to biblical piety the greatness and sublimity of this invocation of an openness to infinite transcendence speaks for itself. And yet the soul's interest in understanding must draw us to question whether revelation may be received simply and exclusively as a "brute fact, to which nothing in purely human experience corresponds" (Strauss 1989, 304), or whether it must not also be interpreted immediately as a *meaningful fact*, that is, a fact integrated in some way with what is meaningful to human beings as human beings, under one or another understanding of the good by which souls and cities are ordered. The attempt to understand revealed law as altogether absolved from a hierarchically ordered world may be understood as an attempt radically to insulate the soul as agent (under God) from the soul as intellect, or to liberate knowledge of heterogeneity (the differences among kinds of things that must be respected by human action)[12] altogether from knowledge of homogeneity (the unity of the world under some intelligible first things). But must not this radical solution collapse in a manner parallel to Machiavelli's godless version of denial of the rational soul's detachment in favor of the soul's power to act? For the antiidolatrous rejection of all hierarchical and cosmological interpretations of the whole within which human beings act cannot escape the necessity of interpretation; it can only create a teleological vacuum to be filled by progressive-materialist interpretations of the meaning of human action and of "individuality."[13]

If we admit that neither philosophy nor revelation can ever altogether abandon the ancestral good, the pretheoretical intimations of the good variously present in the implicit orientations toward the whole woven into every life-world, then we must question the absolute dualisms into which Strauss casts the differences between philosophy and piety. Most evidently, if, as concerns philosophy, we consider that knowledge and therefore the life of knowledge never achieve absolute autonomy, and if, as concerns piety, we recognize that no comprehensive law, divine or otherwise, is obeyed by a human being without being understood in some way with respect to some world, then it is hard to maintain an absolute distinction between thinking and obeying. Strauss himself notices that Socrates' quest is in one sense— perhaps not wholly ironic, I would say—a response to a divine command. And he has alerted us to the charms of a certain "humble awe" before the mystery of the human good to which political philosophy must not exclusively succumb but which it must in some way preserve. It is not easy to say after all whether in heeding one's higher self's call to the most lucid and rational way of life one is obeying oneself or something higher.[14]

PHILOSOPHY AND THE MYSTERY OF THE SOUL

Leo Strauss devoted most of his scholarly life to the effort to articulate the claims of reason in the governance of human life, giving a fair hearing to the "low but solid ground" of modern rationalism while clearly preferring the classical ideal of serene contemplation. Finally, though, he seems to have agreed with his great rival, Heidegger, that "being is radically mysterious" (Strauss 1997, 328). More than Heidegger, however, Strauss provides us with a framework for understanding that the "mystery" of the human soul cannot be identified simply with the practical and poetic being of man any more than with man's interest in necessary and eternal truths. To attempt to understand or to evoke poetically one dimension of the human soul or of Being in absolute abstraction from the other is to do violence to wisdom as well as to piety. For the mystery that must be respected lies precisely in this duality, that is, in the reality of individual beings who appear at once as wholes and as parts of some larger whole.

To interpret dogmatically the classical rhetoric of serene philosophical autonomy is to court the divorce of philosophy from pretheoretical intimations of the good and the just and thus to risk leaving the "philosopher" with no possible orientation toward heterogeneity or to what is other than the orientation of mastery. To admit such a divorce and thus to freeze classical political philosophy in the rhetoric of the self-sufficient sage would be to lend credence to the "postmodern" claim that classical philosophy is implicated in the "totalism" of the modern project of the end-less mastery of nature. As Strauss must have learned from Heidegger as well as from Machiavelli, the extremes meet: mastery implies humanitarian necessity; rationalism as autonomy shades into instrumental or technological rationalism; the claim of absolute detachment yields a perverse and unnatural attachment, and vice versa. If the humane roots of this Janus-faced rationalism are to be recovered and renewed, if the "philosopher" is seriously to go down into the city, it may now be necessary for philosophy itself to encounter Jerusalem as well as Athens.

More particularly, I will conclude by suggesting that the thinker must meet Rome on the way to Greece.[15] If Christianity claims the attention of political philosophy, this is not only because the historical question of the meaning of its appropriation by modern rationalism remains open, or simply because the positive truth of its revelation cannot in principle be excluded on rational grounds. Rather, Christian belief concerns the reality of the human soul as knower and as agent, and therefore points to problems and possibilities that the student of the whole and therefore of the human soul cannot afford to ignore. For example, the powerful and dangerous strategy that Machiavelli adapted from Christianity must reveal something about the human soul, and therefore about "the whole." The challenge of Christianity to political philosophy lies in the fact that both address and are addressed to human beings.

WORKS CITED

Mansfield, Harvey C. 1996. *Machiavelli's Virtue*. Chicago: University of Chicago Press.

Strauss, Leo. 1989. *An Introduction to Political Philosophy: Ten Essays by Leo Strauss*. Edited by Hilail Gilden. Detroit: Wayne State University Press.

——. 1991. *On Tyranny*. Edited by Victor Gourevitch and Michael S. Roth. Rev. and expanded edition. New York: Free Press.

——. 1997. "Why We Remain Jews." In *Jewish Philosophy and the Crisis of Modernity: Essays and Lectures in Modern Jewish Thought*. Edited by Kenneth Hart Green. Albany, N.Y.: State University of New York Press.

Strauss, Leo and Joseph Cropsey, eds. 1987. *History of Political Philosophy*. Chicago: University of Chicago Press.

NOTES

1. Most notably, perhaps, in his *Machiavelli's New Modes and Orders* (Ithaca, N.Y.: Cornell University Press, 1979).

2. Leo Strauss, *Natural Right and History* (Chicago: University of Chicago Press, 1953), 323.

3. See Pierre Manent, *La cité de l'homme* (Paris: Fayard, 1994), 224, 226: "La nature enveloppe la liberté; elle est plus forte qu'elle. Pour autant, elle la nie. La philosophie moderne, en niant le libre arbitre, nie cette négation et libère la liberté. . . . Affirmer la nécessité des actes humains, c'est rendre possible l'affirmation d'une pure liberté; pour autant, c'est affirmer celle-ci." Compare Strauss's discussion of Machiavelli's assumption of an Archimedean point outside of nature in *Thoughts on Machiavelli* (Glencoe, Ill.: Free Press, 1958), 297.

4. This passage is quoted and seems to provide the linchpin of Stanley Rosen's reading in "Leo Strauss and the Quarrel between the Ancients and the Moderns," in *Leo Strauss's Thought: Toward a Critical Engagement* (Boulder, Col.: Lynne Rienner Publishers, 1991), 161. For his part, Rosen appears utterly convinced that this statement represents Strauss's true, esoteric teaching. But he seems to encourage us to doubt whether it was also Plato's teaching by quoting from *Philebus* 28C, where Socrates says, "All the wise agree, thereby exalting themselves, that intellect is king for us of heaven and earth. And perhaps they speak well." I suppose that Rosen supposes that the "perhaps" must be understood in relation to "thereby exalting themselves."

5. Strauss argues further in these pages that the philosopher's need to put in question the prejudices of his own philosophical sect by engaging political opinions is concealed today by the "modern substitute" for the sect, that is, the "Republic of Letters." This association is characterized by relativism or by a "soft eclecticism," for which Strauss shows very scant respect: "A certain vague middle line, which is perhaps barely tolerable for the most easy-going members of the different persuasions if they are in their drowsiest mood, is set up as The Truth or as Common Sense. . . ." (Strauss 1991, 195)

6. In *An Introduction to Political Philosophy: Ten Essays by Leo Strauss*, ed., Hilail Gilden (Detroit: Wayne State University Press, 1989), 249–310.

7. Strauss seems to have reinvented this classical rhetoric to stiffen the spine of the late enlightenment. Contrary to Heidegger, he appears to believe that modern nihilism is best resisted not by deconstructing the spiritual links between classical reason and modern rationalism but by reinforcing them. This rhetoric is not without beauty, because it is not without truth. But it is perhaps permitted now to reconsider the judgments implicit in Strauss's rhetorical choices. Can the praise of the autonomy of philosophy today continue to point to a possibility beyond the dominant dogmas and habits of the age without unduly contributing to the complacency or insulation of "philosophy" as an academic sect, a mere counteraristocracy, or, rather, counter-elite? And can the rhetoric of the good moderate the modern passion for justice without respecting the sources of that passion as expressed in revealed religion?

8. In the title essay of "What Is Political Philosophy" (Glencoe, Ill.: The Free Press, 1959), 38–39.

9. Edited by Leo Strauss and Joseph Cropsey, Chicago: University of Chicago Press, 1987.

10. "The *Republic* presents a practical discussion of theory . . . [in the *Statesman*,] the theoretical discussion of the highest practical knowledge . . . takes on a commanding character. . . ." (Strauss and Cropsey 1987, 77)

11. Consider the passage in Plato's *Theaetetus* (173b–177e) to which Strauss refers us in concluding his account of the *Statesman*. Here the dignity of the philosopher, ignored by the "rabble" or the "maidservants or the uneducated" who mock his practical incompetence, is appreciated "by everyone whose breeding has been the antithesis of the slaves," or by one "who has learned to wear his cloak like a gentleman, or caught the accent of discourse that will rightly celebrate the true life of happiness for gods and men." See Hamilton and Cairns, eds., *Plato: Collected Dialogues* (Princeton, N.J.: Princeton University Press, 1971), 880.

12. In *Jewish Philosophy and the Crisis of Modernity*, ed., Kenneth Hart Grave (Albany, N.Y.: SUNY Press, 1997).

13. Consider in this connection Strauss's strikingly unqualified denial in the "Restatement" that "man as man is thinkable as a being that lacks awareness of sacred restraints. . . ." (Strauss 1991, 192)

14. Surely Strauss knows that more than modernity is at stake in the "ultimate" question of the "status of individuality." His awareness of the vulnerability of "individualism" to progressive-materialist (and therefore ultimately Machiavellian) interpretations no doubt underlies his tendency to dismiss any more high-minded genealogies of individualism. But once we see that there is indeed such a philosophical and spiritual question, and that "the individual" can by no means be simply identified with the attachment to one's own body, then might not theory as well as practice be better served by paying more philosophical respect to the spiritual sources of individualism, whatever their vulnerability?

15. Cf. Jacques Derrida, *The Gift of Death*, trans. David Wills (Chicago: University of Chicago Press, 1995), 45–52.

16. Pierre Manent, *La cité de l'homme*, last section, 294–95.

5

Metaphysics and Religion: Francis Bacon's Critique of the Ancients

Jerry Weinberger

Francis Bacon's criticism of the ancients is well known. The ancients preferred theory to practice, contemplation to action. The mind's perfection was for them a kind of rest far removed from the hustle and bustle of art and even from prudence. Because these ancients were followed and revered for two thousand years, knowledge, like water, never rose above its ancient sources, and the human race was unable to tap the hidden powers of nature and bend them to human ends, and in particular to the relief of man's estate. Moreover, most of what was contained in the ancients' supposed wisdom simply was not true. The ancients may have known a thing or two about politics and morals, but they knew nothing of the hidden courses of nature. And mastery of nature—the true goal of reason—so alters the political world as to make the ancients' political and moral wisdom, useful as it once might have been, now otiose. The classical divide between theory and practice actually retarded practice and distorted theory. In fact, according to Bacon *real* contemplation—by which he means a true grasp of the world as it actually is—is possible only through modern science, in which reason actively puts nature on the rack. A case can even be made for the superiority of such real contemplation to mere practice. As Bacon says in the *Novum Organum:*

> And again, if the usefulness of just one particular invention has so impressed men that they deemed superhuman the man who could secure the devotion of the entire human race through some benefit he brought, how much loftier will it seem to discover something that will enable all other discoveries to be readily made? And yet, to tell the whole truth, just as it is thanks to light that we can go our ways and practice our arts, read, and recognize each other, while actually seeing the light is more excellent and beautiful than all its manifold uses; in

the same way, surely, the very contemplation of things as they are, without superstition or imposture, error or confusion is in itself more praiseworthy than all the fruit of inventions.[1]

According to Bacon, the ancients erred because they were unable to discern the separate domains of being that make up the world. Consequently, the ancients did not sufficiently distinguish between final cause—purpose and end—and material and efficient causes. This confusion had two effects: first, "the handling of final causes mixed with the rest in physical inquiries, hath intercepted the severe and diligent inquiry of all real and physical cause and given men the occasion to stay upon these satisfactory and specious causes, to the arrest and prejudice of further discovery." We see this effect especially in Aristotle's teleology, where circular and scientifically sterile judgments such as "eyelashes are for protecting sight" were found to be so full an explanation of nature that the corresponding and much more fecund judgment regarding material and efficient causes, "hairiness is incident to wet orifices," was overlooked.[2]

Second, the ancients' preoccupation with final causes led them to misconceive the character of formal cause. This error was especially prominent in Plato. He understood the intelligible forms of nature as if they were the perfect, independent, and changeless originals of the things we encounter in everyday practical and moral experience. As there are many ephemeral cats, so there is one eternal and perfect essence of cat—the *eidos* of cat. The same for "bed." And the same for human relations: as there is justice as it emerges from and is relative to this or that particular situation, so there is the changeless essence of justice, the *eidos* of justice. The *eide* are linked to the particulars of which they are *eide*, because in each case they are what the particulars in some way or other strive to be; but the *eide* are not and cannot be identical to any particular thing or relation. Moreover, as there is cat and rat, so there is a relation of rank from high to low of the *eide* of cat and rat. As cat eats rat, so the *eidos* of cat orders the *eidos* of rat. What else can we conclude from the argument that there is such a thing as the *eidos* of the good that is the cause of all existence and being and the "cause of all that is correct and noble in everything"?[3]

Aristotle repeated this conceit, although with more sobriety. Aristotle's understanding of formal cause in terms of substance (a thing having independent existence, as indicated by the fact that in speech it can be a subject but not a predicate) avoided the Platonic extravagance of total abstraction of form from material particulars. Indeed, for Aristotle, a particular and material thing, such as this Socrates right here, is a substance. But Aristotle still approached nature as if to know it is to grasp the character of things as they first appear to us in our everyday experience. As a result, Aristotle no less than Plato conceived of nature as a hierarchy of rat, cat, and man. As Bacon says, even the empirically minded Aristotle conceived of nature as "pregnant with final causes."[4] In confusing final and physical causes and in misconceiving the intelligible forms that really operate in nature, the ancients understood the world not as it is but as they wanted it to be. They imagined a worldly environment that answered to their moral hopes and somehow told them how to live.

In a nutshell, Bacon argued that the ancients were moved by the false assumption that the natural and the human realms were of a piece and to be understood in the same ontological terms. The result was that the ancients were blind to the real causes that operate in the world and are the real objects of knowledge. Why such a monumental failure? Because the ancients, says Bacon, were in thrall to the inbred tendency of the human mind to see things as ordered and connected when in fact they are not (what he terms the Idols of the Tribe), to the inclination of men to love their own ideas (the Idols of the Cave), and to the peculiar tendency of the philosophers to think that nature must conform to their abstract theories (the Idols of the Theatre).

In Bacon's contrary understanding, physics investigates the variable and respective causes that operate in nature. These causes are material and therefore transitory, and "suppose in nature only a being and moving": fire is the variable and respective cause of hardening in clay and softening in wax. Fire is the efficient cause, and wax and clay are the material causes. Metaphysics, for Bacon, is the study of "the abstract and the fixed in nature." It is the study of formal and final cause, which supposes in nature "a reason, understanding, and platform." In *Advancement of Learning* Bacon rejects the skeptical opinion that we cannot find out essential forms or true differences of things, but he adds that Plato erred in considering forms as absolutely abstracted from matter and not confined and *determined* by matter (my emphasis). If, however, we keep our eyes upon action, operation, and use—on material things and practice—we can discover the forms that really exist and that can be fruitful for the state of man.

Turning implicitly to Aristotle, Bacon remarks that it is only of man that we can know the *substance*—the essence of the thing as it is given to us in everyday experience. We can know man's substance because God created man directly, as opposed to all other creatures that God had the earth and water bring forth. Of the latter, the "forms of substances" (the essential whatness of things, such as cat, rat, and bed), as we encounter them in everyday experience, are "so perplexed" as not to be inquired. Thus "to enquire the form of a lion, of an oak, of gold, nay of water, of air, is a vain pursuit." But we can inquire of and understand "the forms of sense, voluntary motion, vegetations, colors, gravity and levity, density, tenuity, heat, cold, and all other natures and qualities" that are finite and *"of which the essences (upheld by matter) of all creatures do consist"* (my emphasis). Physics treats these natures and qualities, but only as regards their material and efficient causes.

If we ask the cause of whiteness in snow and froth, and say that it is the subtle intermixture of air and water, we have given the efficient and material causes of whiteness, not the form of whiteness. The form of whiteness is the state of any matter such that it causes in our sight the experience of the color white, and such that this state is itself the product of phenomena or natures other than and more general than whiteness. The form whiteness is the operation of the material and efficient causes of whiteness, but considered in the light of the more general natural motions that underlie whiteness and things other than whiteness.[5]

Bacon says that this part of metaphysics, the study of formal causes as just described, is "most excellent" in two respects: (1) it abridges the infinity of individual experience as far as truth will permit, and (2) it remedies the problem that art is long and life is short. In true natural philosophy, natural history is the basis for physics, and the vertical point, above physics, is metaphysics. But metaphysics as the enumeration of the natural forms is not a vertical point of knowledge in the sense of disclosing an ordered world as our home or of penetrating the ultimate purpose of the world. Of things such as the fit between the world and our needs, and ultimate purposes and ends—"the work that God did from beginning to end"—Bacon says that we do not know if we can comprehend them (which is not to say that we cannot). Even so, the three stages of knowledge (natural history, physics, and metaphysics as the elaboration of true forms) are holy in three respects: (1) they describe God's works, (2) they show the connections of God's works, and (3) they show the union of God's works in a perpetual and uniform law. Metaphysics is thus the worthiest knowledge for two reasons. First, it is charged with the least multiplicity and considers the simple forms or differences of things and the degrees and coordinations of all the variety. Second, it "enfranchises the power of man unto the greatest liberty and possibility of works and effects." While physics can at best give light to new invention in similar materials, the knowledge of any form discloses the "utmost possibility of superinducing that nature on any variety of matter [i.e., not just water or snow] and so is less restrained in operation" by matter and efficient cause.[6]

But again, the natural unity and connectedness revealed by Baconian metaphysics are not the unity and connectedness of man and world. Baconian forms are not the perfect models of the things making up the world of experience, nor are they natural moral stars by which we can take our bearings. They are, rather, the most general, latent motions of nature that course below the mere appearances of things and that can be grasped and bent to human will. Metaphysics is the peak of knowledge, not in the sense of being a crown or in being concerned with the meaning and purpose of the whole, but in the sense of being the simplest and most powerful tool that serves the infinitely variegated realm of physics.

The other part of metaphysics is inquiry into final causes. It has not been omitted in the course of history, says Bacon, so much as it has been misplaced. But this misplacing is not just a matter of mere order; it has ruined the sciences and hidden the truth about formal and material causes, because it harbors a false assumption about what can be known of the relationship of natural causes and human purposes. To repeat: "The handling of final causes mixed with the rest in physical inquiries, hath intercepted the severe and diligent inquiry of all real and physical causes and given men the occasion to stay upon these satisfactory and specious causes, to the great arrest and prejudice of further discovery." Bacon does not deny that the causal courses of nature serve human ends. Do not animals and vegetables nourish us? Is not the material organ we call the brain also the site of consciousness and the soul? Bacon thus says that if the true boundaries between metaphysics and physics be honored, we are "deceived" if we think there is some conflict between final and physical causes. There is no conflict between the statements "eyelashes are for protecting sight" (judgment of final cause) and "hairiness is incident to wet orifices" (judgment of physical cause). Both are true and compatible, he says: the one (physical cause) "declares an intention" and the other (final cause) "declares a consequence."[7]

We can see the brute facts of natural intention and consequence for man, but we cannot understand or penetrate the means by which they are connected. The divide between physical and final cause reflects the limits of *human* understanding. Therefore, the divide does not, says Bacon, impugn divine providence. On the contrary. For just as in civil affairs the greater politician is the one who gets people to do things without their knowing it, so the wisdom of God is the more admirable when nature intends one thing and providence draws forth another, "than if he had communicated to particular creatures and motions the characters and impressions of his providence."[8] We don't know how and why natural intention regarding wet orifices turns out to protect the human capacity for sight; that's God's doing. The metaphysical account of final cause thus describes the effects of divine will, but how and why that will actually works we cannot know. Trying to know the unknowable (the divine) blinds us to the extraordinary workings of nature to the extent that nature is available to the light of the human mind. Final cause concerns only human purpose and not the intelligible courses of nature. The factical harmony between nature and our purposes is determined by two forces: inscrutable divine providence, and the transformative power of human art.

As I said, this argument is fairly well known. What is less well known, or at least less often remarked, is that Bacon does not simply accuse the ancients of being wishful and thus poor philosophers. He says something more radical. When he criticizes Plato's extravagant doctrine of the ideas, Bacon says not only that Plato viewed forms as too abstracted from matter, but also that in doing so Plato "turned his opinion upon theology, wherewith all his natural philosophy is infected."[9] Rather than say the heaven is a stove and men are charcoals, as Socrates was accused of doing, Plato said rather that the *eidos* of bed is, if not a god, at least godlike![10] Even Aristotle, for whom piety was not a virtue worthy of discussing in the *Nicomachean Ethics*, who denied the immortality of the soul (by saying it is a thing of the second intention), and who corrupted natural philosophy and the true understanding of nature's forms by "constructing the world out of categories," was in fact no less moved by theology. It appears that Aristotle, who impregnated nature with final causes, had no need for a god. But not really, says Bacon. Rather, Aristotle "left out the fountain of final cause, namely God, and substituted nature for God: and took in final causes themselves rather as the lover of logic than of theology." Aristotle *substituted* nature for God.[11] Nature, in Aristotle's account, shares many characteristics with the gods who guide our lives.

Thus Bacon says ultimately that the ancients were not really philosophers at all. Despite their claims to be apostles of reason, they were in fact in thrall to the religion of their time and ultimately no less gods-besotted than the ancient heathen poets. In fact, the ancient philosophers were less wise, as regards religion, than the ancient poets. The problem with all pagans, philosophers and poets alike, is their opinion that "the world is the image of God and that man is an extract or compendious image of the world."[12] But the ancient poets, says Bacon (quoting Homer), were wise enough to know that the world's being an image of God does not disclose God's will and thus the appropriate worship of God. Not so for the ancient philosophers, whose account of the world had concrete implications for what the gods are and will, and who (at least in Plato's case) said much about the character of worship. When paganism and philosophy mix, reason, already infected by the idols of the mind, is further emboldened to speak about matters it can know nothing about.

Bacon tells us, in other words, that the ancients were guilty of the charge Athens brought against Socrates: that of introducing new gods to the city. As so-called natural philosophers, the ancients were not atheists, but heterodox pagans. According to Bacon, modern science is free of such theological contamination, which is surely good for science and scientists and for reason in general. It is true, says Bacon, that natural theology is a legitimate part of the sciences in general and that natural theology is the "knowledge of God that can be had by contemplating God's creatures."[13] But the content of natural theology is very limited: no light of nature, says Bacon, can declare the will and thus the true worship of God. Just as any work of art shows the power and skill of the artisan, but not his image (who he is and why he made the artifact), so the natural works of God show his power and wisdom, but not his image—not his will and purpose. Therefore, since we learn nothing from nature about who God is, we learn nothing from nature about how to worship him. Bacon says that natural theology "sufficeth to convince atheism" and then restates this claim in a weaker form, saying that the "light of nature might have led him [an atheist] to confess a God." Only miracles can reveal what is on the divine mind. This is why, Bacon says, God never works miracles to convince atheists, but only to convert idolaters and the superstitious.[14] For Bacon, modern science and the technological mastery of nature are not just compatible with Christianity; they are in an important way dependent on the "sacred truth." Christianity teaches that the world is but a created thing and (with the exception of man) is thus in no way itself divine or an image of the divine. Science need not revere nature, and as a consequence modern science can see material causes for what they really are, and, by the way, can investigate, penetrate, and manipulate the hidden courses of nature without offending piety and devout opinion. Outside the Christian worldview, the object of science is taken as divine. Such piety tempts reason beyond its ken, confuses the investigation of nature, and opens natural philosophy to the enmity of the orthodox believers.

Now, as striking and powerful as this critique is, Bacon leaves a small but significant fly in the ointment. In his discussion of the various ways and means of transmitting knowledge—what he calls the "methods of tradition"—Bacon says that one diversity of method is a pair he calls exoteric and acroamatic (or enigmatical).[15] The exoteric method is for addressing the vulgar many. The acroamatic (i.e., esoteric) method excludes the vulgar from the secrets of knowledge. The ancients as well as later writers used these two methods. Now the term "acroamatic" means "for listeners" as opposed to readers—for those who hear spoken discourses rather than read written ones. Consequently, says Bacon, for the ancients the acroamatic method concerned "principally," and so not exclusively, the publication of books rather than the method of writing. That is, for the most part either some books were circulated secretly while others were made public for the vulgar, or for the most part some doctrines were spoken in private while others were written and published for the vulgar. Bacon, however, is careful to say that he understands the acroamatic method to refer precisely to the method of writing, not the facts of publishing or circulation. By acroamatic method he means a calculated mode of obscurity meant to exclude the vulgar from the hidden truth contained in a writing while making that truth available to those few who "have wits of such sharpness as can pierce the veil." Moreover, he adds that the ancients used the acroamatic method, understood as this method of writing, "with judgment and discretion." They did not prostitute this method by writing obscurely for the sake of obscurantism, as later writers have done, but only to speak of things that would have been harmful or dangerous had they been addressed with candor.

Now, Bacon's extraordinary remarks about the ancients' use of the acroamatic method—their esotericism—raises some very provocative questions.

First, if questions of faith and religion are among the most controversial a thinker can address, then is it not possible that for some of the ancients their theological proclivities were more apparent than real—the exoteric surface rather than the esoteric teaching to be had in their writings? Second, if some did theologize only exoterically, why did this result in heterodox opinions rather than more conventional views? The reason for their choice of heterodoxy may be that they could not communicate properly without *some* provocativeness, but they could get away with this provocativeness, in the guise of heterodoxy, because of the relative fluidity of paganism that made heterodoxy less abhorrent (although easier to prove and still serious enough) than atheism. In the essays "Of Atheism" and "Of Superstition," Bacon argues that heresy is worse than atheism, because since human beings tend by nature to belief, atheism is rare and is anyway convinced by the manifest order of nature.[16] But Bacon speaks to Christians, for whom atheism is surely bad but for whom heresy is the more general danger because it means schism in a religion that claims to be unitary and universal. For paganism, heterodoxy is bad, but never so bad as it is for Christianity. And it is possible that the ancients learned how to make their apparent heterodoxy into a workable shield to hide the atheism of their doctrines. Given the fluidity of Greek religion, the appearance of heterodoxy could be managed, while a reputation for atheism was the kiss of death.

By telling of the ancients' well-used esotericism, Bacon makes us consider that the ancients were, beneath the surface of their writings, genuinely free of theology. But if indeed they were, this freedom did not prevent their natural philosophy and its historical legacy from being affected as if they were not. Perhaps their preoccupation with the question of religion deflected their interests from genuine natural science. Or perhaps the rhetorical circumstances of their pagan environment somehow limited their ability to see nature clearly and for what it was. Whatever the case, Bacon argues that the advent of Christianity was absolutely crucial for the true flourishing of reason and natural science. The condition of reason is thus inseparable from the condition of religion. Bacon thus prompts us to ask him: does Christianity in fact liberate reason by freeing the understanding and penetration of nature from the danger of trying to know the unknowable and, thereby, of treading on divine toes? Is modern science therefore indifferent to and immune from the claims of faith *when* that faith is the true faith? Or does modern natural science, despite all appearances to the contrary, pose a threat to religion and Christianity? And conversely, does religion somehow pose a threat to natural science in particular and to the claims of reason in general?

These questions go far beyond the limits of this essay. But raising them calls for some suggestions about Bacon's answers. Recall his remark about natural theology. In *Advancement of Learning* Bacon says, "no light of nature extendeth to declare the will and true worship of God." Nature discloses the *power* and *wisdom* of the maker, but that's all. Well, not quite. A few lines later Bacon says, "by the contemplation of nature to induce and inforce the acknowledgement of God, and to demonstrate his power, providence, and goodness, is an excellent argument, and hath been excellently handled by diverse."[17] In these remarks Bacon clearly relaxes the stipulation that we learn nothing of divine will from nature. For surely the facts of providence and goodness are aspects—indeed among the most important aspects—of divine will. In the *De Augmentis* Bacon goes considerably further. Here Bacon says that the contemplation of nature discloses that God exists, that he is supremely powerful, that he is good, that he is a rewarder, that he is an avenger, that he is an object of veneration.[18] Providence requires rewards and punishments. But in *Advancement*'s discussion of theology, Bacon says that we cannot, with the light of nature, understand the creation and the redemption and likewise the moral law truly interpreted—the law that enjoins us to love our enemies, to do good to those who hate us, and to be like our heavenly father who lets the rain fall on the just and the unjust.[19] So it seems, after all, that nature by itself does not disclose God to be a rewarder and avenger: the rain falls on good and bad alike; the good die young and the wicked live to ripe old age.

The contradiction alerts us to the simple fact that nature is indifferent to our merits. The law of nature—at least as regards all manner of living things—is the law of the jungle or, at worst, the law of the casino, where winners and losers are determined ultimately by sheer luck. (Did a feeble-minded wretch *do* anything to deserve this sad fate?) Science, including natural theology, is utterly incapable of establishing the fact of God's providence. Only miracles can do that. The problem for believers is, as Bacon acknowledges in several places, that miracles can be faked. In *New Atlantis*, a miracle of divine revelation occurs.[20] One of the wise men of Salomon's House (a natural scientist) proclaims that God has given to man (i.e., to natural science) the power to discern among "divine miracles, works of nature, works of art, and impostures and illusions of all sorts." Armed with this power, the wise man certifies to the multitude that the miracle is genuine. Bacon never explains, however, how science can do this. That there is no scientifically known cause for an apparent miracle does not establish that it is in fact a miracle, rather than just something we cannot *yet* explain by recourse to nature (including psychology). But this argument cuts in the other direction as well: there is no way demonstrably to rule out the possibility that an apparent miracle not *yet* explained away may not, in fact, be a miracle. Bacon's move in *New Atlantis* is a sleight of hand. He depicts a society in which people believe that science can prove the existence of miracles. But science cannot prove or disprove the occurrence of miracles, just as it cannot prove or disprove God's providence.

For Bacon, science is one thing and the true faith is another. It seems then that science has nothing to fear from faith: miracles don't change the laws of nature; they just jump over these laws, and only rarely. And faith has nothing to fear from modern science, since miracles and the courses of nature, though related, are two different things. So why Bacon's misleading picture of science as the basis of faith? The reason is fairly simple. The idols of the human mind are not so easy to dispel, especially from the vast majority of human beings. These idols incline most men to a kind of natural paganism in this sense: human beings are by nature inclined to mix up the realms of being and to see connections where there are none, or else to think that unknowable connections can in fact be known. Hence science is said to establish miracles and nature is said to disclose some rudiments of divine will. Stated otherwise: perhaps belief is never really enough for men to accept the existence of miracles; perhaps men always need to *know* that miracles are real in order to ward off some doubt that always haunts them.[21]

But that science and Christianity are not obviously at odds for Bacon does not mean he thinks there is no crucial overlapping of science, reason, and religion. We cannot assume that he was an atheist, but we cannot simply assume his piety or believe the sincerity of his pieties. Bacon was, after all, a genuinely nasty character. As Ben Franklin said of him by way of Alexander Pope, "If parts allure thee think how Bacon shined, the wisest, brightest, meanest of mankind."[22]

Bacon gives us some important clues to his ultimate view of the relations among science, reason, and religion. In *New Atlantis* the scientist who certifies the miracle makes a most unusual pronouncement. After saying that God has vouchsafed to his ilk the power to penetrate nature and to discern genuine miracles from frauds, the wise man of Salomon's House says, "I do here acknowledge and testify before this people, that the thing which we now see before our eyes is thy Finger and a true Miracle; and forasmuch as we learn in our books that thou never workest miracles but to a divine and excellent end (for the laws of nature are thine own laws, and thou exceedest them not but upon great cause), we most humbly beseech thee to prosper of it in mercy; which thou dost in some part secretly promise by sending it unto us."

The important point is not that nature is exceeded by any miracle, but rather that a miracle is done only for an excellent end. Divine miracles must be for the good. To believe in miracles is thus to presume God's goodness and providence: the fact that he is a rewarder and an avenger. True, Bacon does say that the ways and means of divine providence are inscrutable. We may not be able to understand why, in the short run, the good suffer and the wicked prosper. But he also tells us that Providence cannot be ultimately for some end we know to be evil, and at the end of days must be for the good as we human beings understand the good (and evil). Bacon also tells us that the new science of nature applies to all the human things, including the nature of good and bad, justice and injustice.[23] It follows, then, that if reason and modern science can grasp the good and the bad, then reason and modern science can tell us something important—perhaps essential—about miracles, divine intention, and the divine itself.[24] Bacon has much to say about politics and morality.[25] It is by investigating these subjects—well within the ken of reason as Bacon understands it—that we can discern his understanding of faith, miracles, and revelation.

NOTES

1. *Novum Organum,* trans. and ed. Peter Urbach and John Gibson (Chicago: Open Court, 1994), 1:129. It is not clear just *how* seeing light itself could be superior to all of its uses, such as going on our ways, practicing our arts, reading, and recognizing each other. Is seeing the light that illuminated Bathsheba more excellent and beautiful than seeing Bathsheba? The answer is not obvious. Perhaps the sequel offers a clue. On what grounds could seeing things as they are, "without superstition or imposture, error or confusion," be "more praiseworthy than all the fruit of invention"? Perhaps on the grounds that the fruits of invention are themselves attractive only because their promise is always ultimately based on superstition, imposture, error, or confusion. When we understand just what the appearing of Bathsheba really is, we cannot be moved by Bathsheba as we were before that understanding. No wonder Bacon describes real contemplation as "more praiseworthy" than the fruit of inventions, rather than "more excellent and beautiful."

2. *Advancement of Learning,* vol. 3 of *The Works of Francis Bacon,* ed. James Spedding, Robert Leslie Ellis, and Douglas Denon Heath, 14 vols. (London: Longman and Co., 1857–74), 357–59. See also *Novum Organum* 1:45–52, 52–58, 61–67.

3. *Advancement of Learning,* 355–57; Plato *Republic* 509b–c, 517c; see also 476d, 505a–509b, 531c–534c.

4. *De Augmentis* 3:4, *The Works of Francis Bacon,* vols. 4 and 5.

5. *Advancement of Learning,* 354–59; *Novum Organum* 2:4.

6. *Advancement of Learning,* 356–57.

7. *Advancement of Learning,* 357–59.

8. *Advancement of Learning,* 359; *De Augmentis* 3:4.

9. *Advancement of Learning,* 355.

10. Aristophanes, *Clouds* 95–100; Plato, *Republic* 509c–11e. See Heidegger, *The Basic Problems of Phenomenology,* trans. Albert Hofstadter (Bloomington: Indiana University Press, 1982), 112–17.

11. *Novum Organum* 1:63; *De Augmentis* 3:4.

12. *Advancement of Learning,* 350.

13. *Advancement of Learning,* 349–51.

14. Bacon's waffling on this issue raises very interesting questions. If the light of nature suffices to convince atheists that there is a God, then God has no need to convince atheists—or anyone else, for that matter—by means of miracles. But if the light of nature only "might" lead an atheist to confess a God, then some atheists might not

be convinced by the light of nature, and the question arises as to why God does not use his miracles to prevent this fact. Is he unable to do this? If so, why? Perhaps he does not need to bother, since such atheism is rare and thus not really dangerous to other men. But then does God not care for the atheist? Again, if the light of nature convinces most but not all men that there is a God, what accounts for the difference? Perhaps the difference springs from the prior *credulity* of most men. And so, perhaps belief in miracles presumes such prior credulity. See Leo Strauss, "Progress or Return?" in *The Rebirth of Classical Rationalism*, ed. Thomas L. Pangle (Chicago: University of Chicago Press, 1989), 265–70.   ·

15. *Advancement of Learning*, 404–5; *De Augmentis* 6:2.

16. But see note 14.

17. *Advancement of Learning*, 349–51.

18. *De Augmentis*, 3:2.

19. *Advancement of Learning*, 479–80.

20. *New Atlantis*, ed. Jerry Weinberger (Arlington Heights: Harlan Davidson, 1989, rev. ed.), 47–49.

21. And so, perhaps credulity is not just simplemindedness. See notes 14 and 16.

22. From *Poor Richard Improved, 1749*. Benjamin Franklin, *Writings* (New York: The Library of America, 1987), 1252–53.

23. See *Advancement of Learning*, 420, 475–77.

24. Indeed, as Bacon surely knows, men were not just made directly by God but also, alone from among all the things in nature, reflect the image of God.

25. And with respect to the question of Providence, see in particular his discussion of Machiavelli's "evil arts," *Advancement of Learning*, 471–73.

6

"Christian Kings" and "English Mercuries": *Henry V* and the Classical Tradition of Manliness

Paul A. Cantor

> You have allied yourself with Christ—and yet will you slide back
> into the ways of Julius and Alexander the Great?
>
> —Erasmus, *The Education of a Christian Prince*

I

The chorus that begins act V of Shakespeare's *Henry V* provides a remarkable moment in Elizabethan drama, one that helps reveal in concrete terms what the Renaissance meant to Shakespeare and his contemporaries. Celebrating Henry's triumphant return from his victory at the battle of Agincourt, the chorus draws two parallels, one looking back and one looking ahead in time:

> How London doth pour out her citizens!
> The Mayor and all his brethren in best sort,
> Like to the senators of th' antique Rome,
> With the plebeians swarming at their heels,
> Go forth and fetch their conqu'ring Caesar in;
> As by a lower but by loving likelihood,
> Were now the general of our gracious Empress,
> As in good time he may, from Ireland coming,
> Bringing rebellion broached on his sword,
> How many would the peaceful city quit
> To welcome him! Much more, and much more cause,
> Did they this Harry. (V.Cho.24–35)[1]

The chorus views the great English conqueror, Henry V, on the model of a Roman predecessor, Julius Caesar, and then goes on to compare both to a contemporary hero, the Earl of Essex, sent by Queen Elizabeth to subdue an Irish rebellion.[2] Shakespeare seldom is this explicit in drawing a parallel between one of his characters and one of his contemporaries. The ease with which this passage weaves together references to Henry V, Julius Caesar, and the Earl of Essex is a striking reminder of the fact that at the core of the Renaissance lay the hope of reviving the political forms of classical antiquity and perhaps of rivaling the martial greatness of ancient Rome in modern terms. Exploring in *Henry V* the political and military career of England's greatest foreign conqueror to date, Shakespeare seems to be raising the question of how England might follow in the footsteps of Rome as an imperial power.

The hopes expressed in this passage for Essex's success in his Irish campaign were of course soon dashed, and the earl in fact ended his career in disgrace. But his fate should not blind us to the larger significance of the Caesar-Henry-Essex parallels Shakespeare draws. Where Essex failed, later Englishmen were to succeed (though on different battlegrounds) and win for their nation an empire that could brook comparison with Rome's. Like Spenser's *The Faerie Queene,* Shakespeare's history plays helped provide the English with a vision of national greatness, and that vision was largely based on Roman models. As Machiavelli teaches in his *Discourses on Livy,* Rome's greatness was ultimately based on the energy of its republican mixed regime, which combined monarchical, aristocratic, and democratic elements in an unstable equilibrium and thereby kept its ambitious citizens alert to possibilities for glory.[3] What distinguishes Henry V as a king in Shakespeare's portrayal is precisely his ability to create a mixed regime on a Roman model. As the act V chorus suggests, Henry won the allegiance of his nobles and his people by giving both ranks an active role in his rule and his military campaigns. Above all, Henry's common touch makes him an effective leader of his largely citizen army and gives his rule the force and effectiveness that come from incorporating a significant popular element. Although Henry's monarchy obviously differs from the Roman republic, he follows certain basic Roman principles as articulated by Machiavelli. Like ancient Rome, Henry's English regime manages to channel the ambition, spiritedness, and contentiousness of its citizens away from domestic conflict and into foreign conquests.[4]

The glory of Rome hovers in the background throughout Shakespeare's history plays, perhaps most poignantly in *Richard III,* when the young Prince Edward wonders about the Tower of London, in which he is soon to meet his doom at the hands of his evil uncle:

> *Prince.* Did Julius Caesar build that place, my lord?
> *Gloucester.* He did, my gracious lord, begin that place,

> Which, since, succeeding ages have re-edified.
> *Prince.* Is it upon record, or else reported
> Successively from age to age, he built it?
> *Buckingham.* Upon record, my gracious lord.
> *Prince.* But say, my lord, it were not regist'red,
> Methinks the truth should live from age to age,
> As 'twere retail'd to all posterity,
> Even to the general all-ending day. . . .
> Julius Caesar was a famous man;
> With what his valor did enrich his wit,
> His wit set down to make his valure live.
> Death makes no conquest of this conqueror,
> For now he lives in fame though not in life.
> I'll tell you what, my cousin Buckingham—
> *Buckingham.* What, my gracious lord?
> *Prince.* And if I live until I be a man,
> I'll win our ancient right in France again,
> Or die a soldier as I liv'd a king.
>   (III.i.69–77, 84–93)

The Tower of London serves as a living monument to the continuity between Rome and England. The prince's awareness of Julius Caesar's achievement and his sense of how it has endured for centuries fire his own ambition to achieve military victories that might immortalize his fame as an English king.

But the prince's mention of "the general all-ending day" reminds us that the horizons of his cosmos extend to the Last Judgment and thus well beyond Julius Caesar's. Like all Shakespeare's English characters, the prince lives in a Christian universe, and thus can never look at the world through purely Roman eyes. A simple return to the ancient Roman world is impossible for Shakespeare's Englishmen; classical antiquity can at most be revived, and that means re-created in a new context, a Christian context. Mirroring the complexity of the Renaissance itself, *Henry V* blends classical and Christian elements, no mean feat when one considers how antithetical the two traditions are. Suggesting that the play shows us two different faces at once, several critics have argued that *Henry V* is ambiguous and equivocal.[5] This perplexing duality may well be rooted in Henry's effort to create a single whole out of two conflicting visions of the human ideal, a complex mixture of the classical and the Christian reflected in the chorus's image of Henry's army: "Following the mirror of all Christian kings, / With winged heels, as English Mercuries" (II.Cho.6–7). Henry V is a kind of Renaissance man, trying to synthesize opposing realms of value: the public and the private, the active and the contemplative, the ambitious and the humble, the ferocious and the merciful. But however promising, this synthesis turns out to be deeply problematic, and in his would-be comprehensiveness Henry exposes the often buried tensions in Renaissance efforts to make one whole out of the classical and the Christian traditions. As *Henry V* reveals, the classical tradition was a living and powerful force for Shakespeare, but one that could not be incorporated into Christian Europe without creating profound contradictions, inner divisions that were soon to provide the dramatic basis for some of Shakespeare's greatest tragedies, most notably *Hamlet*. Above all, the classical elements in *Henry V* are in tension with the Christian because they are linked to a tradition of martial virtue, a tradition of manliness at odds with Christian ideals of meekness and forbearance.

II

The classical tradition of manliness is embodied in the very poetic texture of *Henry V*, which is perhaps the most epic of Shakespeare's plays. This epic quality is clearly evident in the choral interludes, beginning with the prologue, which sounds like a Homeric invocation of the muse:

> O for a Muse of fire, that would ascend
> The brightest heaven of invention!
> A kingdom for a stage, princes to act,
> And monarchs to behold the swelling scene!
> Then should the warlike Harry, like himself,
> Assume the port of Mars.
> (Prol.1–6)

Shakespeare repeatedly presents military greatness in *Henry V* in terms of precedents from classical mythology and history. The most vocal spokesman for the classical tradition is the pedantic Welshman, Captain Fluellen, who, carrying his enthusiasm for the ancient world to an almost comic extreme, judges all military matters according to the strict standards of "the disciplines of the pristine wars of the Romans" (III.ii.81–82). As a result, Fluellen often finds his contemporaries lacking in martial virtue: "If you would take the pains but to examine the wars of Pompey the Great, you shall find, I warrant you, that there is no tiddle taddle nor pibble babble in Pompey's camp" (IV.i.68–71).

By the same token, when Fluellen wishes to compliment a soldier, classical references come readily to his lips: "The Duke of Exeter is as magnanimous as Agamemnon. . . . There is an aunchient lieutenant there at the pridge, I think. . . . he is as valiant a man as Mark Antony" (III.vi.6–7, 12–14).

But Fluellen's vision of classical greatness becomes deeply problematic when he presses his comparison between ancient and modern heroes too far. Like a latter-day Plutarch, Fluellen sets up parallels between the lives of Henry V and Alexander the Great:

I think it is in Macedon where Alexander is porn. . . . There is a river in Macedon, and there is also moreover a river at Monmouth. It is call'd Wye at Monmouth; but it is out of my prains what is the name of the other river; but 'tis all one, 'tis alike as my fingers is to my fingers, and there is salmons in both. If you mark Alexander's life well, Henry of Monmouth's life is come after it indifferent well. (IV.vii.22–23, 26–31)

Up to this point, Fluellen's parallels may seem weak and even forced, but at least they are innocuous and redound to Henry's credit. But as Fluellen continues, he compares Alexander's murder of his friend Clytus with Henry's treatment of Falstaff. Fluellen manages to wriggle out of a potentially embarrassing situation; he quickly points out that whereas a drunken Alexander killed his friend, a sober Henry merely banished Falstaff from his company. But earlier in the play Hostess Quickly said of Henry's treatment of Falstaff, "The King has kill'd his heart" (II.i.88). Thus Fluellen's Plutarchan parallels may reveal more than he himself realizes.[6] If Henry has indeed modeled himself on ancient warriors, something of their pagan fierceness and cruelty may have rubbed off on him.

Fluellen's association of Henry with Alexander becomes an even more dubious compliment as a result of the Welshman's unfortunate mispronunciation:

Fluellen. What call you the town's name where Alexander the Pig was born?
Gower. Alexander the Great.
Fluellen. Why, I pray you, is not "pig" great? The pig, or the great, or the mighty, or the huge, or the magnanimous are all one reckonings.
(IV.vii.12–17)

In Fluellen's heavy Welsh accent, the classical virtue of magnanimity becomes indistinguishable from piggishness.[7] Fluellen inadvertently reduces the boundless ambition of the great-souled man seeking to conquer the world to the insatiable appetite of a barnyard animal.

As Fluellen's miscalculated efforts to praise Henry reveal, many of the classical virtues, especially the martial virtues, become suspect when transposed into Christian contexts. The manliness that makes a classical hero victorious on the battlefield may seem evil or even demonic to Christian eyes, as John Milton's portrait of Satan in *Paradise Lost* shows. Henry's effort to combine classical and Christian virtues thus becomes a delicate balancing act. His masterpiece of battlefield rhetoric, his St. Crispin's day speech, makes a revealing admission: "if it be a sin to covet honor, / I am the most offending soul alive" (IV.iii.28–29). In Christian terms it surely *is* a sin to covet honor, and yet faced with the task of rousing his badly outnumbered troops to heroic exertions, Henry must call upon their manly sense of honor to overcome their fear. Wartime makes extraordinary demands upon men, forcing them as Henry realizes to transform their peacetime selves completely:

> In peace there's nothing so becomes a man
> As modest stillness and humility;
> But when the blast of war blows in our ears,
> Then imitate the action of the tiger;
> Stiffen the sinews, conjure up the blood,
> Disguise fair nature with hard-favor'd rage;
> Then lend the eye a terrible aspect.
> (III.i.3–9)

Here we begin to see the formula for Henry's synthesis of the classical and the Christian. Peacetime calls for the humane virtues of a Christian saint, wartime for the beastly ferocity of an epic warrior. Henry's use of terms like *imitate, disguise,* and *lend the eye* suggests that he thinks of the dual roles of peacetime saint and wartime hero as actor's parts, identities he can slip into and out of as circumstances demand.[8] The siege of Harfleur gives Henry a chance to demonstrate his flexibility. Standing before the gates of the city and trying to get it to surrender, Henry sounds like Christopher Marlowe's tyrannical hero Tamburlaine.[9] He threatens the cruelest treatment of his enemies with no sense of Christian restraint:

> The gates of mercy shall be all shut up,
> And the flesh'd soldier, rough and hard of heart,
> In liberty of bloody hand, shall range,
> With conscience wide as hell, mowing like grass
> Your fresh fair virgins and your flow'ring infants.
> What is it then to me if impious War,
> Arrayed in flames like to the prince of fiends,
> Do with his smirch'd complexion all fell feats
> Enlink'd to waste and desolation?
> (III.iii.10–18)

The ferocity of Henry's rhetoric has the desired effect. Just as his speech reaches its emotional climax in an implied comparison between himself and the archetypal anti-Christian tyrant, Herod (III.iii.40–41), the French decide to surrender the town. Henry is able to return to the role of peaceful Christian, scale down his rhetoric to gentler accents, and instruct his troops to act like lambs rather than tigers: "Use mercy to them all" (III.iii.54). Mercy seems in fact to be an essential component of Henry's strategy for conquering France:

> We give express charge that in our marches through the country there be nothing compell'd from the villages; nothing taken but paid for; none

of the French upbraided or abus'd in disdainful language; for when
lenity and cruelty play for a kingdom, the gentler gamester is the soon-
est winner. (III.vi.108–13)

Notice, however, that Henry's seemingly Christian preference for lenity over
cruelty is not based on its intrinsic merit, but on its superiority as a means to
achieve a desired end. He embraces mercy as a principle only when it is better policy to do so; as we have seen, when he thinks it prudent he is perfectly
capable of proclaiming, "The gates of mercy shall be all shut up."

Shakespeare seems to have contrived Henry's exercises of mercy in the
play carefully to suggest that political prudence and not religious conviction
is his governing principle. In act II, Henry insists on showing mercy to a man
who spoke out against him (he cites drunkenness as an excuse for the of-
fender). Though Henry's leniency provokes a caution from one of his counsellors, the king stands by his judgment:

> *Scroop.* That's mercy, but too much security.
> Let him be punish'd, sovereign, lest example
> Breed, by his sufferance, more of such a kind.
> *King.* O, let us yet be merciful.
> (II.ii.44–47)

It soon becomes clear, however, that Henry has been using this public display of mercy to set a trap for a group of traitors among his counsellors.[10]
Having just argued against the king is showing mercy to offenders, Scroop,
Cambridge, and Grey can hardly appeal for mercy for themselves when they
are accused of treason, as Henry himself points out to them:

> The mercy that was quick in us but late,
> By your own counsel is suppress'd and kill'd.
> You must not dare, for shame, to talk of mercy,
> For your own reasons turn into your bosoms,
> As dogs upon their masters, worrying you.
> (II.ii.79-83)

Merciful at one moment (to an insignificant man who poses no real danger
to him), Henry can turn around and be deaf to all pleas for mercy (from three
powerful nobles who do in fact threaten his safety). Henry is neither merciful nor cruel by nature; rather he seems able to adapt himself to either role
according to the changing political situation.

Henry's flexibility stands him in good stead during the darkest moments of
the battle of Agincourt. From listening patiently and sorrowfully to an account of the deaths of his noble warriors, he can cold-bloodedly order the

slaughter of his prisoners of war, an act contrary to the laws of arms but necessary in his militarily precarious situation. Tears come easily to the Christian monarch's eyes, even in the midst of battle, but he can still be ruthless when he has to be:

> For hearing this, I must perforce compound
> With mistful eyes, or they will issue too. *Alarum.*
> But hark, what new alarum is this same?
> The French have reinforc'd their scatter'd men.
> Then every soldier kill his prisoners.
> (IV.vi.33–37)[11]

The alternation between pity and ruthlessness in this scene is explicitly presented as a contrast between womanliness and manliness.[12] Exeter feels that in weeping for his fallen comrades, he has let his masculine reserve yield to womanly weakness:

> But I had not so much of man in me,
> And all my mother came into mine eyes
> And gave me up to tears.
> (IV.vi.30–32)

Throughout Shakespeare's career, as early as his *Henry VI* plays and as late as *Macbeth,* he tends to associate Christian pity with the feminine side of human nature and martial virtue, especially of the classical variety, with the masculine.[13] Henry's comprehensiveness as a human being is reflected in the way he can embrace both the masculine and feminine sides of human nature, even in a single moment. Like one of his nobles, the king "is as full of valor as of kindness" (IV.iii.15). No wonder Henry puzzles critics. But what makes it hard for them to capture Henry's character in a simple formula is precisely what makes him successful as a king. One might even think of Henry in terms of Nietzsche's paradoxical conception of his *Übermensch*: "the Roman Caesar with Christ's soul."[14] Such comprehensiveness may be beyond even Henry's grasp, but he is able to move smoothly between wartime and peacetime, cruelty and mercy, classical manliness and Christian tenderness.

III

We are introduced to Henry in the play in terms of the ideal of synthesizing opposing realms of value. In the first scene, Canterbury and Ely, the two prelates worried about the king's policy toward the church, praise Henry and especially his sudden and total reformation from a libertine into a pious ruler. They picture him precisely as a kind of Renaissance man, who has mastered every field of human endeavor and seems like an expert in each:

> Hear him but reason in divinity,
> And all-admiring, with an inward wish
> You would desire the King were made a prelate;
> Hear him debate of commonwealth affairs,
> You would say it hath been all in all his study;
> List his discourse of war, and you shall hear
> A fearful battle render'd you in music.
> (I.i.38–44)

In particular, Canterbury views Henry as a philosopher-king, who has derived his comprehensive wisdom from his active experience of life: "So that the art and practic part of life / Must be the mistress to this theoric" (I.i.51–52).[15] Combining the virtues of the active and the contemplative lives, Henry seems to be a Renaissance dream come true, the ideal monarch, in control of himself and of his nation (I.ii.241–43).

With his comprehensiveness as a human being, Henry stands above the tragic divisions that usually destroy Shakespeare's political figures. Henry's father, for example, finds himself trapped in a conflict between public and private values. Henry IV's situation as a father is at odds with his situation as a king. As a father he loves his son, but as a king he feels he must reject Prince Hal, whose licentious behavior seems to threaten the future of the realm. In *Henry V*, by contrast, public and private values come to be in harmony: the king apparently manages to fall in love with just the woman whom political considerations dictate he should marry, the French princess Katherine. The episode of Henry wooing Katherine allows Shakespeare to give a comic shape to the plot of *Henry V*: the play moves toward a marriage and concludes with a good deal of amusing banter and byplay.[16] Once again Henry proves adept at making a transition, from the wartime role of soldier to the peacetime role of lover.[17] He himself has doubts at first, fearing that he is too fierce to prevail in a gentler form of combat: "Now beshrew my father's ambition! he was thinking of civil wars when he got me; therefore was I created with a stubborn outside, with an aspect of iron, that when I come to woo ladies, I fright them" (V.ii.224–28). But Henry is able to turn his manly bluntness to an advantage, and he wins Katherine on the strength of his energy and good humor.[18]

Henry V is a rare figure in Shakespeare, one of the few rulers to achieve satisfaction in public and private life at once. Tragic heroes such as Othello, Macbeth, and Coriolanus cannot make such smooth transitions from wartime to peacetime. Instead, they find that the very virtues that make them great on the battlefield unfit them for success in other areas of life and especially in what we would call domestic politics. Analyzing the comic pattern of Henry's career helps to highlight the tragic patterns of Shakespeare's later heroes. While Henry is able to synthesize opposing realms of value, the later heroes are tragically caught in their contradictions. What Henry manages to put together tears them apart.

Even within *Henry V,* Shakespeare hints at the instability and fragility of the king's achievement. The closing chorus pointedly remarks that the empire Henry created soon fell apart after his death:

> Henry the Sixt, in infant bands crown'd King
> Of France and England, did this king succeed;
> Whose state so many had the managing,
> That they lost France, and made his England bleed.
> (Ep.9–12)

Henry V's empire required a person with his unique combination of talents to rule it. When his son prematurely came to the throne, he was, as Shakespeare had already portrayed him in his First Tetralogy of history plays, too purely Christian, too tender and merciful, to maintain power. As Shakespeare has Queen Margaret describe Henry VI:

> But all his mind is bent to holiness,
> To number Ave-Maries on his beads;
> His champions are the prophets and the apostles,
> His weapons holy saws of sacred writ,
> His study is his tilt-yard, and his loves
> Are brazen images of canonized saints.
> I would the college of Cardinals
> Would choose him Pope and carry him to Rome,
> And set the triple crown upon his head—
> That were a state fit for his holiness.
> (*2 Henry VI,* I.iii.55–64)

Later in the play, the usurper York reiterates the point that Henry VI's pious Christianity unfits him to rule England:

> That head of thine doth not become a crown:
> Thy hand is made to grasp a palmer's staff
> And not to grace an aweful princely sceptre.
> That gold must round engirt these brows of mine,
> Whose smile and frown, like to Achilles' spear,
> Is able with the change to kill and cure.
> (*2 Henry VI,* V.i.96–101)

Notice that York lays claim to the crown by comparing himself to Achilles, the model of classical manliness and martial virtue. The unmanly tenderness of

Henry VI eventually allows the realm to fall into the hands of the merciless and brutal tyrant Richard III. The lamblike and tigerlike qualities Shakespeare conjoined in Henry V he divided between Henry VI and Richard III in his First Tetralogy.

In Henry V, then, the seemingly contradictory virtues of the manly classical warrior and the tenderhearted Christian saint somehow manage to fit together. But as the subsequent history of England indicates, most men are either tigers or lambs and cannot balance cruelty and mercy in the right proportions. As if to make this point within *Henry V*, Shakespeare includes a character who seems to parody the king's ideal synthesis of classical and Christian virtues. In his explosive speech, the Irishman Macmorris moves back and forth between the language of the manly warrior and the language of the merciful Christian. At one point he reacts violently to the army's decision to retreat: "By Chrish law, 'tish ill done! The work ish give over, the trompet sound the retreat. . . . I would have blowed up the town, so Chrish save me, law, in an hour!" (III.ii.88–92). Macmorris has something of Henry's versatility to be able to speak of blowing up a town and being saved by Christ in the same breath. The point is subtle, and one might be tempted to pass over it, if Shakespeare did not seem to emphasize it through repetition: "We talk, and, be Chrish, do nothing. . . . So God sa' me, 'tis shame to stand still. . . . And there is throats to be cut, and works to be done, and there ish nothing done, so Chrish sa' me, law!" (III.ii.109–13). Macmorris speaks the same way when he rejects Fluellen: "I do not know you so good a man as myself. / So Chrish save me, I will cut off your head" (III.ii.132–33).

Obviously Macmorris has no intention of creating a Renaissance synthesis of classical and Christian virtues. What Henry does consciously, as a matter of policy, Macmorris does unconsciously, as a matter of habit. Henry is a rare case; Macmorris is more typical of humanity. He is presumably not even aware of the contradictions in his values, much less capable of synthesizing something greater out of them. Macmorris is a soldier and he would undoubtedly call himself a Christian. But he has probably never given any thought to the tension between his values as a soldier and his values as a Christian. In a moment of excitement, he can juxtapose unthinkingly the utmost martial brutality with conventional expressions of Christian piety. Macmorris's pagan spiritedness is probably the core of his character and his Christianity only a veneer. Perhaps Henry knows that he needs such fierce and manly soldiers in his Christian army if he is to win battles against overwhelming odds.

With his colorful language Macmorris reveals something about human nature: men are capable of harboring the most contradictory values because they would rather not think about the incompatibility of the different goods they cherish. Ordinary circumstances permit them the luxury of this kind of ignorance. But moments of crisis tend to expose these contradictions of values, thus providing the basis for genuine dramatic conflict. The Renaissance was a particularly fruitful time for producing such clashes of values, since by attempting to revive classical antiquity within Christian Europe, it ended up highlighting the tensions between the two great ethical traditions that go to make up what we know as Western culture. It was Shakespeare's genius to see how these tensions could be dramatized. Successfully synthesized, as in Henry V's ability to combine classical and Christian virtues, the two traditions permit a comic outcome. But even in *Henry V* this synthesis seems precarious, and we must remain awake to the possibility that the two traditions might not always fit together harmoniously. To dwell upon the contradictory demands of classical and Christian ethics yields tragedy in the Hegelian sense of the conflict of two goods. Shortly after writing *Henry V* Shakespeare was to turn to a hero who strives for totality the way Henry does, but fails to achieve it, a hero torn between a pagan revenge ethic rooted in the classical tradition of manliness and a Christian outlook on life that leads him to doubt the efficacy of any action in this world. The result was *Hamlet,* the tragic inversion of Henry V's comic career as Renaissance man.[19]

NOTES

1. All quotations from Shakespeare come from G. Blakemore Evans, ed., *The Riverside Shakespeare* (Boston: Houghton Mifflin, 1974). References are to act, scene, and line.

2. Some critics have argued that this passage refers not to Essex, but to his successor in Ireland, Charles Blount, Lord Mountjoy. See Herschel Baker's introduction to *Henry V* in *The Riverside Shakespeare,* 930. Since viewing this passage as referring to Mountjoy would push the date of *Henry V* up to 1603, most Shakespeare scholars continue to believe that Essex is the "general" in question. But whether Shakespeare had Essex or Mountjoy in mind, my basic point about the contemporary relevance of *Henry V* remains the same.

3. See especially *Discourses,* book 1, chapters 2–8. Harvey Mansfield has been our most informative and insightful guide to Machiavelli's understanding of the republican regime. See his *Machiavelli's New Modes and Orders: A Study of the Discourses on Livy* (Ithaca, N.Y.: Cornell University Press, 1979), his *Machiavelli's Virtue* (Chicago: University of Chicago Press, 1996), and the translation of the *Discourses* he did with Nathan Tarcov (Chicago: University of Chicago Press, 1996). For Shakespeare's understanding of the Roman republican regime, see my *Shakespeare's Rome: Republic and Empire* (Ithaca, N.Y.: Cornell University Press, 1976), especially 42–43, 55–77.

4. The comic subplot of the play reflects this theme. Bardolph is able to end the domestic conflict between Pistol and Nym by uniting them against a common foreign enemy: "Come, shall I make you two friends? We must to France together; why the devil should we keep knives to one another's throats?" (II.i.90–92). See also IV.i.222–24.

5. See, for example, Norman Rabkin, "Rabbits, Ducks, and *Henry V*," *Shakespeare Quarterly* 28 (1977): 279–96, revised and reprinted under the title "Either/Or: Responding to *Henry V*" in his *Shakespeare and the Problem of Meaning* (Chicago: University of Chicago Press, 1981), 33–62.

6. For further discussion of this moment and a general treatment of Shakespeare and Plutarch, see my essay "Shakespeare's Parallel Lives: Plutarch and the Roman Plays," *Poetica* 48 (1997): 69–81.

7. See David Quint, "'Alexander the Pig': Shakespeare on History and Poetry," *boundary 2*, vol. 10 (1982): 49–67. For a more detailed comparison of Henry V and Alexander, see Ronald S. Berman, "Shakespeare's Alexander: Henry V," *College English* 23 (1962): 532–39, and Judith Mossman, *"Henry V* and Plutarch's Alexander," *Shakespeare Quarterly* 45 (1994): 57–73.

8. On Henry's skill as an actor, see Pamela K. Jensen, "The Famous Victories of William Shakespeare: *The Life of Henry the Fifth*," in *Poets, Princes, & Private Citizens: Literary Alternatives to Postmodern Politics,* ed. Joseph M. Knippenberg and Peter Augustine Lawler (Lanham, Md.: Rowman & Littlefield, 1996), 237, 254.

9. On this point see Rabkin, "Rabbits, Ducks," 292 (rev. *Shakespeare*, 55).

10. On this point see Jensen, "Famous Victories," 242, and Vickie Sullivan, "Princes to Act: Henry V as the Machiavellian Prince of Appearance," in *Shakespeare's Political Pageant: Essays in Politics and Literature,* ed. Joseph Alulis and Vickie Sullivan (Lanham, Md.: Rowman & Littlefield, 1996), 134.

11. The historian Raphael Holinshed, Shakespeare's principal source for *Henry V,* notes the contradiction in the king's behavior: "he doubting least his enimies should gather togither againe, and begin a new field; and mistrusting further that the prisoners would be an aid to his enimies . . . contrarie to his accustomed gentlenes, commanded by sound of trumpet, that everie man (upon paine of death) should incontinentlie slaie his prisoner." See Geoffrey Bullough, ed., *Narrative and Dramatic Sources of Shakespeare* (London: Routledge and Kegan Paul, 1962), 4:397. For a modern historical account of the killing of the prisoners at Agincourt, see John Keegan, *The Face of Battle* (New York: Viking Press, 1976), 107–12.

12. For other examples of the alternation between manliness and womanliness in the play, compare II.i.98 with II.i.117, and consider the implications of Queen Isabel's remark at V.ii.93–94.

13. For the masculine/feminine dichotomy in *Macbeth*, see my essay "'A Soldier and Afeard': *Macbeth* and the Gospelling of Scotland," *Interpretation* 24 (1997): 309–10.

14. Friedrich Nietzsche, *The Will to Power,* trans. Walter Kaufmann and R. J. Hollingdale (New York: Random House, 1967), sect. 983, 513.

15. On this point see Berman, "Shakespeare's Alexander," 535.

16. On the comic ending of *Henry V,* see Jensen, "Famous Victories," 258.

17. This is of course precisely the transition that Richard III is unable to make, as his opening soliloquy makes clear:

> Why, I, in this weak piping time of peace,
> Have no delight to pass away the time,
> Unless to see my shadow in the sun

And descant on mine own deformity.
And therefore, since I cannot prove a lover
To entertain these fair well-spoken days,
I am determined to prove a villain. (I.i.24–30)

18. On Henry's skillful theatricality in this scene, see Graham Bradshaw, *Misrepre-sentations: Shakespeare and the Materialists* (Ithaca, N.Y.: Cornell University Press, 1993), 116–22. Bradshaw notes that Henry self-consciously adopts the role of his ear-lier rival Hotspur in this scene, even to the point of calling his love "Kate."

19. For a fuller discussion of this subject, see my book *Shakespeare: Hamlet* (Cambridge: Cambridge University Press, 1989), especially 1–64.

PART II

THE LIBERAL REGIME

7

"Hobbes," "Socinus," "Spinoza": Esotericism and the Atheist State in Pierre Bayle's *Historical and Critical Dictionary*

Kenneth R. Weinstein

In the history of political philosophy, Pierre Bayle (1647–1706) is best known for being the first to raise publicly the possibility that a society of atheists could exist and prosper. The society of atheists that Bayle proposes in his first political work, *Miscellaneous Thoughts on the Comet* (1682), offers a solution to the foremost political problems engendered by Christianity: intolerance and rebellion. These dangers arise because ecclesiastic authority claims a sovereignty distinct from and higher than the state. This "empire over souls" is especially dangerous because of the paradoxical impact religion has upon behavior. Bayle sees religion as simultaneously almost omnipotent yet impotent: almost omnipotent in fueling political turmoil, almost impotent in generating good behavior. Exposing as an illusion the belief that religion can effectively control behavior, Bayle seeks to restore human sovereignty to politics. Bayle's philosophy is twofold: first, a project of scientific enlightenment to rid man of popular errors and superstition, and, second, a political project to encourage statesmen to rely upon those powers that remain within their control, particularly strict laws and a hidden manipulation of the passions, especially the sense of honor.[1]

But Bayle's project laid out in the *Thoughts*—to rid Europe of the intolerance and rebellion endemic when Christianity offers rewards and punishments stronger than any earthly sovereigns can offer—may be seen as incompatible with certain prominent articles in Bayle's magnum opus, *The Historical and Critical Dictionary* (1697), that directly deal with the question of whether or not society would benefit by reducing the fear of the afterlife. In Bayle's articles on Faustus Socinus (1539–1604) and Baruch Spinoza

(1632–1677), Bayle vehemently denies the desirability of innovation in matters of religion, particularly any attempt to lessen the fear of the afterlife. If one reads these ringing condemnations of Spinoza and Socinus with no knowledge of the principles guiding Bayle's political philosophy, one might come to believe that Bayle has rejected the atheist state as a solution to the political crisis of Christendom. One could even be left with the idea that Bayle opposes all change in questions of religion. But careful examination of these arguments reveals their various smokescreens while unearthing a dialectic that reinforces Bayle's fundamental teaching—and points the way back to Bayle's political master, Thomas Hobbes.[2]

In the article in *The Historical and Critical Dictionary* on Faustus Socinus, Bayle launches a broad-based attack on the rationalist theologian, noting the dangers of the Socinian belief that a just God would not make men suffer eternal punishments in the afterlife. Leaving theological dispute aside, Bayle admits that it surely might "be more comfortable for each individual not to fear the punishments of the next life"; yet this view could hold dangers for society. Though we sleep at night more easily not having to fear eternal damnation, we nevertheless will feel "much more uncomfortable having to deal everyday with people who do not fear" such penalties. In this argument aimed ostensibly at nonbelievers, Bayle feigns to overlook the essence of his political philosophy: only ignorance and a sloppy examination of human motivation lead men to believe that those who do not fear the afterlife are dangerous. Asserting the social utility of the afterlife, in opposition to much of what he stated in his writings from the *Miscellaneous Thoughts* on, Bayle declares that "it is therefore not at all in the interest of individuals that any dogma that is capable of diminishing the fear of hell be established."[3]

As Bayle continues, his rejection of the Socinian position that a just God would not submit men to eternal damnation shifts grounds. Bayle argues that, indeed, "it is quite probable that preachers of this type of leniency will always shock the public much more than they please it."[4] Bayle thus restates the problem: it is not so much that society is endangered by the attempt to diminish the fear of the afterlife, as that society would be outraged by that attempt.[5] That shock itself in fact posed a danger to the Socinians, who, as history recounts, were forced to flee from their native Poland. However, the shocking character of the Socinian doctrine does not imply that more crimes will result from it.

Bayle shifts ground once more to argue why the fear of the afterlife should not be diminished. Whereas an evil man may not wish to believe in punishments in hell so that he may lie, poison, and commit adultery with impunity, he would be greatly perturbed if his "mother, wife, sister and nieces defamed themselves by their lewdness."[6] Here, Bayle's discussion leads us to think of the *Reflections,* where he argued that religion precisely fails most of all to control the bodily passions: the sense of shame and other earthly forces are what keep women under control.[7]

It should be noted that this specious argument is directed against those who would seek to do evil: those "atheists of practice" who deny the existence of God in order to serve their desires better. Bayle is a modern Epicurean, but not an exuberant atheist of the variety of the century that would follow. Bayle presents the atheist state as a sober alternative to the mindless killing of the wars of religion, not as a new era of human development and liberation.

His sleight of hand aside, Bayle never rejects the theoretical basis of the society of atheists: while the fear of hell and pangs of conscience should prevent crimes, they fail to do so, since abstract beliefs do not control our behavior. The belief that religion prevents crime and lewdness may seem sensible, but does not prove itself empirically.[8] Bayle repeats the point in the *Dictionary* when he rejects the argument that belief in the mortality of the soul would bring men to all sorts of crimes. To disprove the point, Bayle cites an even stronger argument, one "founded on the fact"—"a large number of rogues and scoundrels believe in the immortality of the soul while several saints and just men do not."[9]

Moreover, if these "rogues and scoundrels" reasoned according to Bayle's principles, they would realize that just as religion does not keep them under control, there is no reason to think it will keep others with similar inclinations under control. Bayle then offers a sophistic argument: the evil man should realize the benefits of belief in the afterlife, as he himself is more likely to fall victim to crime than to profit from it.

Bayle concludes his attack on the Socinian view of the afterlife by reformulating his earlier argument regarding individual interest. First, Bayle stated that it was not in "the interest of individuals that any dogma capable of diminishing the fear of hell be established." Admitting that "preachers of this type of laxity [such as Socinians] will always shock the public much more than they please it," Bayle now refines what sort of doctrine self-interest requires, noting that "it is therefore in the interest of each individual that a morality very capable of intimidating the conscience be taught."[10] The abysmal failure of Christianity to control morals, however, proves that strict religious principles do not intimidate the conscience to effect good behavior. Bayle's conclusion, unstated here, remains that the most effective way to be intimidated into good behavior is through strict laws and manipulation of the sense of honor.

Bayle's condemnation of Spinoza goes further than his attack on Socinus's doctrine. Bayle's criticism of Spinoza is primarily centered upon Spinoza's monism—Bayle claims that in the *Ethics,* Spinoza argues that "God and the world are one single being." Bayle in essence argues that by making God everything, Spinoza deprives God of his divine status. A God who is not transcendent but who is all the things in the universe is at best imperfect and contradictory: God, Bayle derisively notes, therefore becomes not merely

Spinoza himself, but the Jew who in pious anger tried to murder Spinoza on the steps of the Amsterdam synagogue. In one of Bayle's most memorable lines, he says that in Spinoza's system rather than speaking of, say, a battle between Germans and Turks in Hungary, one needs to say that "God modified as Germans killed God modified as ten thousand Turks."[11]

Aside from attacking Spinozistic pantheism for making God imperfect and contradictory, Bayle accuses Spinoza of being unable to resolve three major problems: how matter, eternal in Spinoza's system, could be distinct from an eternal God who himself is material; the mystery of how this matter came about; and, the problem of theodicy.[12] Having pointed to these problems in Spinoza's philosophy, Bayle asks us to "counterbalance on a proper scale" the "results" of Spinoza's hypothesis with the problems he sought to avoid. Spinoza's hypothesis, Bayle notes, fails to solve the difficulties Christianity creates while suggesting new ones that Christianity does not create. These weaknesses alone suffice to reverse the "edifice of this atheist": "good sense requires that custom be maintained" against innovators, "unless they provide better laws." "Submit yourself to custom," Bayle declares, "or give us something better."[13]

Comparing Christianity to Spinoza's "philosophic hypothesis," Bayle declares that if the difficulties on both sides were equal, one should choose Christianity. He notes that "besides the privilege of possession," Christianity "still has the advantage of promising us great goods for the future and leaving us a thousand consoling resources in this life." The belief that God hears our prayers leaves us consolation in times of trouble and hope for rewards for our troubles on earth.[14] This consolation, Bayle tells us, is a major reason why true atheists—as opposed to those strong thinkers who wish to be distinguished by their wit—do not attempt to disabuse their neighbors and relatives of their religious beliefs.[15]

Asserting the solace offered by belief in the afterlife, Bayle shifts grounds, returning to an argument close to that he made in his article on Socinus: he says that "it is a great consolation only to hope that other men defer . . . to the instinct of their conscience and the fear of God."[16] Bayle thereby declares the "ordinary hypothesis is at the same time both more true and more comfortable than that of impiety." The Christian hypothesis, moreover, "promises us an infinite good after this life and procures for us a thousand consolations in this life." Spinoza's system "promises us nothing outside of this world, and removes the confidence we place in our prayers and the pangs of conscience of our neighbors."[17]

Like the argument against Socinus, this one too fails to ring true, for Bayle's rejection of Spinoza's atheism does not imply a rejection of atheism per se.[18] Bayle does not truly counterbalance the Christian system with Spinoza's. Despite Bayle's stress here on the consolations of the afterlife, he admits elsewhere that the afterlife may not be altogether a consoling idea, for we may be predestined to suffer eternally, a fate far worse than mere death itself.[19] Furthermore, men who hope that others will defer to their conscience misplace their hope; the conscience is not necessarily guided by notions of equity. This misplaced hope could lead to great danger. On earth, Christianity does undeniably bring consolation in times of trouble. But it also brings undeniable cruelty: persecution, rebellion, and civil war.

Moreover, though Bayle believes that innovators ought to be silent unless they have better laws to propose, he does believe that better laws have been proposed: Hobbes' system to strengthen the hold of the sovereign over his citizens. To appreciate fully Bayle's reading of Spinoza and Socinus, it must be contrasted to his reading of Hobbes. Then one sees what is particularly curious about Bayle's condemnation of Socinus and Spinoza: the fact that so many of the charges he leveled against them could also be leveled against Hobbes. In contrast to these loud condemnations, Bayle's gentle treatment of Hobbes' theology could be understood as a part of a deliberate strategy to protect Hobbes.

Like Socinus, for instance, Hobbes denies the eternity of punishments in the afterlife.[20] Like the Socinians and Spinoza, Hobbes gives God a body.[21] Indeed, several of the works Bayle cites to criticize Spinoza's metaphysics and theology likewise attack Hobbes.[22] In his attack upon Spinoza, Bayle highlights Christian Kortholt's work, *De Tribus Impostoribus,* with a special footnote to let us know that the three impostors whose atheism Kortholt attacks are Herbert of Cherbury, Spinoza, and Hobbes.[23] Kortholt's book, Bayle tells us, allows one to "know better the replies and equivocations that Spinoza made use of to avoid showing his atheism clearly."[24]

But unlike his relentless criticism of Spinoza's atheism, Bayle's presentation of Hobbes' conception of God toys with these "replies and equivocations" in order to de-emphasize Hobbes' own atheism. Speaking of Hobbes' religious views, Bayle assures us that "those who have written of his life, argue that he had very orthodox opinions on the nature of God."[25] Bayle condemns the calumny of the "infinity of small minds or fiendish people," who hurl the charge of atheism at all who stray from popular religious conceptions. But in the next footnote, after this loud albeit spurious defense of Hobbes' piety and condemnation of those who accuse others of atheism, Bayle himself accuses Hobbes of atheism. Restating his position in the midst of a discussion about whether, as some alleged, Hobbes actually feared ghosts, Bayle abruptly condemns Hobbes along with Spinoza and Epicurus: materialists who deny the existence of God are incapable of denying magic and devilry by the same principles. A philosophy that denies the existence of substances distinct from matter is unable to deny the possibility that small pieces of matter are able to form inside of our minds. This objection, as we have noted, is irrelevant for Bayle's political purposes.[26]

Bayle's attempt to prevent meddling in politics by the clergy can be seen as a radical fulfillment of Hobbes' absolutist project to diminish the importance of the divine law and subordinate it to the civil law.[27] Bayle stressed the significance of Hobbes above all others to the study of politics; Bayle declared that Hobbes' *De Cive* "obliged the most far-sighted judges to admit that the foundations of politics had never before been so well uncovered."[28] *De Cive* "destroyed forever the doctrine of the lawfulness of subjects conspiring and rebelling against their sovereigns and the monstrous opinions of overthrowing and executing princes."[29] Bayle's atheist state is therefore best understood as a Hobbesian attempt to make the fear of the sovereign prevail over the commotion in civil society caused by the fear of hellfire. But in arguing that religion was politically unnecessary, Bayle drew out the implications of Hobbes' thought to a degree that Hobbes never did openly.

Hobbes' system secures the state from revolution by "restoring to the civil powers those rights of which they had been robbed by ecclesiastics in the ages of ignorance, and [by] heroically subduing that cruel hydra of the sectarians . . . the limitless liberty of conscience."[30] Though Hobbes' system in practice would face some difficulties, the opposite system contains within it the seeds of the greatest of political evils, civil war. Inherent in the political system of Hobbes' day are the seeds of rebellion and confusion.[31]

Tolerance and obedience cannot be brought about as long as religious belief continues to exercise its present influence on politics. The sovereignty of civil power must reassert itself over the rival claims of ecclesiastic forces. If not, men will obey their clergymen rather than their princes.[32] Fear of violent death at the hands of the sovereign alone "cannot bring to peace those moved to fight by an evil worse than death," those divided about the path necessary for salvation.[33] As "no man can serve two masters," the civil sovereign's power ends where the subject prefers to obey the ecclesiastical forces that menace him with fear of eternal damnation.[34] This fear of eternal damnation thus has to be reduced while the fear of the civil sovereign is augmented. In addition to disobedience, intolerance will gradually disappear as enlightened men, i.e., men free from religious motivation, come to rule.

We have seen that the earliest public advocate for the society without religion does not treat all atheists equally. Bayle reacts rather differently to Hobbes and Spinoza, the most publicly decried atheists of his day. One possible reason for Bayle's boisterous denunciation of Spinoza (as well as Socinus) could lie in the fact that Bayle had been accused of Socinianism and Spinozism by his colleague and friend turned archenemy, the Calvinist Minister Pierre Jurieu (1637–1713), who saw to it that Bayle was removed from his teaching post at the École Illustre of Rotterdam.[35]

But fear of persecution, which Bayle certainly faced, does not adequately account for Bayle's more gentle reaction to Hobbes' atheism. A theoretical question thus arises: why should an advocate of atheism be perturbed by the different theoretical bases for atheism? Such grounds, after all, might appear to be the irreligious equivalent of what the early modern advocates of toleration termed indifferent matters, i.e., those practices, nonessential to the Christian faith, over which churches fought endlessly. Perhaps Bayle focuses his fire on Spinoza's conception of God rather than Hobbes' because, at the end of the day, Bayle realized that Spinoza's religious views were open to the possibility of misinterpretation. Unlike Bayle's or Hobbes', Spinoza's presentation of God as all things opens the door to both rationalist and irrationalist theologians: rationalist theologians seeking to reconcile faith and reason through science as well as the pantheists of the next century who would mistakenly hail the atheist Spinoza as their spiritual father.[36] Hobbes' theology leaves us no such legacy—and thus better opens the door to the atheist state that Bayle sought.

NOTES

1. For a synoptic view of Bayle's political philosophy, see my article "Pierre Bayle's Atheist Politics," in *Early Modern Skepticism and the Origins of Toleration,* ed. Alan Levine (Lanham, Md.: Lexington Books, 1999), 197–223.

2. In a footnote in *Natural Right and History,* Leo Strauss mischievously shows himself to be the first and only interpreter of Bayle to have grasped the full significance of the *Dictionary*'s articles on Socinus, Spinoza, and Hobbes. Strauss claims that Bayle's atheistic society was a "most important implication" of Hobbes' call for popular enlightenment as a means to eliminate "the fear of powers invisible" (Leo Strauss, *Natural Right and History* [Chicago: University of Chicago Press, 1953], 198). In a footnote to that claim, Strauss suggests that the reader would do well to connect "Bayle's famous thesis with Hobbes's doctrine rather than with that of Faustus Socinus." (At first glance, by denying Socinus's influence, Strauss appears to be asserting the importance of political philosophy over theological disputation, for the Socinians rejected the eternity of hellfire, albeit for theological reasons.) In his footnote, Strauss directs the reader to the footnote in the *Historical and Critical Dictionary* in which Bayle praises Hobbes as the most penetrating student of politics (198–99, footnote 43). By mentioning Faustus Socinus in passing in his footnote on Bayle, Strauss draws our attention to Bayle's important article on Faustus Socinus in the *Historical and Critical Dictionary.* What is significant about Bayle's article on Socinus is that, as we shall see, Bayle there appears to contradict directly what Strauss asserts his project is: the attempt to reduce the fear of hellfire. The Socinus article, in turn, is widely cross-referenced to Bayle's article on Spinoza, in which he likewise seems to challenge the need to reform the fear of the afterlife. (These stark condemnations, as we shall see, stand in contrast to Bayle's silent acquiescence to Hobbes in the *Dictionary*.) These arguments, as we also shall see, need to be downplayed, for Strauss's entire discussion takes place in the context of a passage in *Natural Right and History* where Strauss notes that fear of persecution, i.e., the fear of powers visible, drove philosophers such as Hobbes to be so circumspect that they would at times silently acqui-

esce to unconventional or impious ideas that they would vocally reject in other passages. Strauss seems to encourage the reader to discount this conventional viewpoint
by noting in reference to Hobbes, "Many present-day scholars who write on subjects
of this kind do not seem to have a sufficient notion of the degree of circumspection
or of accommodation to the accepted views that was required, in former ages, of 'de-
viationists' who desired to survive or die in peace" (198–99). In his gentle yet powerful manner, Harvey C. Mansfield helped me to begin to comprehend the great subtlety of the relevant passages in the *Dictionary,* which I take to be the key to
understanding Bayle and his method of writing.

   3. "Socin, Fauste," note I, in Pierre Bayle, *Dictionnaire historique et critique,* 5th
ed., 4 vols. (Basel: Jean-Louis Brandmuller, 1738). Subsequent citations will be for article and note or page number. All translations are mine unless otherwise indicated.

   4. "Socin, Fauste," note I.

   5. "Socin, Fauste," note I.

   6. "Socin, Fauste," note I.

   7. Pierre Bayle, *Pensées diverses sur la comète* (henceforth *P.D.*). Edition cited is
Pierre Bayle, *Oeuvres diverses* (henceforth *O.D.;* Hildesheim: Georg Olms, 1965),
3:104.

   8. *P.D.,* §145, *O.D.* 3:93.

   9. "Pomponace," note H, cited in Jean Delvolvé, *Religion, critique et philosophie
positive* (Paris: Félix Alcan, 1906), 385; see also "Periander," note B.

   10. "Socin, Fauste," note I.

   11. "Spinoza," note N.

   12. On Bayle's Spinoza, see Gianluca Mori, "Sulla Spinoza di Bayle," *Giornale
Critica della Filosofia Italiana* 69 (1988): 348–68; Paul Vernière, *Spinoza et la pensée
française avant la Révolution* (Paris: Presses Universitaires de France, 1954),
286–306.

   13. "Spinoza," note O.

   14. "Spinoza," note O; "Théon," note A.

   15. "DesBarreaux," note F.

   16. "Spinoza," note O; compare to "Socin, Fauste," note I.

   17. "Spinoza," note O.

   18. Jean-Pierre de Crousaz, *L'examen du pyrrhonisme ancien et moderne* (The
Hague: Pierre DeHondt, 1733), 356; Pierre Jurieu, *Le Philosophe de Rotterdam, Ac-
cusé, Atteint, Convaincu* (Rotterdam: n. p., 1706), 130; Vernière, *Spinoza et la pensée française,* 293–94.

   19. "Sommona-codum," note A; "Pauliciens," remark F.

   20. Letter to Jacob Bayle, 26 December 1678, *Nouvelles lettres de Monsieur Bayle*
(The Hague: Van Duren, 1739), 2:53–54.

   21. Letter to Jacob Bayle, 26 December 1678; see also Bayle's *Objections to Pierre
Poiret* in *O.D.* vol. 5, chap. 1, pp. 16–17, 28, 30–31. Depending on how one reads
Hobbes' famed debate with Bishop Bramhall, Hobbes' science of bodies in motion
presents God as resembling either the Socinian concept of an extended but nonetheless limited body or Spinoza's view of God as encompassing the entire universe
(Thomas Hobbes, *English Works,* ed. William Molesworth [London: J. Bohn, 1840],
4:349). According to Bayle himself, either concept is impious; in addition to "Socin,
Fauste" and "Spinoza," see Pierre Bayle, *Continuation des pensées diverses* (henceforth *C.P.D.*), §141, *O.D.* 3:392. The *Encyclopédie,* which draws heavily upon Bayle's

accounts of Hobbes and Spinoza, concludes that even if Hobbes "were not an atheist, one has to admit that his own God differs very little from that of Spinoza" ("Hobbes," in Denis Diderot and Jean Le Rond d'Alembert, *Encyclopédie ou dictionnaire raisonné des sciences, des arts et des métiers* [Neuf-Chastel: Samuel Faulache and Compagnie, 1765], 8:241). In his dictionary of free thought, Trinius declares that for Hobbes, "the entire world is God (Johann Trinius, *Freydenker Lexikon, oder Einleitung in die Geschichte der Philosophie der neuern Freigeister* [Leipzig: Christoph Cörner, 1759], 36). Leibniz, on the other hand, separates Hobbes' notion of God as an extended mass from Spinoza's pantheism (Ludwig Stern, *Leibniz und Spinoza: Beitrag zur Entwicklungsgeschichte* [Berlin: George Reimer, 1890], 308–10.) Unlike Socinus and Spinoza, however, Hobbes leaves open the question of the eternity of matter (Thomas Hobbes, *English Works,* ed. William Molesworth [London: J. Bohn, 1839], 1:414).

22. See, for instance, Franciscus Cuyper, *Arcana atheismi rivelata, philosophice & paradoxè refutata, examine Tractatus theologico-politici* (Rotterdam: Isaacus Naeranus, 1676). In his *Tractatus de culti naturali et origine moralitatis oppositius Tractatus theologico politico* (Rotterdam: Rainier Leers, 1680), Lambert van Velthuysen originally contrasted Spinoza's impiety with Hobbes' piety; upon realizing his error, van Velthuysen wrote a subsequent work aimed at denouncing Hobbes. Whereas Noel Aubert de Versé sides with Hobbes against Spinoza in his *L'impie convaincu ou Dissertation contre Spinoza dans laquelle on refute les fondements de son athéisme* (Amsterdam: J. Crelle, 1684), he argues as a Socinian who limits the size of God's body (see Maria Emmanuella Scribano, *Da Descartes a Spinoza: Percorsi della teologia razionale nel Seicento* [Milan: Franco Angelo, 1988], esp. 145–50, 191, 205, 229–40).

23. "Spinoza," note 86. This work should not be confused with the more famous one of the same title, widely circulated among the *philosophes,* that attacked Moses, Jesus, and Mohammed as the three imposters.

24. "Spinoza," note M.

25. "Hobbes," note M.

26. "Hobbes," note N; see also *C.P.D., §18, O.D.* 3:210.

27. Letter to Jacob Bayle, 28 December1678.

28. "Hobbes," note E.

29. "Hobbes," note E.

30. "Hobbes," note E.

31. Compare "Hobbes," note F, with "Loyola," note S.

32. *P.D. §81, O.D.* 3:52.

33. "Hobbes," note C.

34. Thomas Hobbes, "De Cive," in *Man and Citizen,* ed. Bernard Gert (Garden City, N.Y.: Anchor Books, 1972), 179.

35. Jurieu, *Le Philosophe de Rotterdam,* passim.

36. In contrast to Spinoza, Hobbes offers no comprehensive theology. In "On the Basis of Hobbes's Political Philosophy," Strauss contrasts the barrenness of Hobbes' "dry atheism" with the misguided offspring of Spinoza's atheism who transformed him into the "father of a church of pantheism" ("On the Basis of Hobbes's Political Philosophy," in Leo Strauss, *What is Political Philosophy?* [Chicago: University of Chicago Press, 1959], 171). (On this and other matters, I am indebted to Hillel Fradkin for graciously sharing his insights.)

8

Rousseau on the Problem of Invisible Government: The *Discours sur l'économie politique*

Clifford Orwin

> *Il est certain, du moins, que le plus grand talent des chefs est de déguiser leur pouvoir pour le rendre moins odieux, et de conduire l'état si paisiblement qu'il semble n'avoir pas besoin de conducteurs.*
>
> —Rousseau[1]

Among Harvey Mansfield's signal achievements is to have exposed the preoccupation of modern thinkers with the art or science of invisible government, of that government which governs best because it least seems to govern.[2] As the citation above confirms, Rousseau shares this preoccupation. At the same time, he appreciates the ambiguity of the matter: will invisible government expedite good government, or will it merely cloak usurpation? Today we view the transparency of government as a crucial element of its accountability: democratic parties of whatever hue vie to outdo each other in "openness." Rousseau too is averse to machinations of certain kinds, the "petty and contemptible ruses" that go by the names of *maximes de l'état* and *secrets du cabinet* (253). Yet the disguise of power to render it less odious is a tactic he ascribes to *legitimate* statesmen. So the problem remains. If the secret of good government is to possess the ring of Gyges, must not the possession of that ring prove so corrupting as to subvert good government? It is for elucidation of this problem that we turn to Rousseau's sole work devoted to the theme of government.

I

The *Discours sur l'économie politique* of 1753–54 is the least commented upon of Rousseau's political writings. And no wonder: it first comes to sight as *Hamlet* without the prince, the *Social Contract* without the social contract. Others, noting the absence from the *Discours* of any discussion of the state of nature, have regarded it as an immature work, anterior in conception to the *Discours sur les origines de l'inégalité,* the publication of which preceded it.[3] Its most obvious distinguishing positive feature merely brands it as the most anachronistic of Rousseau's writings. The long concluding section, devoted as it is to the promotion of a premodern agrarian economy on the model of a purified republican Rome, seems an exercise in futility, a road left untaken, thank you, by subsequent radical thinkers.[4]

In this essay I will not discuss Rousseau's economics in the narrower sense of that term current in the present day. By *économie* Rousseau himself means government, in the broadest sense of that term (241). In light of this choice of topic, the omissions noted are justifiable—as is the work's claim to be worthy of study in its own right.

The *Discours* was Rousseau's contribution to the *Encyclopédie,* that great enterprise of Enlightenment edited by his then friend Diderot; otherwise we know little about the circumstances of its composition. While commissioning Rousseau to write on political economy, Diderot had reserved for himself the entry on *Droit.* In his own article, therefore, Rousseau discusses politics without treating systematically the question of right, which necessarily leads back to that of origins and hence of the contract.[5] He takes men "as they are" not by nature but by history: he takes them as men in civil society, afflicted by the needs of civil society (248).

The social contract is in any case not the whole of Rousseau's political teaching: at most it establishes the indispensable framework for the resolution of the problem of legitimate authority. The problem it addresses is that of avoiding the domination of society by a particular will or wills. Under the terms of the contract, whereby each alienates to the whole his natural right to rule himself, not a particular but rather the general will is to prevail: none will rule others because all will rule all. But Rousseau of course distinguishes rule or the exercise of sovereignty from government or the enforcement of the laws. While the rule of some by others is out, the government of some by others remains entirely necessary. If law is needed, so too are the execution and interpretation of it, and the vesting of these in a distinct body chosen for its superior qualifications for these tasks.

There thus reemerges within society the problem that confronted us on the threshold of society. The very "realism" of the argument for the social contract—viz., that the utter untrustworthiness of every human being to rule another entails their agreement on the sole set of terms that precludes that outcome—itself implies the difficulty of implementing the contract. If men's unreliability as rulers bids us limit them to the role of magistrates, so it requires us to impute to them a constant tendency to usurp rule under the cover of magistracy.

From this we might expect that Rousseau would place a higher premium than his predecessors on the *visibility* of government. For how restrain a government that operates invisibly? Yet though plausible this conclusion would be wrong. As we have already seen, the Rousseau of the *Discourse on Political Economy* not only praises invisibility but declares it certain that it is the greatest talent of leaders.

II

The discourse begins with a torrent of definitions and distinctions, of which the first is that between *économie générale ou politique* and *économie domestique ou particulière*. Rousseau elaborates at length the disparallelisms between the government of the family and that of the state. The crowning one is that while nature supports the good government of the family, it subverts the good government of the state. "Far from the leader's having a natural interest in the happiness of private individuals, it is not rare for him to seek his own in their misery" (243). Nature "is for the magistrate only a false guide, which works ceaselessly to lead him astray from his duties, and which drags him sooner or later to his ruin and that of the state, if he is not restrained by the most sublime virtue" (243). In moving from domestic to political economy we leave the realm of nature for that of virtue, with the latter understood not, as in Aristotle, as the perfection of the former, but as its antidote.

On "realistic" grounds, then, Rousseau rejects as facile the realism of his fellow moderns. The gulf between nature and politics is greater than they have grasped. It is not, as they have thought, a question of harnessing natural selfishness for the common benefit—"the masterpiece of the policy of our century"[6]—but of forming statesmen who will prefer the common benefit to the gratification of their natural selfishness. If Rousseau's earlier writings had presented nature as good and society as corrupt, he here condemns nature as the corruptor of society. Good government is against nature: to this extent Rousseau endorses the modern project of the conquest of nature.

The crucial task to be addressed is the formation of real statesmen: "Thus it is that nature has produced a multitude of good fathers of families, but it is doubtful whether since the world has existed human wisdom has produced ten men capable of governing their fellows" (243–44). The question of *économie politique*, the knowledge appropriate to statesmen, points to that of "human wisdom," the knowledge required to form them. Having distinguished political economy from that in economy which is not political, Rousseau distinguishes it from that in politics which is not economy.

> I beg my readers also to distinguish carefully *public economy,* of which I am to speak, and which I call *government,* from the supreme authority, which I call *sovereignty*—a distinction that consists in the latter having the legislative right and in certain cases obligating the very body of the nation, while the former has only the executive power and can obligate only private individuals. (244)

Rousseau proceeds to sketch, although not to demonstrate as he will do in the *Social Contract,* the authority of the general will. His argument begins from the primacy and moral indefeasibility for each being of its own good. Offering a version of the hoary figure of the body politic ("a comparison that is not very exact"), he concludes that what defines both bodies, the natural human one and the artificial political one, is a *moi commun au tout.* As a composite the state is a mortal being and "thus also a moral [one] which has a will; and this general will, which tends always toward the preservation and well-being of the whole and of each part, and which is the source of the laws, is—for all the members of the state in relation to themselves and to it— the rule of just and unjust. . . ." (245).

By a moral being Rousseau evidently means one that has a will, and if that being is mortal its will must tend to its preservation. There is thus far no conflict between the morality of a being and its selfishness: morality begins at home. The moral authority of the general will follows precisely from its "selfishness" in the indicated sense. Were it the will of another therefore tending to the good of that other, it would have no claim on us. As our own will, however, tending to our own good (in common with that of the other citizens), it binds us as only our own will can do. The general will is authoritative for all because common to all, for the same reason, in other words, that it tends to the preservation of all.

Because the general will tends to the good of all it is the rule of just and unjust for all—the just is strictly subordinate to the good—so there can be no right on the part of the governors to invoke any other rule of just and unjust as an excuse for deviating from it. That would be to prefer their will to the public will. Thus the search for a transcendent standard of justice is in itself an act of injustice. *[margin note: natural right]*

On reflection, this very case for the supremacy of the general will implies the difficulty of obtaining the submission of the government to it. For as the general will of a particular society is authoritative only for the members of that society, and not for foreigners, who do not share in it—while just in relation to the former it may be unjust in relation to the latter (545)[7]—so will the same problem arise within each society. Factions will form, each actuated by a will common to the members but unjust in relation to the society as a whole.

The will of these particular societies always has two relations: for the members of the association, it is a general will; for the broader society, it is a particular will, which is very often found to be upright (*droite*) in the first respect and vicious in the second. A given man may be a pious priest, or a brave soldier, or a zealous lawyer, and a bad citizen. A given deliberation may be advantageous to the small community, and most pernicious to the large one. It is true that since particular societies are always subordinate to those that contain them, one ought to obey the latter rather than the former. . . . But unfortunately personal interest is always found in inverse ratio to duty, and increases in proportion as the association becomes narrower and the engagement less sacred—invincible proof that the most general will is also always the most just, and that the voice of the people is in fact the voice of God. (246) *the more despotic the rule the more exactly the votes those rules desired*

As a vindication of the general will this is problematic. As already noted, the good of another has no claim on my allegiance. The general will is authoritative for me only because it intends the good of all. If, however, "personal interest is always found in inverse proportion to duty," the question arises why one should prefer duty, supported as it is by an appeal to the broader but less intense interest, to the dictates of the narrower but more powerful one. If what is good for me is less my good the more numerous the others with whom I share it, then the very "realism" that grounds Rousseau's teaching on justice now appears to subvert it. This problem is structural: it is doubtful whether he satisfactorily solves it.

Just as we can count on a given people to prefer its interest to that of the human race as a whole, so we can count on a given government to prefer its interest to that of the people as a whole. Not the widespread observance of the general will but merely an inconsistency in the widespread neglect of it confirms its supreme authority for us (247). Not surprisingly, this section of the *Discours* concludes with a statement of the intransigence of the problem of government.

In establishing the general will as the first principle of public *economy* and the fundamental rule of government, I have not held it necessary to examine seriously whether the magistrates belong to the people or the people to the magistrates, and whether in public affairs one ought to consult the good of the state or that of the leaders. For a long time this question has been decided in one way in practice and in the other by reason, and in general it would be great folly to hope that those who are in fact masters will prefer another interest to their own. It would therefore be appropriate to divide public *economy* still further into popular and tyrannical [branches]. The former is that of any state where there reigns between the people and the chiefs unity of interest and of will; the other will exist necessarily wherever the people and the chiefs will have different interests and consequently opposing wills. The maxims of the latter are inscribed all through the archives of history and in the satires of Machiavelli. The others are found only in the writings of philosophers who dare to assert the rights of humanity. (247)

The perfidy of the chiefs is as completely necessary as is their loyalty to their interests; there can be a common will only where there is a common interest. Again this follows from the very realism that anointed the general will in the first place: if each "moral" being, natural or corporate, wills its own good, none can be expected to sacrifice it to that of another.

The trick then would be to devise a political system that yokes the interest of the magistrates to that of the people. This would not be easy, for short of dispensing with the very existence of a distinct body of magistrates—the solution that Rousseau describes in the *Social Contract* as democracy and there repudiates as suitable only for angels—one will always have to contend with a corporate will of the magistrates in tension with the general will.

The record offers little encouragement to expect a solution of this crucial problem. Consider Rousseau's strict dichotomy between the annals of history and those of philosophy. There is evidently no historical example of a state so constructed as to harmonize successfully the interests of the government and the people. There is none, then, whose magistrates have not acted (and "necessarily") on the maxims of *l'économie tyrannique*. The true maxims of government have come to light *only* in the writings of philosophers. If we are to take Rousseau at his word here, even Sparta and Rome, taken as examples of "popular" statecraft, are the inventions of such philosophers. Rousseau thus appears to assign the *Discourse* itself to a genre far removed from the description of politics as actually practiced. For without further ado he plunges into the elucidation of the maxims of "popular" political economy, to this devoting the remainder of the work (247ff.). Must we in fact place him among the heralds of imaginary principalities? True, we cannot conclude from what he has said so far that the problem of harmonizing the interests of the government and the people is, strictly speaking, insoluble. We need only conclude that its solution still lies in the future. Given, however, the intransigence of Rousseau's statement of the problem, we must ask if the rest of the *Discours* sheds further light upon the possibility of such a solution.

III

It follows from what Rousseau has said so far that "the first and most important maxim of legitimate or popular government . . . is . . . to follow the general will in all matters" (247). Rousseau assumes, if only for the sake of his argument, magistrates submissive to the general will. He proceeds, however, to stress the very great difficulty of discerning it. He suggests that the onus is on the chiefs to decipher it, rather than, as we might think, on the people to express it. Our perplexity on this score is if anything heightened by the powerful praise of the rule of law that follows, and which establishes the law as the inviolable standard for the magistrates no less than for the ordinary citizens (248–49). For if it is law that is the organ of the general will, the magistrates need look no further than the law to determine the dictates of that will. Can it be that the law too (perhaps because wise laws must be proposed by the magistrates to the people) depends on the magistrates' prior discernment of the general will?

It is in his discussion of law if anywhere in the *Discours sur l'économie politique* that Rousseau shoulders the task of reconciling particular interest (including that of the corps of magistrates) with the general will. It is in the interest of each that none (and so not himself) should be exempt from the law, for only then will all (including himself) enjoy its protection.

[margin note: interest in his capacity as citizen, not individual man?]

> By what inconceivable art could the means have been found to subject men in order to make them free; to use in the service of the state the goods, the strength, even the lives of all its members without constraining and without consulting them? . . . How can it be that they obey and that no one commands; that they serve and have no master; all the freer, in fact, because under what appears as subjection, each loses only so much of his freedom as might harm the freedom of another. These marvels are the work of the law. . . . It is this celestial voice that announces to each citizen the precepts of public reason, and teaches him to act according to the maxims of his very own judgment and not to be in contradiction with himself. (248)

[margin note: Marvels]

[margin note: voice of people = voice of God]

It is only as agents of the law that the magistrates can avoid the appearance and reality of seeking to impose their will on that of the people. Appearance matters, for it is only for so long as the citizens perceive the magistrates as not their rulers but their servants (because the executors of the law) that they will willingly obey them. Yet the reality matters also, for we are not speaking here, as in Machiavelli, of a mere appearance of abstention from rule. Rousseau emphatically presents the rule of law as an alternative to the rule of men: where all rule themselves through law, no man rules another. So long as magistrates respect the law, they are part of the only solution to the otherwise intractable problem of human authority; from the moment they depart from it, they are part of the problem.

Once again the Hobbesian tincture of Rousseau's argument is clear. The benefit (however great) to be derived from flouting the law never offsets the dangers to which one exposes oneself thereby. Inasmuch, moreover, as the legitimate authority of the magistrate depends entirely on law, he has not less but much more incentive to respect it than the ordinary citizen. "The most pressing interest of the chief, as well as his indispensable duty, is then to see to the observance of the laws whose minister he is, and on which all his authority is founded" (249).

Q.E.D.? Yet again we are struck by the defective realism of this Hobbesian approach as evinced by the historical record. If obedience to law is even more in the interest of magistrates than of ordinary citizens, why is it that as a matter of fact they, as Rousseau has already conceded, can be so depended on to flout it? Rousseau's reasoned paean to law seems rather to expose the weakness of reason than the strength of law. In moments of temptation, he asks us to accept our phantom will as more authoritative than our real one, or as he might prefer us to put it, our general and constant will as more real than our merely particular and ephemeral one. The law divides in order to rule, but can it count on our rational self to prevail over our passionate one?

It is perhaps with this difficulty in mind that Rousseau, after stressing that the law must both be reasonable and be seen to be so (a position he associates with Plato), goes much further.

> But although the government is not the master of the law, it is much to be its guarantor and to have of a thousand means of making it loved. It is in this alone that the talent of reigning consists. An imbecile . . . can . . . punish crimes: the true statesman knows how to prevent them. It is over wills still more than over actions that he extends his respectable empire. . . . It is certain, at least, that the greatest talent of leaders is to disguise their power to render it less odious, and to guide the state so peaceably that it seems to have no need of guides. (250)
>
> If it is good to know how to use men as they are, it is much better still to make them what one needs them to be. The most absolute authority is that which penetrates within man and is exerted no less on his will than on his actions. It is certain that peoples are in the long run what government makes them. Warriors, citizens, men when it wishes; mob and rabble when it pleases. Every prince who disdains his subjects dishonors himself in showing that he has not known how to make them estimable. (251)

The conventional wisdom in our societies is that we get the leaders we deserve. This deprives the people of all right to complain of the badness of their governors: they have only themselves to blame. Rousseau maintains the opposite. The people would be right to complain not only about the badness of their leaders but about their own badness; the leaders are to blame for both. The people are always what their education in the broadest sense makes them, and that education is always in the hands of the government. What is required of the magistrates is something more (if also, in a sense, less) than reasoning with the citizens.

> Form men, then, if you wish to command men. If you wish the laws to be obeyed, make them beloved, and that for people to do what they ought, it suffices that they think that they ought to do it. This was the great art of the governments of antiquity, in those faraway times when philosophers would give laws to peoples, and would use their authority only to make them wise and happy. From this [arose] so many sumptuary laws, so much regulation of *moeurs,* so many public maxims admitted or rejected with the greatest care. (251–52)

virtue defined

108   *Clifford Orwin*

In distant times, evidently, philosophers emerged from the pages of their books to give laws to peoples. They betook themselves not only and not primarily to reasoning with these peoples, but to supervising their behavior and opinions with an eye to fostering rectitude. An appeal to the self-interest of the citizens conceived as rational individualists—the Hobbesian approach with which Rousseau has flirted earlier in the *Discourse* and even in his recent vindication of law—did not figure in the repertoire of these philosopher-lawgivers. The task is to kindle love of the law, and it is to this task that no Hobbesian line of reasoning—or any line of reasoning —is equal. Hence Rousseau's second maxim of *l'économie publique*, "no less important than the first": "Do you want the general will to be accomplished? Arrange that all particular wills are related to it; and since virtue is only this conformity of the particular will to the general, to say the same thing briefly, make virtue reign" (252). *virtue is de-rating par excell*

To foster love of the law one fosters virtue, which is nothing other than the conformity of the particular to the general will. The abolition of the tension between the two is the real touchstone of statesmanship. The virtue of the citizen does not consist in a painful self-overcoming—a constant daily struggle between his particular will and his civic or general one—but in the education of the former to conform with the latter. He does not merely submit to the law, he loves it. At issue is the transformation of the man Marcus— who as a man is a natural whole—into the citizen Marcus, who is fully a part of the greater whole of the city. Virtue and the love of law pass from statesmen to peoples, rather than vice versa. If the statesmen can leave it to the *moeurs* to govern, their own task is largely accomplished. It is the statesmen's gift for this sort of education that renders their government invisible. Government is visible when it compels, and the conformity of particular wills to the general will renders compulsion superfluous.

Rousseau thus saddles leaders with an awful responsibility, while crediting them with an awesome power. It is the extreme plasticity of peoples that affords the opportunity for grand statesmanship. It is because the power of the statesman/educator extends to wills that he is able to achieve the conformity of those wills to the general will; it is because he is able to penetrate inside the subject that he need not rely primarily on threatening or badgering him from outside. In a well-governed republic the citizen experiences the will of the government as his own. If the wills of the magistrates coincide with the general will, then so will those of the citizens the magistrates form; if the wills of the magistrates are corrupt, they will contrive to corrupt those of the citizens. What this means, however, is that in the *Political Economy* Rousseau has succeeded only in displacing the political problem of virtue or the conformity of private wills with the general will from the people to the magistrates. The work falls into two unequal parts, of which the first defines the science of "popular" political economy. This proves to be distinguished from its "tyrannical" counterpart not by its methods but by its intention (cf. *virtue is understood in terms of plasticity + not in terms of natural end* the reference to ancient tyrants as the evil twins of the ancient philosophers [252]). The second part proceeds to advise adepts of the public-spirited science. What is missing is the link between the two, the necessary discussion of how to assure the public-spiritedness not of the citizens (for that must be the work of the statesmen) but of the statesmen themselves.

We must conclude that those who will govern invisibly must themselves be governed invisibly; that those whose charge it is to form the very wills of the citizens must themselves have submitted (no less unwittingly) their wills to the authority of another. It might seem that Rousseau anticipates a virtuous circle: the magistrates form the wills of patriotic citizens, from whose ranks their successors as magistrates emerge, who will in their turn form the will of the subsequent generation of citizens, etc. Yet this circle must have a noncircular beginning: chronologically, as well as conceptually, virtuous magistrates are for Rousseau prior to virtuous citizens. Behind the governors, then, lurks the figure of the immortal legislator; behind the account of governance, the necessity of an account of the origins that is not exhausted by recourse to a presumed social contract. Exposition of that contract could suffice only if political rationalism could suffice. Yet such rationalism can at most suffice within a civic framework that it cannot establish. Laws must be explained to citizens (to this extent Rousseau is a rationalist). The citizens whom law presupposes, however, must be created not by rationality but by that education of the sentiments on which invisible government depends. Nor can that government on whose integrity civic education depends be rendered upright by argument.

The influence of the Legislator is the truly invisible government, to which even the visible magistrates are subjects and of which even they must remain unaware.[8] Good government is humanly possible when originating in a superhuman founder. At a certain point realism must become magic, and this is no abandonment of realism but a necessary consequence of its dictates. Precisely if we take men as they are, there is no turning back from the conclusion that only in the hands of a Legislator will they ever become what they might be. This argument, which Rousseau will make explicit in the *Social Contract,* is already implicit in the *Political Economy.* Advice to good governors can carry one only so far, or to put it more precisely, can carry one only from a certain point. The question, as always in Rousseau, is whether we can get back there from here.

NOTES

The remote origins of this chapter lie not only in the teaching and writing of Harvey Mansfield but in his generosity in inviting his graduate students to live in his summer home at Stone Pond in Marlborough, New Hampshire. It was there that I gathered many years ago with Arthur M. Melzer, Robert P. Kraynak, and Harold B. Ames for a reading group on the *Discours sur l'économie politique* that launched all of my subsequent reflections on the work.

1. *Discours sur l'économie politique,* in *Oeuvres complètes, Tome III: Du contrat social; écrits politiques,* ed. Robert Derathé et al. (Paris: Editions de la Pléiade, 1964), 250. Unless otherwise noted, all references in the text to the *Discours sur l'économie politique* and Rousseau's other political writings will be to this edition. Translations are my own.

2. "In the great dispute between Machiavelli and Aristotle, two philosophers who sought, in Machiavelli's phrase, 'to acquire the world,' I make out a distinction between direct and indirect government. Direct government, that of Aristotle's regime, is essentially as it appears, and it publicly tells the world who rules. In Machiavelli's indirect government the rulers do not appear but try to hide themselves; and since princes of some kind always rule, it is defined not by *who* rules but by *how* they rule." Harvey Mansfield, *Machiavelli's Virtue* (Chicago: University of Chicago Press, 1996), xiv. For elaboration, see the studies collected in the volume just cited; Harvey Mansfield, Jr., "Hobbes and the Science of Indirect Government," *American Political Science Review* 65 (1971) 97–110; and Harvey Mansfield, Jr., *Taming the Prince: The Ambivalence of Modern Executive Power* (New York: Free Press, 1989), especially the discussion of the "neutrality" of the modern executive.

3. René Hubert, *Rousseau et l'Encyclopédie* (Paris: Gamber, 1928). For trenchant critiques of this view see Michel Launay, *J.-J. Rousseau, écrivain politique* (Grenoble: ACER, 1971), 221–22, and Roger D. Masters, *The Political Philosophy of Rousseau* (Princeton, N.J.: Princeton University Press, 1968), 265–71.

4. See Yoav Peled, "Rousseau's Inhibited Radicalism: An Analysis of His Political Thought in Light of His Economic Ideas," *APSR* 74 (1980) 1034–45. Launay, op. cit. 222–23, stresses the "progressive" aspects of Rousseau's approach to public finance.

5. Cf. *Discours sur l'inégalité,* preface and introduction (122–27, 131–33).

6. *Préface du Narcisse,* in *Oeuvres complètes, Tome II: La Nouvelle Héloïse etc.,* ed. Bernard Guyon et al. (Paris: Editions de la Pléiade, 1964), 968.

7. On the insoluble problem that the existence of distinct societies poses for Rousseau, see Pierre Hassner, "Rousseau and the Theory and Practice of International Relations," in Clifford Orwin and Nathan Tarcov, ed., *The Legacy of Rousseau* (Chicago: University of Chicago Press, 1997), 200–19.

8. See Christopher Kelly, "'To Persuade without Convincing': The Language of Rousseau's Legislator," *American Journal of Political Science* 31 (1987): 321–35.

9

Rousseau, Nationalism, and the Politics of Sympathetic Identification

Arthur Melzer

Why is there *nationalism?* Neither the word nor the thing is much more than two hundred years old.[1] If one looks at the other mass movement that has dominated our century, Communism, one finds that no one expresses puzzlement at its very existence. Radical and strange as it may be, it involves the perennial conflict between rich and poor, which is never far from the core of politics—especially modern, materialistic politics. But nationalism surprised virtually everyone—and continues to do so. We still don't quite know what it is, where it will appear or disappear next, or what new forms it will take. It seems to be on the rise in Eastern Europe, as many had predicted, but in surprising decline in Western Europe, where for the first time in history peoples have calmly voted away major elements of national sovereignty in the name of transnational union. Yet at the same time, in Europe and especially in the United States and Canada, nationalist ideas and passions have been reasserting themselves in the new form of multiculturalism and identity politics—what might be called "minority nationalism." Regarding the latter movement in particular, was there a single observer of Western politics writing, say, forty years ago who predicted its rapid rise and current importance?

There is nothing new, of course, in the division of humanity into distinct "nations," that is, into loose groupings defined not by any common enterprise or actual union, but purely by *felt similarity,* whether of language, race, culture, or history. Nor is the existence of national sentiment—of an affectionate identification with the nation—new. But for most of human history, these phenomena, while present, were not a significant force on the political stage. In the late eighteenth century, however, suddenly the national grouping came to be seen as the most fundamental source of men's charac-

111

ter and identity and as the necessary object of their primary loyalty, so that the state or political union could be legitimate and healthy only if it coincided with and built upon this preexisting national group. These powerful new beliefs and sentiments comprise nationalism.

The republican city-states of the ancient world, to be sure, were famous for their patriotism. But nationalism differs from ancient patriotism in having as its primary object the people and not the land or the republic—and the people, not as it is organized by any common enterprise or hierarchical order, but merely as it is linked by the perception of cultural similarity. "Similarity politics" is what is new. Only through it did the state come to regard as its highest mission something that formerly was hardly a goal at all: not only the resistance to nonnational rule, but the incorporation of all distant parts of the nation, through imperialism if necessary, and the exclusion or expulsion of all minority nationalities within.

Furthermore, this strange and late-arising movement, once arisen, spread very far and very fast. The formation of one nation-state, France, ignited a yearning for nationhood in its near neighbors—Germany, Italy, and Hungary—then in the rest of Europe, and eventually in most of the non-Western world. Today, the concept of the nation-state is so firmly entrenched that the words "state" and "nation" are essentially synonymous.

As it has spread, however, nationalism has changed and mutated. Thus, some profoundly different phenomena are now conjoined under this single term. Indeed, the theme "nationalism" is like that of "religion": in different times or places, radically different beliefs and hopes have been pinned on the concept of "nation" as on the idea of "God." Thus, any full account of either of these phenomena would have to abandon the plane of generality and proceed on a case-by-case basis. Nevertheless, it is possible to speak in general of the "natural seeds of religion" (in Hobbes' phrase) and similarly of the seeds of nationalism—although, in view of the historical ubiquity of religion and the late rise of nationalism, these seeds would seem to be emphatically historical rather than natural. In particular, it seems clear that the seeds of nationalism were somehow—and unwittingly—planted by the rise of the modern state. But how?

It is often claimed that nationalism first arose from Europe's experience and resentment of French imperialism under Napoleon (just as Third World nationalism would later arise from European imperialism). But imperialism, like the national groupings it violates, has existed since the dawn of civilization without giving rise to nationalism. "Irish peasants and gentry," as Kenneth Minogue observes, "felt all manner of grievances against English rule for centuries, but they felt these grievances as an oppressed class, or religious community, or locality."[2] Some new cause is needed to explain why they (and so many others at the same time) suddenly came to interpret and experience these age-old grievances—and indeed, the general phenomena of human partisanship, conflict, and oppression—no longer in terms of economics, politics, or religion but nationality. The strangeness of this transformation, which we tend to forget, is nicely stated by Ernest Gellner: "Life is a difficult and serious business. The protection from starvation and insecurity is not easily achieved. In the achievement of it, effective government is an important factor. Could one think of a sillier, more *frivolous* consideration than the question concerning the native vernacular of the governors? Hardly: and men have seldom had time or taste for such curious frivolity."[3] How did the politics of cultural similarity suddenly arise and take such firm root?

Since nationalism is not merely a sentiment—as patriotism is—but an ideology, one can try to answer this question by tracing its intellectual history. That is certainly a useful thing to do.[4] But the world is full of ideologies. Therefore, the prior question, the "seeds" question, is: why was the modern state so surprisingly *receptive* to this particular ideology?

The answer most often given is: democracy.[5] Nationalism grows out of the democratic idea with its doctrine of popular sovereignty, its deification of the will of the people, the *volk. Vox populi vox Dei.* Yet, again, there were democratic ideas and states in the premodern world—as the medieval provenance of that expression indicates—but no nationalist ones.

But surely modern democracy is unique, one might urge, still seeking the seeds of nationalism. It is *liberal* democracy, a society of independent *individuals,* born free of all the supposed duties stemming from natural inequality or sociality, indeed of all duties not originating in their own will or consent. And following from this, it is a democracy based on the individual's *self-interest*, which tends to mean on materialism or commerce.

But these defining features of the modern state only deepen the puzzle. Of all things, how could individualism be the source of the collectivist idea of nationalism? And how could material self-interest generate a passion for an immaterial thing, the nation, a passion that most often ignores or runs counter to economic rationality? Commerce, and the interest-group pluralism that it tends to produce, is a force more likely to erode than to foster nationalism, as the term "multinational corporation" implies. In sum, if we had only theory to look at, and history didn't get in the way, we might predict that nationalism was a staple feature of the traditional state—arising from its emphasis on homogeneity and on selfless devotion—which finally disappeared with the advent of the modern individualistic, pluralistic, commercial republic.

"Why is there nationalism?" is thus a question not only about nationalism but above all about the modern state that spawned it. How could we ever claim to understand the latter correctly until we comprehended this most powerful and surprising of its inner tendencies?

Perhaps the best place to look for such understanding is in the thought of Jean-Jacques Rousseau, who is generally credited with being the father or grandfather of nationalism, just as he is the father of secular compassion, communitarianism, the cult of sincerity or authenticity, and the proto-Kantian conception of justice as fairness. He is the progenitor, in short, of the whole new world of moral ideas and longings that has grown up on the basis of, and yet in reaction to, the modern state.

Rousseau promoted these particular cultural transformations not only because he saw them as potentially salutary but also as *possible;* that is, as movements that could successfully be made to grow out of the very modern, individualist principles they were needed to correct. It was largely the remarkable penetration and accuracy of Rousseau's analysis of the *receptivity* of the modern state—of what things could and could not be made to grow from it—that gave his thought such unparalleled historical influence. We turn to him, then, not in order to trace this influence but to understand that analysis. We turn to him, that is, not so much as a "father of nationalism" but as a prescient political scientist, as a profound analyst of modernity who, without the aid of the last two centuries of history, managed to foresee what we, with its help, still struggle to understand: nationalism as a powerful inner tendency of the modern state.[6]

SELF-INTEREST RIGHTLY UNDERSTOOD

How is the modern state to be understood? Let us begin from its most familiar feature, which is also the one that renders its relation to nationalism most puzzling: it builds on material self-interest. Rousseau certainly agrees with this characterization: "Ancient politicians incessantly talked about morals and virtue, those of our time talk only of business and money."[7] But this famous doctrine of self-interest is almost always misunderstood.

The complexity of the doctrine becomes most visible in Rousseau, who strongly opposes the reliance on self-interest in one sense, while strongly endorsing it in another. He repeatedly attacks the modern state based on "business and money" as a conflict system generating deceit, crime, and exploitation. Yet his own doctrine of the state, as its very title proclaims, posits a social contract concluded by self-interested individuals seeking the preservation of their lives and goods. And within this state, "it is certain that the right of property is the most sacred of all the rights of citizens, and more important in certain respects than freedom itself."[8] As often happens with Rousseau, there is an appearance of contradiction that has its ultimate root not in a latent confusion in his thinking, but in ours. His argument, if we will follow it closely, shows that the familiar formula of "building on self-interest" conceals two different, indeed opposite conceptions.

To follow Rousseau's analysis of the origin and foundation of society, it is useful to track its agreement with that of Hobbes. Both thinkers begin from the assumption that men are by nature "individuals," who neither have nor feel any obligations except those stemming from agreement or consent. (It is probably false, of course, that men are always or by nature individuals in this sense, but it is true that they are this way in modern societies, as Tocqueville, for one, reports.) Both also agree in claiming that the state does *not* arise naturally from our material needs or acquisitive desires, for the simple reason stated by Hobbes: "if any two men desire the same thing, which nevertheless they cannot both enjoy, they become enemies."[9] Since material goods are not in their nature shareable, material interests do not naturally unify but divide individuals. Men may profit, of course, from cooperation with others, but never so much as from cheating, robbing, or exploiting them. Again, Hobbes: "Though the benefits of this life may be much furthered by mutual help; since yet those may be better attained to by dominion than by the [cooperative] society of others, I hope no body will doubt, but that men would much more greedily be carried by nature, if all fear were removed, to obtain dominion, than to gain society."[10] What, after all, does their famous denial of the naturalness of the state mean? It means not only that we do not naturally seek and enjoy society for its own sake, but also this: our selfish interests do not spontaneously fit together, do not form a common good. As Rousseau puts it, "what private interests have in common is so slight that it will never outweigh what sets them in opposition."[11] Material interests do *not* lead to cooperation and society but to competition and war.

But if there is no common interest, how does the state ever arise? The war produced by the natural opposition of men's interests, because it threatens the life and property of everyone, creates for everyone a *new interest:* peace or the collective security of these private goods. Unlike material possessions, peace is a private good that is shareable—and more: one cannot have it unless all have it. So then there *is* a common interest, after all, that can ground the state—only it is based on a fundamentally new kind of self-interest that must be clearly distinguished from all our other interests. Two characteristics define it: it is a "negative" and a "reflexive" common interest arising precisely from the *lack* of a common interest in the "positive" and "primary" sense.

The self-interest grounding the state is *negative* because it involves a forced reversal in our natural orientation in life: away from the pursuit of good and toward the avoidance of evil. In society, good divides, but evil unites. The state can only arise as a negative union: a uniting against and not a uniting for. Men form communities not to produce some new, positive social good, but to prevent the loss of the private goods and individual rights they already have—their lives, liberty, and property. They unite not because all have something to contribute but because all have something to lose. This explains, for example, Rousseau's comment above regarding the sanctity of property. Property is the basis of society not because we all have positive hopes for commercial gain and getting ahead, but because property is "easier to usurp and more difficult to protect than one's person."[12] It is the point of our greatest personal vulnerability and thus the strongest basis for a negative union. The bond of society is not acquisitiveness but fear of loss.

But precisely what is the evil against which men unite in this negative union? It is not primarily some *external* enemy, but themselves, their own spontaneous, natural interests. The enemy is us. All unite against each. The new, common interest is thus *reflexive* or secondary or reactive because it is formed in reaction against—on the rebound from—the conflict of our *own* primary interests. The principle of order is fear of our natural disorder. We unite because we are enemies. Thus, in uniting, we do not follow our direct, natural impulses but react against and break with those impulses, which lead to chaos. The state is reflexive because it saves us from ourselves, our own primary impulses. In other words, the common interest is not only negative—formed in opposition—but, as it were, a double negative: men unite in opposition to their natural opposition.

In view of all this, it should be clear that to speak in general of "self-interest" is to obscure the whole theory of the modern state. That theory, as presented by Hobbes and Rousseau, is based on a radical distinction between two different, indeed opposite kinds of self-interest. One unites, the other divides—indeed, the one unites only because the other divides. The state is built on the one precisely because it is not and cannot be built on the other.

Having clarified this distinction and its connection to the state's foundation, one might go on to raise a subordinate question: within the state based on self-interest in the negative and reflexive sense—fear of our natural conflict—what does or should become of our social relations based on self-interest in the positive sense, our acquisitive passions? Rousseau, for one, maintains that the latter must still be kept to a minimum. (That is why the distinction of the two interests remains most visible in his thought.) He favors a social-contract state, but not a commercial republic. While the state exists to protect our lives and property, it must discourage economic interdependence and (so-called) cooperation. Thus, he seeks an agrarian economy, where the division of labor is minimized and the independence and self-sufficiency of yeoman farmers is maximized.

But it is also imaginable that, once the state has been well-founded on the fear of natural disorder, then men's positive material interests can, with the state's help, be forcibly harmonized. There is considerable disagreement on this question. Hobbes and Locke—still more, Hume and Smith—argue that the economic benefits of working together plus the sanction of reputation and public opinion plus the vigilance of the police will suffice to ensure that, within the state, most people most of the time will find their true, long-term self-interest in honest cooperation. Tocqueville gives his famous account of the American faith that honesty and virtue flow from self-interest rightly understood—while indicating that he himself does not wholly share that faith. But Rousseau loudly declares that where acquisitive passions have been lib-

erated, dishonest practices—crime by the poor, exploitation by the rich—
will always remain more lucrative than honest ones, that reputation will go
to the successful and not the decent, and that the police, hirelings of the rich,
will always be corrupt as well as ineffectual.

No doubt the amount of crime, corruption, and exploitation in a given society will vary widely depending on the state of its economy, government,
and mores. Throughout most of history, many, perhaps most, states have fit
Rousseau's description; but in the advanced liberal democracies, with their
rapidly expanding economies, the Lockean account would seem to have
proved truer.

Be that as it may, the modern state is a multilayered phenomenon, and our
interest here is with the question of the state's primary layer or foundation.
The crucial point, from this perspective, is that this harmony of acquisitive
interests—whatever its precise measure—is and remains an artifact of the
state, wholly dependent on the latter's enforcing power; and therefore, it is
not itself the foundation, the principled basis or primary bond, of the modern state. The real foundation remains the negative and reflexive interest,
which an adequate theory of the modern state must continue to distinguish
from our acquisitive interests—especially because, if the Lockean view is
right, this distinction will tend to become blurred for those living within the
state. We must strive to remember that all the forms of human harmony that
do indeed arise within the modern state are ultimately made possible by a
recognition of our fundamental, natural disharmony. At bottom, we are
competitive individuals. Thus, the harmonistic theory that there is a natural
agreement of acquisitive interests and that this grounds the state is the very
opposite of the modern view, as presented by Hobbes and Rousseau, because the negative and reflexive common interest upon which they rely
comes into being precisely in reaction against the terrifying *lack* of a primary
and positive common interest.

Indeed, to posit the existence of such a natural harmony and positive common good is to return to a materialistic version of the traditional conception
of the state as presented, for example, in Plato's *Republic:* the view that the
state is natural, arising from the division of labor, from the spontaneous fitting together of men's different but complementary abilities and interests.
But on this traditional view of the state, those who, having superior abilities
and resources, make a larger contribution to the common good (assumed
here to be economic gain) and thereby also display a greater fitness for the
job of ruling the economy, are naturally owed a greater share of public authority. As a matter of right—of distributive justice—the rich should rule. In
short, the view that there is a natural common good rooted in our economic
interests would lead to the classical argument for oligarchy. And clearly this
argument—and the view of a harmony of material interests on which it is
based—is not the foundation of the modern, liberal democratic state (how-

ever oligarchic it may sometimes be in practice). In a word, it is not as pro-
ducers or consumers that we are bearers of equal rights.

   To be sure, in quiet times we take peace and security for granted and focus
on our positive hopes for material advancement. These hopes are a real
source of attachment to the state and especially of our willingness to work
hard, get an education, pay taxes, and so forth. But even in such times no
one thinks that, say, Bill Gates is owed special political rights, whereas people do often suggest that those who are most vulnerable and in need of protection, like disadvantaged minorities, should receive special rights. This
whole tendency of our society toward "victimology," while certainly a dis-
tortion, is nevertheless an indication of the true basis of the state. Our political rights and Constitution are fundamentally derived not from the requirements of commerce, however much they may facilitate it, but from those of
the security or inviolability of the individual.

THE POLITICS OF SYMPATHETIC IDENTIFICATION

It was necessary to spend so much time distinguishing the two self-interests
or the two layers of the modern state—fear of natural disorder and commerce—because of their opposite relation to nationalism. The second layer,
by encouraging materialism, social differentiation, and pluralism, points
away from nationalism, whereas the first and deeper layer, by creating (as
we will see) homogeneity, equality, and identification, is what produces it.
Because of our failure to make this crucial distinction, the following view of
history prevails today: the traditional state was characterized by unity, homogeneity, and identity, and the modern, liberal state by pluralism, heterogeneity, and difference. But this view, which makes it impossible to understand the modern rise of nationalism, has it precisely backward. In its
foundations, the modern state involves what I will call the politics of identification, as opposed to the politics of difference or complementarity characteristic of the traditional state. And the politics of identification, I will argue,
is the sought-for seed of nationalism.[13]

   The unique character of the modern state can be seen most clearly in its
contrast with the traditional state. The latter understood itself to be a naturally or divinely ordered whole built around a positive and primary common good. One citizen was united with another not primarily by a direct relation of similarity, but through their common relation and subordination to
the whole, to the political order (as well as to the land, the ancestors, and
the gods). But the fundamental principle of this political order, as Plato
points out, is "difference": "each of us is naturally not quite like anyone else,
but rather differs in his nature; different men are apt for the accomplishment
of different jobs."[14] The social order is a union of functionally differentiated

parts, each suited for the performance of some particular and socially necessary job (whether economic, military, or political), all fitted together for the good of the whole. As Aristotle puts it: "a community is not formed by two physicians, but by a physician and a farmer, and, in general, by people who are different and unequal."[15] Human beings naturally organize into states, as into families, because through their differences they naturally complement and complete one another. Thus, each individual has citizenship and status and worth only because he makes a contribution. And in accordance with distributive justice, different contributions are owed different degrees of honor and standing. Thus a person's status, indeed his very name and identity, flow from his differentiated contribution and social role as soldier, farmer, artisan, and so forth. This man is a Smith, that man a Cooper or Baker.

To be sure, the traditional state put great emphasis on unity and agreement (*homonoia*). There was very little freedom of the individual in the modern, liberal sense. Everything foreign and alien was suspect. Everyone had to fit in. But the crucial point, from the standpoint of nationalism, is that you did not fit in by being the same as others, but precisely by being different in the right way. You belonged because you made a difference. (It is only under the reign of individualism that everyone becomes alike.) There was no similarity politics in the traditional state. Rather, as Tocqueville remarks of the old regime, "among an aristocratic people each caste has its opinions, feelings, rights, mores, and whole separate existence. . . . They have not at all the same way of thinking or feeling, and they hardly manage to think of themselves as forming part of the same humanity." In the traditional state, unity came from difference, and to the extent that cultural characteristics played a unifying role, it was not at all to unite fellow nationals through a sense of similarity and shared nationality, but precisely to demarcate and legitimize the elaborate internal *differentiation* of roles, ranks, and classes that made the state a whole.[16] As every reader of Tolstoy knows, for example, the Russian aristocracy spoke French a good deal of the time: they used culture to unify the whole, not by grounding their status as Russians but as aristocrats.

In the modern state—especially as interpreted by Hobbes and Rousseau—although the same division of labor exists (indeed, infinitely extended), this differentiation of role, class, or contribution is seen as strictly derivative and not as the basis of the state or of the individual's membership, rights, and identity. Rather, deep down, we are all the same. The premise of the modern state is that we are self-interested individuals and, therefore, despite all our differences and inequalities, no one is by natural or divine right the ruler of another. More generally, there is no natural cooperative order to unite us through our differences, hence to give a moral/political definition, meaning, and value to our differences. By nature, we are the same because undifferentiated, a collection of independent individuals, each made for and ruling himself. We are not completely unrelated to one another, however, but rather competitors—especially for the common material necessities that must be our primary focus due to the lack of natural order and cooperation. Now, co-operation arises from and develops our differences, but competition springs from and accentuates our similarity. Human beings are in systematic conflict because they have identical interests: each wants the same thing for himself. They are "competitive individuals," who stand opposed because they are mirror images of each other, identical in their otherness.

Men are the same not only in their self-interestedness but also in their vulnerability. They may differ in what they can do *for* each other, as the traditional state emphasizes, but are the same in what they can do *to* each other—which is necessarily the primary consideration for beings whose natural condition is not cooperation but enmity. Beneath all the differences men so eagerly assert and create—their talents, wealth, honor, and status—they remain fundamentally the same: frail little bodies, so easily destroyed that "the weakest has strength enough to kill the strongest."[17] We are the same because equally threatened and equally threatening.

The war produced by men's identity can be ended, Hobbes argues, only by the full awareness and acknowledgment of that identity. Each must contract "to lay down this right to all things, and be contented with so much liberty against other men *as he would allow other men* against himself."[18] The essence of the social contract is *not consent* as such (which could, after all, involve an unequal exchange), nor is it even *equality* (which could involve the exchange of equal but different concessions), but rather this complete reciprocity or *fairness,* through which each treats the other as identical and interchangeable with himself. Each recognizes the other as his "opposite number," standing in the identical position as himself, with the same selfish interests and the same essential force and vulnerability. Each agrees to the contract only in order to get the other to agree, and each sees that he cannot expect the other to make any concession that he himself would not make, that he cannot demand more for himself than he is willing to allow to the other. In other words, the essence of the contract is the agreement to limit one's selfishness with the thought: What if everyone did that? This is not mere equality, it is fairness; and fairness is rooted in identification.[19]

Once we have concluded the contract, our mutual identity, which was the source of our conflict, becomes the bond of our union. It is only because the other wants for himself just what I want for myself that we both agree to guarantee it for each. I see myself in the other and recognize in his rights and self-seeking the security for my own. Thus, the ground of our mutual respect or cooperation is not consent as such nor equality but rather this sense of equivalence or identity. As difference and complementarity were the ground of the traditional state, so identification and fairness are the fundamental ground of the modern state.

Still, one may ask whether the latter principles only concern the founding of the state or whether they play a role in the constitution and ongoing functioning of the government. To begin with Hobbes' discussion of the issue, the contract culminates in the reciprocal agreement to "authorize" a sovereign: "to appoint one man or assembly of men to bear their person, and every one to own and acknowledge himself to be author of whatsoever he that so beareth their person shall act." One promises not merely to obey the sovereign but, in some legal sense, to "identify" with him, to regard his will and person as one's own. "This is *more than consent,* or concord; it is a *real unity* of them all, in one and the same person"[20] (emphasis added).

These striking claims constitute the first formulation of the modern doctrine of representation. But what is the purpose of this doctrine? It obviously does not have the familiar purpose of creating "accountability," since Hobbes claims that consent, once given, is irrevocable. Rather, it would seem to have the purpose (among other things[21]) of keeping the subjects in mind of that humble acknowledgment of mutual identity that is the core and sum of the natural law and the foundation of the state. (Although *we* must keep in mind that the identity of the subjects with each other is real, while that of the subjects with the sovereign is a legal fiction.) Through the contract, all the subjects—being identical—are collapsed into one. The modern state is not a differentiated whole, an articulated order or organism, but a *one,* a unit, a collective "person" with a single self and will. *E pluribus unum.* Similarly, the sovereign's authority is not based on his difference from the people, his superior wisdom or virtue, but on his identity with the people, his claim to *be* the people. He claims for himself not the authority of the good, but of the self: the arbitrary authority that every being, individual or collective, has over itself. In other words, modern government is *representative* in a sense more fundamental than "accountability": it is based on identity rather than difference. It replaces the age-old "noble lie" that the rulers are divinely or naturally superior with the "legal fiction" that they are you. Thus, even in Hobbes, the principle of identification remains a major feature of the ongoing functioning of the state—of "representative government."

As the term "legal fiction" suggests, however, the structural flaw of the modern state, especially in its Hobbesian form, is the merely conventional or fictional character of the identification of the people with the sovereign. They are not really the same, from which two problems result: the lack of a sufficient motive for the sovereign to benefit the people—and for the people to obey the sovereign. All later theorists would see their task as somehow making the fiction more real.

Rousseau attempts to do just that through his doctrine of the general will. We have seen that the warlike conditions of the state of nature compel men to conclude an equal and fair social contract, wherein all agree to "will generally," that is to will a general contract that applies equally to each. For that one moment, the "fiction" is real and the people is ruled by a sovereign that is themselves, united and animated by a will that is single and unanimous because general. But, whereas Hobbes would have the first and only act of this general will be the transfer of sovereignty to a king, Rousseau would keep it in the hands of the people, which would continue to have and express a unanimous, general will so long as it continued to be compelled—through the help of certain rare institutional and moral conditions—to rule itself exclusively through general laws that came from all and applied identically to each. Thus, Rousseau's doctrine of the general will, which many regard as a metaphysical conceit alien to modern politics, is only Hobbes' contract doctrine taken to its logical extreme. Indeed, it constitutes the theoretical perfection of the modern state: by extending the principle of fairness and mutual identification into the ongoing workings of the sovereign, it creates a sovereign that is identical to the people. The fiction at the core of modern politics becomes a reality.

Still, Rousseau's scheme, as he well knew, is too perfect for this world, as Hobbes' is too imperfect. We must turn to Locke to see the politics of identification in the form in which it is actually at work in the contemporary liberal state. Locke makes the sovereign power's representativeness—its identity with the people's will—more genuine and less fictional, first, by making it elective and thus accountable to the people, but also, if less obviously, through the separation of powers. Locke makes the legislative power supreme and separates it from the executive so that the legislators "are themselves subject to the laws they have made, which is a new and near tie upon them to take care that they make them for the public good."[22] As a separated and exclusively legislative power, subject to the laws it makes, the sovereign is forced, in Rousseauian language, to generalize its will, to think of all, including itself, as essentially identical and to rule through general laws that any citizen would will if he were in its place. Properly understood, the famous Lockean doctrines of legislative supremacy and separation of powers, at the core of the modern liberal "law-state," are precisely the doctrine of the general will in its most practicable form. Through these doctrines—through the rule of self-imposed law as such, formal generality—the modern state attempts to solve the problem of tyranny by extending the basic principle of the social contract, fairness and identification, into the constitution and ongoing functioning of the government.

NATIONALISM

Our discussion of the shortcomings of the Hobbesian state—and of Rousseau's and Locke's solutions—has focused exclusively on the first of its problems: how to ensure that the sovereign will benefit the people. But there is a second problem: how to motivate the people to obey the sovereign. The doctrine of social contract is an abstract and legalistic theory, useful for many purposes, but not for inspiring men with strong sentiments of devotion or obedience. For the latter purpose, Hobbes would rely mainly on fear of the sovereign, to which Locke would add the desire for respectability and honest profit among commercially minded men. But Rousseau, the first and greatest theorist of the liberal "moral deficit," considers these self-interested motives too cold, calculating, and ineffective. Genuine, heartfelt patriotism is needed if citizens are to obey the laws without cheating, to treat their fellow citizens with genuine respect, and to risk their lives, if necessary, in defense of the fatherland. It is also needed in a democracy—to return to the first problem—to ensure that the citizens, in their capacity as members of the sovereign, will possess the mutual trust, respect, and willingness to compromise as needed to ensure just rule. Finally, it is needed for its own sake: to give the atomized, self-interested individual something larger than himself to love, to warm and expand his heart with the joy of community and with the exquisite, sentimental delight that arises from attachment to one's native customs and ways.

For all these reasons, Rousseau passionately rejected the cosmopolitanism and atomism characteristic of Enlightenment thought and liberal politics, and sought to return to the ancient ideal of patriotism. This "Romantic reaction" against liberalism is the most familiar and easily understandable root of the turn toward nationalism. But the always neglected *prior* question is: what *within* liberalism makes this reaction against it successful? How is it possible to produce such a self-forgetting, collectivist passion in the soul of the modern, liberated, disencumbered, materialistic individual, living in the social-contract state expressly founded on theoretical individualism? In other words, what is it within the modern state that self-mutates into nationalism? The answer to that question would deservedly be called the seed of nationalism.

We have already seen how individualism, leading to war, overcomes itself into political union through a contract based on fairness or the acknowledgment of identity. Thus, if we are to induce a patriotic sentiment of some kind to grow out of and harmonize with the basic principle of this individualist political union, it too would have to be based on identity and not on some opposite principle, like difference or hierarchy. This new, modern form of patriotism could not be (at least not on the deepest level) the sort of organic love that a part feels for the whole or for another, different, and complementary part. Nor could it be the religious deference and awe that pagans once felt toward the sacred land of their ancestors. To be consistent with the contract based on identity, it would have to be a love—if such a thing is possible—for those similar to oneself for no other reason than *that they are similar.* (Just what we mean by nationalism.) That is the precise sentiment called for by the rational structure of the modern state, by the politics of identification. But does it exist?

In his understanding of human psychology, Rousseau follows Hobbes in denying the reality of pure selflessness and devotion, but rejects Hobbes' consequent reduction of all human motivation to self-preservation, finding this theoretically (as well as politically) unsatisfactory. A second principle of human nature would seem to be required, especially to explain more persuasively than Hobbes does the *appearance* of selflessness and devotion. That principle, Rousseau suggests, is "identification"—an answer similar to the principle of "sympathy" postulated by Hume and Adam Smith at about the same time. Unlike them, however, Rousseau can explain how this second principle actually grows out of the first. Self-preservation, he argues, is not merely a fear or resistance to death, as Hobbes claims, but a positive love of life—a desire to experience, prolong, and even increase the delightful sentiment of our own existence. And one of the ways we "increase" our existence is by expanding or extending it over others—through identification—so that, seeing ourselves in others, we feel more broadly and are more vividly present to ourselves. But this impulse to expansion and identification—a formless energy, *élan,* or libido—has no fixed object or natural end, so it is highly malleable and susceptible of receiving a number of different forms.

Through this crucial doctrine, Rousseau shows that there is a near-perfect correspondence between the theoretical principle of the modern, social-contract "law-state"—fairness or identification—and the (second) psychological principle of human nature: the expansive impulse to empathetic identification. If this is correct, then the modern social-contract state contains this unique potential: it can produce, for the first time, a genuine harmony or alignment between the only true psychological basis of social attraction and the moral principle of political union, for both are rooted in identification. This new psychological-political alignment is what gives rise, in the modern state, to its marked "identificatory culture." It gives great and unique power to every form and manifestation of the human impulse to identification—for example, to conformism or to the voyeurism and self-disclosing "sincerity" of our TV culture—but principally and most importantly to *fairness, compassion, and nationalism,* which are the three dominant moral forces of modern life (beyond self-interest and the bourgeois virtues).

As Rousseau emphasizes, however, compassion and nationalism, while both forms of identification, are in certain respects opposed to one another. The one tends to universalistic humanitarianism, the other to national particularism. When our expansive impulse is directed toward others with an eye to our shared vulnerability and suffering—a posture encouraged by the "negative" common interest, the emphasis on fear, at the basis of the social contract—the result is pity or compassion. And since all humans are ultimately the same in their weakness and mortality, compassion tends to "humanity."

But we can also identify with others on the level of their positive sentiment of existence. For this more particular and intimate connection, however, we must find others whose existences are especially transparent to us, who speak our language, whose every gesture and tone we understand, whose inner experiences and feelings we can see and share. These people feel just what we feel when hearing this music, seeing this countryside, smelling this air, tasting this food. Their memories are the same as ours, of victory and defeat. They celebrate and mourn as we do. We do not necessarily need others with the same God as we have, but the same self and existence: others whose lives feel to them as our lives feel to us. The loving identification with others based on this felt similarity, this profound, prerational, prepolitical sense of common existence—when aligned with, and so uniquely strengthened by, the fact or hope of modern "identificatory" political union—is nationalism.

Or, rather, it is the basic *seed* of nationalism, because, while it determines the essential form or direction of modern public-spiritedness and devotion—the love of those who are like us simply because they are like us—it is by no means responsible for all of the different passions, ideas, and interests that have attached themselves to it, producing the whole complex panoply of nationalisms. For example, once the sentiment of nationality is, as it were, put into play by the above considerations, then men extend to this new entity their sense of honor, and this generates a whole new layer of passions: in some conditions, a calm sense of national pride, but in others—in those where nationalism becomes most visible—a fervor for national redemption, resurgence, or revenge. (In this sense nationalism, like compassion, reflects the negative orientation of the modern state, building on sometimes sentimental, sometimes resentful feelings of shared loss, suffering, or humiliation.) A further layer comes from the twin modern movements of industrialization—which causes great social disruption and deracination in its early stages and spiritual malaise in its later ones—and secularization, which not only leaves a general spiritual hunger but which removes the natural outlet for the radical fears and longings engendered by industrialization. Under these circumstances people came to attach to the nation their fervent hopes for social transformation and spiritual transcendence, encouraged in this also by the historical turn of modern philosophy which bestowed on the nation a kind of metaphysical or quasi-religious significance. The crucial point, however, is that these various, accidental, and exogenous passions, which might have taken any number of different directions, all flowed into nationalism only because the latter was there, ready to receive them—as it was not in earlier centuries—having sprouted from the elemental seed we are discussing, a seed deriving from *within* the very essence of the modern state.

Again, this is not to deny that there always existed some notion and sentiment of nationality (as distinguished from full-blown nationalism). But the

Arthur Melzer

whole principle of order and legitimacy in the premodern state—based, as it was, on inequality, difference, and complementarity—was in fundamental conflict with the impulse to identification at the root of nationalist sentiment. Men were hindered from identifying with others by the differences that merged them together. To be sure, the natural identificatory impulse was not simply absent, but it was subordinated to the difference principle: one identified with one's family and one's class, but this only served to strengthen one's differentiation from the other families and classes. And it was ultimately through one's difference that one was a member, a part.

But the modern state, based on self-interest—rightly understood—liberated the individual from his "differentiation," his prescriptive role and contribution, even as it (on the surface) vastly increased differentiation, specialization, and pluralism. Because we are selfish, competitive individuals, there is no positive common good, no natural cooperation, to unite us through our differences. We can unite only negatively and reflexively: from fear of our natural opposition. And as opponents—as distinguished from helpers and contributors—we are all the same. Of course, within the state and because of it, we may cooperate with others, but the underlying basis of the state itself, and thus the condition of all cooperation, is the fear of general disorder and conflict: What if everybody did that? The foundation of the state, therefore, is the initial agreement and ongoing commitment to claim for oneself only what all can claim— fairness, which involves the recognition of the essential equivalence or identity of all individuals. The modern state is an identificatory union. Thus, not only does the state's principle of order or legitimacy no longer hinder the natural impulse to identification, but it seconds, strengthens, and builds upon it. It thus gives rise to similarity politics and an identificatory culture—to strong sentiments of fairness, compassion, and, in different ways in different circumstances, to nationalism.

The seed of nationalism, in sum, has a natural component—"sympathy," or the impulse to identify with our similar—and an historical one. The latter, unique to the modern state, is—paradoxically—individualism, for in keeping us from merging with others, it compels us to identify with them.

NOTES

1. The first use of "nationalism," according to the *Oxford English Dictionary*, was in 1844—a fact all the more striking given the ubiquity and ancient provenance of "nation," which is found, in something like its modern meaning, in Middle English (*nacioun*), Old French (*nacion*), Latin (*natio,* also *gens, populus*), and Greek (*ethnos, genos*).

2. *Nationalism* (London: B.T. Batsford, 1967), 25.

3. *Thought and Change* (London: Weidenfeld and Nicolson, 1964), 153, emphasis in the original.

4. The classic effort at an intellectual history of nationalism is Eli Kedourie, *Nationalism,* 4th ed. (Oxford: Blackwell, 1993).

5. See, for example, Hans Kohn's standard work *The Idea of Nationalism: A Study in Its Origins and Background* (New York: Macmillan, 1944).

6. In what follows (which draws upon "The General Will as the Foundation of a New Science of Politics," chapter 10 in my *The Natural Goodness of Man* [Chicago: University of Chicago Press, 1990]), my aim is not to describe Rousseau's political prescriptions, his influence, or his specific expectations for the future of Western politics, but simply to use some of the principles of his political science as an aid in explaining the course of our own political history.

As for Rousseau's political prescriptions, while he prepared the way for nationalism, he was not, in the end, himself a nationalist. His highest goal was not national union but political freedom—direct democratic self-rule—and such freedom was inseparable from the small city-state, he believed, and thus incompatible with the large nation-state. See Melzer, 1990, 195–97; see also Anne M. Cohler, *Rousseau and Nationalism* (New York: Basic Books, 1970); and Marc E. Plattner, "Rousseau and the Origins of Nationalism" in *The Legacy of Rousseau,* ed. Clifford Orwin and Nathan Tarcov (Chicago: University of Chicago Press, 1997).

7. *First Discourse,* in *The First and Second Discourses,* trans. Roger D. Masters and Judith R. Masters (New York: St. Martin's Press, 1964), 51. See *Discourse on Political Economy,* in *On the Social Contract with Geneva Manuscript and Political Economy,* trans. Judith R. Masters, ed. Roger D. Masters (New York: St. Martin's Press, 1978), 216–17.

8. *Political Economy,* 224–25.

9. *Leviathan,* ed. Edwin Curley (Indianapolis: Hackett Publishing, 1994), chap. 13, para. 3, p. 75.

10. *De Cive* in *Man and Citizen,* ed. Bernard Gert (Garden City, N.Y.: Doubleday and Co, 1972), chap. 1, para. 2, p. 113. See the similar point by Rousseau at *Second Discourse,* 194–95.

11. *Emile, or On Education,* trans. Allan Bloom (New York: Basic Books, 1979), bk. IV, 312n.

12. *Political Economy,* 225.

13. It should be said that the second layer—commerce and acquisitiveness—is not in every respect opposed to nationalism. While commerce does promote economic differentiation, it can also contribute—especially within a modern, industrial economy—to the rise of social mobility, equality of opportunity, mass education, the breakdown of traditional classes and distinctions, all of which help to produce the homogeneity of modern mass society. This homogenizing tendency of commerce helps to strengthen the politics of identification at the root of nationalism. (See Ernest Gellner, *Nationalism* [New York: NYU Press, 1997], who places primary emphasis on this factor.) Furthermore, to the extent that a competitive, commercial society heightens the experience of our natural opposition, it also works to strengthen the first layer.

14. *The Republic of Plato,* trans. Allan Bloom (New York: Basic Books, 1968), 370a.

15. *Nicomachean Ethics,* trans. Martin Ostwald (Indianapolis: Bobbs-Merrill Co., 1962), 1133a17.

16. *Democracy in America,* trans. George Lawrence (Garden City, N.Y.: Anchor Doubleday, 1969), pt. III, chap. 1, 561. See Gellner *Nationalism,* 19–21.

17. *Leviathan,* chap. 13, para. 1, p. 74.

18. *Leviathan,* chap. 14, para. 5, p. 80; emphasis added.

19. This use of fairness involves a fundamental innovation. Traditionally, "fairness" meant simply to apply some preexisting standard of justice in an unbiased manner, without regard to persons. But starting with Hobbes, and reaching full development in Rousseau and Kant, justice becomes derivative from fairness (and the contract based on it), where fairness is constituted by treating all as equivalent or identical.

20. *Leviathan,* chap. 17, para. 13, p. 109; emphasis added.

21. See Harvey C. Mansfield, Jr., "Hobbes and the Science of Indirect Government," *The American Political Science Review* 65 (1971): 97–110; Harvey C. Mansfield and Robert Scigliano, "Representation: The Perennial Issues," pamplet published by the American Political Science Association (1978), 15–23; and Clifford Orwin, "On the Sovereign Authorization," *Political Theory,* 3.4 (Feb. 1975): 26–44.

22. *The Second Treatise of Government,* ed. Thomas Peardon (New York: Liberal Arts Press, 1952), para. 143. Montesquieu makes the same point; see *The Spirit of the Laws,* trans. Anne Cohler, Basia Carolyn Miller, Harold Samuel Stone (Cambridge: Cambridge University Press, 1989), bk. XI, chap. 6.

10

Kantian Idealism

Susan Meld Shell

I will argue in what follows that Kantian idealism, both in its origins and in its goals, has a more complicated relation to realism than is generally supposed. My general aim is to begin to recover Kant as a thinker who is both more "realistic" and more helpful as a guide to liberal politics than some of his current heirs, especially in matters (to name a few) of constitutional law, civic education, and the possibilities and limits of international relations.

By what is politics, in the most basic sense, to be guided? Machiavelli famously urged men to renounce "imaginary republics," and to take their bearings from what is rather than what ought to be. "It is necessary," as he put it, "for a prince, if he wants to maintain himself, to learn to be able to be not good, and to use this and not use it according to necessity."[1] In so urging, however, Machiavelli arguably failed to supply an adequate account of the necessity that underlies his own activity. (Why seek glory and/or truth?) Machiavelli here assumes that men wish, or can be brought to wish, to maintain themselves above all else. But does this assumption—that men wish, above all, to prevail—adequately reflect our genuine needs as human beings? One recalls the story of the king faced with a miscreant who proffered the excuse "Your majesty, one must live"—to which the monarch replied, only half in jest, "I do not see the necessity."

Kant seizes on the ambiguous necessity on which early modern thought relies and stands it on its head. Laws of nature may permit us to calculate effects, and hence the effectual truth; but the necessity they display is based, finally (as the skepticism of Locke and Hume brought home to Kant) on constructions of the mind. Is there not a more powerful and incontrovertible necessity, then, in conscience—the very "ought" that Machiavelli endeavored to erase? Is not the goodness of goodwill—the sole thing good without lim-itation, according to Kant, that it is possible to think—a surer basis for a phi-losophy that seeks an unconditional ground than any foundation that early modern thought was able to unearth? Kantian "idealism" shares with its im-mediate, "realistic" predecessors a conviction that the necessity that under-lies empirical knowledge is a construction or invention—a means, as *they* see it, grounded finally in utility or convenience. Kant departs from them in his insistence on the *necessity,* if science is to be possible at all, that under-lies this world-informing construct, and in the opening he sees in it for a re-covery, and, indeed, enhancement of traditional moral claims concerning virtue and justice. The appeal to necessity by which earlier moderns sought to combat pious belief, emerges, from the crucible of doubt thereby un-leashed, as a weapon in its favor.

To be sure, the content of traditional claims concerning virtue and justice undergoes, in Kant, significant revision, and in an egalitarian direction. Thanks in part to Rousseau and in part to Kant's own metaphysical excur-sions, Kantian morality is itself informed by a peculiar conception of worldly necessity—a conception I will describe in some detail for the rational au-thority that it lends his notion of morality, independent of the testimony of conscience itself.

A world, for Kant, is a whole whose elements cohere not (as with scholas-tic schemes) as form and matter, ruling part and ruled, but as coequals united by bonds of mutual or reciprocal necessitation. (The world of nature, for example, is informed by something like Newton's second law of motion, according to which for every action there is an equal and opposite reac-tion.) There simply is no other way, as Kant conceives matters, to under-stand how ordinary experience—the "common world that we inhabit when awake"—is possible. But this model of reciprocal equality proves all too elusive, according to Kant, to our theoretical understanding. It is impossible to conceive the simple unity of substances other than on the analogy sup-plied by mind or consciousness, i.e., as something radically inward. And it is impossible to conceive the reciprocal interdependence of substances other than in terms of relations that are spatial or external. In short, we can-not entertain a notion of the whole (the world as a totality), without slipping into self-contradiction. One would be driven to conclude that reason is un-reliable and that the whole as such is unintelligible (in which case one could not reasonably gainsay the authority of priests) *except* that reason can cor-rect itself (as Kant's critique of pure reason shows) by relinquishing the claim to know things as *other* than appearances.

As a consequence of this correction, Kant reinterprets the traditional philosophic pursuit of knowledge of the whole (however distant and re-mote) as a case of misguided, because not fully self-guided, overreaching. The idea of the whole (*Ganz,* in German, or *Totalität*) is not something real that can be known (however haltingly and tentatively) but an "idea," understood as the *"focus imaginarius"* of reason's essential—even defining—capacity to impose necessities on itself in the form of principles or laws. In the case of reason in its theoretical employment, those principles are conditional and "regulative" rather than (as with reason in its practical employment) unconditional or categorical. (In the case of rules constitutive of ordinary experience, the mind's rule setting goes on unconsciously, without reason's active intervention.) Theoretical knowledge is not, for Kant, what Kierkegaard called the "one thing needful," but an exercise whose goodness rests on its ability to further goals certified by reason in its capacity as moral legislator. Reason—"factually" announcing itself in conscience —lays down the law and in so doing establishes the final ends of human action.

But what does reason as lawgiver demand? Realization of the very "intelligible world" all theoretical claims to which were given up—albeit an "intelligible world" configured in practical or moral terms. The Kantian idea of justice, for example (an idea he defines as maximum freedom of each consistent with the maximum freedom of the rest), is reciprocal community grasped not theoretically, but via conscience—the worldly "necessity" in question supplied not by nature, but by the reciprocal and inherent rights and obligations of all parties who make up a universal "general will" and hence a whole through which they are simultaneously recognized as separate and autonomous persons.

Virtue, on the other hand, consists for Kant in the principled adherence of the will to self-made law—an autonomous freedom whose *self*-necessitating bonds transcend the *natural* necessity to which we are otherwise subject. Once again, Machiavelli's break with the tradition is seized on and inverted (or in the language of poker, seen and raised). If overcoming nature is the standard, then Kantian virtue, rather than Machiavellian *virtu,* seems the more potent vehicle of human daring. Kant pushes further the wedge that Machiavelli drove between "is" and "ought" to replace Aristotle's moderating equivocations as to the relation between choice and necessity or nature. "Nothing is more reprehensible," Kant says, "than to derive the laws prescribing what *ought to be done* from what *is done,* or to impose on them the limits by which the latter is circumscribed" (emphasis his).[2] Moral choice—the only choice, for Kant, that ultimately counts—makes its own necessity.

KANT'S CONSTITUTIONALISM

But not entirely. Ideas, for Kant, are not objects of intellectual or aesthetic contemplation (as Platonism wrongly claims or encourages us to believe) but the *foci imaginariai* of tasks that we, as finite rational beings, impose upon ourselves. Ideas are nothing *real* (in the sense of actual) except insofar as we make them so by realizing them (approximately). (Since ideas are such that "nothing can ever be met with in experience that is congruent with [them]"[3] [as per the "idea" of the whole], their realization in worldly time and space can at best approach perfection asymptotically.) This is true in a special way in the case of justice as the idea of a perfect constitution, which Kant treats in *Critique of Pure Reason* as *the* Platonic idea, in which natural and moral necessity, so to speak, join forces:

> *The Platonic Republic* has become proverbial as a striking example of vision-ary [*erträumten*] perfection, which has a seat only in the brain of an idle thinker; and [Plato has been ridiculed] . . . for maintaining that a prince can govern [*regieren*] well only insofar as he participates in the ideas. We would do better, however, to follow up this thought, and (where the great man leaves us without help) to place it, through new exertions, in the light. . . . *A consti-tution of the greatest human freedom according to laws, which makes it so that the freedom of each can stand together with that of all the rest* [empha-sis his], (not of the greatest happiness, for this will follow of itself) is yet at least a necessary idea, which one must lay as foundational [*zum Grunde legen*] not only in the first plan/projection [*Entwurfe*] of a state constitution, but also in all laws. . . . Indeed, nothing can be more harmful or less worthy of a philosopher than the vulgar [*pöbelhafte*] appeal to supposedly adverse ex-perience. . . . Whether or not [a perfect state] . . . can ever come into existence, the idea remains entirely correct, which advances this maximum as an arche-type, in order to bring the lawful constitution of men ever nearer to its great-est possible perfection. For what the highest grade may be at which humanity must remain, and hence how large may be the gap necessarily remaining over between the idea and its execution [*Ausführung*]—that no one can and should determine, because the issue on which it hinges is freedom, which can over-come every specified [*angegebene*] limit.[4]

The idea of the republic, rightly understood, must be taken as laying the ground for the plans of all actual state constitutions. Without it, states and laws (i.e., necessitating bonds not based on natural force alone) are, as he puts it, without a "thinkable foundation." (Why that foundation must be "thinkable" is a matter I will return to.)

Like the "ground laying" [*Grundlagen*] of the metaphysics of morals, Kant's constitutional ground laying is a kind of founding execution, albeit one to which names attach only to the extent that "great men" like Plato serve as midwives to an idea whose proper owner is humanity.[5] And yet, if that idea is to be executed to the greatest possible extent, it must first be led out of the pregnant darkness and confusion of philosophy's (pre-Kantian) history—a consideration whose "appropriate execution [*gehörige Aus-führung*]," according to Kant, "makes up philosophy's authentic dignity."[6]

Now to the question of why and in what sense the foundation of a civic order must be "thinkable": the perfect republic (unlike the kingdom of ends, its purely ethical counterpart) does not presuppose, or even strive directly to inculcate, the moral virtue of its members. Its aim is rather the harmonious coexistence of free rational beings in a position to affect one another. Such harmonious coexistence does not require agreement of ends and means (as would be the case for a true kingdom of ends, or ethical commonwealth) but merely reciprocal noninterference, i.e., that each desist from affecting others (either directly or through their external property) in ways they do not in principle or practice consent to.

Such a system of reciprocal noninterference (whose content makes up what Kant calls "private right") requires public enforcement for reasons that lie "a priori in the idea" and without reference to empirical claims as to the supposed evil or untrustworthiness of human nature. Be men ever so "benign and justice-loving," the right of each to do what *"seems right and good to him"* (emphasis his) means that none can be secure from violence.[7]

To be affected against my will by a well-meaning saint is no less a violation of right than to be so affected by an ill-meaning sinner. Even more importantly, to "love" justice, in Kant's view, is not necessarily to do it; indeed, it may instill one with a sense of self-righteousness that makes the rendering of justice all the more doubtful. Perhaps most significantly of all, the violator of right cannot be punished in the state of nature without violating *his* right to do justice as he sees fit.[8] I can repel an evil, if necessary preemptively; I cannot retribute, and thus treat it as a crime. To assert my *right* to life and property (not just defend them) brings me up against the right of my assailant to do what seems right and good to him without "being guided in this by the opinion of another."[9] Prior to the existence of a tribunal that can judge with "force of right," no one can assert a right without implicitly denying it.

Public authority, whose three powers [*Gewalten*] Kant describes as legislative, executive [*aufübend*] (or, alternatively, directive [*regierend*]), and judicial,[10] make good this defect of the "state of nature," above all by making it possible to claim respect without disrespecting others. The Hobbesian *bellum omni contra omnis* to which Kant implicitly subscribes rests not on the natural malignity of human beings but on a concept of right as mutual recognition that is fundamentally Rousseauian in inspiration. It is not only the shortness and brutishness of life that drives men from the state of nature, but also the impossibility therein of carrying out what Kant calls the first duty of right—to live honestly or honorably (*"honeste vive"*). Hence, civil society, for Kant, is an escape less from nature's unpleasantness than from the dialectical instability that naturally infects the impulse, as Kant once put it, to be *"mehr als Mensch"*—that is, to be "more (or more than) human."[11]

Civil power [*Gewalt*] "authorized to judge with force of right"—and, hence, *retribute* crimes, rather than just deterring or preventing them—overcomes the juridical contradiction by which men in the state of nature are *conceptually* beset to the extent that they demand respect from others. Along with his

Rousseauian stress on popular legislative sovereignty, and a Hobbesian emphasis on executive enforcement, Kant adds a Lockean (and Montesquieuian) insistence on the importance to free government of an impartial punitive judiciary.[12] All three powers or dignities [*Würden*] are contained implicitly in any state insofar as it is "to be thought of as legitimate." This means that in judging the legitimacy of anything that claims to be a state, the essential question in the short run is not "did the people consent to it?" (for the social contract, as such, is a goal to be aimed at, not an historical event to which any state need, or even could, trace its origin), nor even "are my rights (or those of others) protected?" but "is this government carrying out policies to which the people *might* have consented without publicly degrading themselves?"[13]

Citizenship, in other words, is even more a matter of civic recognition (and hence of the impartiality of government) than of participation or enjoyment. Kantian liberalism emphasizes the *neutrality* of public authority at the expense, where necessary, of its effectiveness and wisdom. It is more important, from a Kantian perspective, that people be able to credit the public fiction that the ruler *means* them no harm than that he not actually harm them. This, and not only Kant's increasingly tenuous political circumstances, helps explain the enormous circumspection that surrounds his various discussions of the powers of government. Who is to count as head of state, and where the effectual sovereignty lies, is a matter of some delicacy, into which the people may not inquire "with any practical aim in view."[14] Only in the case of war and peace does Kant forthrightly demand a popular legislative voice, to offset the willingness of rulers to transform their subjects into cannon fodder (i.e., literally "consume" them like the sheep and cattle that "paternalistic" rulers take them for). The people's authority, in principle, to make laws through their representatives reduces for all practical purposes to the ability to veto a decision for war—an ability which Kant makes the effectual test of whether or not a state is genuinely republican. (This is important, for Kant, not only because offensive wars needlessly destroy the lives and property of citizens but, even more crucially, because such use of citizens by heads of state is an abuse comparable to cannibalism—a reduction of humanity to a consumable product, that, as he once put it, "overturns the purpose of creation itself."[15]) In the end, Kant is less interested in formal arrangements of office than in the "spirit" that animates a properly constituted civic body. For this, indeed, an absolute monarch like Frederick the Great, who at least called himself servant of the people, may be preferable to a constitutional monarch (like Britain's) who manipulates the people's representatives into doing his unrestricted warlike bidding. Constitutional form is less a matter of visible order and arrangement than of inner rational structure, which separates the universal and particular while uniting them, and thus combines natural and moral necessity without conflating them.

As for executive [*aufübende*] power (or, alternatively, "directive" power [*rectoria*]), Kant is understandably vague about the extent to which heads of state (=monarchs) are or are not subject to the lawmaking power of citizens. Sometimes Kant treats every particular application of the law in the most general sense as properly within the executive power, turning "execution" into what Rousseau calls "government." At other times the power of the Kantian executive is considerably diminished—reduced, as he puts it, to the "minor premise" of a practical syllogism, with the "major premise," and "conclusion" (or "judgment") assigned to the legislative and judicial powers, respectively. Perhaps Kant means thereby to encourage gradual transformation from republicanism in the spirit to republicanism in the letter, by not calling directly into question the legality of despots willing to govern "in a republican spirit." One notes that the Latin *rector*—one of Kant's terms for the executive—can mean "ruler" and "commander in war," but also "director" (as in the director of a firm), or even less muscularly, "tutor." Perhaps in a system of republics of the sort that Kant proposed, such direction and guidance on the executive's part is all that would be necessary.

In any case, it is also worth remembering Kant's other German word for "execution" [*Ausführung*], a term he generally reserves for the execution (or "leading-out") of *ideas,* and especially associates with the activity of philosophers.[16] Since philosophers, as Kant liked to put it, cannot be kings, nor kings philosophers (inasmuch as power always corrupts), he divides executive power, both verbally and functionally, into ruling the people (or carrying out the general will) and teaching or enlightening them (by helping to "lead out" the idea that the people, insofar as they are rational/moral beings, already know, however dimly). In so dividing rulership and civic education, Kant not only discourages would-be enlighteners from playing tyrant; he also helps relieve the paradox that enlightenment otherwise involves.

KANT'S PROGRESSIVISM

That paradox is this: enlightenment means awakening in each of us awareness of autonomy, or the law of our own rational will, as the principle of conscience, which we are inclined to link with the authority of others, outside and above us. To be enlightened is thus, in the first and most important instance, to relinquish one's dependence on the authority of others. But how teach without encouraging that dependence in the very act of teaching? One answer—the autonomy the educator has in view—will not suffice, for prior to the achievement of that end, the student must, it seems, be made subject to the teacher's will. Indeed, given the radical transformation aimed at, such education seems to make the student dependent on another's will to a heightened—and even unsurpassable—degree: to free man utterly it is first

necessary to enslave him utterly. By dividing the roles of rulership and enlightenment Kant forestalls this fatal chain of reasoning—in which natural
and moral necessity again collide—a chain that erstwhile followers like
Fichte and Marx were only to eager to complete. The philosopher is neither
a governor nor tutor (in the Rousseauian sense)—terms suitable for instruc-
tors of the young, or naturally immature, but not those whose immaturity is
"self-incurred." The enlightening philosopher exercises no authority over
those to be enlightened (to whom he stands in a relation of perfect civic
equality), other than that conferred by their awakening awareness of their
rights as citizens and human beings. This is not to say that politicians cannot
be moral educators (nor that presidents, for example, cannot assume the
bully pulpit). It is to say, however, that *as* moral educators they must lay
down their maces and scepters. To be sure, Kant had few illusions that rulers
would in the short run take his advice, especially in a time of revolutionary
upheaval. But freedom of expression *for philosophers* (above all, in a university setting), could, he believed, accomplish the same goal indirectly and
in the long run no less surely.

Habits of personal responsibility and self-reliance, instilled in if not by a
decreasingly paternalistic state, would, Kant believed, also serve to encourage men's civic and moral self-awakening. Both indirectly and directly, then,
progressive realization of free self-government both improves the human
condition and heightens prospects, themselves civilly and morally empowering, for the ethical transformation of the species. Still, for all his institutional hopes, and, not least, for universities, Kant's progressivism is always
tempered by a certain pessimism as to the gap between cultural improvement and true moral betterment—a gap traceable, in the last analysis, to the
existence of two realms of necessity. We are *"cultivated,"* as Kant insisted, "to
a high degree; we are *civilized* . . . almost to excess. But to take ourselves to
be already *moralized*—for that much is still lacking" (emphasis his).[17]

Kantian education is less a matter of scientific discovery and advance than
an execution of ideas already planted in the depths of the human soul—
philosophy, in other words, as consciousness-raising. Such an education
could remind one of Socrates' pedagogical experiments with the slave boy
(who learned by remembering), except that the *principle* idea in question for
Kant pertains not to geometry but freedom, and hence to self-emancipation
(no very suitable subject for a slave boy). Kant's immediate audience was the
wardlike population of Germany and a wider Europe whose peaceful self-
emancipation he hoped crucially to advance if not to witness. But even the
arrival on the scene of true republics, Kant believed, would not relieve
philosophers (or, as he once called them, "free professors of law") of their
perpetual responsibility to do battle with the enemies—implicit in the
human heart itself—of reason as autonomy. This hectoring role, which Kant
placed in the service of a politics severe in its emphasis on individual self-

reliance, was hijacked almost immediately by those (like Fichte) who urged a more robust use of state power in the name of education.

But there is another, more genuinely Kantian, option that is perhaps best reflected in Lincoln's celebration of the Declaration of Independence as the "golden apple enframed by a silver constitution," i.e., of a certain understanding of equal liberty as the defining goal uniting us as a "people." On such a view, the actual constitution as written is less important than the idea of one that we aspire to—though this too has its basis in an originating moment to which our government traces its legitimacy. (We are, as Lincoln puts it, "a *nation,* conceived in liberty, and dedicated to the proposition that all men are created equal.") Lincoln, who also stressed the value of self-employment, less as a source of wealth than as a resource of citizenship, shows, at its very best perhaps, the potential alliance of rule and intellect that Kant hoped for without quite relying on. There is no reason to think that Lincoln ever read Kant or was directly influenced by him. Still, some notable Americans familiar with German philosophy were unashamed to see him in that light, going so far, in the case of William Harris, the first U.S. Commissioner of Education, as to regard Lincoln (in terms echoing a Kantianized Hegel) as a "world-historical" figure. And Kant, for his part, had a high opinion of the American people and its Constitution.

It was the United States he most likely had in mind when in 1790 he praised "the recently undertaken complete metamorphosis of a great people into a state." Of that newly formed "organization," he said, "each member is not just a means but also an end," and each "contributes to the possibility of the whole" the "idea of which determines each member's place and function."[18] His idealism in this context embraces his faith in the power of the idea of a social contract to engender and maintain the civic order that it calls for. Yet as Kant also notes in the same passage, the association in question is more often found in the "idea than in the reality." It is no wonder that Kant, from his own berth in an increasingly repressive and bellicose Prussia, looked with special interest and concern on the opportunities and risks opened up by the idea of a community of nations.

KANT'S COSMOPOLITANISM

Kant is, of course, famous for championing a federation of states, which he deemed a "surrogate" for the world republic with which his name is also commonly associated. The ideal of a world state, traceable to the Stoics, and implicit in much Christian jurisprudence and theology, takes a republican turn in Kant, who once referred to cosmopolitanism so conceived as his pet idea (or *Lieblingsidee*). In his mature writings at least, Kant is emphatic in his rejection of an actual world state any time prior to the moral transformation of the species that would make it both possible and, in a certain sense, un-necessary. His preferred goal is instead an expanding (but always fragile) al-liance among republics, and states verging on becoming so, as the only pos-sible foundation for world peace, or hedge against world catastrophe, that is available to us. To a large extent, Kant's argument is now the prevailing wis-dom: liberal democracies (or republics in roughly the Kantian sense) are es-sentially safe in one another's company but have much to fear from some nonrepublican states that tend, as republics do not, toward expansiveness and bellicosity. Kant's rejection of the goal of equilibrium among great pow-ers as intrinsically unstable seems all the more prescient and attractive with the end of the Cold War (and in light of World War I and its unhappy after-math.) At the same time, Kant's resolute insistence that nations neither inter-fere in the domestic affairs of other nations nor morally coerce them tempers his endorsement of cosmopolitan rights as claims human beings may de-mand from any state into a moderate plea, morally and culturally potent but legally unenforceable, for cosmopolitan justice, claims that have encouraged international commerce and discouraged and discredited European empire.

Less often noticed is Kant's almost equally strong resistance to the forces of what is now called globalism. The idea of a world republic is, according to Kant, to guide only as the implicit focus, never directly to be striven for, of his republican alliance. Its premature actualization would only be, he thought, a "soulless despotism" that would almost immediately give rise to anarchy. (Note again the emphasis on complex wholes or on unity with inner boundaries.) Each nation-state is itself a sovereign, right-bearing per-son, uniquely constituted by the customs (especially language and religion) of its people and the laws by which the individuals comprising it are united as a will empowered to submit itself to public authority. That this authority is above all judicial, empowering "judgment with force of right," suggests the limits to which globalism, for a Kantian, may be stretched. The "spirit of com-merce," which breaks down barriers among states, may "sooner or later put an end to war"; authority to punish (and hence the power to resist extradi-tion even by a "world court") remains the ultimate test, for Kant, of national sovereignty. Kant's identification of state power with authority to punish points to the *priority* of nation-states over every other sort of political group-ing, whether regional or global; it also furnishes a firm basis for distinguish-ing between legitimate cultural/economic influence and illegitimate hege-mony. (Americanization, in other words, is not true empire, (or "Amerika" as we put it in the sixties.)

One is, to be sure, compelled to wonder whether Kant's tentative hopes for an ever growing republican alliance (or what George Bush called a "new world order") pay sufficient attention to the religious or linguistic differ-ences that sustain the public life of individual nations, whose robust diver-sity he both counted on and mostly took for granted. Kant's cosmopolitan idea anticipates the strengths and weaknesses of the liberal internationalism it helped inspire, walking a fine line between a moralizing, and ultimately impotent, universalism and the celebration of diversity whose most memorable nineteenth- and twentieth-century supporters were anything but impotent. Still, if something *better* than the nation-state—conceptually, politically, and morally—is available, no one, to my knowledge, has yet discovered it.

CONCLUSION: KANT'S REALISM

Kant, as I suggested at the outset, deepened the wedge between "is" and "ought" that Machiavelli opened, but he also strove, as our brief survey of his moral and political teaching shows, to bring them back together.[19] Taking to heart the Machiavellian critique of imaginary republics, Kant insisted that ideas, as well as laws, be "executable." Kant's idealism thus goes hand in hand with a realism foreign to the spirit of ancient political philosophy, which did not subject ideas to the litmus test of their effectual truth. Still, it was part of Kant's genius to grasp the inadequacy of the very dualism to which the struggle between moral certitude and scientific doubt gives rise. Kant called himself *both* "a transcendental idealist and an empirical realist"— an unsteady compromise that represented, as he believed, the *only possible* solution to the rationally seated conflict between dogmatic idealism and the skeptical realism that necessarily calls it into question. If he demands the seemingly impossible (e.g., no lying, whatever the circumstances), he does not expect it (and especially not in presidents).

The problem of setting up a state is "soluble," as he famously put it, "even for a nation of devils (if only they have understanding.)"[20] In the end, however, Kant places his trust not in selfishness alone but in a combination (of unspecified proportions) of "love of honor" and "well-understood self interest."[21] Neither in devils nor in angels, in other words, but in ordinary human beings, who not only want to be happy but also, at least sometimes and at some level, to be estimable.

Kant is realistic in another sense. For all his moral rigor and rigorism, Kant lowers the standard of human aspiration in a decisive respect: however difficult, what is worthiest of esteem must in principle be universally attainable. It was this lowering above all, one suspects, that turned Nietzsche against the "Platonism" that he associated with the (false) distinction between the real and ideal worlds—an attack whose more immediate and proper target was Kant. Kant lowers virtue from a quality of character that few can muster to an ethic of playing by the rules in a game that all human beings are equipped, by definition, to win. Still, for all his democratic ease (if anything in Kant can be called easy), Kant's idealism recognizes the centrality of honor to political life, and in doing so enhances the luster that democratic citizenship cannot do without. This too is a necessity to which Kant calls attention.

NOTES

1. Harvey C. Mansfield, Jr., trans., *The Prince,* 2d ed. (Chicago: University of Chicago Press, 1998), 61.

2. *Critique of Pure Reason,* A/319=B/375. In citing the *Critique of Pure Reason,* I refer, as is customary, to the pagination of the original "A" (1781) and "B" (1787) editions. All other references to Kant's work cite the volume and page number of the Akademie edition (*Kants Gesammelte Schriften,* ed. Königliche Preußiche [later Deutsche] Akademie der Wißenschaften [Berlin: Walter de Gruyter, 1902–]). Translations are my own.

3. *Critique of Pure Reason,* A/313=B/370.

4. *Critique of Pure Reason,* A/317=B/373–74.

5. *Ausführung* also means to lead out, as in "e-ducate." Cf. J.-J. Rousseau, *Emile.*

6. *Critique of Pure Reason,* A/319=B/375. It is to be distinguished from *Ausübung,* Kant's translation of the Latin "execution," in the sense that Achenwall and others use it.

7. *Metaphysics of Morals,* VI 312.

8. The necessity to establish civil authority derives from what Kant refers to as "the rational idea of such a (not-just [*nicht-rechtlichen*]) condition" (*Metaphysics of Morals,* VI 312)—a phrase that is, so far as I know, unique to Kant's published work in not being able to be spoken aloud. The content of the rational idea is what might be called a positive *negation* of right (rather than the mere absence of right—e.g., the condition obtaining among animals or among rational inhabitants of mutually inaccessible planets). Such a positive negation of right is nonetheless "ideally rational," inasmuch as it contains the moments (to use Hegelian terms) by which that contradiction is (to be) superseded.

9. *Metaphysics of Morals,* VI 312.

10. Cf. Achenwall (whose *Natural Right* Kant lectured from), who divides state authority into the legislative, executive, and inspectory [*inspectoria*].

11. Albeit one that already presupposes (as Rousseau's earliest state of nature does not) a concern with recognition of one's status on the part of others.

12. Kant's emphasis is on judicial impartiality, not judicial independence. Securing liberty is less a function of governmental checks and balances than of making public recognition of the social contract—the "idea" of which (in the minds of governors and governed alike) legitimate government presupposes—increasingly explicit. For an elucidation of the primacy of this aspect of the just state, see Alexandre Kojève, *Phenomenologie du droit.*

13. Examples of policies or laws to which no people could consent are those involving a public declaration as to the intrinsic inferiority (as distinguished from a merely statutory or historical inferiority, which may be supported for a time for reasons of prudence) of any individual or group vis-à-vis the rest. The most extreme

version—a declaration on the ruler's part that the people as such have no rights against the ruler, whose moral relations to the people are therefore purely ethical (i.e., a matter of benevolence)—is, according to Kant, one that no ruler has ever made or ever will, out of foreknowledge that the people would "immediately rise up against him in fury." See *Conflict of the Faculties,* VII 87n.

14. *Metaphysics of Morals,* VI 318.

15. *Conflict of the Faculties,* VII 89.

16. Compare, however, *Perpetual Peace,* where separation of the governing (or *auführende*) and legislative powers is said to constitute the essential difference between republicanism and despotism. Perhaps, in Kant's view, executive power under a genuinely republican constitution is less like conventional rulership and more like philosophic execution, which "leads out" without dominating.

17. *Idea for a Universal History,* VIII 24–25, prop. seven.

18. *Critique of Judgment,* V 375.

19. See Harvey C. Mansfield, Jr., *Taming the Prince: The Ambivalence of Modern Executive Power* (Baltimore: Johns Hopkins University Press, 1993), 293. Originally published by the Free Press, 1989.

20. *Toward Eternal Peace,* VIII 366.

21. *Conflict of the Faculties,* VII 92.

11

Political Philosophy and the Religious Issue: From the Ancient Regime to Modern Capitalism

Peter Minowitz

It was to prevent the appropriation of the classical regime and its claims of justice by the city of God and the "Christian republic" that he [Machiavelli] directed the attention of both republics and principalities toward worldly gain. (*Machiavelli's Virtue* 292)[1]

In the Aristotelian understanding as Hobbes saw it, the regime was left exposed to the capture of religious parties, who used it with tyrannical zeal and made it the prize of civil war. We may suppose, then, that the impersonality of the modern state was the chosen instrument of secularization. (*Machiavelli's Virtue* 284)

Hobbes invented modern representative government as an attack on Christianity. It is an indirect attack, because he opposes a necessary consequence of Christianity, the independent priesthood, rather than Christianity itself. ("Hobbes and the Science of Indirect Government" 109)

It is hardly possible to exaggerate the importance of the religious issue for modern politics, and Locke's particular solution has formed our understanding of government by consent. (*Taming The Prince: The Ambivalence of Modern Executive Power* 194)

Modern constitutionalism as we see it in Hobbes, Spinoza, and Locke does not have a solution for the religious issue. A solution would be a society in which the highest human aspiration, the divinity in man, would thrive while human freedom was preserved. . . . [D]id they correctly reckon the cost in human irresponsibility—even to their own project—when men are no longer required or expected to take care of their souls? (*America's Constitutional Soul* 114)

Communism is dead, but can the world uncover a sustainable path between a religious fundamentalism more brutal than anything known in the Middle Ages and a relentless capitalism that enshrines greed, inflames consumerism, and erodes the autonomy of nations? As a preliminary step to answering this question, let us examine the efforts of Harvey Mansfield to scrutinize the relationship of constitutionalism and liberalism to "the religious issue." After elaborating some of his key themes—the Aristotelian approach to regimes, and the post-Christian departures from Aristotle that were engineered by Machiavelli and subsequently incorporated into liberalism—I shall explore their implications for the study of Adam Smith, the consummate philosopher of both "worldly gain," in the form that is typically pursued today, and economic liberalism. Compared to the pre-Smith philosophers discussed in detail by Mansfield as "captains" in Machiavelli's army and as founders of liberalism (Hobbes, Spinoza, Locke, and Montesquieu), Smith departs still further from Aristotle in minimizing the regime and promoting invisible or indirect government, the substitute pioneered by Machiavelli. Although this enterprise leads Smith to present an account of modernity's historical development that clashes dramatically with Mansfield's, Smith drops hints that suggest an underlying kinship.

ARISTOTLE AND THE REGIME

Mansfield's lengthiest published discussion of an ancient philosopher is the two-chapter analysis of Aristotle's *Politics* in *Taming the Prince*[2]; on many of the fundamentals, of course, Aristotle follows Plato. To bring out the contrast with modern representative government, Mansfield emphasizes Aristotle's claim that the *polis* is defined "above all" by the regime, *politeia* (1276b11), with political assertions being "arguments about what politics requires, setting forth claims to be worthy of ruling or sharing in rule for good reason" (*Taming the Prince* 32). Aristotle proceeds in book III of *The Politics* to introduce political philosophy as the umpire of competing definitions of citizenship, specifications of the common good, and claims to rule, especially those put forward by democrats (complemented on a philosophical level by claims on behalf of natural necessity) and oligarchs (complemented on a philosophical level by claims on behalf of human choice). When Mansfield elsewhere invokes Aristotelian rulers who "promote themselves in a partisan view of the whole that is typically theirs" (*Machiavelli's Virtue* 283), he again implies that such rulers have distinct visions of the cosmos or nature as well as of the community they rule: "With the claim to rule other men, men must also claim to rule all other things" (*Taming the Prince* 39).

In interpreting the vexing discussion of *pambasileia* that concludes book III of *The Politics,* Mansfield likewise intermingles political and metaphysical

claims. For example, he argues that Aristotle has tacitly constructed a parallel between absolute kingship and the human soul in order to suggest or establish "the reconciliation of nature and man" (*Taming the Prince* 35–36, 41).
Mansfield arrives at the striking conclusion that the "best man," in Aristotle's
account, "chooses according to nature as if nature were his own will. He also
chooses as if human choice, especially past human choices bound up in custom, were nature's (1287b5–8)" (43). Mansfield is now ready to crystallize
the fundamental distinction between Aristotelian ruling and modern executive power:

> This assumption of nature, law, and custom, which is part deference, part pre-
> sumption, is what it means for men to *rule:* they make themselves the beginning
> principle (*archē*) of themselves and of things. This is the very opposite of the
> notion of executive power, in which the ruler presents himself as an agent of
> some other power . . . or as forced into action by brute necessity. (*Taming the
> Prince* 43)

Rulers rule in broad daylight, and the order of a society is visible in stable
forms or institutions that enable and oblige "political science" to discern "the
intent of the founders as made visible in the form of the constitution or
regime" (*America's Constitutional Soul* 205).[3]

The sophistication of Mansfield's discussion of kingship is echoed in his
account of the way executive power in Aristotle moves from political structures to theology. The first step is to fathom how Aristotle in book VI includes but depreciates the fundamental institutional manifestations of what
we now call executive power. Although every regime is compelled to enforce deeds against the condemned and to keep prisoners, this task is not
noble, and the "office" is best exercised by a rotating group of individuals.
To inflate and unify such offices would be to invite a "punitive theocracy."
Thus, although Aristotle begins with "an uncompromising argument for
virtue in his notion of kingship," he proceeds to prevent such kingship from
becoming an "angry god" who intimidates respectable people and empowers potential tyrants (*Taming the Prince* 69).

Mansfield complements these striking remarks about Aristotle's implicit
posture toward theocracy and the angry god by alluding to the marginal status of priests in an Aristotelian regime (*Taming the Prince* 308n21, 316n31).
In the chapter that immediately follows the two chapters on Aristotle, we
read that Aristotle's "precautions against the excesses of the sacral city were
carefully muted" (86), and that "political scientists" in the Christian era could
not follow Aristotle by "covering up the theologico-political question" (89),
the latter being Spinoza's term for "what is perhaps *the* permanent question
of politics" (90). Mansfield elsewhere defines this question as "whether men
are ruled by God or gods, hence by divine right, or by themselves on principles they discern without necessarily referring to the Word of God in Scrip-

ture"; if "rule derives from divinity, all government is theocracy, more or less" (*America's Constitutional Soul* 101). Given the efforts Mansfield generally makes to resuscitate the relevance of Aristotle, it is striking that he accuses him of "covering up" such a momentous issue.[4]

MACHIAVELLI, SECULARISM, AND INDIRECT GOVERNMENT

We need not detain ourselves here with elaborating the anti-Christian animus uniting the nostrums of Machiavelli that have generated and sustained his reputation as a teacher of evil. More controversial are Mansfield's attempts to demonstrate that Machiavelli's "new modes and orders" include perverse "appropriations" of Christian doctrines, practices, and institutional arrangements that had contributed, from a secular point of view, to the longevity and worldly influence of the church. Most controversial is the hypothesis, previously adumbrated by Leo Strauss, that Machiavelli is the hidden prince of the modern world.[5] *Taming the Prince* is surely one of the most subtle explorations available of Machiavelli's place in the history of political philosophy, so let us examine how, according to Mansfield, "the religious issue" was implicated in Machiavelli's abandonment of the Aristotelian framework.

Taming the Prince identifies seven "elements of the modern executive" that Machiavelli anticipated, prepared, or designed: political punishment, the primacy of war and foreign affairs, execution as universal technique, indirect government, suddenness, secrecy, and *uno solo* (the need for a solitary executive "to take on himself the glory and the blame"; 130–31). Many of Machiavelli's departures from Aristotle are easy to grasp: for example, his reducing the "boastful claims of regimes . . . to their capacity to produce palpable and beneficial effects" (137); his celebration of governmental cruelty, including recurring but "extraordinary" executions against criminals, rebels, or scapegoats; and his endorsement of limitless acquisition. Instead of Aristotelian efforts to mediate and elevate contending speeches of oligarchs and democrats toward a mixed regime infused by moral virtue, furthermore, Machiavelli identifies two "humors" that impel tumults within all societies— one humor driven to dominate (the great), the other to avoid being dominated (the people)—and teaches us how to "manage" or manipulate these humors toward glory for the great and security for the people.

Less easy to grasp is the central topic, indirect government, which is crucial for understanding the indebtedness of modern executive power to Machiavelli's appropriation of Christianity: "the modern Machiavellian executive came into being as a response to the religious issue" (*Taming the Prince* 106). If executive power is "power exercised in the name of someone or something else" (xxiii) or "wielded in someone else's name, not in one's own" (29), the religious version, obviously, is power discharged in God's name. The Machiavellian version is power exercised or wielded in the name of necessity, especially the eternal necessity of acquiring sustenance, security, and glory. Both versions of executive power abandon the Aristotelian vision of men ruling "responsibly according to principles they choose and profess" (140).[6]

The Machiavellian strategy of hiding authority behind necessity, according to Mansfield, is necessarily ambivalent. For one thing, the spectacular executions necessary to deter disobedience and to purge the inevitable resentments that build in the people require government to be conspicuously *visible* (*Taming the Prince* 140). And insofar as the popular humor "constitutes a reluctance to face facts, to face necessity," government confronts "the ambivalent task of bringing necessity home to the people, so that they survive, while concealing it from them, so that they are happy and innocent" (145). Consequently, governments and leaders must employ fraud and conspiracy "as instruments available generally if not routinely, and to be used without hesitation or scruple" (145). The crowning conspiracy would be Machiavelli's new modes and orders; however great his role, Machiavelli obviously is not "*the* prince out *in broad daylight*, where everyone can see him" (*Machiavelli's Virtue* 125).

Many of the concrete manifestations of Machiavelli's indirect government are not elaborated in *Taming the Prince*. Election proves to be a key Machiavellian technique because it makes the people take responsibility for tangible evils such as punishments and taxes. As Machiavelli observes about the mode by which Roman dictators were elected, the "wounds . . . a man does to himself spontaneously and by choice hurt much less than those that are done to you by someone else" (*Discourses* I:34). The people cannot create the security they crave because they lack ambition and exalt goodness (*bontà*), but they can be brought to admit the necessity of government and to accommodate ambition "if they are permitted or required to exercise government in elections or in judging capital cases" (*Machiavelli's New Modes and Orders* 149, 316). An election, furthermore, can function as an accusation whereby the candidate is "humiliated, then released for public service"; and the scapegoating or deserved punishment of some princes, via accusation or other modes, can be construed as an election of the unpunished (*Machiavelli's Virtue* 233, 28–29). Mansfield regards all this as an appropriation or adaptation of Christian doctrines about original sin and divine remission of punishment (*Machiavelli's New Modes and Orders* 116, 183, 343). Contra Aristotle, the common good is "not a compromise of ends" but "a hidden tyranny for the princes and a periodic punishment of ambition for the people" (140).[7] For a "quintessential" election, Mansfield refers us to *Discourses* I:47, involving a Capuan magistrate (Paucuvius) who "forced the people to choose between the luxury of revenge and the necessity of government, but in such a way that by having to choose, the people seemed to have both." Mansfield states that "perhaps all electing is essentially the act of grace in relieving from punishment" (*Machiavelli's New Modes and Orders* 145), and later proclaims that "the purpose of indirect government" is to spread guilt (317).

Machiavelli's most explicit reference to invisible government comes in *Discourses* II:21, to explain why the Romans let certain conquered cities ("those they did not demolish") live under their own laws:

> For those cities especially that are used to living freely . . . remain content more quietly under a dominion they do not see, even though it may have in itself some hardship, than under one they see every day that appears to them to reprove them every day for their servitude. There follows closely from this another good for the prince. Since his ministers do not have in hand the judges and magistracies who render civil or criminal justice in those cities, there can never arise a judgment with disapproval or infamy for the prince.[8]

For Mansfield, Machiavelli's model in such matters is the Christian priests who hide their government behind the providence of God (*Machiavelli's New Modes and Orders* 255). Linking this chapter with the discussion of the supernatural in *Discourses* I:56—among other similarities, the two chapters share frequent usage of the phrase "everyone knows"—Mansfield suggests that Machiavelli intended to perfect invisible government: "when men are shown how to interpret signs so as to forestall the intervention of God and His intermediaries, then government becomes truly invisible because it is truly one's own, freely accepted and in accord with human necessities" (*Machiavelli's New Modes and Orders* 256).

HOBBES, LOCKE, AND LIBERALISM

Complementing his sustained focus on Machiavelli, Mansfield has published studies on the political philosophy of Hobbes and Locke.[9] With Hobbes, Mansfield emphasizes two interrelated inventions, representative government and the *science* of indirect government. Mansfield's interpretations of Hobbes do not constitute an immense challenge to mainstream scholars, most of whom would join our author in making claims such as the following: that Hobbes condemned the unrest and bloodshed he traced to the influence of Christian clerics; that he rejected Platonic and Aristotelian efforts to orient politics with assistance from a *summum bonum;* that he sweepingly transferred from subjects to sovereigns the right to make private judgments about good and evil; that he condoned and perhaps encouraged the human inclination to seek "power after power"; that he belittled the distinctions among the forms of government; that he labored doggedly and creatively to convert government into consent-based representation; and that he strug-

gled to reconcile the formal absolutism of sovereignty with the temporal primacy of natural right that lodges in individuals and denies to sovereigns any
duty "to educate or compel men to live more virtuously than they would
without him, except as virtue is defined as obeying him" (*America's Constitutional Soul* 107).

As elaborated by Mansfield, Hobbes adapts the anti-Aristotelian enterprise
of indirect government in three primary ways: by translating the necessity
that shields the crimes of the Machiavellian prince into the notorious hard-
ships of the state of nature; by establishing representation as a substitute for
ruling; and by conveying a power-based teaching in a systematic form that
invokes the precision of mathematics and physics. The detachment from the
subject matter implied by such a scientific stance, and Hobbes' elevation of
the sovereign's status at the expense of "professionals" who dispense private
judgment "by vocation" (*Taming the Prince* 164), are of course compro-
mised by Hobbes' need to acknowledge a greater role for himself as the
teacher of princes than his formal principles would allow (167, 176–78). And
although Mansfield depicts Hobbes' intentions as being secularizing, anti-
Christian, and dramatically anticlerical, he states that Hobbes did not think it
"possible, or necessary, or desirable to abolish religion" (*America's Constitutional Soul* 108). Rather, Hobbes follows Machiavelli in *appropriating*
Christianity—particularly the Christian view of "human government as a necessary intermediary" that should serve as "the keeper of men's consciences
and the interpreter of men's opinions"—for worldly purposes. Thus, Hobbes
"maliciously borrows his central metaphors from Christianity and uses them,
like Christianity, to disguise his government" ("Hobbes and the Science of
Indirect Government" 109–10).

Only with Locke do we encounter an attempt to solve the religious issue
which summons a liberalism that is economic, political, and constitutional.
Mansfield's writings on Locke, especially in *Taming the Prince,* emphasize
three themes in illustrating the fate of the Aristotelian regime in Locke: the
translation of Machiavellian necessity into the state of nature; the semi-
Aristotelian portrayal of political ends and forms that emerges from Locke's
delicate discussion of the separation of powers; and the theological-political
implications of Locke's account of property.

The first of these themes is the most straightforward. Whereas the harshness
of Machiavellian "beginnings" is manifest in the state of war that Hobbes
equates with the state of nature, Locke distinguishes the two states and posits
a law of nature that proscribes the infliction of harm on others. On the other
hand, self-preservation retains a kind of primacy: although each person is
obliged by the law of nature to "preserve the rest of mankind," this mandate
is binding only "when his own preservation comes not in competition" (*Second Treatise* sec. 6). Echoes of Machiavelli and Hobbes may likewise be heard
when Locke extols the need for human labor and invention to "improve"

upon the wasteful material inheritance that nature or God has provided.[10] In Mansfield's vivid formulation, self-preservation is in effect "the tyrant's end of self-aggrandizement . . . transformed by being placed in the state of nature" where it is made "universal, equal, and modest" (*Taming the Prince* 187). Locke's constitutionalism also promotes the Hobbesian enterprise of taming the opinions that fuel partisanship: "Necessity as revealed in the state of nature will compel partisans to consider what is essential, their self-preservation, and to forsake their partisan opinions about the good or godly life" (185).

Regarding political forms and ends, Mansfield concludes his presentation by distinguishing Locke from Aristotle: Locke's constitution is not Aristotle's regime, in which a part of society gives "form to the whole," but is separated into two powers (legislative and executive) "neither of which has responsibility for the whole" (*Taming the Prince* 210). Compared to Machiavelli and Hobbes, however, Locke has much to commend him. Along Aristotelian lines, "freedom and government by consent are considered good in themselves" (188), and constituted legislative power represents both "the act of its creation and the end it was created for." On the other hand, the end is prepolitical (the preservation of life, liberty, and property), and "the form is not *what* is chosen but the *act* of choosing" (186–87).

Needless to say, "prerogative" is crucial for understanding Locke's status as the author who "gave the executive his modern form" as the "executive power" (*Taming the Prince* 192) while advocating constitutionalist principles (primarily due process and the rule of law) against the "extraordinary" interventions of the Machiavellian prince and the more methodical "absolute arbitrary power" of the Hobbesian sovereign. On the one hand, the supremacy of the legislative promotes the rule of law.[11] On the other hand, the executive is equipped with prerogative power that "enforces the discipline of necessity," reminding a possibly overconfident legislature of "all those chance necessities that get in the way of human intentions" (189).[12] Indeed, Mansfield seems to praise Locke for thus incorporating "the extraconstitutional within the constitution" (204). In addition to demonstrating Locke's delicate unfolding of prerogative, finally, Mansfield captures the general interplay of form and end within Locke's rhetoric:

> Locke's very presentation imitates the difficulty of obtaining consent in politics, a difficulty that consists not in getting the people's agreement to the rule of their betters, as with Aristotle, but acquiescence to necessity, as with Machiavelli. One can gain consent by showing them that they have consented to these powers in the past as being necessary, while retaining for themselves the right of resistance that they have also exercised. This approach to the people is like Locke's to his readers, a rationalization and refinement of actual events. By gradually introducing his readers to the scope of executive power, Locke uses reason to help them appreciate that element in humanity which is not amenable to reason. (*Taming the Prince* 204)

To grapple with our third theme, the theological-political implications of Locke's account of property, let us start with two of Mansfield's articles, "On the Political Character of Property in Locke" (in A. Kontos, ed., *Powers, Possessions, and Freedom*) and "The Religious Issue and the Origin of Modern Constitutionalism" (in *America's Constitutional Soul*). According to the former, "the fundamental question" about property is whether *man* has such a right, not whether some men can have a right against others. Whence the contradictions in Locke's scattered answers to the question of whether we are God's property? Mansfield's answer is provocative but persuasive: "As is his habit in matters of religion, he leaves one trail for the skeptical and another for the pious, the latter more plainly marked but leading in circles" (29). The second article makes the less controversial point that Locke's defense of religious toleration, by leaving the soul in private hands and confining governmental intervention to concrete worldly matters, encourages the deflection of public attention from God to Mammon (103, 113).

In *Taming the Prince*, Mansfield again invokes religion to explain well-known Lockean puzzles. The book, as implied by its subtitle, emphasizes the ambivalence intrinsic to modern executive power: although it is strong, it "always claims to be acting on behalf of a will or force that is stronger" (130). Such ambivalence, Mansfield asserts, explains why every U.S. president is forced "to defend himself by claiming the powers that are formally his" (16). Scrutinizing Locke, Mansfield attributes one root of executive ambivalence to the tension between our "perfect freedom" in the state of nature and our subjection to the law of nature. The ultimate source is again Locke's need "to confront the religious issue" (194). Although our status as God's property would bolster the individual's respect for his fellows ("On the Political Character of Property in Locke" 33), we might end up being subjected to God's vicars, such as priests and fathers (*Taming the Prince* 195). Furthermore, if government could be "established merely by uninstructed consent" without subordination to a law of nature, a "majority religious opinion might suffice to justify a government of divine right"; Mansfield asserts that divine right was the "ground of government that prevailed literally everywhere before Hobbes and Locke set to work" (195). Mansfield, however, states a thesis that may be even more bold: that Locke, intending "to confine and humanize the omnipotent Biblical God who creates by miracle without regard to human necessity," reconceived God as "a workmanlike Maker" who "obeys the same necessity men do when they execute the law of nature" (196).[13]

Mansfield also invokes the religious issue to explain Locke's rejection of the primacy accorded to terror by Machiavelli and Hobbes. Our "spirited naysaying resistance to necessity" would dissolve in fear as we "tremble at the prince's executions and the sovereign's sword." Because the path of terror approaches so closely to the fear of invisible powers that is exploited by advocates of divine right, Locke allows the people themselves to "become strong executives": in the state of nature, the "execution of the law of nature" (i.e., the right to inflict punishment, including capital punishment, on transgressors) is lodged in "every man's hands."[14] Locke's articulation of the "right of resisting" governmental oppression could be defended in similar terms.

In addition to explaining some of the theological concerns that shaped Locke's account of property, Mansfield articulates concerns that are more purely political. Property for Locke not only supplies human needs: it is a "fence" that protects life, that keeps us free ("when life and liberty are at stake, they are already in jeopardy"), that distinguishes political power from despotism, and that protects freedom and consent even against conquerors.[15] Economic inequality can spur conflict, but the convention of property can also unify society, enabling government to function as a "conventional whole" that "secures property for mankind as well as property for each." Property is not only a convention or form that can expand "out of its matter so that it becomes an end in itself"; property is a "whole that includes all members of society as well as all the objects of their desires."[16] Property likewise serves to unite "right and necessity": the need to work is "answered by the virtue of industry," and the property right of each depends on the right of everyone else (*Taming the Prince* 210). This unifying function also strengthens Locke's teaching about resistance and revolution, because "when anyone's property is taken without his consent, property as a whole is attacked and the people as a body can see or can be made to see this clearly."[17] Despite the effort Mansfield devotes to illuminating such depths in Locke, he concludes his discussion in *Taming the Prince* with a stark criticism that invokes Kant as well as Marx: "our experience shows that Locke's convention could not cohere," because "your property does not engage my interest as much as mine," and, moreover, because "my spirit may be more readily engaged by the attack on Property than by its defense" (210).

ADAM SMITH AND CAPITALISM

What light does Mansfield's account of liberalism, property, and the religious issue shed on Adam Smith's *The Wealth of Nations?* Compared with Hobbes and Locke, Smith proceeds further in taming Machiavelli's prince, in diminishing the directness of government, and in resolving (via secularization and other means) the theological-political problem.[18]

Smith stands out in the history of philosophy, even when compared to Hobbes and Locke, for elevating property and the acquisition of wealth as ends in themselves and for correspondingly shrinking the scope of governmental activity. Nevertheless, scholarly disputes continue to rage over the precise balance Smith established between politics and economics.[19] Some manifestations of what could be called Smith's "economism" are direct and obvious: elevating the invisible hand of the market at the expense of the visible hand of the state; reducing the role of government in the name of "natural liberty," primarily the individual's liberty of "superintending" his own interest and industry (*WN* IV.ix.51), of allocating his labor and capital as he sees fit (I.x.a.1, I.x.c.12, IV.ii.10, IV.v.b.16); and combating, on behalf of free trade and global prosperity, the mercantilist exaltation of empire, military power, self-sufficiency, and national pride. It is the indirect aspects of Smith's presentation that have not received the attention they deserve.

Mansfield, as we have seen, argues that Machiavelli, Hobbes, and Locke innovate by hiding government behind necessity and/or nature. In addition to his manifest efforts to tame government on behalf of nature, Smith labors assiduously and imaginatively to hide the type of authority that an *author* can exercise. Smith's presentation of his ideas under the rubric of machine-like "systems"—of political economy, moral philosophy, and natural jurisprudence—goes well beyond Hobbes in anticipating or preparing the detachment and precision pursued by contemporary social science. In certain respects, moreover, Smith's posture reaches an absurd culmination in Marx's appropriation of "iron necessity" for the cause of world revolution. Of the indirect dimensions in Smith's exposition that enhance the prospects for indirect government, I shall amplify four: the delicate ways Smith manipulates readers of *The Wealth of Nations* to regard public enrichment as the ultimate aim; his abandonment of the quest to evaluate different forms of government; his attenuation of opinion as a vehicle to gain knowledge of justice; and his complex juggling of nature and necessity.

Nowhere does Smith sketch a complete explanation of why "the nature and causes of the wealth of nations" deserves the extended investigation he gives it. Equating wealth with a variety of other terms—prosperity, riches, revenue, subsistence, plenty, opulence, and "the necessaries, conveniencies, and amusements of human life" (*WN* I.v.1)—Smith presents political economy as the science of *obtaining* wealth (II.v.31, IV.Intro.1, IV.ix.50), not as a broader science that evaluates wealth's rank among competing human ends. Smith's insinuations on behalf of wealth could fill a pamphlet on the art of exaggeration. The development of roads, canals, and navigable rivers is the "greatest of all improvements"; "the compleat improvement and cultivation of the country" is the "greatest of all publick advantages" (I.xi.b.5, I.xi.1.12); a populous society is a "great society" because it facilitates the division of labor and technological progress (I.viii.57); money is the means by which "every individual . . . has his subsistence, conveniencies, and amusements, regularly distributed to him in their proper proportions" (II.ii.13); bankruptcy is "perhaps the greatest and most humiliating calamity which can befall an innocent man" (II.iii.29); and a "person who can acquire no property, can have no other interest but to eat as much, and to labour as little as possible" (III.ii.9). Smith's massive "Digression concerning the Variations in the Value of Silver during the Course of the Four last Centuries" (I.xi.e–n) likewise illustrates the priorities of *The Wealth of Nations*. Judging by Mansfield's criteria for solving "the religious issue" (*America's Constitutional Soul* 114), one would have to complain that Smith displayed insufficient concern for "the highest human aspiration, the divinity in man," however much he labored on behalf of human freedom and prosperity.

The psychological linchpin of *The Wealth of Nations* is the desire to "better one's condition" that dominates human behavior because no one is ever perfectly satisfied with his situation. Smith's indirectness is provocatively revealed by his elaboration of "the means by which the greater part of men propose and wish to better their condition": increased wealth. In asserting that this conception of betterment is only "the most vulgar and the most obvious" conception (II.iii.28), Smith implies the existence of less vulgar conceptions, but he does not identify them, and his massive treatise caters more or less to the vulgar version.

Let us proceed to the second indirect path by which Smith diminishes the directness of government: his abandonment of the quest to evaluate different regimes that was so important to Plato and Aristotle.[20] In neither of his books, *The Wealth of Nations* or *The Theory of Moral Sentiments,* does Smith provide a typology, much less an evaluation, of the different forms of government. Smith's most complete presentation comes when he sketches the suitability of democracy, aristocracy, and monarchy for deriving revenue from mercantile projects (*WN* V.ii.a.4). Furthermore, only once in his long chapter on the tasks of government (*WN* V.i, "Of the Expences of the Sovereign or Commonwealth"), does Smith frame his policy recommendations with an eye to differences necessitated by variations in the "form of government." This discussion occurs in a minuscule "Part" of the chapter—"Of the Expence of supporting the Dignity of the Sovereign"—whose brevity signals how little Smith wishes to encourage individuals or groups to promulgate, in Aristotelian fashion, claims that they are worthy of ruling.

Smith displays no interest in the literal meaning of aristocracy—rule of the best—that informs Aristotle's presentation of the best regime in book VII of *The Politics*. In commenting on the "natural aristocracy" that he uncovers in actual societies, however, Smith provides provocative echoes of both Machiavelli and Aristotle: an Aristotelian appreciation of American rebels who are becoming "statesmen and legislators . . . contriving a new form of government," and a Machiavellian insistence that politics in every country is dominated by a class of "leading men" who compete amongst themselves for "importance."[21] Smith seems to tame both approaches when he suggests that these "ambitious and high-spirited men" who "draw the sword in defense of their own importance" can be deflected, via union with Britain, from "piddling for the little prizes" of "the paltry raffle of colony faction" into pursuing the prizes yielded by "the wheel of the great state lottery of British politicks" (*WN* IV.vii.c.74). Under the system of natural liberty, perhaps, such men would seek to become captains of industry rather than generals or princes.

Smith's abandonment of the classical regime is also displayed in the way he promiscuously deploys the terms "sovereign" and "sovereignty"—as if no questions could be raised about who possesses or who should possess political authority. Given the prominence of social-contract theories for Smith's contemporaries, it is surprising that he displays so little concern for the thesis that governmental legitimacy is a function of popular consent.[22] His heightened endorsement of economic liberty thus contrasts with his indifference toward what could be described as the political liberty that defines the state of nature, as articulated by Hobbes and Locke, and that infuses (via the general will) the social contract as articulated by Rousseau (we do not know whether Smith was familiar with the *Social Contract*, first published in 1762, but he did anonymously review the *Second Discourse* in 1755). Needless to say, there is nothing comparable in Smith's books to the right of resisting defended by Locke.[23]

For Locke, "natural liberty" is "to be free from any superior power on earth, and not to be under the will or legislative authority of man." Natural liberty is also the premise for liberty in society: "to be under no other legislative power but that established by consent in the commonwealth" (*Second Treatise* sec. 22). Smith's "natural liberty" is defined in terms of security and economic freedom rather than political consent.[24] Even under a "free" government, needless to say, the "natural liberty of a few individuals" must yield to "the security of the whole society" (*WN* II.ii.94). And when Smith praises the liberty possessed by the American colonists "to manage their own affairs their own way" (IV.vii.b.51), economics intrudes as an end—Smith is here trying to explain why colonies can make such rapid progress toward "wealth and greatness"—and perhaps also as a means, insofar as the affairs to be managed are chiefly economic (how people should employ their capital and industry "in the way that they judge most advantageous to themselves"; IV.vii.b.4, IV.vii.b.44).

Given his ubiquitous, casual invocations of sovereignty, Smith certainly cannot be accused of erasing government or even of drastically reducing its visibility. Most of Smith's eighteenth-century readers, presumably, imagined kings when he mentioned sovereigns, and he neither attacks nor defends monarchy, whether hereditary or elective. Smith seems to smile upon "civilized monarchies" like France, and he certainly conducts no Lockean diatribe against absolute monarchy.[25] As we have seen, furthermore, he also refrains from reducing government to a mere agent of the people, as in the indirect, representative scheme emphasized by Mansfield. But all this still leaves Smith in a position very different from that assumed by the Aristotelian political philosopher who mediates competing claims to rule supported by competing definitions of citizenship.[26] Sovereignty becomes an empirical phenomenon divorced from provocative claims about either society or cosmos. Government's tasks, under "the obvious and simple system of natural liberty," become "plain and intelligible to common understandings"; this system even "establishes itself of its own accord" upon the removal of systematic governmental intrusions (*WN* IV.ix.51). Smith's system would allow a society to proceed smoothly along a "natural progress" toward wealth and "civilization" (II.iii.31, III.i, IV.i.33, IV.ix.28, V.i.a.1–11), but the lion's share of the credit would be granted to nature, not to rulers who "make themselves the beginning principle (*archē*) of themselves and of things" (*Taming the Prince* 43). Such ambitions, in any case, would often be frustrated by the unintended consequences that, according to Smith, explain so many watersheds in human history (*WN* I.ii.1, III.iv.10,17, IV.vii.a.21, IV.vii.c.80). With the ongoing extension of the division of labor, finally, the typical citizen would have still less awareness of how a nation or an economy—not to mention the cosmos—operates as a "whole" (I.i, V.i.f.50–51). Social contract theory may tame the prince by making government representative, but perhaps it still encourages people, more than Smith prefers, to exaggerate the arenas that can be shaped by conscious human choice.

In elaborating the ways Smith manipulated his readers to exalt public enrichment and abandoned the classical quest for the best regime, I have suggested that he intended to increase the indirectness of both government and political philosophy. Additional support for my account can be drawn from his treatment of justice, in which he conveys elements of historicism and economism that undermine the regime-oriented, dialectical approach used by Plato and Aristotle.

Justice stands out in *The Wealth of Nations* as the virtue that government is obliged to support and that limits the scope of economic freedom and competition. Under the system of natural liberty, "every man, as long as he does not violate the laws of justice, is left perfectly free to pursue his own interest his own way" (IV.ix.51). For Smith, the effectual truth of the demands made by justice is a legal framework that enforces debts and contracts and that protects the individual's life, person, and property. Departing from both Plato and Aristotle, Smith shows little or no interest in the justice of competing claims to rule. In substituting a quasi-historical analysis of how "civil government" and a "regular administration of justice" (V.i.b.2) arise "naturally" during the development of society to a more advanced "period" or "state," moreover, Smith depreciates not only partisan claims, natural right, and natural law but differing opinions about the relationship of justice to equality.[27] Although the reader may infer that injustice for Smith means "injury" to property, person, or reputation, nowhere in *The Wealth of Nations* does he answer or even raise the Socratic question "what is justice?" With a similar impetus, he invokes the "faculties of reason and speech" as a source for "the propensity to truck, barter, and exchange" (I.ii.1–2) rather than, following

Aristotle, as a starting point for knowledge of the just and the advantageous (*Politics* 1253a14–15).

In a hunting society, Smith explains, "tolerable" security is available despite the absence of "civil government" or an "established magistrate": given the paltry levels of property that can accumulate, there will only be sporadic or incidental reasons for someone to inflict injury upon another (*WN* V.i.b.2). In referring back to prepolitical beginnings, Smith resembles the social-contract theorists, but he replaces their concern for specifying formal conditions of legitimacy, built upon consent and natural right/law, with his systematic historical account of the "circumstances which naturally introduce subordination" and government in the last three social stages (herding, agriculture, and commerce). Subordination and thus government develop "naturally" along with valuable property as the wealthy shepherd exercises authority over those who depend for sustenance on his surpluses (V.i.b.7).

Smith seems to posit precision, equality, and impartiality as standards to evaluate the administration of justice (*WN* V.i.b.1,15,25)—he elsewhere exalts Britain for its "equal and impartial administration of justice" (IV.vii.c.54)—and he describes certain "corrupt" arrangements as being "gross abuses" (V.i.b.14–15). But he attributes such arrangements to the patterns of judicial funding that naturally develop in a shepherd-stage society, in which government derives substantial revenue from the fees paid by people who petition the courts (V.i.b.13). That is, corruption stems neither from defective opinions about what justice is nor from the defective characters of those who administer it. The remedy, moreover, fits the problem. Smith proposes neither philosophical edification about the nature of justice nor recommendations about how to train judges.[28]

Smith elsewhere stresses that commerce and manufacturing are unlikely to flourish unless there is a "regular administration of justice," that is, unless people have a "certain degree of confidence in the justice of government" (*WN* V.iii.7). The "justice of government," however, does not require that a government be ruled by those who deserve to rule, or that it give to each his due, or that it adhere to any particular distributive principle. For Smith, justice means that people feel "secure in the possession of their property," that contracts are legally enforced, and that the state is known to be "regularly employed" in enforcing debt payment (V.iii.7).

Smith's analysis of justice-administration also provides the setting for his endorsement of the separation of powers. Unless judges are independent of the executive, they will be tempted to sacrifice justice, the "rights of a private man," to "the great interests of the state."[29] The key is again to be found in the historical evolution of funding through the social stages: "The separation of the judicial from the executive power seems originally to have arisen from the increasing business of the society, in consequence of its increasing improvement. The administration of justice became so laborious and so complicated a duty as to require the undivided attention of the persons to whom it was entrusted" (*WN* V.i.b.24).

Although Smith's account of justice can be accused, as Mansfield accuses various modern doctrines, of hiding the punitive function of government behind the mask of necessity, Smith can be more plausibly accused of hiding economic tyranny behind the mask of nature. As we have seen, Hobbes and Locke seem to tame Machiavelli partly by transforming the harshness of "beginnings" (invoked by Machiavelli to justify brutality and cruelty) into the insecurity and penury of the state of nature; in Mansfield's words, self-preservation represents a transformation of "the tyrant's end of self-aggrandizement" into a form that is "universal, equal, and modest" (*Taming the Prince* 187). One can argue that Smith goes even further in softening but extending Machiavellian necessity by transforming it into the universal, unceasing pressure on human beings to labor to "better their condition" and thereby advance the wealth of nations. Smith has in fact been widely criticized for his constant recourse to nature as an impersonal authority that can supplant the need for conscious actions undertaken by political agencies.[30] Nature for Smith seems to mean the way something operates "of its own accord" (*WN* II.v.31, IV.ii.13, IV.v.1.33), without the intrusion of human violence, plan, constraint, artifice, or custom (I.i.4, I.xi.m.9, I.xi.p.8, II.v.32, IV.iii.c.2, V.ii.k.3).

The core accusation leveled by Marx at Smith and legions of other "bourgeois economists" is that they use nature, and/or the liberal political framework of "Freedom, Equality, Property," as masks to conceal economic oppression: the exploitative tyranny by which "capital," like a vampire, brutally appropriates the time and energy of the proletarian masses.[31] Smith might reply with the following points: that the main alternative to commercial society is feudalistic oppression, in which economic power (control of land) translates openly into robust political power (III.ii, III.iv.5–7, V.i.b.7); that the main alternative (within commercial society) to natural liberty is a system of mercantilist privileges that benefit the few at the expense of the many; that in commercial society, *everyone* is dependent on "the assistance and cooperation of many thousands" (I.i.11, I.ii.2, III.iv.11–12); and that certain types of freedom must be diminished or deemphasized if the human species is to advance steadily in population, wealth, security, technology, and scientific knowledge.

In *The Wealth of Nations*, Smith's sole discussion of "the wisdom of nature" (a pervasive theme in *The Theory of Moral Sentiments*) identifies the drive to better one's condition as "a principle of preservation" that maintains the natural progress of the "political body" toward wealth and prosperity (*WN* IV.ix.28). The system of natural liberty, we may infer, helps convert the individual's desire for preservation into the wealth of the nation and the multiplication of the species.[32] Natural liberty in effect augments a Lockean imperative—"securing to every man the fruits of his own industry" (IV.vii.c.54)—with

Machiavellian imperatives of expanding the realm of economic competition and causing more and more people to experience the pinch of economic necessity.[33] We might also infer that, by granting everyone the "liberty to manage their own affairs," the system of natural liberty helps people to comprehend and endorse a range of necessities, including the necessity of a government that uses punitive justice to enforce basic rights. In a variety of ways, therefore, Smith extends the transformation of violent aggrandizement by Machiavellian princes into peaceful acquisition by "the great body of the people." One would have to work harder, however, to unearth in Smith the Machiavellian enterprise of manipulating the popular humor, which craves security, to accept the necessity of ambition.

Despite his diverse and pervasive appropriations of nature, Smith is sometimes surprisingly frank about the coercive or hierarchical relationships that can prevail economically within a formal framework of equal rights. Smith defines exchange value as "command" over the labor of others (*WN* I.v.1); he asserts that workers in "all arts and manufactures" ordinarily need a "master to advance them the materials of their work, and their wages and maintenance till it be completed" (I.viii.8); he identifies merchants and manufacturers as the class of men who put "into motion the greater part of the useful labour of every society" (I.xi.p.10); he proclaims that in most countries landlords and capitalists "oppress" the workers (IV.vii.b.3); and he laments the debilitating effects of the division of labor on the intellectual, social, and martial virtues of "the great body of the people" (V.i.f.49–51).

Although formulations about necessity pervade *The Wealth of Nations,* Smith presents the natural as having less compulsive force than the necessary, and his numerous uncompromising generalizations—e.g., that "in every country it always is and must be the interest of the great body of the people to buy whatever they want of those who sell it cheapest" (IV.iii.c.10), that a famine in Europe "has never arisen from any other cause but the violence of government" (IV.v.b.5), and that "the affluence of the few supposes the indigence of the many" (V.i.b.2)—are coupled with an even larger number of equivocations and qualifications (e.g., his recourse to the word "perhaps"). The all-important economic principles he traces to the manifestly natural imperatives of subsistence and survival, furthermore, lose some of their status when he admits that customary objects of consumption may become "necessaries of life" (I.xi.c.7, V.ii.k.3,10–12). Obviously, philosophers, poets, priests, and politicians can do much more to shape culture than to shape biology. Even Marx concedes something to the power of habits, opinions, and expectations, despite the threat this concession poses to Marx's attempt to uncover economic laws of "iron necessity."[34] To complaints about his own indirectness, finally, Smith could reply that *The Theory of Moral Sentiments* and even *The Wealth of Nations* illuminate how nature pursues *its* dominant purposes—particularly the preservation and propagation of species—in various indirect processes that cannot but confuse human beings whose intellects, emotions, and bodies are so complexly interrelated. Most relevant is the central "Part" of *The Theory of Moral Sentiments,* which contains the book's one mention of the "invisible hand." After describing the "deception" whereby nature "rouses and keeps in continual motion the industry of mankind"—our efforts to subdue the earth, to "invent and improve all the sciences and arts, which ennoble and embellish human life"—Smith invokes the invisible hand, which uses the "luxury and caprice" of the rich to promote "the multiplication of the species" (*TMS* IV.1.10).[35]

PRIESTS, PROPHETS, AND PRINCES

To what degree does "the religious issue" illuminate Smith's anticlassical promotion of worldly gain and indirect government? Can we find in Smith evidence of the rationale Mansfield attempts to uncover in Machiavelli, Hobbes, and Locke: that opposition to Christianity inspired opposition to Aristotle? In attempting to adumbrate an answer to these questions, I shall discuss three themes: the profound but restrained atheism of *The Wealth of Nations,* the opposition to religious fanaticism which stands out in both of Smith's books, and Smith's indirect efforts to extinguish or conceal prophecy (religious and secular). By virtue of the first, Smith adopts the secularizing posture of Machiavelli's new modes and orders; by virtue of the second and third, Smith adapts the indirect government Hobbes, Locke, and others used (according to Mansfield) to prevent "the appropriation of the classical regime" by Christianity.

I have elsewhere argued at length that *The Wealth of Nations* is an atheistic book. This argument has aroused some opposition, but there is no need to recount it here. There is also no need to belabor the meticulousness with which Smith composed his books and later revised them through multiple editions. For our purposes, the key point would be the subtlety of many of the devices Smith uses to intimate his views: the delicate manner in which *The Wealth of Nations* expels God from the cosmos and Jesus Christ from world history; the way it relentlessly but unobtrusively dismisses the prospects of an afterlife, submerging readers in the pedestrian affairs of this world; the way it calmly but cynically ridicules the claims of Christian churches and prelates to piety and holiness; the way it ignores or trivializes the Bible; the way it overlooks the contribution of ceremony and dogma to religious vitality; and the way it reduces the social benefits derived from religion to the moral training that accrues to ordinary people who belong to small sects, in which conduct and character are closely supervised. Smith's indirectness, particularly his use of omission and silence, may promote his intentions by effacing rather than highlighting the traditions he opposed.

Smith, however, neither advocates nor proclaims the elimination of religion, and he is sometimes willing to appropriate it for economic purposes.[36]

Despite their subtlety, the disparagements of religion conveyed by *The Wealth of Nations* are typically more explicit than those conveyed by Machiavelli, Hobbes, Spinoza, Locke, Montesquieu, or Rousseau; compared to such thinkers, indeed, Smith does less to counterbalance or conceal the disparagements by issuing professions that *appear* to be orthodox. Moreover, Smith in *The Wealth of Nations* seems to expect still less by way of social utility from religion than they expected. Such authors might be puzzled about why Smith would encourage the unshackling of the desire for wealth, while abandoning robust religious safeguards as well as the Machiavellian remedy (terror) for corruption. Perhaps Smith thought that the ongoing progress of modernity, if augmented by his system of natural liberty, could deliver sufficient types and quantities of both worldly satisfaction and civic virtue (Smith's historicist side is advertised in his claim that a nation's "style of manners" is generally "suitable" to that nation's "situation" [*TMS* V.2.13]). Even if this explanation is sound, however, a major puzzle remains: how to reconcile the atheistic *Wealth of Nations* with the deistic *Theory of Moral Sentiments*. The puzzle might wither if one were to follow Mansfield—and arouse the indignation of leading scholars of eighteenth-century thought—in trivializing the difference between atheism and deism.[37] One could also argue that Smith regarded deism as a resting point along a longer and more arduous path from revealed religion to atheism. But the religious tone retained by the revised editions of *The Theory of Moral Sentiments* produced *after* the publication of *The Wealth of Nations* in 1776 suggests a more complicated situation. And the differences between his two books remain so broad and, at times, so deep, that it is unwise to assume that Smith regarded the distinction between atheism and deism as inconsequential. Finally, although one must concede that *The Theory of Moral Sentiments* pushes the majesty and utility of *belief* in an afterlife harder than it pushes the *reality* of an afterlife, the prospect of divine reward and punishment imparts vitality to its deism.

Even though *The Theory of Moral Sentiments* conveys a residue of respect for revealed religion that is extinguished in *The Wealth of Nations*, Smith consistently rejects the prospect that God has participated in human affairs via covenant, incarnation, inspiration, prophecy, or any kind of miraculous intervention. Smith's books are also united in highlighting the dangers of religious fanaticism and partisanship. It is no surprise that a "pure and rational" religion, for Smith, would be "free from every mixture of absurdity, imposture, or fanaticism" (*WN* V.i.g.8), and that "the good temper and moderation of contending factions seems to be the most essential circumstance in the publick morals of a free people" (V.i.f.40). It is likewise no surprise that he condemns the Crusades (III.iii.14), the Christian sanctification of unjust conquests in the New World (IV.vii.a.15-17), the "disorder and injustice" of religious persecution (IV.vii.b.61), "the poison of enthusiasm and superstition" (V.i.g.14), and "those absurd and hypocritical austerities which fanatics inculcate and pretend to practice" (V.i.g.34). It may be a surprise, however, that Smith, in lambasting otherworldliness and asceticism, lauds the "liberal, generous, and spirited conduct" endorsed by the moral philosophy of the ancient Greeks (V.i.f.30), and that he invokes Greek natural philosophy in lambasting the scholastic exaltation of "Metaphysicks or Pneumaticks" (V.i.f.28).

Smith's suggestions about the interplay between politics and religion are even more distinctive. Typically, times of "violent religious controversy" include "equally violent political faction," prompting political parties to ally themselves with religious sects (*WN* V.i.g.7–8); from explaining the alliances of party and sect, Smith proceeds to identifying party and sect (V.i.g.33).[38] The specific entanglements of Christianity in the politics of Europe, moreover, explain why the medieval church became perhaps "the most formidable combination that ever was formed against the authority and security of civil government" (V.i.g.24). Although some Protestant arrangements may be benign and even salutary—Smith issues striking praise for the Presbyterian clergy of Holland, Geneva, Switzerland, and Scotland (V.i.g.37–38)—the Reformation was pursued with "that enthusiastic zeal which commonly animates the spirit of party" when attacking established authority, and its biggest weapon was its "zealous, passionate, and fanatical" rhetoric (V.i.g.29).

In elaborating the consequences of the Reformation, Smith provides the book's major statement about the desirability of elections. By granting parishioners "the right of electing their own pastor," Calvinist churches invited rampant "disorder and confusion" and the "corruption" of morals in both clergy and people: the people typically were manipulated by "the most factious and fanatical" pastors; the clergy, pursuing influence over the elections, often became (or pretended to become) fanatical and often encouraged "fanaticism among the people" (V.i.g.35–36). Smith completely ignores the Calvinist vision of rule by a Godly or saintly elect.

These remarks in effect prepare the reflections on union, aristocracy, and democracy that conclude *The Wealth of Nations,* reflections that are redolent with theological-political implications. Political union among Britain, Ireland, and the American colonies (V.iii.68) would bring Ireland "advantages much more important" than freedom of trade. Just as union with England delivered Scotland from an oppressive aristocracy based on "the natural and respectable distinctions of birth and fortune," it would liberate Ireland from the "much more oppressive aristocracy" based on "the most odious of all distinctions, those of religious and political prejudices" (V.iii.89). One might infer that although Smith's earlier accounts of the political authority based on the "respectable" distinctions of birth and fortune would strike most oligarchs or

aristocrats as disrespectful,[39] such distinctions shine in comparison to the political-religious nexus. Smith nowhere specifies the content of these "prejudices," what it is that unites religion and politics, or why they spawn such odious divisions. He says only that religious and political prejudices, more than
any other distinctions, "animate both the insolence of the oppressors and the
hatred and indignation of the oppressed" (V.iii.89).

Smith's next paragraph, however, elaborates his proposal for union with
remarks about *American* democracy that may help us resolve our puzzle.
Union would benefit the colonies because it would "deliver them from those
rancorous and virulent factions which are inseparable from small democracies"; total separation from Britain, correspondingly, would probably end in
"open violence and bloodshed" among the different states and factions.
Union would help because the "spirit of party" is generally weaker in an empire's *provinces:* their distance from the capital, "from the principal seat of
the great scramble of faction and ambition, makes them enter less into the
views of any of the contending parties, and renders them more indifferent
and impartial spectators of the conduct of all" (*WN* V.iii.90). This passage
would stand out merely because it contains the sole allusion in *The Wealth
of Nations* to the "impartial spectator," who, as portrayed in *The Theory of
Moral Sentiments,* plays a decisive role in determining the moral worth of
human actions, emotions, and character traits. There is more at stake, however. From Smith's reservations about democracy, coupled with his apparent
indulgence of a natural aristocracy—those "ambitious and high-spirited
men" who will "draw the sword in defence of their own importance"
(IV.vii.c.74)—one may infer that Smith wishes at least "the great body of the
people" to be absorbed in bettering their condition by lengthy, laborious industry and to be insulated from the "the great scramble of faction and ambition" (V.iii.90) and the other intoxicating elixirs of politics: "splendour and
glory," the "dazzling objects of ambition," the "dazzling object" amidst "the
confused scramble of politics and war," "a thousand visionary hopes of conquest and national glory," "the splendid and showy equipage of empire,"
and so on.[40]

Regarding the "odious" character of certain religious and political distinctions (*WN* V.iii.89), we may further infer that the groupings and subordination
they spawn tend to be, from Smith's perspective, excessively direct, personal,
and divisive. Smith's remarks about America (V.iii.90), meanwhile, support
the hypothesis that he is wary of politics and religion because they both encourage people to pay excessive attention to "wholes." While politics tanta-
lizes us with glory, conquest, and empire, religion—especially the nondeistic
versions that provoked opposition from so many modern philosophers—
attracts us to even larger concerns. Smith elaborates and endorses nature's efforts to direct "the principal attention of each individual to that particular portion of it [the great society of mankind], which was most within the sphere

both of his abilities and of his understanding" (*TMS* VI.ii.2.4); we should en-trust "the good of the whole" to nature's wisdom (VII.ii.1.44–45).[41] Smith per-haps reveals more about his hopes for the future than about his interpretation of the past when he argues that clashing assessments of "the conduct of a third person" or of a "system of philosophy"—apparently even a system that portrays the universe as a "great machine" actuated by "secret wheels and springs"—are unlikely to spur "quarreling" because neither party "can rea-sonably be much interested about them" (I.i.4.2–5).

Smith states that "the great source of both the misery and disorders of human life, seems to arise from over-rating the difference between one per-manent situation and another" (*TMS* III.3.31). For many Christians, of course, heaven and hell constitute "permanent situations" whose difference cannot be overrated. Hence the attractions for Smith of Stoicism, which regards life as a "mere two-penny stake; a matter by far too insignificant to merit any anxious concern" (VII.ii.1.24). In the only chapter or section of Smith's cor-pus that begins with the word "religion," Christianity is initially identified as a sect (III.6.1) and thereafter represented by bigotry and bloody persecution coupled with ridicule of "our Saviour's precept" (turning the other cheek).[42]

The impartial spectator is itself vulnerable to the corrupting effects of reli-gious-based fanaticism: although a reliable remedy to the conflicts of daily life, the impartial spectator is "never at a greater distance than amidst the vi-olence and rage of contending parties," which impute their prejudices to God and "often view that Divine Being as animated by all their own vindic-tive and implacable passions" (*TMS* III.3.43). Here the political-religious nexus appears as the infusion of divine sanction into vicious party disputes. Smith concludes that "of all the corrupters of our moral sentiments . . . fac-tion and fanaticism have always been by far the greatest."[43] In a section of the book added in 1790, however, Smith introduces a different assessment, identifying the disposition to admire wealth and greatness as "the great and most universal cause of the corruption of our moral sentiments" (I.iii.3.1–2). This contradiction, which emerges from Smith's warning his readers of the morally corrupting effects of the ends to which his own science of political economy is devoted, suggests that he regards such corruption as an antidote to a more dangerous corruption associated with religion.

Let us return to the most vituperative remark in Smith's whole corpus: that the church during its heyday "may be considered as the most formidable combination that ever was formed against . . . the liberty, reason, and hap-piness of mankind" (*WN* V.i.g.24). However exaggerated, the accusation is more plausible than what Smith says to explain how the Church became so powerful and how its power ultimately withered. His answers to these ques-tions illuminate his larger strategy of using economic and historical consid-erations both to denude religion of its theological content and to eliminate or conceal the role of prophetic phenomena in shaping human history.

In the aftermath of the chaos brought to Europe by the barbarian invasions, land—the great source of authority and order—was up for grabs (*WN* III.iii.1, III.ii.3, III.iv.7). Under these circumstances, the church was granted (out of "mistaken piety") large tracts that provided it with surplus wealth. This wealth, subsequently augmented by tithes, enabled the clergy, like the feudal barons, to keep the peace in their dominions.[44] Clerical "hospitality and charity," particularly in feeding "the common people," thus brought the priests great "temporal force," but also "increased very much the weight of their spiritual weapons," enhancing the "respect and veneration" they received (V.i.g.22). This exceptional power, which could have "endured forever," was a fusion of bread and spirit: in Smith's words, of "private interests" and "delusions of superstition" (V.i.g.24–25). Even in his day, the institutions of the Catholic church, by engaging clerical "self-interest," did an impressive job of sustaining "the industry and zeal of the inferior clergy"; blandly citing and summarizing Machiavelli's sinister appraisal of the Franciscan and Dominican reformers in *Discourses* III:1, Smith invokes the necessity typically faced by Catholic "parochial clergy" of deriving "a very considerable part of their subsistence from the voluntary oblations of the people" (the acquisitive efforts of the priests were enhanced by confession; V.i.g.2). We may infer that, in Smith's view, the Catholic superstitions were no more captivating than those of other religions except insofar as they were enhanced by the zeal and industry of the inferior clergy. Uniquely Catholic, however, were the "ties of private interest" that came from feeding the people; Smith later invokes the special institutional structures that enabled the clergy to operate effectively as "a sort of spiritual army" under the pope (V.i.g.21).[45]

Smith does state that the authority of every "established" clergy "depends upon the supposed certainty and importance of the whole doctrine which they inculcate" and the "supposed necessity" that people adopt it in order to avoid "eternal misery" (*WN* V.i.g.17). Compared to Hobbes, who conducted, and encouraged others to conduct, an assault on the "fear of powers invisible," Smith avoids a direct confrontation with religious fears.[46] It is difficult to specify the mixture Smith expected his rhetoric to establish among the following sorts of effects: tempering the ardor of readers whose religion was tainted by terror, fanaticism, enthusiasm, or superstition; captivating readers whose religion was already sufficiently tame; and educating the latter (in addition to their more skeptical brethren) about ways of tempering the ardor of the zealous. Smith discourages sovereigns from "instructing the people" about "spiritual matters" (V.i.g.18), and instead seems to explore institutional arrangements—including techniques of "managing" the clergy—that governments could implement to ameliorate or prevent abuses.[47]

In explaining the church's rise and its abiding global impact, devout Catholics would be tempted to invoke interventions by God, including revelations, miracles, and the sacrifice of his son. But Protestants and even secular historians would be tempted to invoke the contribution of religious sentiment as stirred by such things as ceremony, worship, piety, doctrine, charisma, and "the Word made flesh." Smith instead stresses the ways in which "private interest" and "self interest" bound the people to the church and brought the priests the unity and energy needed to acquire and maintain power. Although Smith follows Machiavelli by invoking the poverty of the Franciscans and Dominicans, he omits Machiavelli's comment about their imitation of the *vita di Cristo*. Smith's posture toward what he describes as the "parties or sects" spawned by the Reformation is friendlier, but here too he dwells upon institutional structures at the expense of divine intervention, theological truth, or even religious sentiment (V.i.g.29–38).[48]

Smith's explanation of the church's *decline* is just as idiosyncratic. With the development of foreign trade, the clergy could selfishly squander, on "trinkets and baubles," the surplus wealth they previously used to feed the indigent.[49] The trinkets and baubles were supplied by "the gradual improvements of arts, manufactures, and commerce"—by the "natural course of things." Nature and commerce thus succeeded in breaking the ties of interest that bound the common people to the clergy, and therefore in unraveling "that immense and well-built fabric, which all the wisdom and virtue of man could never have shaken."[50]

Smith's antichurch rhetoric was a commonplace of the Enlightenment, but his explanation of the church's demise would seem to counteract the commonplace Enlightenment expectation that human "wisdom and virtue" can be wielded to ameliorate and perhaps eliminate superstition, fanaticism, and various forms of oppression. In exalting the contribution of nature, Smith depreciates various human initiatives we normally associate with the decay of the church's temporal authority: the schemes of princes, the discoveries of scientists, the writings of philosophers, the sermons of reformers.

Needless to say, Smith's sketch of modernity's development clashes with the account offered by Mansfield, who presents secularization and indirect government as strategies undertaken consciously, if not conspiratorily, in response to the political intrusions of the church.[51] Insofar as Smith denies the singular causes of clerical power, including potent Christian doctrines such as providence and original sin, he would be inclined to deny the efficacy (and perhaps the existence) of the doctrinal responses concocted by Machiavelli and his successors. Smith's books and essays cite major texts by prominent thinkers—among them, Thucydides, Plato, Aristotle, Polybius, Cicero, Machiavelli, Bacon, Descartes, Grotius, Hobbes, Locke, Montesquieu, Hume, and Rousseau—and his discussion of Machiavelli's *Discourses* is provocative, but it is difficult to determine, regarding many of these authors, how deeply he delved into their teachings. Even if we cannot now specify Smith's "rank" in Machiavelli's army, we can easily link many of Smith's doctrines to Machiavelli and/or his alleged captains, especially when those doctrines are juxtaposed to classical and Christian views. His rejection of Christianity, moreover, is far more emphatic than his rejection of the classical tradition; this divergence supports Mansfield's thesis that "the religious issue" inspired modern efforts to promote worldly gain and indirect government.

When Machiavelli proclaims the failure of unarmed prophets (*The Prince,* chap. 6), the reader must wonder about the apparent success of Jesus Christ and about Machiavelli's own efforts to promote new modes and orders. Smith's posture toward Jesus is so exaggerated that one can hardly avoid imputing to Smith a rhetorical intention. Smith offers various summaries of world history, including the history of Christianity, but one can read every word he ever penned—every extant book, manuscript, essay, and letter—without encountering Jesus of Nazareth. One striking example is Smith's discussion of the first three "great revolution[s] in the affairs of mankind of which history has preserved any distinct and circumstantial account": Philip's conquest of the Greek Republics, Rome's ascendancy over Carthage, and the fall of the Western empire (*WN* V.i.a.29, 30, 36). To this one must reply that, even from a secular perspective, history seems to have "preserved" a "distinct and circumstantial account" of another "great revolution in the affairs of mankind" between the rise and fall of the Roman empire. Elsewhere, Smith goes so far as to mistranslate, by removing two references to Jesus Christ, a long passage he quotes from a French bishop (Jean Baptiste Massillon; *TMS* III.2.34). Even the latitudinarian Protestants of Smith's day did not erase Jesus' claims as a Messiah, and who but Smith erased the human Jesus?

Operating on a more general level, Smith's four-stages theory goes beyond secularism—it incorporates neither purposes nor interventions that arise from God—to elevate causes that operate both gradually and impersonally. When he explains momentous historical developments, he typically deprecates the contribution of human intention and foresight (*WN* I.ii.1, III.iv.10 and 17, IV.vii.a.21, IV.vii.c.80, V.i.a.43). Smith, however, sometimes hints at a broader view. For example, the "Article" on religion in *The Wealth of Nations* occurs in book V, chapter 1 ("Of the Expences of the Sovereign or Commonwealth"), and is preceded by sections on defense, justice, and other "publick Works and publick Institutions" (including educational institutions). These previous sections, however, periodically assess the appropriateness of governmental duties within specific stages along the path toward civilization and opulence. But the article on religion—"Of the Expence of the Institutions for the Instruction of People of All Ages"—never utilizes the four stages in this way. One may hypothesize that the sovereign's situation regarding religion has been conditioned if not created by historical developments that cannot be deduced from the "natural progress of opulence." The religion article is likewise distinguished from the rest of the chapter (V.i) by the paucity of its attention to ancient Greece and Rome. Apparently, something happened in the aftermath of antiquity that changed the rules of the game.

Smith's most explicit acknowledgment of prophet-like interventions comes in a passage he added for the 1790 edition of *The Theory of Moral Sentiments*. Speculating in general terms about "the greatest revolutions . . . in the situations and opinions of mankind," Smith asserts that such revolutions have been created by the "founders and leaders of the most numerous and successful sects and parties" as well as by warriors, statesmen, and legislators (VI.iii.28). The "excessive presumption" of such initiators (he mentions Alexander, Socrates, and Caesar) may approach "insanity and folly" and is displayed when they claim a connection with the divine. By proceeding to mention "Prophets" in connection with "the religion and manners of modern times," Smith hints venomously at the impact of Jesus.

Smith's invocation of Machiavelli's *Discourses* in explaining the longevity of church power (*WN* V.i.g.2) is complemented in *The Theory of Moral Sentiments* by the assertion that Hobbes self-consciously formulated doctrines to address theological-political circumstances. It was "the avowed intention" of Hobbes, by propagating his accounts of "self-love" and absolute sovereignty, "to subject the consciences of men immediately to the civil, and not to the ecclesiastical powers, whose turbulence and ambition, he had been taught, by the example of his own times, to regard as the principal source of the disorders of society" (*TMS* VII.iii.2.2).[52] It is reasonable to suggest that Smith sculpted *The Theory of Moral Sentiments* with the hope of completing the liberation of the conscience from "ecclesiastical powers" by subjecting it to nature (via the impartial spectator) rather than the sovereign.

Reflecting on the exaggerations we have been exploring, we must ask why Smith would understate the contribution of charismatic individuals and overstate the gradual and impersonal influence of economic "interests." If we accept Mansfield's account of why and how Machiavelli, joined by various successors, appropriated Christian doctrine, we might hypothesize that Smith, by more or less erasing Christian doctrine—and by using political economy to explain the power of the church—was trying to conceal a taming of religion that, in his mind, was already unfolding through changes in economic practices and ideas. Could he have thought that Machiavelli had succeeded in supplanting Jesus as an unarmed prophet? To the extent that Smith exaggerates the kingdom of nature and the impact of commerce, in any case, his own writings may be regarded as weapons in the battle against the imagined kingdom of God. Whatever the ultimate causes of the church's rise and fall, one may safely conclude that Smith intended his "sciences" of political economy, moral philosophy, and natural jurisprudence to shrink the ideological and institutional breeding ground for any further outbursts of enthusiasm, superstition, and persecution—and to ensure that "the liberty, reason, and happiness of mankind" would never again be crippled by a multinational "combination" (*WN* V.i.g.14).

Let us return to the connection, within Smith's thought, between the religious and political strands interwoven in Mansfield's "history" of secularization and indirect government. Obviously, the tools Smith employs in depreciating religion—primarily his quasi-materialistic philosophy of history, conveyed with the detached tone so prevalent in the social science of our day—are also integral to his exaltation of wealth, his abandonment of the classical quest to evaluate different forms of government, and his refusal to examine justice dialectically (by attempting to ascend from opinion to knowledge). Prophecy is lodged at the nexus of politics and religion, and Smith labors consistently to temper the motivations that inspire ambitious individuals to initiate or support grand transformations of human society. To acknowledge the new modes and orders Machiavelli attempted to legislate, or to highlight one's kinship to the *philosophes* of the Enlightenment, might help to sustain the burning embers of enthusiasm and to open human souls to the sudden, willful, and potentially shattering interventions of the biblical God. Smith would likewise need to mute if not conceal his own ambitions as a secular prophet of liberty, security, and prosperity.

By rejecting divine right, Smith has answered Mansfield's version of "the theologico-political question," but he has hardly resolved "the religious issue" by securing both freedom and "the highest human aspiration" (*America's Constitutional Soul* 101, 114). Should we therefore turn to Marxism? Marx not only labors to reappropriate nature from the liberal economists and philosophers who invoked it on behalf of competition, private property, and freedom of trade; he exhorts the proletariat to expropriate the capitalist class and thereby inaugurate "social" control of the means of production. Marx, however, also radicalizes most of Smith's departures from the classical and Christian traditions: it suffices to mention Marx's dogmatic dismissal of the superhuman and his preposterous prediction that the state will wither. In any case, the toll exacted on human "liberty, reason, and happiness" in our century by the international communist "combination" would itself require Smith to rethink his articulation of "the natural course of things" that he identifies with "the gradual improvements of arts, manufactures, and commerce." And how well could either philosopher explain the carnage people are still inflicting in the name of God? Compared to Marx, Smith is a formidable champion of freedom and divinity along with prosperity and the soul, but we also need guidance from wiser princes.

NOTES

1. Works by Harvey C. Mansfield, Jr. referred to throughout this chapter are as follows (in the order in which they first appear in the chapter): *Machiavelli's Virtue* (Chicago: University of Chicago Press, 1996); "Hobbes and the Science of Indirect Government," *American Political Science Review* 65 (1971); *Taming the Prince: The Ambivalence of Modern Executive Power* (New York: Free Press, 1989); *America's*

Constitutional Soul (Baltimore: Johns Hopkins University Press, 1991); *Machiavelli's New Modes and Orders* (Ithaca, N.Y.: Cornell University Press, 1979).

2. For other central invocations of the Aristotelian regime in Mansfield's corpus, see *Machiavelli's New Modes and Orders,* 30n4, 38n21, 43, 50, 116, 117n10, 184; *Machiavelli's Virtue,* 235–38, 282–86, 291–94; *America's Constitutional Soul,* 204–5; and "On the Political Character of Property in Locke," in A. Kontos, ed., *Powers, Possessions, and Freedom* (Toronto: University of Toronto Press, 1979), 26.

3. The regime is not "some hidden essence lying behind its territory and people. . . . It is publicly visible in its offices and in the characteristic behavior of its rulers as its ordering (*taxis*)." The rulers neither need nor desire to conceal their rule. Even though there are hidden powers in every society that may temporarily "determine the rule," such powers remain hidden because "they are weaker than the power that does not have to hide" (*Machiavelli's Virtue,* 283, 236). For Leo Strauss's articulation of the classical approach to regimes, see *The City and Man* (Chicago: Rand McNally, 1964), 34–35, 45–48; and *What Is Political Philosophy?* (Glencoe, Ill.: Free Press, 1959), 33–34, 85–86.

4. "The Theologico-Political Executive" is both the title of Mansfield's fourth chapter and the last subtitle of his third chapter (*Taming the Prince,* 85). Mansfield goes on to say, regarding Marsilius's doctrine of "ecclesiastical polity," that it is unclear whether for Marsilius the new doctrine is "an act of prudence" required only in the circumstances facing Marsilius or whether it is "a part of political philosophy essential in any time or place, which Aristotle was able to take for granted in his own singular situation" (104–5). Mansfield's footnote helpfully calls attention to the phrase "within the confines of political philosophy," which appears several times in Strauss's essay on Marsilius (316n32).

5. To defend such a hypothesis, of course, one must first present a definitive interpretation of Machiavelli's texts, and no one could deprecate the energy or acuity that Mansfield has brought to the task. On various occasions, indeed, Mansfield conveys an admirable modesty about the difference between interpreting texts to uncover the intentions of their authors and demonstrating the causes that have shaped history. E.g., in studying executive power in America, "I cannot attempt to perform the historian's task of discovering what influenced the Framers," even if historians have lacked "full awareness of the nature of executive power or the history of its doctrine" (*Taming the Prince,* 248); to address "the causes of the [American] Revolution would require a historical study beyond my capacity" (*The Spirit of Liberalism* [Cambridge, Mass.: Harvard University Press, 1978], 78).

6. Whereas the essays collected in *America's Constitutional Soul* highlight various advantages of modern liberal constitutionalism, perhaps Mansfield's early work on representation suggests a narrower gulf between classical and Christian thought. In 1968, he wrote that government by divine right, although it is "the prototype" of nonrepresentative government, "seems to be compatible with any of Aristotle's constitutions of government"; in a Puritan democracy, e.g., the majority would be free to impose severe moral sanction on the entire community in God's name ("Modern and Medieval Representation," in J. Roland Pennock and John Chapman, eds., *Nomos XI: Representation* [New York: Atherton, 1968], 66–67). Coming from the sublime appreciation of the "forms and formalities" of modern constitutionalism that informs *Amer-*

ica's Constitutional Soul, likewise, the reader might be surprised by the opening of the 1971 article on Hobbes, where Mansfield seems to fault the indirect, representative government that prevails in the contemporary world because such government depreciates the "direct political question." The direct question is whether "the law or the command by an officer of the law that a citizen encounters is decent, good, or useful" ("Hobbes and the Science of Indirect Government," 97). In any case, *Taming the Prince* does reiterate the distinction between ancient ruling and modern representing (15, 29).

7. Mansfield's most concentrated analysis of the institutional mechanisms of indirect government comes in "Machiavelli's New Regime," the tenth chapter in *Machiavelli's Virtue.* Mansfield here highlights the gap between the maxims in *Discourses* I:7–8 concerning accusation and calumny and the details about Coriolanus and Manlius as portrayed in the original texts of Livy (and as noted by Machiavelli elsewhere in *The Discourses*). It turns out that accusation "is more an order or arrangement than a precise law" because it "depends on enforcement by prudent princes whose prudence seems very unobtrusive" (243); Mansfield later sketches a variety of institutional "disguises" under which the "kingly arm" of the Senate ruled the Roman republic (247–53). Cf. *Machiavelli's New Modes and Orders,* 60.

8. Machiavelli, *Discourses on Livy,* trans. by Harvey C. Mansfield and Nathan Tarcov (Chicago: University of Chicago Press, 1996), 177. "A dominion they do not see" translates *uno dominio che non veggano.*

9. We cannot here scrutinize the chapter in *Taming the Prince* on Montesquieu, another predecessor of Adam Smith whom Mansfield uses to explain the development of Machiavelli's new modes and orders into liberalism and constitutionalism. On Spinoza's role in the saga, see *America's Constitutional Soul,* 108–11.

10. As Mansfield elsewhere observes, the point of Locke's famous passage on the loaf of bread (*Second Treatise,* sec. 43) is not the division of labor, as often proclaimed, but "the mixing and reconstitution of natural materials in a human product that sums them up"; men do not "seek out and assume the purposes of nature so as to carry them out" ("On the Political Character of Property in Locke" 35), but are forced to remedy the defect of their natural inheritance by acquiring with "their own arms."

11. The rule of law for Locke is rule by "*declared laws*" of the legislative power "which must therefore be both supreme and public"; it is the "rule of lawmaking by a *due process* visible to all" (*America's Constitutional Soul,* 113; emphases his).

12. Locke condones such manifestations of "arbitrary power" (*Second Treatise,* secs. 166, 210) by nodding toward Machiavellian movement—"Things of this world are in so constant a flux that nothing remains long in the same state" (157)—rather than toward the Aristotelian critique of law's generality (that law cannot allow for the best case; *Taming the Prince,* 202–3). Mansfield also faults Locke's regime for its inability to mimic the Aristotelian regime by providing a model for the soul; without the "possibility" of kingship over all, people lose the sense of responsibility for a whole that comprises both desire and necessity (211).

13. The concluding section on Locke in *Taming the Prince* addresses some difficulties posed by Locke's *Essay Concerning Human Understanding* for his *Two Treatises on Government.* Mansfield continues to emphasize Locke's effort to combat "religious fervor" and to ensure "the exclusion of revelation from political life" (208–9). He elsewhere asserts that Locke, by examining distinct disciplines (politics, psychol-

ogy/epistemology, and biblical criticism) in separate books, does not force his read-
ers "to confront the religious issue and to oppose religion with constitutionalism"
(*America's Constitutional Soul,* 111). On the theological-political issues in Locke,
one should also consult the comprehensive account in Thomas Pangle, *The Spirit of
Modern Republicanism* (Chicago: University of Chicago Press, 1988), 131–275; for
Pangle's criticisms of Mansfield, see 307n4.

14. Locke, *Second Treatise,* sec. 7; Mansfield, *Taming the Prince,* 196. The remarks
about *thumos,* "naysaying," and bodily separateness in *Taming the Prince* warrant a
longer discussion than there is here space to provide. For a preliminary account, see
18, 23, 35, 37, 49–51, 66, 116, 127, 237, 245, and the extensive cross-referencing in the
index. On the implications for slavery, see 304n8 and "On the Political Character of
Property in Locke," 26–28, 36.

15. Locke, *Second Treatise,* secs. 17, 174, 193–94; Mansfield, "On the Political
Character of Property in Locke," 37.

16. Mansfield, "On the Political Character of Property in Locke," 32; *America's
Constitutional Soul,* 207.

17. Mansfield, "On the Political Character of Property in Locke," 38; Locke, *Second
Treatise,* secs. 221–22 (cf. 208).

18. Smith's works will be cited according to the system employed in the Glasgow
Edition of the Works and Correspondence of Adam Smith, published by Oxford University Press, 1976–1987, and reprinted by Liberty Press. *WN = An Inquiry into the Nature and Causes of the Wealth of Nations* (first published in 1776), ed. R. H. Campbell
and A. S. Skinner; *TMS = The Theory of Moral Sentiments* (first published in 1759), ed.
A. L. Macfie and D. D. Raphael; *LJA* and *LJB = Lectures on Jurisprudence,* student notes
from 1762–63 and 1766, ed. R. L. Meek, D. D. Raphael, and P.G. Stein.

19. I have examined Smith at length in my *Profits, Priests, and Princes: Adam
Smith's Emancipation of Economics from Politics and Religion* (Stanford, Calif.:
Stanford University Press, 1993). Other books that stress Smith's efforts to deflect political philosophy toward economics include the following: Joseph Cropsey, *Polity
and Economy* (The Hague: Martinus Nijhoff, 1957), and *Political Philosophy and the
Issues of Politics* (Chicago: University of Chicago Press, 1977), 53–89; Vivienne Brown,
Adam Smith's Discourse: Canonicity, Commerce, and Conscience (London: Routledge, 1994); Stewart Justman, *The Autonomous Male of Adam Smith* (Norman: University of Oklahoma Press, 1993); and Peter McNamara, *Political Economy and Statesmanship: Smith, Hamilton, and the Foundation of the Commercial Republic* (Dekalb,
Ill.: Northern Illinois University Press, 1998). Books that interpret Smith as conveying
a more comprehensive treatment of politics include Athol Fitzgibbons, *Adam Smith's
System of Liberty, Wealth, and Virtue* (Oxford: Oxford University Press, 1995); Knud
Haakonssen, *The Science of a Legislator* (Cambridge: Cambridge University Press,
1981); Jerry Z. Muller, *Adam Smith in His Time and Ours: Designing the Decent Society* (New York: Free Press, 1993); and Donald Winch, *Adam Smith's Politics* (Cambridge: Cambridge University Press, 1978). A sophisticated recent addition to the literature is Charles L. Griswold Jr., *Adam Smith and the Virtues of Enlightenment*
(Princeton, N.J.: Princeton University Press, 1999). For additional reflections by me on
the evolution of political philosophy from Machiavelli to Marx, see "Machiavellianism
Come of Age? Leo Strauss on Modernity and Economics," *Political Science Reviewer*
22 (1993): 157–97.

20. Machiavelli, Hobbes, and Locke anticipated Smith's approach in various respects. Mansfield has written more than enough to demonstrate Machiavelli's pervasive effort to blur the distinction between king and tyrant, not to mention the distinction between principality and republic; recall his argument that Machiavelli reduced the "boastful claims of regimes . . . to their capacity to produce palpable and beneficial effects" (*Taming the Prince,* 137). Along these lines one could also invoke the brief and perfunctory character of Locke's chapter, "Of the Forms of a Commonwealth" (*Second Treatise,* chap. 10), in which the distinctiveness among the different forms is so trivialized that Locke, despite the polemics that he conducts in the rest of the *Second Treatise,* seems to condone absolute monarchy. In *Leviathan,* Hobbes deemphasizes the distinctions among the forms of government—and ridicules the Aristotelian effort to determine whether regimes are *orthos* based on their attachment to the common good (*Politics* 1279a25–31)—but Hobbes provides a modest analysis and evaluation of the forms in chap. 19.

21. *WN* IV.vii.c.74. Smith's largest appropriation of Aristotelian terminology comes in a section of *TMS* added in 1790. Particularly relevant are his definition of "constitution," his agenda for "the highest effort of political wisdom," and his encomium to "the reformer and legislator of a great state" (*TMS* VI.ii.2.7, 12, 14).

22. In his jurisprudence lectures, Smith does articulate the Humean critique that contract theory is untenable because it clashes with history (*LJA* iv.19, v.114–19, v.127–89; *LJB* 15–18); the lectures also provide a fuller account of the forms of government (*LJA* iv.1–179; *LJB* 12–64), culminating in a detailed and sympathetic analysis of English political institutions (*LJA* v.5–31). Without here entering into a longer polemic I have provided elsewhere about how much priority should be assigned to these lectures, let me point out only that Smith doggedly arranged to have his own notes, along with all but a few of the other unpublished documents he had written, burned upon his death. Two sets of student notes to his classes at Glasgow University were subsequently discovered and published, one in 1896 (*LJB*) and the other in 1978 (*LJA*); for a detailed analysis of the lectures that emphasizes their disjunction from *WN* and *TMS,* see Brown, *Adam Smith's Discourse,* 100–42. Even in the lectures, finally, Smith does not so much evaluate the different forms as illuminate the historical phenomena that spawn them.

23. Smith in *TMS* asserts that "Kings are the servants of the people, to be obeyed, resisted, deposed, or punished, as the public conveniency may require" (I.iii.2.3), but he nowhere insists on mechanisms by which the public will may be formulated, voiced, or provided with institutional power. *LJB* 91–99 does provide a qualified endorsement of the "right of resistance."

24. *WN* II.ii.94, IV.ii.42, IV.v.b.16, IV.ix.51. Echoing Montesquieu, Smith identifies the liberty of the individual with "the sense which he has of his own security" (V.i.b.25). On Montesquieu, see *Taming the Prince,* 221–23, 234.

25. Cf. *WN* IV.vii.c.52, V.ii.k.74. Smith does chastise absolute governments like those of Spain and Portugal for failing to provide the equality of rights that secures "to every man the fruits of his own industry" (IV.vii.c.54). Although France too is an "absolute" monarchy, it partakes of the security, legality, and gentleness that characterize the British system (IV.vii.b.52, V.ii.k.78). Smith is more explicit than Locke is in employing Britain as a model (on Locke, see *Taming the Prince,* 190–93).

26. Regarding economic theories, however, Smith proceeds in a more Aristotelian fashion. Although book IV of *WN* is dominated by criticisms of mercantilist opinions and policies—including denunciation of the fitness of merchants and manufacturers as rulers (IV.iii.c.9, IV.vii.b.11, IV.vii.c.104)—it offers some dispassionate and balanced assessments of the clash between two extant "systems of political economy," mercantilism and physiocracy. In any case, Smith's "system of natural liberty" drifts somewhat abstractly above or beneath the fray, with nature gaining credit that might, under an Aristotelian scheme, be granted to human groups that promulgate claims to rule.

27. Elsewhere in *WN,* Smith links justice and equality as pillars of the system of natural liberty (I.viii.36, IV.vii.c.87, IV.viii.30, IV.ix.3).

28. Although Smith in *TMS* treats justice (and a range of other virtues that *WN* depreciates) in much greater detail, an anticlassical thrust remains, including the eclipse of opinions about the whole by natural "moral sentiments." Needless to say, Smith's jurisprudence lectures, which correspond to the "theory" sketched at the conclusion of *TMS*—a theory of "the general principles which ought to run through, and be the foundation of, the laws of all nations"—convey an extensive analysis of justice.

29. On the tensions between "the ordinary laws of justice" and "reasons of state," see *WN* IV.v.b.39; on the contributions the executive power can make to despotism, see V.i.d.16; on the inherent role of the executive power in managing "the general revenue of the state," see V.i.d.18; on the contribution to liberty made by a representative assembly that "overawes the executive power," see IV.vii.b.51; on the role of legislators in a "free" government, see IV.vii.b.54; on the "management" of parliaments by British and French kings, see IV.vii.c.69, V.i.g.19; on the connection between military command and political authority, see V.i.a.26,40–41,V.i.b.7,11; on the historical development of representative institutions in the European monarchies, see III.iii.11.

30. One of the more comic instances of Smith's naturalism is his ironic invocation of nature—and his use of the passive voice—in the last sentence of *WN* book IV. About Montesquieu's poem to the Muses that commences the book on commerce (book XX) in *The Spirit of the Laws,* Mansfield observes: "The self-executing constitution needs to be set in work with a flick of its author's finger" (*Taming the Prince,* 244). Regarding Smith's system of natural liberty, the poetic contributions of the author are advertised only by his single reference to the "invisible hand," but his fingers were perhaps as busy as Montesquieu's. Cf. *Taming the Prince,* 167, 176–78 on Hobbes' posture as a "teacher of princes"; on the "poetry underlying modern prose," also see Strauss, *What Is Political Philosophy?,* 50.

31. Marx, *Capital,* trans. Ben Fowkes (New York: Random House, 1976), 280; cf. 279–80, 680, 719, 799, and 899, especially the remark about "silent compulsion" and "invisible threads." Space limitations do not permit me to address Mansfield's provocative article on Marx, in which he reconstructs the debate with Aristotle that infuses Marx's treatment of forms in *Capital* and suggests that Aristotle rather than Hegel is the book's main antagonist. See Mansfield, "Marx on Aristotle: Freedom, Money, and Politics," *The Review of Metaphysics* 34 (December, 1980): 351–67. On Marx, also see Minowitz, *Profits, Priests, and Princes,* chap. 11.

32. Cf. *WN* I.viii.22–23, 36–40; *TMS* II.ii.3.5, VI.ii.2.4.

33. *WN* I.vii.9 and 27, I.ix.20, I.x.c.1–2, I.xi.b.5, II.iii.12 and 36, III.ii.7–9, III.iii.12, III.iv.11–13, IV.ii.4 and 42, IV.v.b.3–4, V.i.e.30. Smith's possible use of the system of

natural liberty to conceal rule and to appropriate necessity is complemented by his attribution to "commercial society" of many features of what we today would call a capitalistic society. Commercial society, in which the division of labor is highly advanced and "every man thus lives by exchanging, or becomes in some measure a merchant" (I.iv.1), culminates the "natural" four-stage progress of social development.

34. The "value" of labor power, unlike that of other commodities, "contains a historical and moral element" (Marx, *Capital,* 275, 341, 376). On the compulsion exerted by economic laws, see 91–92, 381, 394–95, 465, 635, 739, 742, 783–84, 798–99, 927–30.

35. The chapter concludes by showing how intellectual models of the social mechanism can be employed to stimulate people's "interest" in the public welfare (*TMS* IV.1.11). Cf. Mansfield, *America's Constitutional Soul,* 82.

36. Consider Smith's application of the term "sacred" to property rights and economic liberty (*WN* I.x.c.12, I.xi.c.27, IV.vii.b.44). Smith is more imaginative when he employs Puritan language of piety, consecration, and profanity while assessing the contrasting effects of parsimony and prodigality on the accumulation of capital (II.iii.18–19); his account establishes a kind of eschatology, subordinating present enjoyment to a destiny linking "forefathers" with the future. One might also speculate about possible appropriations of Christianity in Smith's paeans to love and benevolence (*TMS* I.i.5.5, I.ii.5.1, III.6.1, VII.ii.3.4,14–15) and in his concern for "the great society of mankind." Along these lines, compare Mansfield, *America's Constitutional Soul,* 110, with the following passages: *WN* I.i.9, I.ii.4–5, I.viii.36, I.xi.p.9, V.i.f.28,51; *TMS* I.ii.2.6, III.2.20,35, VI.iii.31.

37. Mansfield boldly states that the "sole purpose" of the deist God is "to foreclose the possibility of any relation of governance between God and man, so as to destroy every system of divine right." In addition, he argues that deism can promote secularism, and comments pithily that "natural religion" combines "the power of the impotent, rational Aristotelian God" with "the reason of the mysterious, omnipotent Christian God" ("Modern and Medieval Representation" 71). Given the centrality of Scripture in Mansfield's above-discussed definition of "the theologico-political question" (*America's Constitutional Soul,* 101), he would judge that, even in *TMS,* Smith portrays men as ruling themselves rather than being ruled by "God or gods, hence by divine right."

38. In *TMS,* Smith likewise unites parties and sects (VI.iii.28), and implicitly defines a "heretic" as a person who belongs to the "weaker party" once violence has commenced (III.3.43).

39. *WN* V.i.b.7,8,11; cf. III.ii.1–7, III.iv.10, and the discussion above of the mastery and oppression implicit in modern economic relationships.

40. *WN* IV.vii.c.75,81,85; V.iii.37,92; cf. I.xi.c.36, III.3.15, IV.i.11,19; V.i.d.16; the parade of such terms is still longer in *TMS.* Even within the sphere of economics, Smith tends to demote "extensive projects," "golden dreams" (*WN* II.ii.69), "the grand and the marvellous" (II.ii.77), monopoly, pageantry, the precious metals, "glittering baubles," and wild speculation. On the faction and "clamour" that afflicted the democratic courts of Athens, see *WN* V.i.f.44.

41. In a similar spirit, *TMS* condemns reformers who attempt to "arrange" citizens as if they were chess pieces (VI.ii.2.17), and *WN* insists that "no human wisdom or knowledge could ever be sufficient" to provide the sovereign the capability of "su-

perintending the industry of private people" and "directing it towards the employments most suitable to the interest of the society" (IV.ix.51).

42. *TMS* III.6.12–13. Smith scholars who emphasize the diverse variants of Christianity that had emerged by the eighteenth century typically fail to assimilate his use here of "sect."

43. *TMS* III.3.43. Smith later highlights the vulnerability of "natural" sentiments and judgments to "a false religion" and "false notions of religion" (III.6.12).

44. The tenants on the land were "entirely dependent on their immediate lords, and therefore liable to be called out at pleasure, in order to fight in any quarrel in which the clergy might think proper to engage them" (*WN* V.i.g.22). On the contribution of land ownership to feudal and shepherd-stage authority, see *WN* III.ii.1–3, III.iv.5–10, V.i.b.7–12.

45. Smith says nothing to suggest Machiavelli's appreciation of how the church managed, via elections, to energize old "orders" with new lords or princes (*The Prince*, chaps. 11 and 19 [end].)

46. Recall Mansfield's above-discussed remarks about Locke's attempt to quell the terror encouraged by Machiavelli and Hobbes (*Taming the Prince*, 196).

47. *WN* V.i.g.8–9,12-20,26–34,37–38; cf. V.i.f.28–35,46,54–61.

48. A similar retreat from theology and philosophy to secular history may be uncovered in Smith's praise of the "pure and rational religion" (V.i.g.8)—Smith specifies the absence of "absurdity, imposture, or fanaticism" rather than the presence of any particular doctrines—and in his defense of religious toleration. Whereas Locke's *Letter on Toleration* offers sustained arguments that toleration would promote both salvation and civic health, Smith speculates only about the civic benefits, and his analysis proceeds hypothetically: he explains what "probably" would have occurred "if politicks had never called in the aid of religion" (*WN* V.i.g.8). Smith, however, had just finished describing why and how politics *did* summon religion. The firmest civic benefit of toleration, in any case, would be the attention to "character" that could, via the proliferation of small sects, prevent anomie among "the common people"; Smith seems indifferent to the content of their faith (V.i.g.9–12).

49. Smith explains the decline of the feudal nobility in similar terms (*WN* III.iv.4-17).

50. *WN* V.i.g.24–25. The key developments occurred "even before the time of the reformation" (V.i.g.28), although the Reformation further strengthened the hand of the state against the church (V.i.g.30).

51. Smith's debts to Montesquieu are widely acknowledged, although insufficiently fathomed. In Mansfield's words, Montesquieu strives "to reduce the intensity of the drama of modernity"; modernity did not begin "as a heroic project, but rather established itself insensibly through a series of unplanned, unlegislated causes" (*Taming the Prince*, 216).

52. Smith would presumably sympathize with Mansfield's emphasis on Hobbes' efforts to transfer from subjects to sovereigns the right to make private judgments about good and evil; for Mansfield, Hobbes was thereby appropriating, for worldly purposes, the Christian view of "human government as a necessary intermediary" that should serve as "the keeper of men's consciences and the interpreter of men's opinions" ("Hobbes and the Science of Indirect Government," 109–10).

PART III

AMERICA, CONSTITUTIONALISM, AND STATESMANSHIP

12

Things Which Independent States May of Right Do

Jeremy Rabkin

The United States is unlike other nations, we are often told, because it was founded on a universal doctrine, proclaimed in the country's founding document, the Declaration of Independence. Our founding doctrine of natural rights can be seen as a liberating doctrine. But it has often been dismissed, for that reason, as naive, unpolitical, or fanciful.

What most readers of the Declaration overlook, however, is that it actually starts and ends with a doctrine about international affairs. Whether that doctrine is finally seen as sunny and optimistic or as cold and calculating is open to question—and the question must shadow any conclusions one hazards about the significance of the Declaration's assertions regarding the natural rights of individuals.

I

The stirring rhetoric of the Declaration's final line—where its signers "mutually pledge" their lives, fortunes, and "sacred honor"—is merely a flourish to the preceding sentence. It is that next-to-last sentence that sums up the actual argument of the text. And the summation is notably legalistic in tone: As America's "political connection" with Great Britain "is and ought to be totally dissolved," the United States must "have full Power to levy War, conclude Peace, contract Alliances, establish Commerce, and to do all other Acts and Things which Independent States may of right do."

If the "rights" of independent states can be enumerated in such detail, then there must already be some body of law that governs the relations of states with each other. And that is just what the opening sentence of the Declaration asserts: "When in the course of human events, it becomes necessary for one people to dissolve the political bands which have connected them with another," the "one people" must then "assume among the Powers of the earth, the separate and equal station to which the Laws of Nature and of Nature's God entitle them. . . ." So there seems, indeed, to be a prior law, a law independent of human will, which guarantees to each independent nation a "separate and equal station" in the world.

Yet if "Nature's God" imposes a law for states—a sort of rudimentary international law—there appears (from the Declaration, at least) to be no comparable law for citizens in their own states. The famous second paragraph of the Declaration asserts, as "truths" which are "self-evident," that "all men are created equal," that they "are endowed by their Creator with certain unalienable rights," that governments are "instituted among Men" in order "to secure these rights . . . deriving their just powers from the consent of the governed." We hear about "rights" and "consent" but not about "law" in the discussion of government's relation with "the people."

The rest of the second paragraph follows in the same spirit. The "right of the People to alter or abolish" their government arises "whenever any Form of Government becomes destructive of these ends"—when government violates its "ends," not when it violates the law of nature. When government does abuse its "ends," the people may "institute new Government, laying its foundation on such principles and organizing its powers in such form, as to them shall seem most likely to effect their Safety and Happiness." The explicit teaching of the Declaration, then, is that in the international arena, there is a "Law of Nature and Nature's God," but in domestic constitutional arrangements, there is only "the consent of the governed" and a disputable opinion about what is "most likely to effect their Safety and Happiness" in the future.

At first sight, this seems a very strange doctrine—that a transcendent law governs the relations between independent states, while the relations of people to their own government are matters of opinion and choice. One might be tempted to dismiss it as a mere rhetorical flight in Jefferson's text. Yet the doctrine proved quite enduring. Fifty years later, James Kent, who was celebrated throughout the nineteenth century as the American successor to Blackstone, closely echoes Jefferson's Declaration in his *Commentaries on American Law*. Kent begins his comprehensive, wide-ranging commentary with an extended exposition of "the law of nations," in an ordering which suggests that the law of nations is somehow prior to the Constitution and the rest of American law. Kent then offers a summary of the relevant law that is virtually a paraphrase of the Declaration:

Nations are equal in respect to each other. . . . This perfect equality, and entire independence of all distinct states, is a fundamental principle of public law. It is a necessary consequence of this equality, that each nation has a right to govern itself as it may think proper, and no one nation is entitled to dictate a form of government, or religion, or a course of internal policy, to another.[1]

If one traces the argument back to earlier authorities, however, one finds that the version of "Nature's Law" invoked in the Declaration was by no means a long-established tradition in the law of nations. Grotius, writing in the early seventeenth century, discoursed at great length on the "rights" of sovereign states, but nowhere in *De Jure Belli ac Pacis* (The Law of War and Peace) does he affirm that all states are "equal." Rather than affirming the claim of states to a "separate station," moreover, he begins his work by emphasizing, on the authority of ancient writers, that man has "an impelling desire for society" (Prol. §6) and concludes that the law governing the conduct of states toward each other "had in view, the advantage, not of particular states, but of the great society of states" (Prol. §17).[2]

If one seeks the immediate philosophic source for the Declaration's "Law of Nature," one will find it in *Le Droit des Gens* (The Law of Nations), the mid-eighteenth-century treatise by the Swiss diplomat Emmerich de Vattel.[3] Compared to its predecessors, Vattel's treatise relied far less on ancient example and far more on modern theory. He dismissed the notion that states could be seen as partners in a great society in these terms:

I recognize no other natural society among nations than that which nature has set up among men in general. It is essential to every civil society that . . . there should be some authority capable of giving commands, prescribing laws, and compelling those who refuse to obey. Such an idea is not to be thought of as between nations. Each independent state claims to be, and actually is, independent of the others. (Preface, p. 9a)

Regarding the equality of states, Vattel is equally emphatic:

Since men are by nature equal, and their individual rights and obligations the same, as coming equally from nature, nations, which are composed of men and may be regarded as so many free persons living together in a state of nature, are by nature equal and hold from nature the same obligations and the same rights. Strength or weakness, in this case, counts for nothing. A dwarf is as much a man as a giant is; a small republic is no less a sovereign state than the most powerful kingdom. (Intro., §16, p. 7)

Vattel's stress on the equality of sovereign states, for all its pleasing resonance to American ears, implies that there is no natural ordering principle among states: they are equal, because equally independent, equally free to reject the lead or influence of other states. Where did Vattel get this notion?

He tells us in his preface: "Hobbes, whose work, in spite of its paradoxes and its detestable principles, shows us the hand of the master—Hobbes, I repeat, was the first, to my knowledge, to give us a distinct though imperfect idea of the Law of Nations." (5a) What Vattel seems to have admired in Hobbes was precisely the latter's insistence on a sharp distinction between the "law of nations," as a law between independent states, and the law that obtains within states.

The Roman jurists had applied the term *jus gentium* to the basic norms observed *within* all nations and hence associated it with a vague notion of "natural law." In *De Cive,* Hobbes presents the "law of nations" as a special application of natural law, now understood as the law that would apply in the absence of higher authority. As such, Hobbes emphasizes, it is a law that applies only to independent states. But he also makes it plain that the only law fully worthy of the name is the law that is enforced by authority, hence only the internal law of states is truly law—and the "law of nations" is not a real law.[4]

In fact, Vattel is not quite so far from the "paradoxes" of Hobbes. While insisting that the "necessary law of nations," founded on the "law of nature," requires states to respect each other's rights, he acknowledges that the strict requirements of that law are only binding on each nation's "conscience" and "it is for each nation to decide what its conscience demands of it, what it can or can not do; what it thinks well or does not think well to do; and therefore it is for each Nation to consider and determine what duties it can fulfill towards others without failing in its duty towards itself." (Intro, §16). What other nations can insist upon is not the "necessary law" but the "voluntary law," the set of practices that nations have consented to by long-accepted custom. So a state has, by the "necessary law," a duty to maintain freedom of commerce, but under the "voluntary law," no other nation can protest if a state restricts trade for its own advantage (bk. II, chap. 2). And where the "necessary law" limits the justifications for war, the "voluntary law" holds that all war must be acknowledged as lawful on both sides. "Let each sovereign make the necessary law the constant rule of his conduct; he must allow others to take advantage of the voluntary law of nations" (bk. III, chap. 12).

J. L. Brierly, perhaps the leading British commentator on international law in the early part of this century, protested with some justice the logic of Vattel's exposition: "This exaggerated emphasis on the independence of states had the effect in Vattel's system of reducing the natural law, which Grotius had used as a juridical barrier against arbitrary action by states towards one another, to little more than an aspiration after better relations between states. . . . By making independence the 'natural' state of nations, he made it impossible to explain or justify their subjection to law."[5]

II

One might try to ignore the awkward implications of Vattel's exposition and then—as the Founders themselves seem to have done—to take Locke rather than Hobbes as "master." Hobbes, in his rationalist enthusiasm for cataloging categories and distinctions, makes a place for a "law of nations" and then denies it. Locke characteristically seems to fumble past the topic and assume it by indirection. But he does allude to it.

Locke's *Second Treatise* follows Hobbes in grounding the rights of individuals in the claims they might make in a state of nature, prior to the establishment of government. And like Hobbes, Locke insists that the state of nature is a verifiable reality, still exemplified by the relation of independent monarchs or governments with one another. Hobbes depicts a state of nature so awful that even submission to an absolute sovereign seems a rational escape. Locke depicts a state of nature which is not quite so bad—and would not justify escaping into "civil society" if that turns out to bring untrammeled despotism. In particular, Locke's state of nature already has some arrangements that make possible the acquisition of private property, so that Locke can claim, again and again, that men institute government—later on—in order to secure their property (paras. 88, 94, 95, 120, 139, 222). The principal arrangement is the "tacit consent" to accept gold and silver in exchange for perishable produce, and this seems to be an agreement, as Locke suggests, that requires no government to define or enforce (para. 50).

In what is probably the longest and most tangled sentence of the *Second Treatise,* Locke then moves from this first transnational convention to a different one, by which different communities establish boundaries between themselves—as it appears, after all, that local laws are necessary to make property titles secure. So we are told that in "some parts of the World, (where the Increase of People and Stock, with the *Use of Money*) had made land scarce and so of some Value, the several *Communities* settled the Bounds of their distinct Territories, and by Laws within themselves, regulated the Properties of the private Men of their Society, and so *by Compact* and Agreement, *settled the Property* which Labour and Industry began. . . ." And in the same ramshackle sentence, presumably elaborating the same twisting train of thought, Locke then proceeds to notice "the Leagues that have been made between several States and Kingdoms, either expressly or tacitly disowning all Claim and Right to the Land in the other Possessions" and so "given up their Pretences to their natural common Right, which originally they had to those Countries, and so have, *by positive agreement, settled a Property* amongst themselves, in distinct Parts and parcels of the Earth . . ." (para. 45, Locke's italics).

Locke thus suggests that the security of property rights is related to the security of national boundaries: one's own government can guarantee precise title to land because the governments of other countries acknowledge its right to do so, within its own borders, and the other countries agree in turn to the borders. It is all somehow done by "compact" and "positive agreement"—and property itself ultimately rests on such agreement, as Locke's italics seem to emphasize. This story appears much more convincing if one assumes that all nations are agreeable.

But that would imply that the state of nature is itself quite agreeable, which, Locke concedes at various points, it is not. And he also stipulates that "not every compact . . . puts an end to the State of Nature between men, but only this one of agreeing together mutually to enter into one community and make one Body Politick" (§14), which suggests that agreements between independent sovereigns are by no means entirely reliable.

Locke thus seems to offer alternate visions of the fundamental realities. On the one hand, there is the vision of a world where individuals can trade freely across boundaries and where governments, instituted for the security of property, are barely more than facilitators of the trade that property makes possible. On the other hand, there is the vision of a world in which strong communities are the only reliable guarantors of property, so consent to government is not so much an unconstrained choice as a recognition of necessity.

III

The Declaration of Independence might indeed seem to take a rather optimistic view of human affairs, expressed in an optimism about the relations between states. It is easy to see why this outlook would appeal to the men who offered the "pledge" of their "sacred honor" in support of Jefferson's Declaration. Revolution looks more plausible if reversion to the state of nature—or the risk of a reversion to the state of nature—is not an entirely horrifying prospect.

There is also a more immediate and practical point. The Declaration asserts that "the people" can decide for themselves what government to have. Yes, the British are already "making war" on America, but the Declaration seems to take for granted that in defending themselves, "the people" of "these united colonies" will remain united among themselves in the same united territory. If the revolution fails, the result will be "tyranny" or "despotism." But the possibility of a partial success—accompanied by a splintering of "the people" and their territories—is passed over in silence, as is the possibility that any other power (apart from the British) might launch intrigues or aggressions to exploit such divisions. The people seem to come with a preestablished territory. Here again, the assumption against foreign meddling, the clear identification of "the people" with "their" territory, makes it more plausible to think of government rooted in consent.

It was the great good fortune of the American founders to have a nearly empty continent in which to assert their claims to "government by consent." In the revolutionary war France gave open support to the Americans, and other European powers gave implicit support (by welcoming American trade), rather than taking the occasion to attempt their own conquests at the expense of a fragile new nation. Those inclined to optimism could imagine that such a world would be a comfortable place for a new republic.

Not all Americans thought so. The Federalists, who sought a stronger national government, proceeded almost immediately after the ratification of the new Constitution to impose a tariff and establish a national bank to improve federal finances and then used the improved credit to begin the building of an American navy. But Jefferson himself led an opposition party that resisted almost every element of the Federalist policy. His party denounced the tariff and the new national bank and the standing army and the ambitions for a navy. Calling themselves "Republicans," the followers of Jefferson denounced the schemes of their opponents as a path to the restoration of monarchy. The Republicans sought to defend the states against the federal government and the federal legislature against the executive. Their program was, in a way, all about the safeguarding of popular consent. Jefferson's party was eager to stress the right of the people to give or withhold consent and thus sought to keep government as close as possible to the preferences of local majorities.

There is some logic in associating this outlook with the surface optimism of the Declaration of Independence. The more the world looks orderly, the more plausible it is to think that government can really rest on consent—on unconstrained preference. And also, perhaps, on a strong notion of individual rights. An unhampered commerce, it was hoped, would dissolve ancient prejudice and soften the relations between states. (On "the subject of money and commerce, Smith's Wealth of Nations is the best book to be read," Jefferson advised in 1807.[6])

Hence, Jefferson, as a party leader and then as a president, was eager to see the world as moving toward greater harmony. In 1785, while serving as a diplomat, he hailed a new trade agreement with Prussia as "humanizing by degrees" the law of nations.[7] As president, he lowered the tariff and dismantled the navy. He insisted Britain was wrong to interfere with American shipping, because belligerents should not interfere with the rights of neutral nations in time of war. But at the same time, he insisted that it was not necessary to go to war to support these rights. Jefferson's secretary of state, James Madison, published a very learned, closely reasoned legal appeal against the British doctrine. It appealed to "the progress of the law of nations, under the influence of science and humanity." It insisted that this "law" was already "mitigating the evils of war and diminishing the motives to it, by favoring the rights of those remaining at peace rather than those who enter into war."[8] And it had no effect on British policy. "As an argument," a disgruntled critic noted, "it was but a shilling pamphlet against eight hundred British ships of war."[9]

Jefferson persuaded himself that an embargo would force Britain to rescind its policies, as British merchants protested to their own government over the loss of trade. Jefferson looked to the solidarity of commerce to overcome the differences between states. When Madison, his faithful lieutenant, entered the presidency and finally acknowledged the failure of the embargo, he still did not think it proper to ask for a declaration of war. President Madison simply advised Congress of this option, for its "early deliberations" as a "solemn question which the Constitution wisely confides to the legislative department of the Government." Congress then took nearly three weeks to conclude for war. Madison did not ask for war measures; the country was totally unprepared for war; and a British army subsequently drove President Madison and the rest of the government out of Washington, leaving the White House and the Capitol building in smoking ruins. Jefferson, from retirement, consoled Madison that he had followed the right principles and simply been ill-served by subordinates.[10]

So there is a side of Jefferson's thought that did embrace optimism about international affairs and did find in this the basis for a greater optimism about republican government. It is probably no mistake to associate this with the Declaration. But it is only one side of Jefferson's outlook and only one side of the Declaration.

IV

Even Jefferson was enough of a practical statesman to recognize that "human events" do not always lend themselves to free choice. In the 1790s, he continually reproached the Federalists for invoking foreign threats to aggrandize the power of the federal government and the federal executive. After attaining the presidency for the opposition Republicans, however, Jefferson himself did something still more dramatic—and still more constitutionally dubious, by his own understanding of the Constitution. When New Orleans and the Louisiana territory shifted from enfeebled Spain into the energetic grip of Napoleon Bonaparte, Jefferson at once saw the necessity of taking the port and the territory into American hands. He negotiated its purchase, with strong hints to the French that the United States might seize the territory by force if it were not promptly sold. At one stroke, he doubled the size of the United States and removed any local threat to U.S. dominance on the American continent.

Yet for all the obvious benefits of the Louisiana Purchase, Jefferson regarded it as a violation of the Constitution. Jefferson's first thought was for Congress to "appeal to *the nation* for an additional article to the Constitution, affirming & confirming an act which the nation had not previously authorized" (Jefferson's italics).[11] His constitutional scruples, now utterly forgotten, were not simply a doctrinaire extrapolation from the abstract dogma of "strict construction." Noting that the Constitution "expressly declares itself to be made for the U.S.," Jefferson argued that the Constitution must have meant to authorize the admission of new states to the union only "out of the territory for which & under whose authority alone [the Framers] were then acting. I do not believe it was meant that they might receive England, Ireland, Holland, &c. into it. . . . [There are] those who consider the treaty making power as boundless. If it is, then we have no Constitution."[12]

This was not simply a legalistic point for Jefferson. If the Constitution is understood as, in some sense, an expression of a social contract among Americans, it could not be open-ended about a total change in the character of the country. In his *Notes on the State of Virginia,* Jefferson argued against encouraging immigration: "Every species of government has its specific principles. Ours perhaps are more peculiar than those of any other in the universe. . . . [Immigrants] will bring with them the principles of the governments they leave, imbibed in their early youth. . . . In proportion to their numbers, they will share with us the legislation. They will infuse into it their spirit, warp and bias its direction and render it a heterogeneous, incoherent, distracted mass."[13]

Nonetheless, Jefferson acted to purchase Louisiana, with its existing population of foreigners, and agreed with his followers in Congress not to raise the constitutional issue in public. He bowed to a greater "necessity." He bowed to necessity, too, in approving federal undertakings beyond his initial conception of a federal government limited strictly to matters of foreign policy. And so did his followers. The Bank of the United States, which had been a great bugbear of Jeffersonian opposition, was quietly reestablished with Madison's approval after the War of 1812, when experience showed its necessity. The doctrine of state nullification—that states could oppose improper federal law on their own authority—was implicitly repudiated. Both Jefferson and Madison quietly accepted that there could not be a foreign policy without a united nation. The law of nations could not govern the relations of U.S. states with each other.[14] At least at some times and for some purposes, there would have to be a common authority to lay down the law.

But this was not simply the fruit of experience. The underlying point had been recognized long before. It is the central argument in the central paper of *The Federalist,* number 43, a paper, as it happens, written by Madison. In what the opening line describes as a survey of "miscellaneous powers," this paper brings together a series of awkward compromises between "necessity" and consent. Struggling to justify the provision in Article VII, allowing the new Constitution to go into effect with only the ratification of nine states, Madison appeals to a higher law—or rather, a justification transcending law. It is the one passage in the entire series of *The Federalist* that directly echoes the first line of the Declaration and deploys it in this way: "The . . . question is answered at once by recurring to the absolute necessity of the case; to the great principle of self-preservation; to the transcendent law of nature and of nature's God, which declares that the safety and happiness of society are the objects at which all political institutions aim and to which all such institutions must be sacrificed."

This is a troubling thought, because it indirectly affirms that even "consent"—on which all American institutions are supposed to be grounded—"must be sacrificed" to the dictates of "absolute necessity," which are equivalent in some way to "the law of nature and of nature's God." But other portions of the paper keep returning to the same point. Thus, in defending the "republican guarantee" clause in Article IV, Section 2 of the new Constitution, Madison explains why it may be necessary to use force against state governments that stray into nonrepublican forms: "At first view, it might seem not to square with the republican theory to suppose either that a majority have not the right, or that a minority will have the force, to subvert a government. . . . But theoretic reasoning, in this as in most other cases, must be qualified by the lessons of practice." The paper proceeds to question whether "force and right are necessarily on the same side in republican government" and then notes: "May it not happen, in fine, that the minority of citizens may become a majority of persons, by the accession of alien residents, of a casual concourse of adventurers, or of those whom the constitution of the State has not admitted to the rights of suffrage?"

After a veiled allusion to the danger of slave revolts, the paper goes on to extol the role of the federal government as a moderator: "Happy would it be if such a remedy for its infirmities could be enjoyed by all free governments; if a project equally effectual could be established for the universal peace of the world!" But the same paper goes on to explain, in a slightly different context, why this "project" of a "universal peace" cannot be "equally effectual" and must remain merely a "happy" dream. The point is made regarding the existing Articles of Confederation: having been ratified only by state legislatures, the Articles can pretend to no higher authority than that of "a compact between independent sovereigns," and such "a league or a treaty" has no staying power, because any infraction of its particulars by one state "absolves the other" parties and "authorizes them, if they please, to pronounce the compact violated and void." Stable government cannot rest on treaties. Only where a government can exercise a reliable force can it be a reliable guarantor of peace—and consent must be tempered to this fact.

In fact, Jefferson's language in the Declaration of Independence already gives tacit recognition to the point. Though the text always uses the plural form regarding the United States ("the United States *have* the right. . . ."), the body of the text refers to Americans as "one people" and "the people." It reports the British abuses of particular colonies as if they all shared necessarily in the misfortunes of each, as if they were already "one people." The Declaration, in other words, already hints that a common stance toward the outside world implies common—and substantial—authority within.

In his last years, Jefferson gave much thought to the curriculum at the University of Virginia. On the "distinctive principles of the government of . . . the United States," he urged, "the best guides are to be found in, 1. The Declaration of Independence, as the fundamental act of union of these States."[15] Of course, the Declaration does not say it is a "fundamental act of union," but Jefferson seems to have taken this as a necessary implication. And he could be quite comfortable with such reasonings from necessity. After the Declaration, he immediately added in second place for his prescribed university readings, "The book known by the title of 'The Federalist.'"

V

To sum up, the surface doctrine of the Declaration of Independence seems to be that the world is safe for government by consent, because all the "Powers of the earth" are bound by a "Law of Nature" that obliges them to respect each other's sovereign rights. The deeper thought seems to be that the internal unity of nations—which is also requisite to government by consent—rests on a recognition of conflict and uncertainty in the outside world. So the law of nature may be favorable to nations—and to republican government—precisely because it does not guarantee them anything.

The Declaration does not actually mention the state of nature. Perhaps the phrase would direct too much attention to the awkwardness of explaining how the thirteen colonies could present themselves to the world as "one people." The Declaration leaves the state of nature in the background, out of sight but not quite out of mind. The Declaration begins instead with what Locke (following Hobbes) invoked as the enduring model of that state—the relations between independent states to each other, where there is no established higher authority. The more one takes an optimistic view of these relations, the more plausible it is to think that real authority—the coercive strength of national governments—is of secondary importance. But the thought of the Declaration has no certain trajectory in that direction.

On the contrary, there is a logic in the Declaration that reminds inevitably of Machiavelli. Professor Mansfield notes that Machiavelli begins his *Dis-*

courses by emphasizing "the difference between native and foreigner." In doing so, Machiavelli veils his own quite emphatic recognition that this distinction is at some level entirely "conventional and subject to swift and ruthless change." The distinction is crucial to lend force to the dictates of "necessity": "If they could rely on the protection of nature or God, [men] would not have to separate themselves into natives and foreigners. If they could consider themselves natives of a mother earth or of an intended home, they could regard themselves as brothers. But necessity forbids it. . . ."[16]

As Mansfield himself acknowledges in another context,[17] the last line of the Declaration seems "to rely more on honor and less on necessity," when it invokes the "protection of divine providence" and the "sacred honor" of the signers. It is probably more consistent with Jefferson's thought to see this as a hope for the progress that allows room for honor, rather than a pious faith in an assured reward for the righteous.[18] Still, the whole burden of the Declaration speaks distrust of power, justifying revolt.

After its opening nod to "the course of human events," the first phrase in the Declaration is "it becomes necessary." The word "consent" appears only in the third sentence, only after acknowledging the separateness of nations and the unalienable rights of separate men. First there is the reckoning with the natural "course," and only then consent.

So the dream of freedom is firmly rooted in the fear of conquest. Doctrines of equality—among sovereign states as among free individuals—may encourage the dream. But in theory as in history, the dream still seems to draw its strength from the fear. Declaring independence seems as much an impulse of fear as of hope.

The connection between the optimistic and the fearful view is this: consent looks like the solution to all problems only if conquest or coercion is the ultimate root of all problems. There is sentimentality in this view and also a brake on sentimentality. Both are entailed in making "independence" the founding principle.

NOTES

1. Kent, *Commentaries on American Law,* 14th ed. (Boston: Little, Brown, 1896), 21.

2. Grotius, *De Jure Belli ac Pacis,* trans. Francis Kelsey (Washington, D.C.: Carnegie Foundation, 1925). Originally published 1625.

3. Vattel, *Le Droit de Gens,* trans. Charles Fenwick (Washington, D.C.: Carnegie Foundation, 1916). Originally published 1757.

4. Hobbes, *De Cive,* chap. 14, para. 4.

5. J. L. Brierly, *The Law of Nations,* 4th ed. (Oxford: Oxford University Press, 1949), 39, 41.

6. Letter to John Norvell, June 14, 1807, *Writings,* Merrill D. Peterson, ed. (New York: Library of America, 1984), 1176.

7. "Reasons in Support of the New Proposed Articles in the Treaties of Commerce," in *The Papers of Thomas Jefferson,* J. P. Boyd, ed. (Princeton, N.J.: Princeton University Press, 1950), 7:491.

8. Madison, "An Examination of the British Doctrine, Which Subjects to Capture a Neutral Trade, Not Open in Time of Peace," in *Writings of James Madison,* Gaillard Hunt, ed. (New York: Putnam's Sons, 1908), 7:207.

9. Henry Adams, *History of the United States of America during the Administrations of Thomas Jefferson* (New York: Library of America, 1986), 679. Originally published 1889.

10. Henry Adams, *History of the United States of America during the Administrations of James Madison* (New York: Library of America, 1986), 1071. Originally published 1890. On the burning of public buildings in Washington, Adams notes that the British army did nothing of the kind in all its European battles of the previous twenty years: "They burned the Capitol, the White House and the Department buildings because they thought it proper, as they would have burned a negro kraal or a den of pirates. Apparently they assumed as a matter of course that the American government stood beyond the pale of civilization, and in truth a government which showed so little capacity to defend its capital, could hardly wonder at whatever treatment it received" (1014).

11. Jefferson, letter to John C. Breckinridge, Aug. 12, 1803, *Writings,* 1138.

12. Jefferson, letter to Wilson Cary Nicholas, Sept. 7, 1803, *Writings,* 1140.

13. Jefferson, Query VIII, *Writings,* 211.

14. See Peter Onuf and Nicholas Onuf, *Federal Union, Modern World: The Law of Nations in the Age of Revolutions, 1776–1814* (Madison: Madison House, 1993). For an account of how Jefferson and his followers gradually abandoned the notion that the "law of nations" could regulate the relations of state governments with each other within the United States.

15. Jefferson, *Writings,* 479 (quoting an extract from a resolution of the University of Virginia Board of Governors, which seems to have been drafted by Jefferson).

16. Mansfield, *Machiavelli's Virtue* (Chicago: University of Chicago Press, 1996), 69.

17. *The Spirit of Liberalism* (Cambridge, Mass.: Harvard University Press, 1978), 87.

18. It is perhaps revealing that Jefferson's own original draft made no mention of "firm reliance on the protection of divine providence," but simply appealed "for the support of this declaration" to the "pledge" by the signers of "our lives, our fortunes and our sacred honor." On the other hand, the Continental Congress struck out Jefferson's closing peroration in the previous paragraph, ending with these proud lines that cast a rather different light on Jefferson's view of national honor: "We might have been a free and a great people together [with Britain]. . . . The road to happiness & glory is open to us too. We will tread it apart from them. . . ." Jefferson reproduced the original draft in his "Autobiography": *Writings,* Peterson, ed., pp. 19–24.

13

The Common Law Spirit of the American Revolution

James R. Stoner Jr.

Whether we Americans would make our Revolution again if we had to, whether we understand and accept its principles, preserve its spirit, and possess the prudence to know when and how to fight, are questions not often asked by modern scholars. In the first place, such questions imply that the Revolution was a clear-eyed choice and a common project, and both these notions are suspect to historians ironic about human intentionality and cynical about the existence of any common good. In the second place, questions like these suppose continuity in American ideas and circumstances, and it must be admitted that our circumstances at least seem vastly altered in the past 225 years, in no small part as a result of the Revolution's own success. Whether the Constitution written at the Revolution's close can be understood and should be applied according to its original understanding is a question more frequently debated in recent years. To be sure, ironists, cynics, and progressives similarly dismiss its plausibility, but the notion that a law must be understood in light of the intention of its makers runs deep in our legal culture and continues to have authority, even in Congress and the Supreme Court of the United States, while the founding fathers still engage the imagination of the American people.[1]

Though the question of fighting the Revolution today might seem quaint and the question of interpreting the Constitution by its original intent might be controversial, the Declaration of Independence remains a touchstone of American political ideas. In fact, this understates its meaning, for the ideas announced in the Declaration concern founding government by choice and thus declaring it by words; the Declaration, in other words, does what it talks about. Through the Declaration, the United States is founded upon universal principles—human equality, natural rights, government by consent—announced to all mankind and recommended for adoption by other peoples, indeed by all the rest. Proclaiming themselves to establish a "new order of the ages," the founders rejected the notion that kings rule by divine right, attributing to God the creation of man and of his rights and asserting for themselves the business of forming government. Relieving Providence of responsibility for the state, they likewise claimed for men the right and the ability to pursue their earthly fortune, couching in the phrase "pursuit of happiness" and planting in their strong support for rights of property and enterprise the seeds of a dynamic economy that has changed the face of the world. These, then, are the liberal moments of the Revolution and the Declaration that explains it, liberal both in the ancient sense of being generous, for the Declaration shares a promise with all mankind, and liberal in the modern sense of being founded philosophically on the political theory of natural rights and promoting the political economy of human progress.

If America was once exceptional for having made a Revolution in the name of universal principles and for having explained them to the world and to themselves, the American Revolution today seems exceptional for having avoided the disasters, not to say the crimes, of subsequent revolutions likewise boasting universal import. The American Revolution did not devour, but rather exalted those who made it; they governed for half a century and have their names attached across a continent. Likewise, in this century, the United States has seemed exceptional, or exceptionally disappointing, to many scholars for never having developed a serious socialist movement, and now the world witnesses the apparent growth of American influence in the wake of socialism's retreat.[2] Tocqueville's explanation of the first phenomenon, and even of the second, which he already foresaw, was that Americans had been born equal instead of having to become so; equality was planted in the circumstances of our beginnings and in our earliest institutions, and so our Revolution, important though it was in suppressing vestiges of aristocracy, avoided the deep resentment and hatred among the classes that poisoned European politics for the next two hundred years. If the circumstances were fortuitous and ultimately fleeting, the institutions were essential, and to Tocqueville the principal among these were our religion, our practices of self-government, and our law.[3] Though I will have a word or two to say about religion in the final pages, I concentrate in the essay that follows on the other two, which together form what I call our common law constitutionalism. American politics have been neither Jacobin nor Burkean because our constitutionalism has preserved, at least until only yesterday, a special form.

COMMON LAW CONSTITUTIONALISM

Common law is rarely spoken of in political science today, and if it is, it is defined as modern lawyers define it, as "judge-made law." This definition apparently causes little consternation in the legal profession, but every citizen not a member of that caste intuitively thinks otherwise, unless persuaded by sophisticated political science or plain cynicism to ignore the principle of the separation of powers and to see all officials as policymakers pushing their preferences as far as they can. Oliver Wendell Holmes Jr. is responsible for redefining the common law as judge-made, and he meant his definition to be paradoxical or indeed, as he says of his definition of law itself (as the bad man's prediction of what the courts will do), that it is "cynical acid."[4] To understand common law as it figures in the Revolution and more generally at the founding, the indispensable beginning point is a willingness to suspend Holmes' cynicism and our modern sophistication and to recognize that, while the founders may not have lacked Holmes' insight, they never gave his opinion authoritative voice.

What, then, is common law, as it was understood at the founding and for one hundred years or so before and afterward?[5] In the first place, common law is unwritten, customary law, originating in England and carried over by the colonists to the New World, where it was applied insofar as it was consistent with American circumstances and not contradicted by statutes here devised. Although unwritten in principle, common law could be declared in writing and commonly was, necessarily in the decision of cases, additionally in legislative statements such as bills of rights. The decision in a case was understood to draw upon unwritten law in settling a particular dispute, while a legislative declaration was more general in its form but was thought no less deferential to existing standards in its substance. Like legislative declarations, judicial decisions provided evidence of what was common law, but neither was thought necessarily to introduce new law. Legislatures could, of course, remedy mischiefs that arose in the common law and so make new law, but in interpreting a statute it was always a question whether the aim was to legislate anew or just declare in writing the good old law.

The two characteristic institutions of common law are the rule of precedent and trial by jury, and together they prove the common law a sort of mixed regime. At common law, the decisions in previous cases count as law in a new but similar case; in common law practice much of the argument in a case involves drawing analogies and distinctions, and precedents become the vocabulary of lawyers and judges. Trial by jury, traditionally of "twelve good men and true" chosen more or less by lot, insures that precedents cannot grow so arcane as to divorce customary law from the community whose custom is in question; more precisely, it makes difficult a verdict that runs against community sentiment. The roles of judge and jury were in general understood to be, respectively, the determination of the law and the judgment of the facts, but it was apparently characteristic of American juries in the colonial era to venture confidently into questions of law.[6] Actually, especially where precedent has the force of law, the line between questions of law and fact is not easily drawn, for a precedent might be defined strictly by the facts of the case, while the law of evidence determines what facts can count in court.

Common law was generally understood to be distinct from natural law or the law of reason, although this too is unwritten law. The traditional doctrine was that there was nevertheless nothing in common law that was against natural law, or in other words, nothing against reason; a precedent that went against reason, that is, against the whole more or less consistent order of maxims, rules, or precedents, was not good or valid law in court. The orthodox doctrine of the common law fits squarely within the medieval or Thomistic tradition, for it sees in natural law a minimal restriction on the actual determination of most legal rules, even while involving reason in the definition of law. The seventeenth-century English judge and legal writer Sir Edward Coke, still considered authoritative to our founders, said of the common law that it was "an artificial perfection of reason . . . fined and refined by an infinite number of grave and learned men," and he contrasted this legal art with the mere "natural reason" of a private man.[7] The common law was amenable to reason, in other words, but it understood reason to work within a tradition, not as an independent or radical force.

Common law in England and in America was often called the law of the land, and indeed it concerned itself first and foremost with land law. By the eighteenth century and especially in the early nineteenth, it absorbed as well the law merchant, or in other words, the law of contracts and the many instrumentalities of commerce. Trespasses or wrongs by individuals against one another were subject to action at common law; this is what now goes under the name of torts. The law of the family belonged for the most part to common law, especially as the jurisdiction of the ecclesiastical courts was narrowed in England, while of course in America there were never officially established ecclesiastical courts. Finally, the common law defined many crimes and the procedures for their prosecution; while the eighteenth century saw continued pressure for crimes to be defined by statute (a movement the common law judges had encouraged from the start), the various protections for criminal defendants established at common law and implied in the phrase "due process" were jealously guarded in common law jurisdictions and admired elsewhere as enlightened institutional forms.

Common law is law as it appears from the point of view of a judge faced with the need to decide a particular case or to frame a question for the jury, not from the point of view of a policymaker trying to solve a social problem. It is, as it were, law viewed from below and so looked up to or discovered,

although in the practiced judge it is assimilated into his whole way of thinking and becomes a part of his professional art. Unlike modern positive law,
whose paradigm is, as Hobbes understood, the sovereign's command, common law has as its paradigm the community's traditional sense of right and
wrong. Common law is, in other words, morality insofar as it operates in a
court of law. The proviso is a strong one, for common law was skeptical of
the urge to condemn and thus solicitous in its protection of the accused. But
it did not have an overall principle such as Mill's "very simple" one of limiting legal interference to other-regarding actions, designed to leave a whole
sphere of human life essentially lawless.[8] Common law was woven through
the fabric of society; it was not ubiquitous, but it was not confined, except
by the prerogatives of the king in England, the jurisdiction of other courts,
and the limits inherent in its own way of proceeding.

Now, if this is common law, what is common law constitutionalism as it
figures in the American Revolution? The first thing to note is that the unwrit-
tenness of the English constitution makes sense when seen as part of or as
companion to unwritten common law. Though Americans would famously
pioneer written constitutions, in colonial times the closest thing they had to
these were colonial charters, and like other legal instruments, these were
construed in the midst of a common law tradition, so great principles could
be found in them and given legal force. The constitutional issue of the Revolution, after all, was that there could be no taxation without representation.
This was not a quibble involving charter interpretation, but a conclusion on
the level of political institutions of the common law principle that property
could not be taken without due process of law. Because the English constitution was unwritten and was seen on the analogy to the common law, in
short, the colonists could claim as their own not just the provisions in their
charters but the leading maxims and principles of English political liberty, so
exalted in the eighteenth century.

The second thing to note is that the colonists made recognition of their
common law rights an explicit political demand. This was put most succinctly in the Declaration and Resolves of the First Continental Congress in
1774, especially the fifth article: "That the respective colonies are entitled to
the common law of England, and more especially to the great and ines-
timable privilege of being tried by their peers of the vicinage, according to
the course of that law."[9] Though many of the specific points of common law
differed in America, especially where the absence of a titled nobility accompanied in most states a more egalitarian land law and where the newness of
things made acquisition a more important source of property than inheritance, Americans had already their own common law judiciaries in the
colonies. The British threat to these, seen especially in the removal of trials
away from local communities in response to the Boston Massacre and the
Tea Party in the early 1770s, made trial by jury a rallying cry alongside the
political demand for taxation by consent.

In short, the colonists saw their dispute with England in a constitutional and legal perspective. It was not, or not only, that the British were making foolish policy with harsh consequences; it was that they were violating the colonists' rights, their legal privileges and liberties, even or especially in passing little taxes. The disproportion between the policy objected to and the eventual remedy of a war of independence is what makes the Revolution so incomprehensible to modern scholars and why a scholar like Bernard Bailyn finds a need to discover a whole ideology of conspiracy that he thinks threw gasoline, so to speak, on harmless sparks. Yet Americans were in the grips of no perverse ideology; perception of a dangerous precedent in a small step in the wrong direction is the natural consequence of seeing politics through the common law frame of mind. Edmund Burke, in his "Speech on Reconciliation with America" in 1775 saw it best:

> another circumstance in our colonies, which contributes no mean part towards the growth and effect of this untractable spirit [in the colonists is] their education. In no country perhaps in the world is the law so general a study. The profession itself is numerous and powerful; and in most provinces it takes the lead. The greatest number of the deputies sent to the congress were lawyers. But all who read, and most do read, endeavor to obtain some smattering of that science. . . . This study renders men acute, inquisitive, dexterous, prompt in attack, ready in defense, full of resources. In other countries, the people, more simple, and of a less mercurial cast, judge of an ill principle in government only in an actual grievance; here they anticipate the evil, and judge of the pressure of the grievance by the badness of the principle. They augur misgovernment at a distance; and snuff the approach of tyranny in every tainted breeze.[10]

To be sure, most of the most prominent founders were, like Burke, fully capable of giving events a political rather than a narrowly legal interpretation and of shrewdly considering what should be done from a policy perspective, not just within a legal frame. But it was a part of their prudence to encourage Americans generally to understand the dispute with England in legal or constitutional language, as perhaps the noblest, perhaps the safest available to the generality of men on whose behalf they claimed to act.

COMMON LAW CONSTITUTIONALISM AND THE DECLARATION OF INDEPENDENCE

To ask where the common law constitutionalism I have just sketched appears in the Declaration of Independence is almost to answer already, for it is obviously in the long bill of grievances against the king and Parliament, in the middle of the document, that is so often overlooked today. The celebrated opening theoretical paragraphs have great clarity and power, and I will return to them presently, but the bulk of the Declaration is devoted to showing why the right of revolution should be invoked in the situation at hand. A govern-

ment that becomes destructive of its ends, that evinces a design of establishing absolute despotism, must be replaced: so much the theoretical principles
make plain. But the evidence of such destructiveness and design is found not
in abstract moral wrongs but in constitutional violations. The king has abused
his veto power, his right to assent to legislation. He has thwarted the right of
representation, by refusing to redistrict as population moves westward and by
suspending legislative sessions. He has "obstructed the administration of justice" and violated judicial independence. He has inserted into American affairs a standing army without the colonists' consent, thereby rendering the
military superior to the civil power. He has "combined with others to subject
us to a jurisdiction foreign to our constitution and unacknowledged by our
laws; giving his assent to their acts of pretended legislation."

This last complaint, which introduces nine objections to parliamentary acts
and occurs exactly in the middle of the document, ought to give us pause:
what, on July 4, 1776, did the Congress mean by "our constitution"? The Federal Constitution was of course drafted eleven summers afterward, ratified a
year later, and brought into effect only in 1789. The committee that wrote the
Articles of Confederation, our first written federal constitution, was appointed after the Declaration was adopted, and though the Articles passed
Congress in 1777, they lay unratified by the required unanimity of the states
until 1781—leaving the Continental Congress to operate without a formal
written instrument for the entire course of the Revolutionary War. Though
Jefferson's initial draft has "constitutions" in the plural, "our constitution"
cannot refer to the written constitutions of the states, not only because Congress adopted the singular form but because the states had themselves just
begun writing constitutions, the first permanent document having been
passed by the legislature of Virginia the week before.[11]

Congress, then, must have had in mind by the term "our constitution" the
unwritten constitution of British North America. What it entailed, at least
from their perspective, can be inferred from the entire bill of grievances, but
especially from the complaints against parliamentary legislation: due
process of law, no forced quartering of troops, free trade, no taxation without representation, trial by jury, and the right to preserve their forms of government and make their own laws. That the constitutional whole must be
inferred from an enumeration is characteristic of the common law way of
thinking; if the core of the law is unwritten, it is not subject to summary or
definition in a single paragraph or phrase. In the course of the American
Revolution, Americans established a tradition of written constitutions, but in
making that Revolution they drew upon, depended upon, and structured
their arguments and choices according to an unwritten constitutional tradition, anchored in a British constitution they thought betrayed by the home
government and in a common law they had carried across the ocean with
them and made their own.

This common law constitutionalism finds its way into the Constitution of 1787, not only in the technical language—a point still accepted by all parties today—but throughout the design of its institutions, for these are made partly on the basis of established patterns, partly to remedy the mischiefs experienced in these. The story is a complex one, for the Constitution of 1787 redresses not only the grievances against the king and Parliament, insuring they will not be repeated by the federal government against the people, but also the mischiefs seen to arise under the Articles of Confederation; and, in a pattern that recurs in American history, the constitutional experience upon which the framers drew includes their experience in the states as well as in Congress. Still, if all we knew of the founding depended on the principal documents alone, the continuity between the Constitution of 1787 and "our constitution" of 1776 would be striking, for nearly every grievance listed in the middle of the Declaration is addressed in the Constitution or in the first ten amendments, called the Bill of Rights. To list them all would be tedious, but consider just these answers to the grievances mentioned above. To prevent abuse of the negative, Article 1, Section 7 provides that a presidential veto can be overridden by a two-thirds vote in both houses of the national legislature. Article 1, Section 2 establishes a decennial census and apportionment of representatives among states by population, while Article 4, Section 3 provides for the admission of new states, thus obviating the danger that the central government would "refuse . . . the accommodation of large districts of people." Setting a date for an annual meeting of Congress and putting adjournment and meeting place under Congress's control in Article 1, Sections 4 and 5 repairs the irregularities imposed by the British in calling and dissolving assemblies. Making judges dependent on something like the royal will becomes impossible once Article 3, Section 1 establishes that federal judges hold office upon good behavior. The keeping of standing armies is limited by the restriction in Article 1, Section 8 to biannual army appropriations. Forced quartering of troops is confined by the third amendment. Taxation with consent is protected by Article 1, Sections 7 and 8. Trial by jury is secured by Article 3, Section 2, and Amendments 5, 6, and 7. And there is more.

My point here is not to emphasize the little details, though each can become important politically in the right circumstances. Rather, I mean to suggest that politics itself, as seen by the American founders, appears in a common law frame. It is not in the first place a matter of imagining utopias or even public programs and then inventing a process or implementing a public policy; politics was first of all the business of alleviating troubles, of righting wrongs. This is why, in the various documents leading up to the Revolution, and then again in the First Amendment, importance is placed on the right to petition for the redress of grievances. Revolution becomes necessary when "our repeated petitions have been answered only by repeated injury," says the Declaration, when the specific indictments add up to an intolerable threat. This is a judgment call, of course, and prudence is needed to know when to make it, but it is neither unstructured rejection of the past and a rush to experiment with the future nor pragmatic groping for some middle way. The grievances are redressed, the mischiefs remedied on a big scale in the Revolution—independence is declared, and written, republican constitutions based on the sovereignty of the people are established—but the specific grievances are addressed as well and guarded against for times to come, the founders not supposing that sovereignty forfeits its temptations when it changes its form. And the Constitution that addresses and guards is written in an idiom inherited from the unwritten constitution in the name of which the Revolution was fought.

NOVUS ORDO

To this account of the common law constitutionalism of the founding I can imagine the following objection. In stressing constitutional continuity, have I not overlooked what was genuinely new about the United States? The founding generation, as I alluded to at the outset, adopted as the motto on their great seal, "*Novus Ordo Seclorum*," a "new order of the ages." Moreover, reading the Declaration from the inside out, as it were, downplays if it does not outright ignore the ringing sentiments of the first two paragraphs, announcing the principle of equality and the origins of government in consent; and these, the generative principles of American politics, derive not from the common law tradition, but from the political theory of philosophers such as Thomas Hobbes and John Locke. Let me address this objection by speaking first of the place of novelty in common law and then of its relation to liberal philosophy.

First, though common law is traditional, there is room for new precedent, for the case that raises a question never before squarely presented, the decision of which, if it takes its bearings by the law, can settle that law on a new course. This happens in the Revolution through the turn to republicanism. The political theory of the Declaration does not reject constitutional monarchy as a legitimate form of government; its authors only argue that George III had become a tyrant. Still, by the end of the document, in the stirring call for common action, it is clear that there will be no turning back. At the Philadelphia Convention, if only for strategic reasons, Alexander Hamilton might propose constitutional monarchy for the United States, but defending the Constitution as coauthor of *The Federalist Papers* he would agree with James Madison that, as a result of the Revolution, the genius of the American people demanded republican government, there being now "an honorable determination, which animates every votary of freedom, to rest all our political experiments on the capacity of mankind for self-government."[12] But republican institutions, if not republicanism, were not unprecedented in common law constitutionalism. Consider here the insistence on consent in the grievances concerning taxes and standing armies, not to mention the jury, that most characteristic institution of common law and still the most democratic of our regime.[13]

Insofar as the objection I am addressing depends on the claims of the philosophers, it is more difficult to answer; in fact, in part I admit it, since my claim is not that the Revolution derives only from the common law tradition, but that our constitutionalism is itself a sort of mixed regime of principles both medieval and modern, a coming together or harmonizing (Jefferson's word) of traditions often at odds.[14] Still, my first response is that the common law way of thinking was—unlike some forms of liberalism—able and willing to assimilate different strands, recognizing as it does the extraordinary complexity of human life and insisting on no simple principle of consistency, only that every valid principle have its place. To the common law mind, the theory of Locke and maybe even Hobbes had its use in examining the origin of government and its reestablishment after collapse, but it ought not to swallow up every other legal principle. That tendency was most evident in Hobbes, who thought the danger of anarchy in civil war—he called its ideal type the state of nature—was so great as to require rational men to submit themselves to an absolute sovereign. Locke allows for balance here, but only as a matter of prudence, and his doctrine of prerogative is wide enough to allow the supreme executive to do nearly anything a Hobbesian sovereign might rationally aspire to. Americans, by contrast, have never been willing to admit more than a little presidential prerogative, and that largely hidden, nor to allow a president to be immune to law himself.[15]

Even on first principles, it is important to pay attention to the subtle differences between Locke and Hobbes on the one hand and the Declaration of Independence on the other. First, though they all agree that government arises from human consent, not divine institution, the Declaration makes infinitely clearer than Hobbes or Locke that our rights are an endowment from God, not natural necessity. Second, the Declaration's rights are called inalienable, not just the right to life, as in Hobbes, or the right to property, as perhaps in Locke, but the whole batch of rights to life, liberty, and the pursuit of happiness. To be sure, that last term is a Lockean formulation, but it appears in Locke's *Essay Concerning Human Understanding* as a fact, not in the *Second Treatise* as a right.[16] In any event, while Hobbes and Locke sharply distinguished natural and civil rights, the mixing of these two has been a constant theme in American history, as one might expect of a people who see rights as liberties at common law, where the natural and the civil are not sharply at odds. Third, according to the Declaration, when a government becomes destructive of its ends, citizens have in the Declaration but not so clearly in Locke (and clearly not at all in Hobbes) not only a right but a duty to insist that it be reformed, even by force. To whom that duty is owed will be our final topic.

Before turning to that, however, and as a final word on our objection, it is worth noting that liberalism was, in fact, ambiguous about the American Revolution, for liberalism could foster either William Blackstone's insistence on parliamentary sovereignty or Thomas Paine's demand for simple democratic government.[17] The Americans chose something in between, neither blind veneration nor bitter hatred of all things British, but a sturdy preservation of their ancient liberties. Even sovereignty of the people, in the United States, was to be exercised through a Constitution and, strictly speaking, only in its making. And in that making, for all the self-conscious experimentation, there was, at least until the Progressive Era, rather a reasonable adjustment of inherited forms than a rationalist urge to dismantle and re-create.

LIBERTY AND SACRED HONOR

To whom, then, was the duty owed to fix a government gone bad, to right the wrongs of abuse of power? Let me try to answer that by reference to the Declaration's stirring close. In enumerating inalienable rights at the outset, Jefferson had penned a famous trio, "life, liberty, and the pursuit of happiness," a slight amendment of the formula "life, liberty, and property" that had developed in English constitutionalism. The closing pledge—"to each other, our lives, our fortunes, and our sacred honor"—is an echo of that earlier trio, with a change of order: The right to life becomes their lives, the pursuit of happiness yields them their fortunes, and that leaves liberty to be interpreted as a matter of "sacred honor." Why did they call that honor sacred? I do not think it was just because they imagined themselves to be Romans, awaiting laurel wreaths from pagan gods, though the iconography of the early republic, not to mention the architecture of Washington, D.C., lends plausibility to this claim. They said "sacred honor" because they pledged their word and because they counted this their greatest treasure, trusting one another as their characters had been proven in danger, and also because they thought God's blessings come not in the form of manna from heaven but through lives lived in accord with a common law of right and wrong written upon the human heart. Their sense of duty, in other words, was anchored in the "firm reliance on the protection of divine providence" to which they appeal as they close the Declaration with their pledge.

When John Winthrop wrote aboard the *Arabella* that Puritan New England should be a model Christian commonwealth that mankind, or at least old England, could watch in wonder, he called it a "city upon a hill," coining an image of American exceptionalism that resonates even in our own day.[18] Alexander Hamilton in *The Federalist* similarly voices an aspiration that

America will prove a model worthy of emulation, not for its Christianity but for its political achievement: "It seems to have been reserved to the people of this country, by their conduct and example, to decide the important question, whether societies of men are really capable or not, of establishing good government from reflection and choice, or whether they are forever destined to depend, for their political constitutions, on accident and force."[19] When Ronald Reagan used Winthrop's phrase to invoke Hamilton's project, or its modern-day equivalent, he captured something of the mixture of principles—or should one say, ambivalence?—in American thought. The mixed influence of common law and liberalism in the Revolution is a part of this story on the level of the constitution, for common law was thought in America to incorporate the general principles of religion, or at least not to contradict them. Is it possible that the tension between the traditions of common law and liberalism contributes to the vitality of our constitutionalism, as the tension between Jerusalem and Athens has been said to be the secret of vitality in Western thought?[20]

NOTES

1. The ironic reading of the Revolution is characteristic of Bernard Bailyn, *The Ideological Origins of the American Revolution* (Cambridge, Mass.: Harvard University Press, 1967), and Gordon Wood, *The Radicalism of the American Revolution* (New York: Knopf, 1992). But cf. Harvey C. Mansfield, Jr., "The Right of Revolution," in *The Spirit of Liberalism* (Cambridge, Mass.: Harvard University Press, 1978), chap. 5. On the question of the jurisprudence of original intention, see, e.g., Robert Bork, *The Tempting of America: The Political Seduction of the Law* (New York: Free Press, 1990). But cf. Mansfield, *America's Constitutional Soul* (Baltimore: Johns Hopkins University Press, 1991), where the emphasis is not on the founders' intent but on their political science.
2. See Daniel Bell, "'American Exceptionalism' Revisited: The Role of Civil Society," *The Public Interest* 95 (Spring 1989): 38–56.
3. Alexis de Tocqueville, *Democracy in America* (New York: Harper & Row, 1966), vol. I, pt. 2, chaps. 8–9; vol. II, pt. 2, chaps. 3–4. Originally published 1835, 1840.
4. Holmes, *The Common Law* (Boston: Little, Brown, 1881); "The Path of the Law," in *Collected Legal Papers* (New York: Harcourt, Brace, and Howe, 1920).
5. I develop these observations at greater length in *Common Law and Liberal Theory: Coke, Hobbes, and the Origins of American Constitutionalism* (Lawrence: University Press of Kansas, 1992), esp. intro. and chap. 1.
6. See Shannon Stimson, *The American Revolution in the Law: Anglo-American Jurisprudence before John Marshall* (Princeton, N.J.: Princeton University Press, 1990), and William E. Nelson, *Americanization of the Common Law: The Impact of Legal Change on Massachusetts Society, 1760–1830* (Cambridge, Mass.: Harvard University Press, 1975).

7. Coke, *Institutes of the Laws of England,* part I (1628; reprint, New York: Garland Publishing, 1979), 97b.

8. Hobbes, *Leviathan,* chap. 26; Mill, *On Liberty,* chap. 1.

9. In Jack Greene, ed., *Colonies to Nation, 1763–1789: A Documentary History of the American Revolution* (New York: W. W. Norton & Co., 1975), 245.

10. Burke, "Speech on American Conciliation," March 22, 1775, in *On the American Revolution: Selected Speeches and Letters,* ed. Elliott Robert Barkan (New York: Harper & Row, 1966), 85–86.

11. Greene, *Colonies to Nation, 1763–1789,* 334–35.

12. Jacob E. Cooke, ed., *The Federalist,* no. 39 (Middletown, Conn.: Wesleyan University Press, 1961), 250. Originally published 1787–88.

13. Besides republicanism, the other really new thing about the U.S. Constitution is its prohibition of federal religious tests for office, its rejection of religious establishment, and its protection of religious liberty. I discuss the common law dimension of this issue in "Religious Liberty and Common Law: Free Exercise Exemptions and American Courts," *Polity* 26 (Fall 1993): 1–24, and "Christianity, the Common Law, and the Constitution," in Gary L. Gregg II, ed., *Vital Remnants: America's Founding and the Western Tradition* (Wilmington, Del.: ISI Books, 1999), 175–209. Cf. Mansfield, *America's Constitutional Soul,* chap. 8.

14. See Jefferson's letter to Henry Lee of May 8, 1825, in *Writings,* Merrill D. Peterson ed. (New York: Library of America, 1984), 1501.

15. Hobbes, *Leviathan,* chaps. 13, 17, 29; Locke, *Two Treatises of Government,* chap. 14. Cf. Mansfield, *Taming the Prince: The Ambivalence of Modern Executive Power* (New York: Free Press, 1989), chaps. 1, 10.

16. Locke, *Essay Concerning Human Understanding,* bk. II, chap. 21, sect. 59.

17. Blackstone, *Commentaries on the Laws of England,* bk. 1, chap. 2, introduction to chap. 4; Thomas Paine, *Common Sense.*

18. Winthrop, "A Modell of Christian Charity," in Stewart Mitchell, ed., *Winthrop Papers* (Boston: Massachusetts Historical Society, 1929).

19. *The Federalist,* no. 1, p. 3.

20. Leo Strauss, "Machiavelli," in Strauss and Joseph Cropsey, eds., *History of Political Philosophy,* 3rd ed. (Chicago: University of Chicago Press, 1987), 297; Strauss, "Progress or Return?" in Thomas L. Pangle, ed., *The Rebirth of Classical Political Rationalism: An Introduction to the Thought of Leo Strauss* (Chicago: University of Chicago Press, 1989), 270.

14

The Federalist's Unmixed Republican Government

David F. Epstein

Today, when we "have embraced the view that democracy is the only legitimate form of government,"[1] it is striking to read *The Federalist*'s expressed hope that "popular government" could be "rescued from the opprobrium under which it has so long labored and be recommended to the esteem and adoption of mankind" (10).[2] The future reputation of the popular form, *The Federalist* judged, would depend on the success of an American "experiment" introducing various improvements on previous popular governments. *unusual emphasis for democracy*

Two centuries later, can we judge the experiment a success? Can democracy be esteemed reasonably on the basis of experimental evidence, and therefore recommended to mankind? Or is democracy our "value," embraced even without evidence, with no foundation or applicability beyond *unique as our system* our own culture? Does "esteem" overstate a current attitude toward popular government that might also be described as acceptance or resignation ("the worst form of government except all the others")? Is the dominance of democratic ideas a vindication of the founders' design, or of what evolved later contrary to their design?[3] Or do those ideas demand even further reforms?

Our own perplexities about the justification, development, and meaning of democracy make it instructive to reconsider the account found in *The Federalist*. That book could not complacently or inertially accept popular government because that form had not yet been successful; it had not yet even endured. Recommending popular government as an honorable experiment, *The Federalist* is awake to both its nobility and its weak spots.[4] *The Federalist* does not dogmatically insist that democracy is the only legitimate form of government, but compares it to other forms according to standards rooted in *this is the manual standard* the "laws of Nature." It offers specific prescriptions about how popular gov-

205

ernment should be "modeled" in light of a science of politics based on the prior record of human behavior. *The Federalist* sees virtue and not merely necessity in the substitution of representatives for an assembled people; and it admits the merit of Britain's mixed monarchy. In contrast to the imprecise but open-ended egalitarianism of our day, *The Federalist* speaks of the "unequal faculties" of men as well as of the equality of men, and calls the "equal division of property" an "improper or wicked project" (10).

I will begin by considering the standards to which *The Federalist* holds "all governments." Then I will consider its case for popular rather than monarchical government, and its case for a representative rather than directly democratic form of popular government. To summarize the conclusion: all legitimate governments must serve popular ends and satisfy popular judgment, but not necessarily have a popular founding or wholly popular form. The best form of government has a popular founding and form, but not a popular assembly.

ALL GOVERNMENTS

While *The Federalist* speaks as a "friend of popular governments" and expounds the "genuine principles of republican government" (10, 62), in a few places it explicitly states principles that apply to all forms of government. *The Federalist* follows John Locke (and the Declaration of Independence) in deriving standards for legitimate government from an argument about the "state of nature," mankind's condition without government. In the state of nature "anarchy" reigns: "the weaker individual is not secured against the violence of the stronger" (51). Each man's aim in joining (or creating) "civil society" is to secure his own rights, to live in "repose and confidence" (37); thus it is the "ordinary administration of criminal and civil justice" that most attaches men to government (17). "Justice is the end of government. It is the end of civil society": This is *Federalist* 51's restatement of the Declaration's assertion that "to secure these rights, governments are instituted among men."

So that the civil society necessary for justice can be preserved and prosper, government's practical task is to pursue the "public good." The "public good, the real welfare of the great body of the people, is the supreme object to be pursued; and . . . *no form of government whatever* has any other value than as it may be fitted for the attainment of this object" (45).[5] Borrowing the phrases of the Declaration of Independence, *The Federalist* asserts that "the transcendent law of nature and of nature's God . . . declares that the safety and happiness of society are the objects at which all political institutions aim, and to which all such institutions must be sacrificed" (43). While Locke called the "law of nature" the rule of reason that governs men in a state of nature, the Declaration and *The Federalist* give that name to the reasonable political implications of the state of nature.[6]

The Federalist states a third standard for all governments: "the cool and deliberate sense of the community ought, in all governments . . . ultimately [to] prevail over the views of its rulers" (63). This third standard is a remarkable indication of how substantially these universal standards for government point in the direction of popular government. Not only are government's proper ends the rights and good of all rather than of a privileged or ruling few, government's service of those ends must "ultimately" win the community's approval. This is in the spirit of, but seems to go beyond, the Declaration's right of revolution, which only subjected governments "destructive of these ends" to a usually patient people's verdict. It is not enough that government avoid provoking revolution. No government should use the latitude afforded by the people's powerlessness or inattention to serve them contrary to their own ultimate cool and deliberate sense.

When invoking the state of nature to understand the "end of civil society," *The Federalist* raises a problem that the Declaration and John Locke seem to pass over: the separateness, diversity, and inequality of men. *The Federalist* makes a distinction between "the weaker individual" in the state of nature and "the stronger."[7] They are not equal, but they are both insecure and can agree to form a civil society where both can live in repose and confidence. But this agreement is not simply an agreement to have a government or about who shall rule. It is also an agreement about the ends of rule. "Justice"—the "end of civil society"—means the protection of each man's right to exercise his own "faculties." This end is democratic in that the faculties of each must be protected, but the faculties themselves are "unequal" (10). An equal right to acquire property, for example, can win men's consent, but equal property would have to be imposed by a "stronger individual" or a "stronger faction." This agreement on the proper ends of government is not hypothetical or ancient history; it is reflected in the fact that men will not accept and preserve a government "under the forms of which the stronger faction can readily unite and oppress the weaker" (51).

The Declaration and Locke both begin with the equal rights of each (individual) man as the thing that needs protection; both then shift without emphasis or explanation to the (whole) people's "safety and happiness" as the object of a newly created government.[8] *The Federalist* similarly emphasizes the positive, the case for a government that will serve the "public good." The claims of justice are presented more as a warning: a government unjust to the equal rights of unequal individuals cannot long endure.[9] The case for popular government does not follow from a natural unity or potential uniformity of the people; it must rather surmount the problems posed by the people's natural separateness and diversity.

MONARCHIES AND REPUBLICS

Few governments in history have served justice and the public good and won the people's cool and deliberate approval. Most have "degenerate[d] into tyranny," because they lacked a "communion of interests and sympathy of sentiments" between rulers and people (57). Conceivably, even an absolute monarch could meet *The Federalist*'s standards, if he eschewed the "impious doctrine in the Old World, that the people were made for kings, not kings for the people" (45)—a doctrine that (for example) lets kings make war even when their nation would "get nothing by it" (4). But a monarch is more likely to be devoted to the public good and deferential to the people's cool and deliberate views if he is a limited monarch, sharing power with representatives of the people—as exemplified in the British Constitution. *The Federalist* calls "free government" both wholly popular forms (such as the American states) and partly popular forms (such as Britain's). One representative branch is enough to conclude that "the cool and deliberate sense of the community . . . actually will, in all free governments, ultimately prevail over the views of its rulers" (63). Even though the British monarch is not subjected to the laws he shares in making, his officers and the members of the House of Commons are (70). The popular part of Britain's government can prevent policies that oppress the people, so the government's performance tends ultimately to win the people's approval.

As compared to a purely popular government, Britain's admixture of monarchy appears more favorable to an energetic execution of the laws and the effective collection of taxes (70, 12). And a monarch is less susceptible to corruption by foreign enemies, not from superior virtue but from the strong hold on his loyalty of his opportunity to take unlimited advantage of his subjects' prosperity. Elected officials, never far from a return to private life, may be much more tempted to betray a country they cannot expect to exploit permanently (22). Limited monarchy also appears to exhibit more "stability" than a purely popular government, and to provide some security for the rights of the wealthy minority, although not for the rights of all minorities (37, 51).

The advantages of a mixed form do not suffice to make it acceptable to America. The new American Constitution must be "strictly republican," i.e., "a government which derives all its powers directly or indirectly from the great body of the people, and is administered by persons holding their offices during pleasure, for a limited period, or during good behavior" (39). This rules out a king or lords who are "self-appointed" (51) and hold office for life. Not "all governments" must be republican, but the American one must:

It is evident that no other form would be reconcilable [1] with the genius of the people of America; [2] with the fundamental principles of the Revolution; or

[3] with that honorable determination which animates every votary of freedom, to rest all our political experiments on the capacity of mankind for self-government. If the plan of the convention, therefore, be found to depart from the republican character, its advocates must abandon it as no longer defensible. (39)

The American people's "genius"—or at least their "present genius" (55)[10]— reflects the Revolutionary period's "universal resentment and indignation against the ancient government" (Britain's monarchy), which brought a "universal ardor for new and opposite forms" (49). The "fundamental principles of the Revolution" go beyond antimonarchical ardor[11] and are stated in the Declaration of Independence, but it is not clear that they demand republican government. The Declaration asserts the people's right to institute government "in such form, as to them shall seem most likely to effect their safety and happiness," which seems not to decide on a particular form. Just as puzzlingly, several other passages in *The Federalist* seem to call the Declaration's principles a "republican theory" (43, 49, 78), as if they commanded republican government rather than a choice of forms, or as if they were not dictates of the law of nature and of nature's God but only principles held by the friends of republican government. Does the right of revolution imply republicanism, or presuppose it, or neither?

The Federalist appears to divide into three parts the series of truths the Declaration called self-evident. First and most clearly universal is the principle that the people's happiness is the end of government; this is a "law of nature" (43). The "transcendent and precious right of the people" to alter or abolish existing governments (40) is also universal—it belongs to "every national society" (39)—but it seems to be especially embraced by "republican theory" (43) and understood as a "fundamental principle of republican government" (78).[12] One further step beyond this right of revolution is the people's right to institute new government, to act as the "pure, original fountain of all legitimate authority" (22) and "new-model" the government (49). This last step is a distinctively "republican theory" (49), and this is the theory that Americans will vindicate or refute:

> It has been frequently remarked that it seems to have been reserved to the people of this country, by their conduct and example, to decide the important question, whether societies of men are really capable or not of establishing good government from reflection and choice, or whether they are forever destined to depend for their political constitutions on accident and force. (1)

This third point is "republican" in that the popular founding of a regime presupposes a certain capacity in the people, just as the republican form assumes "the capacity of mankind for self-government." If mankind is "really capable" of instituting good government by reflection and choice, is it not— even a fortiori, because founding is harder than preserving[13]—capable of appointing all officers by direct or indirect election? Without this republican theory, one could preserve a truncated, melancholy version of the right of revolution: tyrannical government may be resisted and overthrown, but no "regular" popular founding can institute a good government to replace it; the people must simply hope that "accident and force" turn up something better.

With this republican theory, a people who feel really capable of founding government will feel that "honorable determination" of man's capacity for self-government that makes nonrepublican forms indefensible. Nonrepublican or partly republican government would not be a people's choice,[14] although it may be accepted as an inheritance if it has been benign or as a matter of necessity if republican government is or proves untenable.[15]

This republican theory of the people's real capability does not loom large in Locke. He allows mixed government or republican government, as either admits of representation, a separation of powers, and rule by law. And in describing the historical origins of government Locke admits that the people have usually made the "simple, and most obvious" choice of monarchy, because families were accustomed to a father's authority, needed a military commander to protect them, and were oblivious to the dangers that would arise later if less virtuous kings appeared.[16] Their failure to choose a more durably benign regime does not, in Locke's view, diminish the people's right to choose; they may try again when the old regime turns bad. To speak of the people's "capacity" reopens an older line of argument (presented in Aristotle's *Politics*), according to which the several alternative regimes were recommended on the basis of the virtues of various claimants to rule.[17] Locke's denial of any natural hierarchy rejected in principle the view that differences in capacity would confer legitimacy on anyone's claim to rule. In *The Federalist* the question of capacity returns in attenuated form. Man's natural freedom poses a problem (insecurity), and this requires that there be some human capacity that permits a solution. Consent to an artificially created rule is the road to peace, but this requires that there be a capacity in human beings to do the creating. No superior capacity in one or a few can bring peace, because their rule would depend on force and accident, and could be challenged by someone else's force or some new accident. Thus the question is not whether the people have the most or highest capacity, but whether they have enough capacity. The "honorable determination" that they do animates the twin American "experiment[s]" of founding by consent (1) and a wholly popular form of government (39).

There is accordingly something "mortifying" about the defects of republican government; these might imply the need for something (like a king) that the people cannot provide for themselves.[18] But the spirit that rejects the creation of a mixed government also undermines mixed governments already in existence. In England, an "infant and humble representation of the people" in the House of Commons gradually gained strength and finally reduced "as far as it seems to have wished, all the overgrown prerogatives of the other branches" (58; see 71); so that in 1788 the king is very unlikely to use his power to veto legislation (73). This history illustrates the "irresistible force possessed by that branch of a free government, which has the people on its side" (63). Once there is a "sufficient portion of liberty," i.e., a popular share in government, there is a "zeal for its proper enlargement" (52). Mixed government does not live up to its own intentions. As a "free government" it evolves in the direction of and comes to resemble republican government.[19] Or, as shown by the example of Sweden, the monarchical element can defeat the republican. Sweden's king became "absolute and uncontrolled" after the representative body was corrupted by foreign powers (22). It does not appear that popular and self-appointed rule can be durably balanced. This may be a case where one cannot mingle desirable elements in their due proportions (37), but must "firmly embrace a rational alternative" (23).[20]

REPUBLICS AND DEMOCRACIES

Mankind's capacity for self-government might seem to permit a "pure democracy," where the people "assemble and administer the government in person"; but *The Federalist* makes clear that that form is inferior to a "republic", i.e., "the delegation of the government . . . to a small number of citizens elected by the rest," encompassing a "greater number of citizens, and greater sphere of country" (10).

While "the people commonly *intend* the PUBLIC GOOD" (71; italics and small capitals in the original), substituting representatives risks introducing some other intention. For this reason "Republican government presupposes the existence of [certain estimable human] qualities in a higher degree than any other form" (55). Republics require virtue more than monarchy, where the king need not restrain himself and is powerful enough to restrain the people, but also more than democracy, where there are no representatives who must be trusted to serve the good of the electors rather than their own good. This republican virtue of trustworthiness is not some "superlative virtue" (75), a "stern virtue [that] is the growth of few soils" and that would follow "duty at every hazard" (73). It seems only to require a sensibility to the prospect of reelection or defeat in the next election, and to the criminal punishments threatened against attempted usurpations in defiance of elections. Unless human nature can supply this minimal trustworthiness, republican government is absurd.[21]

But representation is not just a feasible simulation of an assembled people's self-concern; it is an improvement. Their small size makes pure democracies vulnerable to external conquest, and (in the famous argument of *Federalist* 10) prone to violate the rights of a minority. They have a more general and profound defect: in "collective meetings of the people," "[i]gno-rance will be the dupe of cunning, and passion the slave of sophistry and declamation." Not only does this promise bad decisions, it humiliates the democratic spirit: "In the ancient republics, where the whole body of the people assembled in person, a single orator, or an artful statesman, was gen-erally seen to rule with as complete a sway as if a sceptre had been placed in his single hand" (58). *The Federalist* does not rely on the tactful argument that a large country makes representation necessary; it makes clear that a large country is desirable partly because it makes a democratic assembly im-possible.

These observations may shock modern democratic sensibilities, but they are certainly not "elitist." The diagnosis of human inequality is no more flat-tering to the ambitious few ("cunning," "sophistry") than to the partisan many ("ignorance," "passion"). The good news is that men's behavior is in-fluenced by their situation, and that the Constitution can determine their po-litical situation. In a republic, neither the elected representatives nor the vot-ers at large experience the circumstances, temptations, and vulnerabilities of a democratic assembly. The situations and thus the motives and opportuni-ties of these two groups differ from each other and from the situation of an assembled people, giving republican government its distinct character.

How are elected citizens different from assembled citizens? Elections are intended to "obtain for rulers men who possess most wisdom to discern, and most virtue to pursue, the common good of the society," but *The Federalist* more modestly predicts that those actually elected will be "somewhat distin-guished" by these qualities (57). The specialization of the representative's job gives him the competence that comes from experience (53, 72). Since the representative's electors will have various interests and views, he must con-sider how to "combine" these (35). A democratic assembly tries to effect such a combination in its decisions, but each of its members can begin from his own preferences rather than from any effort to combine. Moreover, an elected representative may suppose that his constituents share his opinions, making him less "timid and cautious" than he would be on his own, and less vulnerable to the mob psychology that overtakes individually timid men when assembled together (49). Above all, the representative is conspicuous and ambitious; he must somehow "build" his "political consequence," per-haps by means of "extensive and arduous enterprises" (46, 72). His motive is to distinguish himself, not to fade into the mass. He is "responsible," mean-ing that he will be judged for his decisions or the apparent results of those decisions (63)—unlike an assembled people as a whole or its individual, anonymous members, whom no one will judge. Moreover, while a demo-cratic assembly acts as one body, representatives can be divided into several bodies to restrain passionate haste (62). And representation makes feasible the American innovation of a written constitution. While no presumed or even known sentiments of the people would justify representatives in violating the constitution until the people have by "some solemn and authoritative act" changed it (78), such a restraint would be less plausible for the assembled people themselves.

As to the unassembled, voting public, most of the time they lack the power to rule according to their immediate impulses. Although the people may be divided into parties (49, 50), because of their "number and . . . dispersed situation" they will not display the "systematic spirit of cabal and intrigue" seen in assembled bodies (76). Their cool and deliberate sense can prevail (or their passionate whims, when they coincide with election time), but since they vote only periodically they must make prospective and retrospective judgments. Representatives are therefore motivated to do what the people will have wished, rather than what they may already wish.

The Federalist's emphatic distinction between representative and democratic government is reformulated less sharply in number 63. The two types of popular government are enough alike that a number of arguments for a senate apply to both; and America should take heed of the fact that all long-lived ancient republics (Sparta, Rome, and Carthage) had senates. In the course of this argument, *The Federalist* notes that even "the most pure democracies" of ancient Greece elected "representatives" to executive offices, and cites several examples of ancient representative bodies that exercised legislative and other authorities. Representation is not strictly speaking a modern invention. The "true" distinction between America and the ancient democracies is not the distinction between elections and assemblies but the distinction between wholly representative (American) and partly democratic, partly representative (ancient) governments.[22] "The distinction, however, thus qualified, must be admitted to leave a most advantageous superiority in favor of the United States."

What is this superiority? Why is representation alone[23] preferable to a partly democratic, partly representative government that might mix the advantages of each practice? At the end of number 63 an answer is suggested. Precisely in those long-lived ancient republics with senates the senates were eventually dominated by the more popular elements of government. The tendency of the most popular branch to prevail, the tendency that unmixes the British government, is what unmixed the ancient democracies. This tendency lets representatives prevail over kings or senates, and assemblies prevail over representatives. The Achaean confederacy, otherwise well designed and very much like the American Constitution, was pulled apart because democratic assemblies governing cities prevailed over an elected representative government for the whole confederacy (18). Only if there is no direct assembly of the people is the most popular representative body the government's most popular part. "But to insure to this advantage its full effect, we must be careful not to separate it from the other advantage, of an extensive territory. For it cannot be believed, that any form of representative government could have succeeded within the narrow limits occupied by the democracies of Greece" (63). Why not? Perhaps a people small enough to assemble would insist on assembling, or would be virtually even if not formally assembled, always at hand to dispute and challenge the rule of their representatives.

The American regime is thus characterized as an "unmixed" republic (14), because all parts are directly or indirectly elected, and there is no admixture either of democratic assembly or monarchical self-appointment. The American form of mixing mixes elements all of which are directly or indirectly appointed by the people. The more permanent branches have a better chance of sustaining themselves because of their "purely republican" foundation. The proud spirit of popular government brooks no opposition, so the Constitution creates nothing more popular than elective institutions to undermine them, and nothing less popular than elective institutions for them to undermine.

CONCLUSION

To assess the fate of this experiment we would need to consider both the sturdiness of the forms invented in 1787, and the degree to which they had the intended effects. The first of these subjects is easier to consider. The Constitutional forms of 1787–88 have not succumbed to the state governments or the House of Representatives, despite the presumed strength of the most popular branches. A number of conspicuous institutional changes of two centuries appear consistent with *The Federalist*'s own arguments: the growth of political parties, the withering of the electoral college, the expansion of suffrage, the abolition of slavery, and the direct election of senators.[24] In particular, *The Federalist*'s emphasis on the honorable human determination for self-government argues against theories of interest aggregation or virtual representation that might condone a restrictive franchise.

Have these institutions had the intended effects? A full answer to this question would require not only an understanding of the actual history of the United States and the causes of that history, and of the "silent and unperceived" (63) influence of the Constitution in preventing things that did not happen,[25] but also the wisdom to judge how far those developments have served private rights, the public good, and popular government. It would have to consider whether the founders overestimated or underestimated the strength of various political impulses set or kept in motion by the Constitution, and whether these constitutional effects were offset or overcome by "informal" forces it was unable (or failed) to control, such as changes in prevailing opinions, technical inventions, or foreign enemies. The Constitutional amendments would have to be understood both as part of the original design, because the provision and procedure for amendments were part of that design, and as revealing its defects (or at the very least its inability to sustain itself against misguided complaints).

On this large topic I offer only a few observations that bear on the question of popular government. The technology that permits public-opinion polling and modern media seems to act as an informal counterweight to the constitutional forms that were designed to encourage patient deliberation as opposed to passionate haste.[26] These developments change the situation of representatives and of the unassembled people, but it is not clear that they are democratizing. Do they rather give new tools to ambitious politicians, teaching them how to "position" themselves, to "focus" popular messages, to deflect responsibility for what is unpopular, and in general more artfully to "build their political consequence on the prepossessions of their fellow-citizens" (46)?

The federal government's size and scope are perhaps cases where one part of the founders' design succeeded too well. Employing politicians who are held "responsible" encourages them to generate or claim accomplishments—even "extensive and arduous enterprises for the public benefit" (72)—rather than to content themselves with the honest, uneventful superintendence of a minimal set of functions. They want to make their mark so as to claim reelection or fame. The Constitution expects such ambition to be restrained by other politicians and by a suspicious people egged on by jealous state officials. But a national government that proves itself benign will calm these suspicions and lay the basis for further activities. The state governments, despite certain advantages for the practice of popular government,[27] take a back seat. And responsibility itself changes. "Responsibility, in order to be reasonable, must be limited to objects within the power of the responsible party, and in order to be effectual, must relate to operations of that power, of which a ready and proper judgment can be formed by the constituents" (62). As the objects of the government increase, a ready and proper judgment becomes more difficult. The people are seen more as consumers of policy than as judges of it.

Some of the federal government's growth was deliberately enacted by constitutional amendment, but some was not. Democratic opinion today is not preoccupied with interpreting constitutional grants of power or with the formalities of constitutional amendment, so long as the substance of policy seems good and the people come to accept it. While this opinion resembles *The Federalist*'s standards for legitimate government, it does not quite preserve in its full glory the republican theory that our form of government is a deliberate choice of a people with the right and capacity to choose and judge their own rulers.

NOTES

1. Harvey C. Mansfield, review of *Athenian Democracy: Modern Mythmakers and Ancient Theorists,* by Arlene Saxonhouse, *American Political Science Review* 92.2 (June 1998): 449.

2. Parenthetical citations refer to essay numbers of *The Federalist.*

3. One historian goes so far as to say that the revolutionary generation's "accomplishments had no calculable links to democracy." Robert H. Wiebe, *Self-Rule* (Chicago: University of Chicago Press, 1995), 14.

4. Mansfield aptly calls this "introspective republicanism." "Returning to the Founders: The Debate on the Constitution," *The New Criterion* (September 1993): 54.

5. Emphasis added. See also number 57: "The aim of *every political constitution* is, or ought to be, first to obtain for rulers men who possess most wisdom to discern, and most virtue to pursue, the common good of the society; and in the next place, to take the most effectual precautions for keeping them virtuous whilst they continue to hold their public trust" (emphasis added).

6. By beginning with an assertion that American independence is justified by the "Laws of Nature," the Declaration implies that the subsequent list of "self-evident truths" that lead to that conclusion are themselves laws of nature. These truths include what *Federalist* 43 calls a law of nature: the standard of "safety and happiness" for new governments, and the idea that existing governments may be "sacrificed."

7. *Federalist* 51. This account echoes chapter 13 of Hobbes, *Leviathan,* ed. C. B. Macpherson (Harmondsworth, England: Penguin Books, 1968), 183. In Locke's state of nature, the reasonable obey and enforce the law of nature and the unreasonable do not, but Locke does not call attention to the "weaker" and "stronger."

8. Compare the Declaration's first and third self-evident truths; and Locke, *Second Treatise,* sec. 131, in *Two Treatises of Government,* ed. Peter Laslett (New York: Mentor, 1965), 398.

9. This rhetorical emphasis was appropriate to the main practical task of agreement on a constitution, which required a sacrifice "of private opinions and partial interests to the public good" (37).

10. Madison and Hamilton both suggested in the privacy of the Philadelphia convention that this genius might change. See Max Farrand, ed., *The Records of the Federal Convention of 1787* (New Haven, Conn.: Yale University Press, 1966), 1:219, 221, 301.

11. Indeed, *The Federalist* describes the "contest with Great Britain" not as a case of monarchical oppression but as one in which "the more numerous part [of the empire] invaded the rights of the less numerous part" (46).

12. Compare number 57, which states "*the*" (emphasis added) "fundamental principle" of republican government as "the right and the capacity of the people to choose their own rulers."

13. While a "variety of interests . . . may have a salutary influence on the administration of the government when formed, yet every one must be sensible of the contrary influence, which must have been experienced in the task of forming it" (37).

14. Thus the Constitutional provision that forbids the people of a state to institute an antirepublican government will "hardly be considered as a grievance" (43).

15. The proud claims of self-government may give way to the humbling needs of security. In dire circumstances, a people becomes willing to risk being "less free" in order to be "more safe" (8). The insecurity of private rights against majority faction could cause even the majority to call for a government "altogether independent of the people." "Justice . . . will be pursued until it be obtained, or until liberty be lost in the pursuit" (51). And apparently because there is no alternative to the national government's full authority over the seat of government, *The Federalist* defends an arrangement for the capital's government that does not comport with its own republican principles (43).

16. *Second Treatise,* sec. 107, p. 382.

17. See book 3, chap. 11 of Aristotle, *Politics,* ed. Carnes Lord (Chicago: University of Chicago Press, 1984), 101.

18. Number 22 observes that "history furnishes us with so many *mortifying* examples of the prevalency of foreign corruption in republican governments," but not in monarchies (emphasis added).

19. Majority rule, a "fundamental maxim of republican government" (22), is also called "the fundamental principle of free government" (58).

20. The fate of Gorbachev's attempt to democratize Communism is evidence on *The Federalist*'s side. On the problem of mixing different principles of rule, see Harvey C. Mansfield, Jr., *The Spirit of Liberalism* (Cambridge, Mass.: Harvard University Press, 1978), 6: "The problem is that attracting the partisans does not diminish but rather increases their desire for democracy or oligarchy unmixed. How can they be weaned away from the very taste by which they are attracted?"

21. If representatives cannot be trusted, democracy might still be feasible. "The people should resolve to recall all the powers they have heretofore parted with out of their own hands, and to divide themselves into as many States as there are counties, in order that they may be able to manage their own concerns in person" (26). But democracy requires some virtue, because a vote in the assembly gives opportunities to abuse minorities or because popular administrative practices are not harsh enough to control a truly wicked people. An exaggerated view of human "depravity" implies not only that representatives are untrustworthy, but that no form of "self-government" is feasible because men will "devour" each other without "the chains of despotism" (55).

22. Thus *The Federalist* sometimes calls the ancient governments "republics" (6, 8, 9, 34, 58, 63), sometimes "democracies" (14, 63).

23. That is, "*the total exclusion of the people in their collective capacity* from any share" in the government (63; italics in original).

24. Note the very lukewarm defense of indirect election of the Senate (62), reinforced by the argument against appointments by a "select body or assembly" (76). The electoral college procedures defended in number 68 are summarized (twice) in number 69 as an election "by the people." While *The Federalist*'s authors might be surprised by the durability, respectability, and moderation of modern parties, they

would not be surprised by their existence (see 50). Even "our Southern brethren" are said to admit that slavery is a matter of "rights which have been taken away" (54).

25. A leading historian neglects the latter issue when he concludes from the scarcity of actual presidential impeachments that that constitutional provision has been "nearly useless" (Jack Rakove, *New York Times,* January 12, 1999, A19).

26. On polls and media, see Harvey C. Mansfield, Jr., *America's Constitutional Soul* (Baltimore: Johns Hopkins University Press, 1991), 156–57 and 163–76.

27. *The Federalist*'s case for the national government as against the state governments included arguments that seem to cut the other way today. Electoral districts can properly encompass six thousand or thirty thousand voters, not just six hundred (57); but today's congressional districts include six hundred thousand inhabitants. The argument that size and diversity favor justice (10) was accompanied by a prediction that the individual states themselves would over time become internally diverse, improving the prospects for state government (56).

15

Responsibility in *The Federalist*

Charles R. Kesler

How can republican government be made responsible? This is the question that *The Federalist,* in its new account and defense of republicanism, answered some two hundred years ago. Its argument is worth revisiting, because today "responsibility," though still a kind of virtue and therefore praiseworthy, seems to lack any sure connection with republican government. Here and there a few of our politicians covet the title—Senator Bob Dole, for example, was proud to be counted as a "responsible Republican," and President Clinton can hardly utter a sentence without urging responsibility on everyone except himself—but it is not exactly clear what the encomium means. "Responsible" appears often to be a synonym for "pragmatic," that is, not an extremist either of the right or the left; but the term has a certain prosaic or uninspiring connotation, too, which is not lost on our media.

So the relation between responsibility and republicanism is nowadays elusive. Responsibility seems to be a quality that republican government needs or can use, but that cannot be found in the Constitution itself. Politicians who are responsible want the government to moderate its ambitions and to live within its means, but their sympathy with the taxpayers has no obvious connection to the Constitution. By contrast, *The Federalist* argues that responsibility is essential to republicanism's success and dignity—and that it is the Constitution that makes responsible republicanism possible. The boldness of Publius's claim is reinforced by the consideration that the very word "responsibility" shows up prominently for the first time in the American political debates of the 1780s; and the term receives its classic definition in its extended discussion in *The Federalist.*

"Responsibility" is thus a fairly new word, thought by the historian Douglass Adair to have been coined by James Madison himself. Adair noticed that the *Oxford English Dictionary* considered the word an American invention and credited its first appearance in the language to Madison's discussion of senatorial responsibility in *Federalist* number 63. Adair's own researches turned up earlier uses by Madison and James Wilson, beginning with "its first obscure appearance . . . in Madison's committee report to the Continental Congress on the Quartermaster Department [July 22, 1780]."[1] In fact, however, the word had already been used by British Whigs arguing for a Parliament responsible to the people and for government ministers responsible to Parliament. It was in America, though, that the term took root and began rapidly to spread. General George Washington, for example, wrote to James Duane (December 26, 1780), "There are two things . . . indispensably necessary to the well being and good Government of our public Affairs . . . greater powers to Congress, and more responsibility and permanency in the executive bodies."[2]

Whoever coined the term, "responsibility" is the noun form of a much older adjective, "responsible," itself related to the verb "respond," meaning to answer; its Latin ancestor is *respondeo,* whose root (*spondeo*) means to promise sacredly or to vow. To be responsible thus means to be answerable to someone else, implying the possibility of punishment if one has not been diligent or faithful. But to be responsible also means to be the cause of something, to be equal to a challenge or obligation, to live up to a vow or solemn promise. If republican government is to be responsible, it must be responsive to the people and answerable to their will; but if it is to be responsible in the more positive sense, it must go beyond mere responsiveness and be able to serve their true interests or their reasonable will. The tension between these two senses of "responsibility" underlay the debate between Anti-Federalists and Federalists over the ratification of the Constitution.

For the Anti-Federalists, responsibility meant primarily and almost exclusively the first sense of the term: the essence of republican government was that it be responsive to the people. Hence responsibility was always, in the words of the Anti-Federalist writer Brutus, "responsibility to some superior power." The "true policy of a republican government" was so to frame it that all its officials were "made accountable to some superior for their conduct in office"; and this "superior power" was ultimately "the People."[3] In one of his great speeches denouncing the proposed Constitution in the Virginia convention, Patrick Henry asked, "for where, Sir, is the responsibility?" "Where is the responsibility," he repeated, "that leading principle in the British government? In that government a punishment, certain and inevitable, is provided: But in this, there is no real actual punishment for the grossest maladministration." Under the British Constitution, malfeasance in office had cost the heads of "some of the most saucy geniuses that ever were"; whereas under the new American Constitution, he charged, "the preservation of our liberty depends on the single chance of men being virtuous enough to make laws to punish themselves."[4]

The problem, as Patrick Henry and many other Anti-Federalists saw it, was that the Constitution, though boasting an elaborate scheme of separation of powers and checks and balances, did not manage to secure the new government against the danger of minority faction, of tyranny by the few men of enterprise, ambition, and wealth. This goal had been achieved, however precariously, in the British Constitution, which was why it had so much appeal to the Anti-Federalist writers. In fact, the whole question of responsibility in government was for them an extension of the British struggle for parliamentary and ministerial accountability, that is, for a freely elected Parliament and for ministers who were answerable to Parliament rather than to the king. Ministerial accountability meant that Parliament had a direct say over the administration of British government, and thus an additional important check on royal power. A Maryland pundit expressed the point so: "In this new Constitution—a complicated system sets responsibility at defiance, and the Rights of Men . . . are left at the mercy of events." For after all, he declared, "Government by Representation (unless confirmed in its views and conduct by the constant inspection, immediate superintendence, and frequent interference and control of the People themselves on one side, or an hereditary nobility on the other, both of which orders have fixed and permanent views) is really only a scene of perpetual rapine and confusion."[5] Except in England, that is, whose mixed regime had achieved a proper balance, though it had once been "hardly a government at all" until "simplified by the introduction and regular formation of the effective administration of responsible ministers."[6]

Indeed, one possibility for securing responsible government was the mixed regime along British lines. Most Anti-Federalists admitted, however, that America did not have the proper materials—most importantly, a well-established class of wealthy aristocrats—out of which to construct a mixed regime along British, much less along classical lines.[7] And given the vicissitudes of British constitutional history, the stability and reliability of even the best modern incarnations of the mixed regime did not look all that promising. The Philadelphia writer Centinel criticized John Adams' elaborate apology for balanced government on the grounds that human wisdom was not equal to contriving such a structure; that even if practicable it would last "not a day," inasmuch as the balance would be upset by the subsequent decisions made by unequal men; and that at any rate "the welfare and happiness of the community" could not be produced by the "jarring adverse interests" actuating the three branches. Besides, even in England, where the "state of society" is much more favorable to balanced government, the tripartite balance is illusory: it is "the sense of the people at large" that forms "the only operative and efficient check upon the conduct of administration."[8]

Given how unlikely it was that any form of mixed government could be created and sustained in America, the Anti-Federalists tended to prefer simple government, based as far as possible upon the people at large. Though they recognized that direct democracy was impossible even for state governments, much less for the national government, they preferred representative forms that approximated direct democracy through such expedients as a numerous representation, short terms of office, and frequent rotation in office (term limits, we call it today). The Federal Farmer, one of the soberest opponents of the Constitution, expressed this ideal of representation as follows: "a full and equal representation, is one that possesses the same interests, feelings, opinions, and views the people themselves would were they all assembled."[9] While conceding the necessity in a representative government of some sort of bicameralism and separation of powers, most Anti-Federalists regarded these devices primarily as means of checking the ambitious few—the enemies or manipulators of direct democracy—rather than as means of restricting legislative power as such and consequently energizing executive and judicial power. Few went so far as Centinel, who advocated a unicameral legislature on the Pennsylvania model. But most would have agreed with him that the form of government that "holds those entrusted with power, in the greatest responsibility to their constituents" is "the best calculated for free men."[10] A Maryland farmer put it succinctly: responsibility is "the only test of good government."[11] The point of the strict separation of powers urged by most Anti-Federalists was, therefore, to keep the government responsible to the people by making the parchment barriers between departments as clear and exact as possible. It would then be up to the people to police those barriers, to keep the executive from encroaching on any part of the legislative power, to keep the legislature from dabbling in the judicial power, and so forth.[12]

Quite different is *The Federalist*'s understanding of the nexus between responsibility and republicanism; and it is to the explication of this relation that the rest of this chapter will be devoted. The term "responsibility" occurs twenty-six times in *The Federalist,* all but once in the book's second part (numbers 37–85). If one adds in the adjective "responsible," the term and its cognate occur thirty-six times, all but three appearances being in the second part.[13] These facts suggest what a careful reading of the book confirms, that what makes American national government responsible is the Constitution proper, not the union (the theme of the first thirty-six papers). Responsibility implies the capacity to answer for oneself, to govern oneself, but it is precisely the ability of Americans to govern themselves as one nation that is in question in *The Federalist*'s first part.[14] In the beginning, Publius stresses that it is difficult to take responsibility for oneself in the face of the powerful necessities that confront the American people—that would confront any people. In the language of *Federalist* number 1, "reflection and choice" must pay their due to "accident and force" if the Americans intend really to establish themselves as an independent people. The most elementary of the necessities that Americans must face up to is "safety" or self-preservation: "Safety from external danger is the most powerful director of national conduct," Publius writes. "Even the ardent love of liberty will, after a time, give way to its dictates."[15] But his objective is to meet this necessity not through Machiavellian crimes but by way of "reflection and choice" on the proper structure of the union and the new, energetic form of government that will pervade it.

These are the themes of *The Federalist*'s first part. Initially it appears that securing the union will be easy, for "Providence has been pleased to give this one connected country to one united people. . . ." But soon it appears that this "band of brethren" is threatening to split up into separate confederacies of states, with each state itself teetering on the brink of tyranny due to the danger of majority faction. By "majority faction" Publius means a majority "of citizens," not just of legislators or elected officials; so that the Anti-Federalists' favorite prescription for the ills of republican government—responsibility to the "superior power" of "the people"—is shown to be inadequate in principle.[16] What if the people, or a majority of the people, wishes to use its power unjustly? The Anti-Federalists' reduction of responsibility to *responsiveness* leaves them without a good answer to this fundamental question. Civic education would be the traditional solution to this perplexity, and the Anti-Federalists did maintain that the states provided, through militia service, established churches, bills of rights, and various forms of direct participation in government, a republican education to their citizens that a national government could not begin to equal.[17] But Publius's point was that civic education as carried on in the states had failed or was failing—else why would the urgent problem of majority faction have arisen?[18]

Of course, the size of the states had something to do with the advent of majority factions, as Publius argues in the famous number 10. Neither direct democracy nor a small republic could solve the problem of majority tyranny, according to *Federalist* 10, because neither was large enough to embrace a saving multiplicity of interests. If one extended the sphere of republican government to include more, and more various, interests, then it would be less probable that any one of them could form the basis for an enduring and impassioned majority. One could get rid of majority faction by getting rid of majorities, or a least those "united, and actuated, by some common impulse of passion, or of interest," adverse to private rights or the public good.[19] Thus it was necessary for the "one united people" of America to utilize and perhaps even foster the divisions of interest among themselves in order to remedy the problem of republican responsibility.

Yet interest checking interest seems to be a formula for irresponsibility: no one (at least, no one after the framers) needs to take responsibility for the common good or for connecting private and public interest. Publius begins his argument in this section by in effect granting the Anti-Federalists' premise: the American people are virtuous and their interests homogeneous enough to sustain republican government. The Americans, he avers in number 2, are "a people descended from the same ancestors, speaking the same language, professing the same religion, attached to the same principles of government, very similar in their manners and customs. . . ."[20] This portrait is somewhat exaggerated, as Publius knows, but he employs it to show that even so, the American people, faced with clever threats and devious temptations from foreign powers, and abandoned by the Articles of Confederation at home, have reached the point that their loyalty to the union and their justice toward one another are fast degenerating. Whatever the strengths of the Anti-Federalists' argument *in abstracto* for the small republic, Publius emphasizes that the reality of government in the states is that the people have learned that they have rights but not how to distinguish those rights from their passions and interests. In short, republican government was degenerating toward extreme democracy.

This is why the real agenda of *Federalist* 10 is to discredit direct democracy as the standard at which popular government ought to aim. Publius says this explicitly: "a pure democracy, by which I mean a society consisting of a small number of citizens, who assemble and administer the government in person, can admit of no cure for the mischiefs of faction."[21] Republican government, i.e., representative government, then becomes the best form of popular government—not just a diluted or second-best form. What is good about republicanism, Publius claims, is two things, representation (the government will be administered by a chosen few) and size (it can cover an extended territory embracing many interests). But Publius wishes to refute direct democracy on the most democratic grounds possible, and so in number 10 he stresses the numbers of interests and sheer extent of territory that are necessary to make popular government work. He does not dwell on the subject of representation, which would lead eventually to a more candid account of the limitations of direct democracy from the point of view of aristocracy.[22] (This is the subject he will treat of in the book's second part, in the discussion of senatorial and executive responsibility; and even there his discussion is quite politic.)

Publius lays the groundwork in number 10 for a new kind of responsibility that means more than reporting back to the people, and for a new kind of republicanism that is more than direct democracy once removed. Indeed, it is on this new basis that Publius, after emphasizing in numbers 6–10 the differences in interests that have arisen and will continue to arise among Americans, returns in number 14 to the theme sounded in number 2—union founded on the unity of the American people. "[T]he kindred blood which flows in the veins of American citizens, the mingled blood which they have shed in defense of their sacred rights," Publius insists, "consecrate their

Union and excite horror at the idea of their becoming aliens, rivals, enemies."[23] The problem of faction recedes and becomes, as it were, an interlude in American unity. But because of the rhetorical structure of his argument, he leaves the impression in these papers that size, virtually alone, will guarantee healthy republican government.

Accordingly, the large territory he lauds remains abstract; he does not discourse on the political subdivisions that might order it, and barely mentions the existing states except to criticize them for being too small and factious. In the remaining papers of the first part, Publius reconstructs—perhaps one should say deconstructs—the union in order to meet the dangers it faces, including, he now explains, threats from the excessive power of the state governments under the Articles of Confederation. To establish a "firm" union, the United States needs an energetic government capable of operating directly on individuals, not merely on the people assembled in the "collective bodies" of the states. In such "collective bodies," men divide up the infamy of their actions; and, exulting in their corporate power, they are driven to fight off all external efforts to restrain or direct them. In such groups, men continue to feel and be moved by their bodily passions, but the means to pursue the objects of their passions are vastly multiplied. In their "collective bodies," men are at their most ungovernable. Therefore, government must be able to reach down to them in their individual bodies in order to overawe them and render them fit for government. Publius's new version of federalism is thus necessarily a rearrangement not only of sovereignty but also of the objects of the people's passions and interests.[24] It affects not only the people's "hopes and fears" but also their habits and so finally their opinions.[25]

Energizing the national government may help to fortify the union, but it does not, by itself, increase republican responsibility. For in this new dispensation the people are acted upon by the government; they are the objects of what Publius does not hesitate to call "coercion." Though collectively men are at their most ungovernable, taken individually men are perhaps too governable, too "timid and cautious" for political freedom.[26] Thus the first part of *The Federalist* does not manage to solve the problem of republican responsibility, certainly not in its higher dimensions. The single mention of "responsibility" in this part of the book occurs in number 23, when Publius declares that it is the federal government, "from the responsibility implied in the duty assigned to it," that ought to have all power necessary to "make suitable provisions for the public defense."[27] Moreover, this power, as well as the power to tax, are essential attributes of sovereignty, and "ought to exist without limitation" because no limitation can in practice be put on the potential dangers and exigencies with which the nation may be confronted.[28] This is an eye-opening statement on responsibility, radically different from the Anti-Federalists' view. Here responsibility arises from a duty, a particular task or job assigned to the national government, and the spirit of the statement suggests that the people cannot reasonably limit the government's exercise of that responsibility in advance, and even in retrospect ought to beware of pious second-guessing. In other words, whereas for the Anti-Federalists responsibility is principally a check on government for the sake of the people's power or right, here responsibility empowers government as an implication of government's duty—and a rather peremptory duty at that.

This is ultimately a duty to the people, however, so that contrast between the two notions of responsibility is not as stark as it may first appear. Still, in number 23 Publius emphasizes the contrast, and argues that the American people really have no choice but to adopt a more energetic government if they wish to survive and prosper. The possible dangers involved in the unlimited rights to tax and "to make suitable provisions for the national defense" are said, in effect, to come with the territory. Only later, in the book's second part, does Publius show how the dangers of unlimited powers may be reduced by constitutionalizing them through the separation of powers, which allows energy in government to be concentrated in the executive branch, guarded by an independent judiciary and a bicameral legislature—one branch of which will be especially concerned with taxation, the other with diplomacy and foreign relations. Only in this later discussion does *The Federalist* show how the state governments may themselves be rehabilitated by becoming parts of the constitutional system.[29]

Turning, then, to the second part of *The Federalist,* one finds that "responsibility" is mentioned once in the account of the House of Representatives, six times regarding the Senate, thirteen times concerning the executive, and thrice in the papers on the judiciary. The great thematic discussions of responsibility occur in number 63 on the Senate and number 70 on the executive. Somehow the nature of republican responsibility seems to be revealed particularly in those two branches.

But the main organizing principle of the whole second part of *The Federalist* is the separation of powers, which is the sine qua non of responsibility in republican government. Separation of powers performs three main functions in Publius's argument. First, it protects against governmental tyranny, especially by restricting the legislature's power—the branch most to be feared, precisely because it is by nature the most powerful in republican government. The Constitution mixes the powers of the three branches in order to keep them separate, but the result is to deprecate the legislature's claim to be in some special sense the people's branch. Instead, the executive and judiciary are made representative, too, though it is now no longer just the people's interests or passions that come to be represented in government.[30] By contrast, the Anti-Federalists understood the separation of powers to cut particularly against the executive, or against energetic government in general, in the name of popular liberty or responsibility.

Second, Publius holds that a proper separation of powers allows each of ꝛ.
the branches to perform its peculiar function well. The Anti-Federalists
thought this desirable, too, but emphasized that the people must be the
judge of constitutional demarcations, hence also of the nature of the three
powers.[31] And finally, *The Federalist* argues that separation of powers pre- ꝛ.
vents or replaces direct recurrence to the people as the means of solving Con.
cases of conflict among the branches. This is an advantage of the separation Con.
of powers that needs some further explanation. The people of the United
States legislate the Constitution for themselves by ratifying it; but they never
subsequently judge or execute it directly. There is no national initiative or
referendum to decide whether a law is constitutional, for example. In fact,
the people are excluded altogether from the administration of the government; that is the job of our elected representatives.[32] To be sure, the people
have the right, under the Constitution, to exercise their sovereign opinion
over the whole government (eventually), through regular elections. The political and constitutional soundness of particular measures is, however, always decided in the course of conflict and cooperation among the departments. To the extent that the public does occasionally pronounce on the
soundness of a particular measure, e.g., the Kansas-Nebraska Act, it does so
indirectly through its choice in representative elections.

In this way, the deliberative give-and-take among the separated branches replaces direct appeals to the people to decide questions of constitutional propriety. This effect of separation of powers, Publius explains in *Federalist* 49,
encourages reverence for the law and veneration of the Constitution to de- Aristotle
velop. Though public opinion or the consent of the governed is the original Politics
authority of the Constitution, the public learns subsequently to measure its
opinions by the Constitution. The Constitution and the public opinion that reflects it—what Publius calls "the reason of the public"—then become sovereign over the government. In the words of number 49, "it is the reason, alone,
of the public that ought to control and regulate the government. The passions
[of the public] ought to be controlled and regulated by the government."[33]

So the reason of the public controls the government, which in turn regu-
lates the public's passions. This is not a formula for the direct rule of reason
over passion in politics. It calls rather for the reason "of the public" to control the passions through the mediation of government. The direct rule of philosophy
reason over passion in politics might be said to dictate the suppression of
rights in the name of duties or virtues. Publius does not endorse that, but neither does he allow rights to sink to their lowest common denominator, to become mere expressions of self-interest or passion. Instead, he calls for the
"reason of the public" to become responsible for the passions of the public:
he defends a form of government that will encourage rights to be claimed
and exercised responsibly. *The Federalist*'s concern for veneration of the

Constitution shows that a purely calculative or self-interested attachment to government is not enough to secure republicanism. To the extent that Hobbes and Locke urge such an approach, their understanding of the social contract is deficient. Instead, Publius emphasizes that the Constitution must attract the loyalty, admiration, pride, and even reverence of American citizens if the rule of law is to be firmly grounded—if republicanism is to be responsible. Therefore, in the end, one needs an opinion of the Constitution's goodness to attract, define, and hold Americans' passions and interests in a decent republican order.

This means a politics of public opinion, not just of fractured interests à la *Federalist* 10. Majority faction, in other words, cannot finally be defeated except by a healthy majority opinion, which it is the chief educational goal, or to put it differently, the ultimate political goal, of Publius to inculcate. This means not so much a politics of virtue as of responsibility, which is consistent with men's equal natural rights but urges that these rights be seen ultimately in light of "the honor of the human race" rather than in light of man's dishonorable necessities.[34] Responsibility lifts up rights toward reason, though it does not close the gap completely. Responsibility comes into its own in particular circumstances when some sort of action must be taken: it strives to bring interest and duty together in order to do the right thing, often in disagreeable situations where someone must take charge, or as we say today, take responsibility. The Constitution provides platforms for this kind of responsibility in the various offices of the separated powers, particularly the Senate and the presidency.

In his discussion of the Senate in number 63, Publius begins by acknowledging what will strike many of his readers, including the Anti-Federalists, as a paradox, namely, that irresponsibility may sometimes result from "that frequency of elections which in other cases produces this responsibility." That is to say, too frequent elections may destroy the responsibility that elections normally produce. Publius here begins to turn the Anti-Federalist catechism against itself: in order to produce true responsibility to the people, responsibility in the stronger, more self-assertive sense may sometimes be necessary. Responsibility, he continues, if it is to be reasonable, presupposes that the objects to be achieved lie within the power of the agent, and if it is to be effectual, that the constituents may form "a ready and proper judgement" of the power's use. The achievement of these conditions is jeopardized by the fact that government has not only "immediate and sensible" objects but also those "depending on a succession of well-chosen and well-connected measures, which have a gradual and perhaps unobserved operation." A Senate is needed especially to attend to the latter class of objects. Without such a select group of representatives enjoying long terms of office, republican government would not be able rationally to pursue long-term objectives, and the people would not have anyone whom they could fairly blame for the neglect. Thus responsibility to the people demands responsibility in the office of Senator. Senators need responsibility to be able to pursue the common good, even against the "temporary errors and delusions" of the people themselves, Publius now adds. The "cool and deliberate sense of the community" ought to prevail in all governments, a fortiori in free ones; but when the people, "stimulated by some irregular passion, or some illicit advantage, or misled by the artful misrepresentations of interested men," prepare to do themselves harm, then "some temperate and respectable body of citizens" has a responsibility to "suspend the blow . . . until reason, justice, and truth can regain their authority over the public mind." Publius does not specify that these temperate and respectable men actually hold office as senators; their authority or responsibility seems to arise from the nature of the case, not from any authorization by the people.[35] Nor does he explore the consequences should "reason, justice, and truth" not soon regain their hold on the public mind. He does invoke Athens as an example of a popular government that could have used a senate, the better to avoid "the indelible reproach of decreeing to the same citizens the hemlock on one day and statues on the next." Thus Publius generalizes the case of Socrates into an indictment of the passionate and mutable justice of Athenian democracy, suggesting that "reason, justice, and truth" *cannot* be counted on to show themselves in the public mind *absent* the institution of a senate. Responsibility requires wisdom, not exactly the wisdom of Socrates but the wisdom that could have saved Socrates.

"the most decent" (vito)

Yet how can the American people in their extended republic be subject to such "violent passions" or to the "danger of combining in pursuit of unjust measures"? Will not America's large size protect it against such distempers? Now Publius revises his famous judgment on this question rendered in number 10. There are disadvantages to a large extent of territory about which we did not hear before. Moreover, not all ancient popular governments (the apparent bane of number 9) had "fugitive and turbulent" lives. "Sparta, Rome, and Carthage" were in fact "long-lived" republics, because each had a senate. Though "as unfit for the imitation as they are repugnant to the genius of America," these examples are nonetheless "very instructive proofs" of the necessity of a senate, of "some institution that will blend stability with liberty." America's continental dimensions do not exempt her from the need for a senate, because the extended republic actually solves neither the problem of governmental tyranny nor that of popular tyranny. Publius makes clear that to cure the defects both of "a numerous assembly frequently elected by the people" and of "the people themselves," what is necessary is not so much an extended territory as a senate.[36]

One might say that republicanism requires more responsibility than was implied in the democratic, almost deterministic account given early in *The Federalist.* This truth is visible most plainly in the presidency. The president, too, must occasionally stand responsibly not only against the legislature but against the people; but he is only one man, and if he is not "timid and cautious" it is because men of "courage and magnanimity" are attracted to so grand an office.[37] The president's expected virtues go beyond the temperance and respectability of the senators; perhaps they go beyond the requirements of responsibility. But they look like responsibility or can be made to look like it in action, because his virtues appear alongside his legal, constitutional powers of office. He has a job to do, and what is more responsible than doing it? Still, he is one, and his virtues and powers raise the specter of monarchy, which Publius takes great pains to exorcise. In a nice twist, Publius appeals to the more democratic or Anti-Federalist version of responsibility to rescue the presidency from anti-republican opprobrium: it is precisely the unity of the executive that makes him so accountable, so easily censured and punished. He has no one to shift the blame to. Hence his office is eminently responsible, is safe "in the republican sense."[38]

Responsibility is the only virtue or quasi virtue that has entered our moral language from the American founding. In large measure, in fact, it is *The Federalist* that has defined and still defines its contemporary meaning. The sense of the term preferred by the Anti-Federalists is still with us, too, but our debt to Publius is larger and more important, as can be seen in the fact that what was principally in *The Federalist* a virtue of statesmen, is now sought among ordinary citizens as well. One does not have to be a statesman to act responsibly. But citizens and statesmen alike must act responsibly if they intend to keep their republic. This is *The Federalist*'s lesson in self-government.

NOTES

1. Douglass Adair, "The Federalist Papers," in Trevor Colbourn, ed., *Fame and the Founding Fathers: Essays by Douglas Adair* (New York: W. W. Norton, 1974), 257.

2. Cf. James Burgh, *Political Disquisitions* (New York: Da Capo Press, 1971; orig. pub. 1774), bk. IV, chaps. 1–3, and bk. V, chap. 4; W. B. Allen, ed., *George Washington: A Collection* (Indianapolis: Liberty Classics, 1988), 178.

3. Brutus XVI, 2.9.197, in Herbert J. Storing, ed., *The Complete Anti-Federalist,* 7 vols. (Chicago: University of Chicago Press, 1981), 2:442.

4. "Speeches of Patrick Henry," June 5, 1788, 5.16.8, in Storing, 5:226.

5. "Address by John Francis Mercer," April or May 1788, 5.5.11, in Storing, 5:105.

6. "Essays by a Farmer," V, 5.1.75, in Storing, 5:45.

7. Cf. "Letters from the Federal Farmer," XI, 2.8.145–46, in Storing, 2:287–88.

8. "Letters of Centinel," I, 2.7.7–2.7.8, Storing, 2:138.

9. "Letters from the Federal Farmer," II, 2.8.15, in Storing, 2:230.

10. "Letters of Centinel," I, 2.7.9, in Storing, 2:138–39. This view of course presupposed that "the body of the people are virtuous, and . . . property is pretty equally di-

vided. . . ." In such circumstances, "the highest responsibility is to be attained, in a simple structure of government," where what is today called the blame game (i.e., passing responsibility from the House to the Senate, or from Congress to the president) cannot be played. "Centinel," I 2.7.9, in Storing, 2:139.

11. "Essays by a Farmer," II, 5.1.34, in Storing, 5:23.

12. Cf. Herbert J. Storing, *What the Anti-Federalists Were FOR*, in Storing, 1:55–63. Storing notes that most of the Anti-Federalists did not advocate reliance on the people "for everyday use" in policing the separation of powers, which is true, inasmuch as elections are a periodic rather than "everyday" check. Storing, 1:61. But most of the opponents of the Constitution were surely not comfortable with the extent to which the Constitution mixed the powers of the three departments in order to keep them separate. This left the Anti-Federalists in a dilemma. Cf. "Brutus" XVI, 2.9.197 and 2.9.202–2.9.204, in Storing, 2:442–43 and 445–46 with *The Federalist Papers,* ed. Clinton Rossiter with introduction and notes by Charles R. Kesler (New York: Penguin Putnam, Inc., 1999), (New York: New American Library, 1961), no. 51, 288–89. And consider William Kristol, "The Problem of the Separation of Power: *Federalist* 47–51," in Charles R. Kesler, ed., *Saving the Revolution: The Federalist Papers and the American Founding* (New York: Free Press, 1987), 100–130, at 120–122.

13. See the relevant entries in the indispensable *The Federalist Concordance,* eds., Thomas S. Engeman, Edward J. Erler, and Thomas B. Hofeller (Middletown, Conn.: Wesleyan University Press, 1980). On the importance of responsibility, see Harvey C. Mansfield, Jr., *The Spirit of Liberalism* (Cambridge: Harvard University Press, 1978), 81; and Harvey C. Mansfield, Jr., *Taming the Prince: The Ambivalence of Modern Executive Power* (New York: Free Press, 1989), 251, 270–71, 291–93.

14. On the significance of the structure of the book's argument, see Charles R. Kesler, "*Federalist* 10 and American Republicanism," in Kesler, 13–39, at 19–21; and David F. Epstein, *The Political Theory of The Federalist* (Chicago: University of Chicago Press, 1948), 7–10.

15. *The Federalist* no. 8, p. 35.

16. *The Federalist* no. 2, p. 6; no. 10, p. 46.

17. Cf. Storing, *What the Anti-Federalists Were FOR,* 20–23.

18. Cf. *The Federalist* no. 10, pp. 45–46.

19. *The Federalist* no. 10, pp. 46, 49, 51. The difficulty of distinguishing between just majorities, whose opinions must direct the government, and unjust majorities, whose passions and interests must be prevented.

20. *The Federalist* no. 2, p. 6.

21. *The Federalist* no. 10, p. 49.

22. For a more complete interpretation, see Kesler, "*Federalist* 10 and American Republicanism," 23–39.

23. *The Federalist* no. 14, p. 72; cf. no. 2, p. 6.

24. *The Federalist* no. 15, pp. 76, 78–79.

25. *The Federalist* no. 16, pp. 84; no. 27, pp. 142–44.

26. Cf. *The Federalist* no. 49, pp. 282–83.

27. *The Federalist* no. 23, p. 123.

28. *The Federalist* no. 23, p. 121.

29. Cf. *The Federalist* no. 17, pp. 87–88; no. 27, pp. 142–45; no. 43, pp. 242–46; no. 45, pp.258–62; no. 46, pp. 262–68; no. 62, pp. 345–46.

30. See *The Federalist* no. 39, p. 209; no. 47, pp. 268–71; no. 48, pp. 277–78.

31. Cf. *The Federalist* no. 48, pp. 276–77, and no. 37, pp. 194–97.

32. *The Federalist* no. 63, p. 355. And see the general discussion in Charles R. Kesler, "Natural Law and the Constitution: *The Federalist's* View," in Sarah Baumgartner: *The United States Constitution in Twentieth Century Politics* (Lanham, Md.: University Press of America, 1988), 155–81.

33. *The Federalist* no. 49, p. 285.

34. *The Federalist* no. 11, p. 59.

35. *The Federalist* no. 63, pp. 351–52; cf. no. 40, p. 221.

36. *The Federalist* no. 63, pp. 352–54.

37. *The Federalist* no. 49, p. 283; no. 71, p. 400.

38. *The Federalist* no. 70, pp. 395–98; and Mansfield, *Taming the Prince,* 264–74.

16

Abraham Lincoln and the Spirit of American Statesmanship

Glen E. Thurow

> As a formal possibility, Aristotle's kingship of virtue remains in the Constitution. Nothing in it prevents the emergence of such a king, except for the same practical problems that stand in the way of Aristotle's king elsewhere . . . constitutional powers broad enough to meet necessities may also be strong enough to satisfy virtue.[1]

Does statesmanship take a particular form and have a particular spirit in the United States? A statesman is one who can lead a community to act for the common good. Statesmanship combines two qualities: the ability to know what the common good is in a particular set of circumstances, and the ability to get people to do what it requires. Each of these abilities is rare, and their combination even rarer. And there may be reasons why Americans do not often elect such men to office even when they do exist.[2] Consequently America, like other nations, has had more mediocre than excellent statesmen. But if there is a form of statesmanship that could rightfully be called American at its best, it would be found in the pursuit of an American understanding of what the common good is and be shaped and limited by the powers its statesmen possess for achieving that good. We might expect to find such statesmanship in the best American statesmen.

Abraham Lincoln is a preeminent example of such a statesman. He is known both for his ability to express in memorable words the heart of America, and for testing the limits of the powers our most powerful office gives its occupant. In Lincoln we can see what an American understanding of the common good is and what powers its statesmen possess to achieve it.

THE MEASURE OF LINCOLN'S STATESMANSHIP

Although Lincoln is today almost universally admired, it is well to remind ourselves that the honor he receives would not be given had the Northern armies not triumphed on the battlefields of the Civil War. Lincoln is praised because it is Lincoln's nation, and not the Confederacy, that still exists. Had Lincoln been the defeated leader, he might be no more generally admired today than is Jefferson Davis. Does Lincoln stand at the apex of American statesmanship only, or primarily, because he succeeded through force of arms in getting people to do what he wanted, rather than because he knew the common good and respected American ways of achieving it? Is success the measure of Lincoln's statesmanship?

Now Lincoln himself did not think that success was the sole measure of statesmanship, nor, indeed, even its principal component. In the peroration of his "Subtreasury" speech, Lincoln sets forth a different standard:

> The *probability* that we may fall in the struggle *ought not* to deter us from the support of a cause that we believe to be just; it *shall* not deter me. If ever I feel the soul within me elevate and expand to those dimensions not wholly unworthy of its Almighty Architect, it is when I contemplate the cause of my country, deserted by all the world beside, and I standing up boldly and alone and hurling defiance at her victorious oppressors.[3]

Lincoln says that he should be judged first not by his success, but by the worthiness of his soul to stand before his maker. And that worthiness is found in his willingness to defend the cause of his country even in the face of certain defeat. (The identification of the worthiness of his soul with devotion to the cause of his country was not one made in a momentary fit of patriotism, but one that Lincoln made throughout his life.[4])

Lincoln, fortunately, did not have to hurl defiance at his country's victorious oppressor, but he did have to defend her in the face of a powerful enemy, sometimes in circumstances in which it appeared that even his friends were deserting him. Did Lincoln's position as president allow his soul to expand to the worthy dimensions he had contemplated in the "Subtreasury" speech? What does his leadership reveal about the spirit of statesmanship fostered or permitted by America?

The political order within which Lincoln worked (the "cause of his country") was not an accidental jumble of institutions, but one that had been deliberately formed by its founders to achieve certain ends and to regulate the means that might be used to achieve them. In the first *Federalist*, Publius uses pride in this fact as a motive for support of the Constitution: "It has been frequently remarked, that it seems to have been reserved to the people of this country, by their conduct and example, to decide the important question, whether societies of men are really capable or not, of establishing good government from reflection and choice, or whether they are forever destined to depend, for their political constitutions, on accident and force."[5] The Constitution was an act of deliberate choice, and the republic it formed would depend on the reflection and choice of the people not only to be founded, but to be perpetuated as well. As a government wholly popular in character, all powers would be derived from the people and all offices would be filled either directly or indirectly by the people for limited terms. At the same time without violating these principles, the new Constitution would remedy the defects that had vitiated all previous republics, chiefly by making the republic wholly representative in character, large rather than small, and ordered by the separation of powers.[6]

The Constitution provides both the end that American statesmen should serve and the means they may use. It is possible, of course, to have officeholders who do not share the spirit of the Constitution but attempt to serve other ends or to circumvent the means provided. It is to hold such men in check that the Constitution, in the words of Publius, provides auxiliary precautions (such as using ambition to check ambition through the separation of powers) to try to ensure that they cannot undermine the whole.[7] But in the best cases the Constitution would empower true statesmanship. The result would be a republic in which statesmanship would not replicate or play upon popular passions, but be able to control and guide those passions. In the words of the *Federalist,* "It is the reason of the public alone that ought to control and regulate the government. The passions ought to be controlled and regulated by the government."[8] In Lincoln's statesmanship we can see not only his personal qualities, but the spirit of the Constitution in action. In contrast, in contemporary American politics the spirit of the Constitution has been eroded, with many far-reaching unfortunate results. One of these is that new roadblocks have been placed in the way of achieving statesmanship of the breadth demonstrated by Lincoln.

LINCOLN AND OBEDIENCE TO THE CONSTITUTION

As president, Lincoln faced a situation in which the American union was more threatened than it ever had been before or ever has been since. To meet this danger, Lincoln used the powers of the presidency to their fullest, and consequently he is credited today with bringing about a great expansion of presidential power. Yet Lincoln never claimed a right to go beyond the powers the Constitution granted to the president. Some actions he might have liked to take he did not because he regarded them as beyond his constitutional powers. When challenged on actions he did take, he always defended them as being consistent with the words, the intentions, and the spirit of the Constitution. Indeed, an overall objective of Lincoln's statesmanship was to increase obedience to the provisions of the Constitution and instill reverence for the instrument as a whole.

Lincoln saw the Constitution as a limitation on what he could do, even limiting actions that he considered in and of themselves to be just. Nowhere is this more clear than on the slavery issue. Lincoln once said, "I am naturally anti-slavery. If slavery is not wrong, nothing is wrong. I can not remember when I did not so think, and feel. And yet I have never understood that the Presidency conferred upon me an unrestricted right to act officially upon this judgment and feeling."[9] In his first inaugural he quoted from one of his previous speeches to declare, "I have no purpose, directly or indirectly, to interfere with the institution of slavery in the States where it exists. I believe I have no lawful right to do so, and I have no inclination to do so." He even goes on to say that it is the duty of officeholders even to uphold that provision of the Constitution which provided for the return of fugitive slaves in spite of his own distaste for it.[10] Obedience to the Constitution took precedence over remedying the great injustice of slavery because free government was the very condition for the possibility of ending slavery.

An even stricter Constitutional limit to what he might do was reached in the case of suspending a presidential election. While a power to declare slaves free might become operable under the necessities of war, there were no circumstances that justified the suspension of an election. If the people could not choose their representatives, free government was at an end. In response to a serenade following his victory in the wartime election of 1864, Lincoln said, "But the Election was a necessity. We can not have free government without elections; and if the rebellion could force us to forego, or postpone a national election, it might fairly claim to have already conquered and ruined us."[11]

When Lincoln did act in novel ways in exercising presidential powers, he was careful to outline their constitutional justification. Two of the most important such cases were his suspending the writ of habeas corpus and his issuing the "Emancipation Proclamation." In the first case he not only had his attorney general issue a careful analysis of its constitutionality, but he himself defended its constitutionality to both the Congress and to critics outside the Congress. His reasoning covered the gamut of possible arguments, from the explicit words of the Constitution, to its intention, to the constitutional justification even if he were wrong about the particular provision in dispute. In speaking of the Constitution's words, he pointed out that they provided for the suspension when "in cases of rebellion or invasion, the public safety may require it," and argued that those were precisely the circumstances they were in. In addressing an issue that the Constitution did not explicitly resolve—whether the power to suspend the writ was given to Congress or to the president, he spoke of its intention:

But the Constitution itself, is silent as to which, or who, is to exercise the power, and as the provision was plainly made for a dangerous emergency, it cannot be believed the framers of the instrument intended, that in every case, the danger should run its course, until Congress could be called together; the very assembling of which might be prevented, as was intended in this case, by the rebellion.[12]

And even if he were wrong in his interpretation of the particular provision, his greatest obligation was to defend the Constitution as a whole. If he could do so only by violating this one particular provision, the whole took precedent over the part: "To state the question more directly, are all the laws, *but one,* to go unexecuted, and the government itself go to pieces, lest that one be violated. Even in such a case, would not the official oath be broken, if the government should be overthrown, when it was believed that disregarding the single law, would tend to preserve it?"[13] Thus Lincoln, in good lawyerly fashion, relied not upon one argument alone, but upon a series of arguments to back up his constitutional position. The clarity and force of these arguments display a spirit of respect for the Constitution and of seeking to make his actions accord with it.

In his defense of his greatest departure from the status quo, the "Emancipation Proclamation," Lincoln proceeded from the necessity of the case to its constitutionality. In the "Emancipation Proclamation," he justifies his actions as an exercise of his powers as commander-in-chief and "as a fit and necessary war measure for suppressing said rebellion."[14] In a reply to a critical letter from James C. Conklin in August of 1863, Lincoln wrote, "You say it is unconstitutional—I think differently. I think the constitution invests its commander-in-chief, with the law of war, in time of war."[15] But this action combined not only necessity and constitutional justification, but justice as well. The "Emancipation Proclamation" proclaims that it is "an act of justice, warranted by the Constitution, upon military necessity."[16] Thus, in his letter to Conklin, he tries to show that it is constitutional, that it is essential to the triumph of the Union armies, and that it is an act of justice to the black man.[17] Lincoln could act in behalf of justice in a way that ultimately moved the Constitution toward greater justice precisely because his action had constitutional warrant.

Lincoln demonstrated in his own actions the obedience and respect for the Constitution that his statesmanship as a whole tried to inculcate in the American people. Early in his career, in analyzing the difficulties the American republic faced and the remedies that might be needed, Lincoln had called for using all of the resources available to foster a "reverence for the constitution and laws."[18] One of the ways he attempted to do this was through the force of his own example.

LINCOLN, CONSTITUTIONAL PRINCIPLE, AND HUMAN VIRTUE

Lincoln's actions show the extensive constitutional powers that may be exercised by the president in situations of grave crisis. But toward what end are these powers to be used? While there are some few actions the Constitution commands the president to do or refrain from doing, such as to take a specified oath upon the assumption of office or not to accept other emoluments than his presidential salary from the United States, for the most part the Constitution grants powers that the president may or may not exercise, and if he does exercise them, may do so in a variety of ways.

Of course it is the president's duty to execute the laws of the United States, as duly enacted by Congress. Beyond that he may exercise his powers to defend or fulfill a constitutional provision or intent. As we have seen, Lincoln argued that his exercise of the power to suspend the writ of habeas corpus was such a case. There are also provisions of the Constitution that require action by either Congress, the executive, or the states, in order to be carried out. The clause calling for the return of those who escaped from labor or servitude was not self-enforcing and hence required action by someone if it were to be effective. While some argued that it should not be enforced, that was not Lincoln's position. He thought there was a positive duty imposed by the Constitution to enforce it; the only issues were who was to enforce it and with what protections for the innocent?[19]

Yet the spirit of Lincoln's statesmanship cannot be understood as simply obedience to the Constitution and laws of the United States. For it was the principles of the Constitution, even more than the Constitution itself, to which Lincoln was loyal. Those principles were summed up in the principles of the Declaration of Independence, especially in the claim that all men are created equal. "The principles of Jefferson," said Lincoln, "are the definitions and axioms of free society. . . ."[20] This "abstract truth" was "*the* word, '*fitly spoken,*' which has proved an 'apple of gold' to us. The *Union* and the *Constitution* are the *picture* of *silver*, subsequently framed around it. . . ."[21] The principles of the Declaration were the bedrock of the nation, and the Constitution was the means to embody those principles—a means at once necessary and yet imperfect because it had to take account of the political realities of its formation.

Lincoln understood the institution of slavery to be incompatible with the principle that all men are created equal, and consequently with the democratic form of government erected by the Constitution. "As I would not be a *slave,* so I would not be a *master.* This expresses my idea of democracy. Whatever differs from this, to the extent of the difference, is no democracy."[22] Slavery was incompatible both with the spirit of the Constitution and with the spirit of free government more generally. Consequently, while he felt himself bound to respect any protection explicitly given slavery by the

Constitution, in any matter on which it was silent he felt free to interpret it in the way most favorable to the antislavery cause, because it was in spite of its compromises at root antislavery. Thus, while he held that he was not free as president under the Constitution simply to abolish slavery, he could oppose its extension into the new territories both as a private citizen and as president. He could oppose it because there was nothing in the Constitution protecting the extension of slavery, and because that extension would have to rest upon principles that undermined the very principles of free government—i.e., that slavery was either a good thing or a matter of indifference.

When Lincoln called for a rebirth of freedom in the "Gettysburg Address," he did not mean simply a rebirth of the original founding order of the United States. He meant a rebirth of that order, in which its great imperfection, the compromises with slavery, was purged and the Constitution purified by its reunion with the principles of the Declaration.[23] The circumstances of the war had permitted Lincoln constitutionally to end slavery, an end that would achieve constitutional status by the Thirteenth Amendment. Lincoln's statesmanship went beyond a defense of the Constitution and laws of the United States to defending and extending the principles of the Declaration that underlay them.

The principle of equality in the Declaration was not merely the fundamental principle of the American Constitution or even of free government in general. Lincoln also understood it to be the fundamental principle of justice. In a speech delivered in Chicago on July 10, 1858, Lincoln attempted to explain what it was that enabled immigrants from many different nations to become one nation. Many Americans could look back to the founders and take pride in their greatness. They could see:

> a race of men living in that day whom we claim as our fathers and grandfathers; they were iron men, they fought for the principle that they were contending for; and we understood that by what they then did it has followed that the degree of prosperity that we now enjoy has come to us. We hold this annual celebration to remind ourselves of all the good done in this process of time, of how it was done and who did it, and how we are historically connected with it; and we go from these meetings in better humor with ourselves—we feel more attached the one to the other, and more firmly bound to the country we inhabit.[24]

But, Lincoln goes on to say, this alone would not necessarily unite us the one to the other. "We have not yet reached the whole." After all, he continues, we have many citizens who cannot look back to those men as their fathers and grandfathers. They, or their ancestors, have come from Europe since the Revolution. They have no common ties of blood to that earlier race,

> but when they look through that old Declaration of Independence they find that those old men say that "We hold these truths to be self-evident, that all

men are created equal," and then they feel that moral sentiment taught in that day evidences their relation to those men, that it is the father of all moral principle in them, and that they have a right to claim it as though they were blood of the blood, and flesh of the flesh of the men who wrote the Declaration, and so they are.[25]

We have a common history, according to Lincoln, because the Union is the triumph of moral principle within ourselves. Hence in working for the preservation of the Union, he was working as well for the principle upon which the Union was based: the "Union *must be preserved in the purity of its principles as well as in the integrity of its territorial parts.*"[26] If the territorial union could be saved only by giving up the principles of the Declaration, Lincoln once said, "I would rather be assassinated on this spot than to surrender it."[27] Lincoln did not believe that the Union was fundamentally united by its territory or institutions, but by a public dedication to a sense of justice whose central idea is the equality of all men.

But even this does not reach the deepest level of Lincoln's understanding and actions as a statesman. The problem is that free people can abandon the principle of equality, the principle of justice (indeed, they had powerful economic reasons for doing so in the case of slavery). Prior to the Civil War, Lincoln noted that the principles of the Declaration "were denied and evaded with no small show of success."[28] Lincoln thought that the truth of equality needed the support that public opinion could give it. He said, "Our government rests in public opinion. Whoever can change public opinion, can change the government, practically just as much." The central idea of that public opinion in the United States is equality. Yet there had been a struggle "to discard that central idea, and to substitute for it the opposite idea that slavery is right. . . ."[29] It is the work of American statesmanship to maintain or restore in public opinion the principles of the Declaration.

It is the object of much of Lincoln's rhetoric, culminating in the "Gettysburg Address," to make the self-evident truth of the Declaration an object of passion and piety. In the poetry of the "Gettysburg Address," Lincoln weaves together the universal principle of the Declaration with the life of this one particular nation, and seeks to seal this union through the sacrifice men have made on the battlefield. The very meaning of life and death are bound up with the continued existence of an American nation dedicated to human equality. The Union is a sacred union.

Not only does Lincoln attempt to make the Constitution and laws of the United States an object of reverence, but he seeks through his rhetoric to raise the sights of Americans beyond politics to the source of their nation in the divine. This effort reaches its height in the "Second Inaugural Address." In it Lincoln attempts to persuade the American people to acknowledge that if the war is a punishment of God for the sin of slavery, God is just. Through this acknowledgment, it is possible to be charitable to all, for both North and South have sinned in the eyes of God. All are equally under God's judgment. He thus leads the people to acknowledge limits to their government. Their actions must be bounded by an order they did not create. The passion for a cold or inhuman justice that would demand an eye for an eye is moderated by a human charity that rests upon divine retribution.[30]

Lincoln gives us an example of how it is possible for a statesman under the constitutional order to reveal and act from his virtue to accomplish great good for his country. Today the constitutional basis of statesmanship has been eroded, as I shall indicate. This erosion has made the kind of statesmanship Lincoln displayed more difficult to achieve.

LINCOLN AND CONTEMPORARY STATESMANSHIP

Lincoln could display his own intellectual and moral virtues because he could interpret the American political order—its Constitution and laws—as aiming at human justice and providing the means to its officials to advance that cause. Today, an understanding of our political order prevails that makes it more difficult both to acknowledge and to praise virtue in public speech and to exercise the powers that might advance it. Paradoxically, this has come about by trying to make a particular understanding of virtue more directly the object of politics, rather than being constrained by constitutional forms.

The decisive change was brought about by Woodrow Wilson, who formulated a new conception of the presidency and of presidential character in relationship to republican government. As is well known, Wilson disliked the American constitutional system and particularly its central feature, the separation of powers, because he thought it hindered the power of statesmen. Although preferring the parliamentary system, he did not bring about its introduction in the United States. He did try, however, to infuse the political order with a new spirit and a new understanding of the role of the president in particular and statesmanship in general. He expressed this spirit in his first inaugural address, in which he portrays his and his party's election as the introduction of a new government, bringing about a new point of view in the nation as a whole. The standards of this new view are not to be found in the Constitution, in the work of the founders, or in knowledge of the true principles of republican government, but rather "in our hearts." What we find in our hearts is compassion. This is a virtue both more democratic and more nonpolitical than the previous standards: more democratic because all can feel pity, less political because compassion can be felt for all and not merely for fellow citizens. It musters the "forces of humanity." Our principles, Wilson says in his second inaugural, are "the principles of a liberated mankind." Attention to forms of government, in contrast, is attention to "mere" politics.[31]

If the true principles are to be found in people's hearts, rather than in an understanding of the principles of republican government, then the supreme task of statesmanship is to articulate what people feel. Hearts do not speak, but statesmen do, and they must say what the heart feels but cannot express. As we would say, they must be charismatic. The president's ultimate task is to express the unspoken desires of the people, not to instruct or govern them. This stands in sharp contrast with Lincoln's view that the people could desert the principle of equality and, if they did, it was the task of the statesman to bring them back to it. The statesman took his measure not from what the people found stirring, but from the principles of the Constitution. In attempting to infuse the presidency with the power of public passions, Wilson's view stripped from the president the main resource he had to resist or to instruct the public.

Wilson did argue that the president must be able to bring an expertise to bear that is not shared by the people. The people not only are unable to articulate their own desires, but they do not know how to fulfill these once they are articulated by others. The president, as head of an executive branch shaped to become the embodiment of expertise, can supply what the people lack. President Carter expressed the Wilsonian ideal, without its charismatic component, when he said in his inaugural address that government should be both "competent and compassionate."[32] Competency and compassion are the virtues of a bureaucrat who cares, not those of a statesman who would lead the American people to live up to their fundamental principles by being principled himself. Adding charisma provides excitement, but no additional direction.[33]

This view has become and remains the dominant view of the presidency and, consequently, of American statesmanship at the highest level. In contrast with Lincoln's understanding, it is an understanding that stands in the way of statesmanship. Virtue becomes reduced to the lowest common denominator at best; at worst, flattery replaces aspiration. Ronald Reagan called upon his fellow Americans in his first "Inaugural Address" to "dream heroic dreams." This did not mean, however, that they would be called to difficult and ennobling tasks. No, Reagan reassured his listeners, "you can see heroes every day going in and out of factory gates. Others, a handful in number, produce enough food to feed all of us and then the world beyond." Even taxpayers, it turns out, are heroes. And then he concludes: "Your dreams, your hopes, your goals are going to be the dreams, the hopes and the goals of this Administration, so help me God. We shall reflect the compassion that is so much a part of your makeup."[34] There is nothing outstanding to admire because even the most *ordinary* American is a hero.

A lowered understanding of virtue makes it difficult to admire and seek publicly the qualities needed for statesmanship. Lincoln could say in his campaign for the Illinois General Assembly, "Every man is said to have his peculiar ambition. Whether it be true or not, I can say for one that I have no other so great as that of being truly esteemed of my fellow men, by rendering myself worthy of their esteem."[35] But in the modern view, the president's virtue stems from his being close to the people, rather than from his demonstrating any unusual virtue. Leadership becomes reduced to the way Jimmy Carter saw it in a speech: "I promised you a president who is not isolated from the people, who feels your pain, and who shares your dreams and who draws his strength and his wisdom from you."[36] One of the difficulties in sorting out the issues with regard to President Clinton's moral and legal failings is that there is no longer an understanding among a large part of the American electorate that the president should be held to a standard any higher than its weaker members might practice.

Finally the predominant view of statesmanship today turns political attention away from principles and character. Indeed, contemporary presidents tend to see their highest function not to be loyal to political or moral principle, but to have a vision or a dream. A vision or dream is not only that human conscious state in which the intellect is least active, it is also the most private of human conscious states. The "vision thing," as George Bush called it, is a replacement for principles. Instead of pointing toward principle and character, judging a president by his vision is to judge him by a creative, individual act, by an act of his will rather than of his reason. President Clinton attempted to capture this vision in his first inaugural, "This ceremony is held in the depth of winter, but by the words we speak, and the faces we show the world, we force the spring. A spring reborn in the world's oldest democracy that brings forth the vision and courage to reinvent America."[37] The image of forcing even the course of nature out of its accustomed path, and of reinventing America (not improving or restoring it), suggests the degree to which American politics has become simply a matter of the will when guided by neither Constitution, principle, nor character.

On the other hand, to form the relationship between the president and the people through the Constitution makes room for virtue. The people may choose to select for its offices persons who have talents and virtues that they may admire and find useful without possessing them themselves. The Constitution is a means for making room for uncommon people in a democratic regime, without undermining democracy. The intention of replacing the Constitution by a direct relationship between the president and the people was to strengthen the presidential office. In fact, however, it has weakened it by undermining the basis of the strength it may gain by being occupied by independent and talented people, who can openly and publicly display their talents and virtues and receive credit for them. Lincoln's statesmanship shows us that the highest possibilities for American statesmanship are to be found not in spite of the Constitution, but by working through the Constitution to deepen its effect.

NOTES

1. Harvey C. Mansfield, Jr., *Taming the Prince: The Ambivalence of Modern Executive Power* (New York: Free Press, 1989), 275.

2. See Alexis de Tocqueville, *Democracy in America*, trans. Henry Reeve (New York: Schocken Books, 1961), 228–31.

3. Roy P. Basler, ed., *The Collected Works of Abraham Lincoln* (New Brunswick, N.J.: Rutgers University Press, 1953), 1:178–79; emphasis Lincoln's.

4. See, for example, the speech Lincoln made at Independence Hall in 1861 on his way to Washington to be inaugurated President. *Collected Works* 4:240.

5. *Federalist* no. 1.

6. *Federalist* no. 9, 10, 39, 51.

7. *Federalist* no. 51.

8. *Federalist* no. 49. See the discussion of the attempt of the American founders to give independence to the executive and the judiciary in Harvey C. Mansfield, *America's Constitutional Soul* (Baltimore: Johns Hopkins University Press, 1991), 209–13.

9. *Collected Works* 7:218; cf. 2:493, 5:388–89.

10. *Collected Works* 4:263.

11. *Collected Works* 8:101.

12. *Collected Works* 4:430–31.

13. *Collected Works* 4:430.

14. *Collected Works* 6:29.

15. *Collected Works* 6:408.

16. *Collected Works* 6:30.

17. *Collected Works* 6:407–9.

18. *Collected Works* 1:115.

19. *Collected Works* 4:263–64.

20. *Collected Works* 3:375.

21. *Collected Works* 4:169; emphasis Lincoln's.

22. *Collected Works* 2:532; emphasis Lincoln's.

23. See the discussion by Eva Brann, "A Reading of the Gettysburg Address," in *Abraham Lincoln, The Gettysburg Address, and American Constitutionalism*, ed. Leo Paul S. de Alvarez (Irving, Tex.: University of Dallas Press, 1976), 41–43.

24. *Collected Works* 2:499.

25. *Collected Works* 2:500.

26. *Collected Works* 2:341; emphasis Lincoln's.

27. *Collected Works* 4:240.

28. *Collected Works* 3:375.

29. *Collected Works* 2:385.

30. *Collected Works* 4:332–33; see a lengthier discussion of this in Glen E. Thurow, "Lincoln and American Political Religion," in *The Historian's Lincoln,* ed. Gabor S. Boritt (Urbana and Chicago: University of Illinois Press, 1988), 125–43.

31. *The Inaugural Addresses of the Presidents of the United States* (Washington, D.C.: U.S. Government Printing Office, 1952), 189–96.

32. Jimmy Carter, "Inaugural Address," *Vital Speeches* 43 (Feb. 15, 1977): 258.

33. For analyses of bureaucracy and charisma, see *America's Constitutional Soul,* 186–92; *Taming the Prince,* 284.

34. Ronald Reagan, "Inaugural Address," *Vital Speeches* 47 (Feb. 15, 1981): 258–60.

35. *Collected Works* 1:8.

36. Speech of July 15, 1979, *Vital Speeches* 45 (Aug. 15, 1979): 642.

37. William Clinton, "Inaugural Address," *Vital Speeches* 59 (Feb. 15, 1993): 258–59.

17

Constitutional Bureaucracy

R. Shep Melnick

So well known is Harvey Mansfield's work in political theory that it is easy to overlook his contribution to American political science. Unlike many "theorists," Mansfield is an avid and astute observer of American politics. From his early work on Burke and political parties to his more recent writing on constitutional government, he has sought to tear down the wall our profession has erected to segregate "normative" and "empirical" studies. The great works of political philosophy, he has shown, offer insights into human nature and the nature of politics that illuminate contemporary politics in ways that behavioral political science cannot.

In a variety of recent essays Mansfield has attempted "to set forth a constitutional view of American politics,"[1] an understanding of American government that recognizes the importance of constitutional forms and formalities. The purpose of this chapter is to call to the attention of students of American politics a few of Mansfield's insights into America's "constitutional soul." Understanding his arguments and applying them to contemporary politics is, of course, not an easy task for those of us who dwell within the pedestrian "subfield" of American politics. Mansfield never offers simplified "models" or cookbook methodologies. (Who could forget his claim that "studying methodology is like practicing seduction on an empty couch"?) Recognizing the risk of vulgarizing his thought, I offer this apology: he has provided valuable lessons from which students of American politics have yet to profit.

I

Mansfield's constitutional vision of American politics shares little with that of contemporary constitutional-law scholars. Today, the study of constitutional law consists primarily of arguments about the merits of Supreme Court opinions on the Bill of Rights and Fourteenth Amendment. It is only a slight exaggeration to say that most academic writing on the subject is devoted to explaining why Warren Court precedents should be expanded and Rehnquist Court rulings reversed. The U.S. Constitution, according to this understanding of constitutionalism, places demands on government—above all that it should strive to guarantee equality—and imposes constraints on government—for example, that it must respect the rights of the accused. Governing—making difficult choices, forcing recalcitrant citizens to obey the law, devising policies that will command the consent of the governed—lies within the somewhat disreputable world of politics. The Constitution rules only in the sense that judges' interpretations of vague constitutional phrases trump decisions of the other branches of government.

Mansfield's constitutionalism, in contrast, examines how our Constitution shapes our politics. Since he is primarily interested in our governing institutions, one might call him an "institutionalist," thus placing him on the cutting edge of our rather dull profession. But as Mansfield points out, the problem with institutionalists—both old and new—is that they rarely offer convincing explanations of why institutions matter. Indeed, institutionalists have "no definition, or even any definite ideas, of *institution* to cling to." One reason behavioralism triumphed so quickly was that old-fashioned institutionalists "had almost nothing to say for themselves, a fact their students noticed."[2] Today's "new institutionalists" use longer sentences and grander words to provide an equally ineffective defense.

Mansfield presents a detailed, if unconventional, explanation of why constitutions (and thus institutions) matter. At the risk of oversimplification, I will reduce this explanation to four propositions. First and most importantly, the American Constitution, and indeed all important institutions, consist of more than a few basic "rules of the game." They express our collective aspirations, shape our individual ambitions, engage our pride, and thus mold our political experiences. For example,

> Being in the office does not ensure that a president will act, as we say, "presidentially"; some presidents have been quite disappointing. But why were we disappointed? Because we had some better notion of the office derived in part from an understanding of the Constitution and in part from the formation of the office by the best presidents. The formal cause is an end that attracts, as distinguished from a motive that pushes.[3]

Powerful institutions do not merely channel and moderate ambition, they establish public standards for evaluating acceptable and honorable behavior. They direct and at times even enlarge the ambitions of those in the public eye.

Isn't it unrealistic to suppose that those who enter politics will pay more than fleeting attention to the "better angels of our nature"? Mansfield's argument is not that politicians will act altruistically, but that their "interests" are more complex than today's political economists recognize. Among the "interests" they pursue are the esteem of their peers and the people; among their greatest ambitions are to be remembered, honored, perhaps even loved. To be honored, one must appear honorable; to be remembered, one must do something memorable. Assuming that politicians act like business entrepreneurs underestimates both their pride and their dependence on public opinion.

Among the most important assumptions employed by contemporary students of Congress is that members can best be understood as "single-minded reelection seekers."[4] Fear of electoral defeat plays the same role in most studies of congressional behavior that fear of violent death plays in *The Leviathan:* it is the reliable motivation that provides a basis for peaceful, orderly, commodious living. This common form of political analysis has proven incapable of explaining some of the most important policy changes of the past several decades, including tax reform, the expansion of social regulation, the elimination of many forms of economic regulation, and the explosion of spending on entitlements.[5] It has an especially hard time explaining why on important occasions pivotal congressmen are willing to take risks and antagonize well-organized interests. Why, for example, did Dan Rostenkowski turn his back on the high-priced lobbyists from "Gucchi Gulch" in 1986 and become a leading proponent of tax reform? Because he wanted to prove that he could be as great a chairman of the House Ways and Means committee as Wilbur Mills and perhaps even a credible candidate for Speaker. Why did Senate Finance Committee chairman Robert Packwood jettison his attachment to the old tax code and traditional interest-group politics to shepherd tax reform through the Senate? Because he was embarrassed about being known as "Senator Hackwood," purveyor of semicorrupt deals.[6] Rostenkowski and Packwood obviously were not men of unalloyed virtue: the former was convicted of fraud and sent to jail; the latter resigned after being censured for repeated sexual misconduct. Institutions are important because they create expectations that even seriously flawed human beings at times seek to live up to.

Second, the powerful norms and aspirations that undergird our formal institutions often shape our informal practices as well. Examples abound. In the early days of the republic, members of Congress developed the committee system not because they wanted to distribute "pork" to their districts (after all, most members of Congress hated Washington and expected to leave after a term or two to pursue more important careers at the state level), but because they believed Congress had a constitutional responsibility to establish national policy without undue influence from the executive branch.[7] Throughout the nineteenth century, presidents assiduously avoided direct appeals to the people, which they saw as inconsistent with the dignity and purpose of their constitutional office.[8] The longstanding norm of balanced budgets sprung from Jeffersonian notions of the threat of monarchical corruption within republican governments.[9] James Sterling Young's wonderful book on early Washington, D.C., explains how the physical and social environment of that city reflected the constitutional views of the first generation: no bridge crossed the tiny Tiber River on Pennsylvania Avenue because contemporaries believed in a strict separation of the legislative and executive branches; the boardinghouses in which most members of Congress lived reflected the primacy of state and regional loyalties.[10] If institutions were mere "rules of the game," they could not penetrate so deeply into our everyday lives and most fundamental political assumptions.

Admittedly, informal practices at times undercut publicly announced principles and procedures: consider how use of the literacy test in the South made a mockery of the Fifteenth Amendment. "Separate but equal" was never anything more than a ruse to disguise the conflict between the equal protection clause and the South's entrenched racial caste system. Of course, the argument that our informal practices are at variance with our formal declarations is a politically potent one, as the words and careers of Abraham Lincoln and Martin Luther King Jr. attest.

Third, those institutions that prove most powerful and enduring are seldom the product of historical accident or ad hoc "interest aggregation." Rather, they are crafted by founders who either consciously design them to achieve a purpose that can be announced in broad daylight or provide a compelling and principled public defense of a political compromise. Such founders give institutions staying power by linking procedural and technical details to broader public goals and beliefs. As Mansfield points out, the notion of founding based on "reflection and choice" assumes a level of political prescience that most social scientists find intolerable. Contemporary political analysis assumes that behind all apparent exercise of reflection and choice lie deeper historical forces that mere reason cannot overcome. Studies of "institution-building" usually offer detailed descriptions of the craftsmen and mechanics involved in this construction, but avoid detailed investigation of the ideas of the architects. One key difference between Mansfield's political science and that of most institutionalists is that he is not afraid to adopt the language and perspective of these statesmen and to expect that they have something to teach us.

Finally, all actual institutions, constitutions, and regimes, however well constituted, contain imperfections, tensions, and blind spots that threaten to

destroy or transform them. Most obviously, the original Constitution toler-
ated slavery, thus creating a house that in the long run could not stand. As
Tocqueville noted, American individualism threatens to undermine the public spiritedness and associational habits that sustain our free institutions.
These tensions and imperfections are best understood by those who have
thought most deeply about competing ideas of justice, about the meaning of
equality and freedom, and about the inherent difficulties of governing
human beings. Thus, to understand the development (or decay) of political
institutions we frequently need the assistance of students of political philosophy. For example, Locke can help us understand both the prerequisites and
the dilemmas of regimes based on the separation of church and state.[11]
Machiavelli can help us understand the hazards and glory of founding new
modes and orders—not to mention the advantages of expeditious execution.[12] And Burke can help us understand the underpinnings, usefulness, and
limits of party government.[13]

II

The remainder of this essay attempts to illustrate this understanding of constitutional government by examining the contemporary federal bureaucracy.
Bureaucracy constitutes a "hard case" for such a constitutional approach to
the study of politics. The subject is barely mentioned in the Constitution itself. For a century and a half our federal bureaucracy remained pitiably small
and weak. Some conservatives claim that our large national bureaucracy is
literally unconstitutional, not only incompatible with the government of limited scope contemplated by the founders, but a constant threat to our most
precious liberties. For years progressives, too, have held that creating a modern state required either explicit or surreptitious constitutional amendment.
Our eighteenth-century Constitution, they have frequently argued, is incompatible with the demands of twentieth-century governance. Indeed, so common is the view that bureaucracy lies outside the constitution of 1789 that it
is regularly called the "Fourth Branch of Government"—the bastard offspring
of an illicit affair among the other three.

Modern social science generally assumes that bureaucratization is inevitable and that it substantially reduces differences among regimes. What
defines government in "advanced industrial democracies" is not the written
constitution or particular traditions of each, but the "legal-rational authority"
and Weberian bureaucracy they all share. Steven Skowronek, author of the
leading analysis of "state-building" in the United States, argues that "expansion of administrative capacities" in both the United States and Europe was
an inevitable "response to industrialization." In the United States our anti-
quated government institutions and political beliefs had to give way:

The modernization of national administrative controls did not entail making the established state more efficient; it entailed building a *qualitatively different kind of state*. . . . To embrace the cosmopolitan bureaucratic remedy in meeting new demands on government, America had to alter course and shed already well-articulated governing arrangements. The expansion of national administrative capacities in the age of industrialism became contingent on undermining the established structure of political and institutional power and on simultaneously forging an *entirely new framework for government operations*.[14]

Welcome to the New American State, where constitutional forms crumble under the weight of a technically rational but ultimately soulless bureaucracy.

This picture of the triumph of administrative government overlooks the extent to which the American Constitution has shaped our public bureaucracy, giving it a unique and resolutely American form. On this side of the Atlantic, bureaucratization did not produce a centralized, hierarchical government. Rather, American government created a decentralized, permeable, entrepreneurial, and occasionally chaotic bureaucracy. The Constitution has prevailed, despite the hopes of progressives, the fears of conservatives, and the prediction of social science.

First consider federalism. When Americans speak of "the state," they do not mean the bureaucracy of the central government, but *their* state— California, New Hampshire, Louisiana, and other peculiar places. Despite the enormous expansion of federal responsibility and spending since 1960, the civilian work force of the federal government is virtually the same size today as it was forty years ago. Total government employment has nearly doubled since the late 1950s, and almost all the increase has come at the state and local level. State and local governments hire 80 percent of government employees.[15]

In the vast majority of national programs federal administrators must work with and through state and local bureaucrats. In some instances states receive federal funds and are subject to only a few constraints. (A leading example is welfare prior to 1968 and since 1996.) In other cases (such as disability insurance), state officials are expected to carry out uniform national policies, but remain capable of blocking unpopular federal demands.[16] Many programs establish national objectives but give states extensive discretion in choosing implementation strategies and enforcing the ensuing regulations.[17] Other programs offer matching funds, and allow states to chose from a variety of policy options and develop their own administrative style.[18] Still others impose legally enforceable mandates (some funded, some not) on existing state and local institutions. Local school systems, for example, are now required to provide a "free appropriate education" to all disabled children; mass-transit systems run by state and local governments must provide ready access to the handicapped. Many of these mandates and "cross cutting requirements" have been interpreted, enforced, and in some cases even created by the federal courts.[19] Those enamored of government efficiency and national uniformity may decry this perplexing hodgepodge of governmental responsibilities. But it reflects our fear of administrative centralization, our faith in the responsiveness of decentralized institutions, our respect for regional differences, and our conviction that no single distribution of power is appropriate for all policy arenas.

Many thoughtful students of federalism have been alarmed at the steady increase of federal control over state and local governments since the 1960s. Clearly federal funding, federal strings, federal mandates, and litigation in federal court have significantly reduced the autonomy of state and local governments. Yet we should not overlook either the amount of formal authority that remains in the hands of state and local governments or, just as importantly, the difficulty federal officials confront in ensuring that state and local bureaucracies carry out federal policies in a uniform manner. For better or for worse, hierarchical controls remain weak; at the "street level" state and local variation remains extensive. Judicial enforcement of federal mandates tends to be episodic and poorly monitored. Despite the powerful political appeal of uniformity, despite the decay of regional differences and local communities, and despite the alleged imperialism of bureaucracy, Americans' attachment to the federal system created by the Constitution remains vital.

Viewed in comparative perspective American public administration is unusual not just for its decentralization, but for the extent of legislative and judicial supervision. Bureaucratization did not (as many expected and as seemed likely in the 1940s and 1950s) reduce the importance of separation of powers. Rather, it created a vast new arena for competition among the three branches. Starting in the 1960s both Congress and the federal courts rejected New Deal norms of deference to administrative expertise. They adopted new doctrines and practices that produced extensive, intensive, and often ideologically driven oversight of administrative action.

The "resurgence" of Congress in the late 1960s and early 1970s has frequently been described by political scientists and journalists. Liberal Democrats wrested control of the House and Senate from the Southern, conservative "committee barons." They instituted "subcommittee government," which gave nearly all Democrats—no matter how junior—a subcommittee chairmanship, significantly more staff, a media soapbox, and an area of policy specialization. Obviously, divided government contributed significantly to these developments: Democrats saw subcommittee government as a mechanism for presenting alternatives to the legislative program of Republican presidents and for countering Nixon and Reagan's efforts to create an "administrative presidency."[20] Electoral considerations were important as well. As countless political scientists have noted, subcommittee government multiplied the opportunities for "credit claiming," "position-taking," and other forms of self-promotion. For two decades incumbents became safer and safer.[21]

The feature of the "New Congress" that is most important from a policy-making perspective—and most frequently ignored or even denied by quantitative political science—is the extent to which members of Congress became deeply engaged in the details and the merits of legislation. To be sure, members of Congress repeatedly demonstrated their capacity to engage in vacuous grandstanding, empty gesturing, and trafficking in particularized benefits. Perhaps a few were content with this, but not many. Most subcommittee chairs (which means most members of the majority party) resolutely staked out their turf, cultivated a national constituency, wrote statutes of ever increasing detail and complexity, defended their program against administrative malfeasance both real and imagined, and thought more about their "legacy" as their seats became more secure. Once criticized (often with good cause) for excessive delegation of legislative authority, Congress is now frequently attacked (again, often with good cause) for "micromanagement." This new "micromanagement" is not just old pork-barrel politics writ large. It usually takes the form of general rules rather than ad hoc, particularized judgments, and it frequently produces entitlements (with cost-of-living adjustments) that *curtail* future opportunities for credit-claiming.[22] Entitlements have crowded out traditional pork-barrel spending, which is now a tiny percentage of the budget.

Those who describe congressional supervision of the bureaucracy simply in terms of the "electoral connection" miss the big picture not because they exaggerate the self-interested nature of members of Congress, but because they systematically underestimate their ambitions. For most of these proud, often vain and self-important people, just sitting in Congress is not enough. To use Harry McPherson's phrase, they long to "cast a shadow."[23] To make their ambitions palatable to their democratic constituents (and perhaps to themselves as well) they feel the need to couch them in constitutional terms: the Constitution authorizes Congress, not nonelected bureaucrats, to make the laws; Congress needed to reclaim its constitutional responsibility for appropriating funds, declaring war, and offering its "advice and consent" on nominations; in general it needed to reduce the power of the "imperial presidency."[24] The "interest of the man," as Madison had planned, was thus "connected with the constitutional right of the place."[25]

At about the same time that these changes were taking place in Congress, the federal courts were overhauling their doctrines on judicial review of agency action. In a few instances these revisions took the form of constitutional law in the conventional sense.[26] But most of the changes took shape in the arcane realms of administrative law and statutory interpretation. Ironically, the lower-court judges who developed these new doctrines tended to understate or even disguise the constitutional implications of their decisions. They were not eager to attract attention from the Supreme Court, which they considered suspiciously conservative. What Richard Stewart has called the "reformation of American administrative law" was based on two shifts of constitutional dimension. First, the courts sought to reform administrative procedures in order to make policymaking more accessible to civil rights organizations, "public interest" groups, and other advocacy organizations, and thus less susceptible to "capture" by vested interests. In Stewart's words,

> Faced with the seemingly intractable problem of agency discretion, the courts have changed the focus of judicial review (in the process expanding and transforming traditional procedural devices) so that its dominant purpose is no longer the prevention of unauthorized intrusions on private autonomy, but the assurance of fair representation for all affected interests in the exercise of the legislative power delegated to agencies.[27]

This meant not just allowing a variety of "public interest" groups to participate in agency deliberations and to challenge administrative rulings in court, but also insisting that administrators pay more attention to "public values" and the "spirit" of remedial legislation and correspondingly less attention to the material interest of established clienteles.[28] The "new administrative law" was designed to "open up" and democratize the federal bureaucracy in much the same way as reapportionment decisions were designed to democratize Congress and state legislatures.

Second, these judicial doctrines on administrative law and statutory interpretation rested on a new understanding of fundamental rights. Preventing unauthorized or excessive government interference in the private realm was no longer sufficient to ensure liberty or equality. In the words of Justice Brennan,

> Government participation in the economic existence of individuals is pervasive and deep. Administrative matters and other dealings with government are at the epicenter of the exploding law. . . . [A]s government continues in its role of provider for so many of our disadvantaged citizens, there is an even greater need to ensure that government acts with integrity and consistency in its dealings with these citizens.[29]

Creation of the modern welfare state requires an expanded understanding of property that places new demands and constraints on government. This "new property" includes not just entitlements such as social security or food stamps, but the right to a safe environment, the right to an adequate education, the right to participate in government decisions that might affect one's life, and even the right to insist that bureaucrats aggressively enforce the law. In the most frequently cited administrative-law opinion of the 1970s, Judge David Bazelon explained that the "new era" of "fruitful collaboration of administrative agencies and reviewing courts" was based on the belief that "fundamental personal interests in life, health, and liberty" have a "special claim to judicial protection, in contrast with the economic interests at stake in ratemaking or licensing procedures."[30] As the "new property" expanded, the old property was demoted to mere (even crass) economic interest.[31]

These new judicial doctrines on the nature of fundamental rights guided the federal courts in their allocation of authority to the various branches and levels of government. During the 1960s and 1970s they created strong presumptions in favor of national uniformity. They also tended to side with Congress and its committees against presidents and their appointees. In the mid-1980s the Supreme Court started to move slowly and haltingly in the opposite direction, contracting the "new property," increasing protections for the "old" property, creating presumptions in favor of state control, and increasing the discretion available to the executive. In each instance there was a strong connection between fundamental rights and institutional arrangements.

A variety of comparative studies have emphasized the pervasive and peculiar role of both judicial review and the language of individual rights in the United States. For example, in their study of regulation of the chemical industry in France, Britain, Germany, and the United States, Brickman, Jasanoff, and Ilgen report that

> U.S. regulators must contend with an extremely active judiciary. . . . Indeed resort to the courts by one or another interest group has become so commonplace that major regulatory issues are seldom settled without litigation. As a result, the courts enjoy an unparalleled opportunity to second-guess the agencies in the implementation of chemical control laws. Even a casual observer is struck by the vastly lower level of judicial involvement in European regulatory processes.[32]

Some writers emphasized the way in which American federalism and separation of powers encourages "rights talk" and "adversarial legalism."[33] Other stress the way in which American political culture (especially its individualism and distrust of centralized power) have shaped our institutions.[34] The important point is not to resolve the chicken-or-the-egg issue, but to note the way in which our beliefs and institutions reinforce each other. One cannot hope to understand powerful institutions without understanding the beliefs that sustain them, or the day-to-day power of political beliefs without seeing how they are embedded in our institutions.

Comparative studies have also noted major differences between European and American patterns of recruiting and training top civil servants and between European and American administrators' understanding of their role. As Fessler and Kettl note, the American higher public service

> is not a close-knit group of people who, by formal organization, shared values, or informal understanding, act in a unified fashion on policy matters and protect their status, salaries, and perquisites. Instead the American public service includes many elites build variously on educational and professional specialization, single-agency attachments, and distinctive congressionally established career services. . . . In this respect our administrative elite contrasts sharply with those of Britain and France, each of which has a narrow recruitment.[35]

Not only is the American higher public service more specialized, diverse, and fragmented than its European counterparts, but it is subject to much more oversight *within* the bureaucracy. In Britain and France new governments appoint only about a hundred top officials. In Germany the figure is about half that. American presidents, in contrast, have the power to nominate three thousand political executives. Most of these political executives stay in office two years or less, thus creating what Hugh Heclo has called "a government of strangers."[36]

These differences in recruitment, training, and tenure contribute to the striking difference in the way American and European administrators view their jobs. In their study of the roles of bureaucrats and legislators in Western democracies, Aberbach, Putnam, and Rockman found that "American exceptionalism dogs our quest for uniformity and uninhibited generalization." To a "startling extent" American civil servants are inclined to see themselves as politicians rather than as technicians. Why?

> To answer this question requires that we begin with institutions, for institutions are in large part responsible for this remarkable fusion. American bureaucrats, to a degree unmatched elsewhere, are responsible for shoring up their own bases of political support. Fragmented accountability forces American bureaucrats to be risk takers and forceful advocates for positions they hold privately. . . . In a political system that rewards entrepreneurs, neither protected by anonymity nor clearly serving a single master, American bureaucrats must find allies where they can. This, in turn, generates an entrepreneurial style of behavior that encourages bureaucratic commitment to clienteles.[37]

To put it another way, American administrators do not see themselves as classic Weberian, rule-applying, record-keeping bureaucrats. They cannot rely on assertions of hierarchical authority, but must constantly work at mobilizing the "consent of the governed" and demonstrating their responsiveness to public opinion.

Such responsiveness is not always a virtue. As Tocqueville noted, this trait can be particularly dangerous in foreign policy. At the extreme it can degenerate into what Theodore Lowi has called "universal ticket-fixing."[38] For better or for worse, American political institutions produce maddening inconsistencies, combining overregulation with underregulation,[39] gratuitous generosity with shortsighted stinginess. It can take years and years to decide whether to dredge Oakland harbor,[40] whether to restrict automobile use in order to lower pollution levels,[41] or even how to establish the minimum number of peanuts in a jar of peanut butter.

James Q. Wilson captures the European-American contrast with a vivid metaphor:

> Policy making in Europe is like a prizefight: Two contenders, having earned the right to enter the ring, square off against each other for a prescribed number of rounds; when one fighter knocks the other one out, he is declared a winner and the fight is over. Policy making in the United States is more like a barroom brawl: Anybody can join in, the combatants fight all comers and sometimes change sides, no referee is in charge, and the fight lasts not for a fixed number of rounds, but indefinitely or until everybody drops from exhaustion.[42]

The disadvantages of this approach become more apparent the larger the government grows, leading to a variety of proposals to nudge us in the European direction. Of course, many Europeans have noted the disadvantages of their model, arguing that their nations should move in the American direction.

If the American regime usually produces bureaucracies that are decentralized, permeable, and subject to a variety of constraints, how do we explain the success of those rare federal agencies that have earned a reputation for influence, effectiveness, and autonomy? Moreover, how do we explain the undeniable fact that in the aggregate the power of the federal administrative apparatus has grown enormously during the twentieth century? Providing adequate answers to these questions requires us to examine the ways successful administrative leaders have tied organizational routines and structures to compelling public purposes, and the ways successful statesmen have subtly given new meaning to inherited constitutional forms and ideals. In other words, they require us to think about how bureaucratic organizations are founded and how political regimes are refounded.

Federal agencies noted for their influence, effectiveness, and autonomy tend to share two attributes. First, as James Q. Wilson has emphasized, they all have had a strong sense of *mission,* that is, a vision of the organization and its goals that is "widely shared and warmly endorsed by operators and managers alike." This sense of mission "confers a feeling of special worth on the members, provides a basis for recruiting and socializing new members, and enables the administrators to economize on the use of their incentives."[43] Second, to use a more traditional term, they have identifiable, often remarkable founders. One could not hope to understand the culture and success of the Forest Service, for example, without examining the teachings

and shrewd maneuverings of Gifford Pinchot. Much the same can be said of
J. Edgar Hoover and the FBI and Hyman Rickover and the nuclear navy.
These founders knew how to protect their turf, to create constituencies, to
build alliances, and to market their product. They also understood the importance of creating strong internal norms, myths, heroes, pride, and mutual
expectations.[44]

No federal agency has left a larger mark on American life than the Social
Security Administration (SSA). Programs proposed, administered, or shaped
by the SSA—social security, medicare and medicaid, disability insurance,
Supplemental Security Income, and what used to be called Aid to Families
with Dependent Children—today account for almost half of the federal
budget. Agency leaders not only helped to write the 1935 Social Security Act,
but played a central role in the remarkable expansion of retirement, disability, and health-care programs over the next half century. As Martha
Derthick's classic study of the SSA shows, the key to its success was the devotion, longevity, and skillfulness of its "program executives," men such as
Robert Ball, Wilbur Cohen, and Arthur Altmeyer who dedicated their professional lives to expanding and perfecting the agency's programs. These program executives were patient and flexible in their political tactics. Wilbur
Cohen, one of the most astute congressional strategists of recent times, was
renowned for his incremental "salami-slicing." Yet SSA program executives
"knew what they wanted; they were very clear about first principles." These
guiding principles were clearly enunciated and frequently repeated:

> The dogmas pertained to operative features of the program. It should be con-
> tributory: people must qualify for benefits by making contributions (paying
> taxes). Having paid their contributions, they or their dependents should get
> benefits as a matter of right. There must be no means test. . . . The program
> should be national in scope and should be run by the federal government. It
> should be universal and compulsory.[45]

Program executives recruited administrators who shared this perspective.
Training within the agency reinforced these norms. Administrators at all levels had to be convinced that social security was not a dole, but "a different
kind of animal—that because of contributions there were certain rights,
statutory rights, that had to be recognized and achieved, and we had an obligation."[46] This rights-based "client-serving ethic" permeated the agency
from top to bottom, creating in the public mind a vision not just of the
agency, but of the entire social security system.

Of course, during the organization's early years social security advocates
could count on the support of a powerful patron: the president of the United
States. Old-age insurance was included in the 1935 act not because the public demanded it (there was no outpouring of support for a program that imposed taxes right away but offered no benefits for several years), but be-

cause Franklin Roosevelt insisted upon it. He also insisted upon a financing system that was consciously designed to "give the contributors a legal, moral, and political right to collect their pensions" and to insure that "no damn politician can ever scrap my social security program."[47] Creating what social scientists today call a "policy legacy" was in this instance a self-conscious act of founding.

As Sidney Milkis has shown, FDR was not just a frenetic, cheerful experimenter, but a man who had given extensive consideration to the crucial question of how one could meld the American political tradition with the modern welfare state.[48] His new constitutional order combined reconstituted institutions—an expanded presidency; a larger, more professional bureaucracy; more pliant judicial and legislative branches; and more centralized political parties—with a new understanding of the basic rights of Americans. The job of modern government is "to assist the development of an economic declaration of rights, an economic constitutional order." "The task of statesmanship," Roosevelt declared, "has always been the re-definition of these rights [announced in the Declaration of Independence] in terms of a changing and growing social order." Statesmen must teach the public "to recognize the new terms of the old social contract."[49]

Toward the end of his presidency FDR laid out these "new terms" in greater detail. His "Economic Bill of Rights" supplemented the "sacred Bill of Rights of our Constitution." It included "the right to earn enough to provide adequate food and clothing and recreation"; the right to "adequate medical care," "a decent home," and "a good education"; and "the right to adequate protection from the economic fears of old age, sickness, accident and unemployment." Each of these rights, Roosevelt added, "must be applied to all our citizens, irrespective of race, creed or color." "What all this spells," he explained in 1944, "is security."[50]

Eighteenth-century liberalism promised security from civil war, anarchy, and arbitrary government action. Its cornerstone was the protection of a realm of private autonomy from government intervention. Contemporary liberalism promises a broader security—security against the vagaries of the business cycle and other hazards created by dynamic capitalism, against the prejudices of private citizens and the consequences of three centuries of racism, against the risks of congenital handicaps and inevitable old age, and against the consequences of poverty and of family decomposition. More than ever before, the protection of fundamental rights rested on "enlightened administration"—such as that provided by the Social Security Administration.

My aim here is not to provide new insights into the New Deal or the Social Security Administration, but simply to apply arguments about constitutional forms made more elegantly and abstractly by Harvey Mansfield. What political scientists are wont to call "institutions" matter enormously not just because they establish the rules that govern bargaining, but because over the long run they shape the expectations, aspirations, habits, and inhibitions of rulers and ruled alike. Most powerful institutions rest on clearly articulated, broadly shared, and vigorously defended political beliefs. Building new institutions or substantially revising old ones usually requires statesmen who can shrewdly link new to old truths and embed them in new programs, procedures, and political organizations. Successful founders are clear about their purposes and aware of the difficulty of their task. As a result, these leaders often have a better understanding of their endeavors than do the social scientists who study them. This means we scholars should be more humble and willing to learn from those we study. The more ambitious the founding, the more likely it is to raise fundamental questions about the meaning of justice, equity, and the purposes of the political community. Because the study of institutions requires us to understand the structure and implications of various arguments about justice, those who study American politics or European politics or the politics of any other region or nation eventually find themselves on the threshold of the "subfield" we now call "political theory."

While it is tempting to conclude this essay with the refrain that careful examination of contemporary politics shows us why we must study the *Republic,* the *Politics,* or *The Prince,* virtually all of the readers of this volume already share that conviction. Rather, I wish to emphasize that by endeavoring to bring political philosophy down from the heavenly city of philosophy departments and the "subfield" of political theory, Harvey Mansfield has not only enriched our understanding of our own regime, but also helped us understand how we can overcome some of the pitfalls and pratfalls of contemporary political science.

NOTES

1. Harvey C. Mansfield, Jr., *America's Constitutional Soul* (Baltimore: Johns Hopkins University Press, 1991), ix. Most of Mansfield's writings on constitutional government are contained in this volume. Several of his earlier essays on American politics are collected in *The Spirit of Liberalism* (Cambridge, Mass.: Harvard University Press, 1978).

2. *America's Constitutional Soul,* 4.

3. *America's Constitutional Soul,* 12.

4. The term comes from David Mayhew's influential book *Congress: The Electoral Connection* (New Haven, Conn.: Yale University Press, 1974), 17.

5. See, for example, Timothy J. Conlan, Margaret T. Wrightson, and David R. Beam, *Taxing Choices: The Politics of Tax Reform* (Washington, D.C.: CQ Press, 1990); Martha Derthick and Paul Quirk, *The Politics of Deregulation* (Washington, D.C.: The Brookings Institution, 1985); Marc Landy, "The New Politics of Environmental Policy," in Marc Landy and Martin Levin, eds., *The New Politics of Public Policy* (Baltimore: Johns Hopkins University Press, 1995); and Aaron Wildavsky, *The New Politics of the Budgetary Process* (Scott Foresman, 1988), esp. chaps. 7 and 8.

6. On Rostenkowski and Packwood, see *Taxing Choices*, 88–92, 112–15, 154–69, 252–55. For similar examples, see *The Politics of Deregulation*, 108–11 (on Senator Howard Cannon), and Joseph Bessette, *The Mild Voice of Reason: Deliberative Democracy and American National Government* (Chicago: University of Chicago Press, 1994), esp. chap. 5.

7. Joseph Cooper, *The Origins of the Standing Committees and the Development of the Modern House* (Houston: Rice University Studies, 1990).

8. Jeffrey Tulis, *The Rhetorical Presidency* (Princeton, N.J.: Princeton University Press, 1987).

9. James D. Savage, *Balanced Budgets in American Politics* (Ithaca, N.Y.: Cornell University Press, 1988).

10. James Sterling Young, *The Washington Community, 1800–1828* (New York: Harcourt Brace & World, 1966), chaps. 4 and 5.

11. Mansfield, "Party Government and the Settlement of 1688," *American Political Science Review* 58.4 (Dec. 1964).

12. Mansfield, *Taming the Prince: The Ambivalence of Modern Executive Power* (New York: Free Press, 1989), chap. 6.

13. Mansfield, *Statesmanship and Party Government: A Study of Burke and Bolingbroke* (Chicago: University of Chicago Press, 1965).

14. *Building a New American State: The Expansion of National Administrative Capacities, 1877–1920* (Cambridge: Cambridge University Press, 1982), 4, emphasis added.

15. James W. Fessler and Donald F. Kettl, *The Politics of the Administrative Process*, 2d ed. (Chatham, N.J.: Chatham House, 1996), 138.

16. See Martha Derthick, *Agency under Stress: The Social Security Administration in American Government* (Washington, D.C.: The Brookings Institution, 1990), 37–48.

17. A good example is air-pollution control. R. Shep Melnick, *Regulation and the Courts: The Case of the Clean Air Act* (Washington, D.C.: The Brookings Institution, 1983), chaps. 2, 6, 7, and 9.

18. A good example is medicaid. See Michael Sparer, *Medicaid and the Limits of State Health Reform* (Philadelphia: Temple University Press, 1996).

19. Robert A. Katzmann, *Institutional Disability: The Saga of Transportation Policy for the Disabled* (Washington, D.C.: Brookings Institution Press, 1986), and R. Shep Melnick, *Between the Lines: Interpreting Welfare Rights* (Washington: The Brookings Institution, 1994).

20. See, for example, Thomas Mann and Norman Ornstein, *The New Congress* (Washington, D.C.: AEI Press, 1981); James Sundquist, *The Decline and Resurgence of Congress* (Washington, D.C.: The Brookings Institution, 1981); Gary Orfield, *Congressional Power: Congress and Social Change* (New York: Harcourt Brace Jovanovich, 1975); Richard Nathan, *The Administrative Presidency* (New York: Wiley, 1983); and Joel Aberbach, *Keeping a Watchful Eye: The Politics of Congressional Oversight* (Washington, D.C.: The Brookings Institution, 1990).

21. Morris Fiorina, *Congress: Keystone of the Washington Establishment*, 2d ed. (New Haven, Conn.: Yale University Press, 1989), chaps. 1–3.

22. See James Q. Wilson, *Bureaucracy: What Government Agencies Do and Why They Do It* (New York: Basic Books, 1989), 241–44; and Kent Weaver, *Automatic Government: The Politics of Indexation* (Washington, D.C.: The Brookings Institution, 1988), chap. 2.

23. *A Political Education: A Washington Memoir* (Boston: Houghton Mifflin, 1988), 18.

24. See Sundquist, *Decline and Resurgence,* esp. chaps. 8–11.

25. *Federalist* no. 51.

26. For example, *Goldberg v. Kelly* 397 U.S. 254 (1970) required administrative hearings prior to termination of welfare benefits.

27. "The Reformation of American Administrative Law," 88 *Harvard Law Review* 1667, 1712 (1975).

28. Martin Shapiro, *Who Guards the Guardians: Judicial Control of Administration* (Athens: Georgia University Press, 1988), 49–54, 79–94, and 115–24. A principal theme of Shapiro's fine book is that administrative-law doctrines tend to reflect the dogmas dominant in political science twenty years before. It thus illustrates and buttresses Mansfield's claim that "Political scientists should recognize that political science has always been essential to American political life, and they should develop greater respect for the consequences of what they think." *America's Constitutional Soul,* 14.

29. "The Constitution of the United States: Contemporary Ratification," in David M. O'Brien, ed., *Judges on Judging: Views from the Bench* (Chatham, N.J.: Chatham House, 1997), 205–6.

30. *EDF v. Ruckelshaus,* 439 F2d 584 at 598 (D.C. Cir., 1971).

31. The term "new property" was coined by Yale Law School professor Charles Reich in a famous law review article, "The New Property," 74 *Yale Law Journal* 1245 (1964). Justice Brennan referred to this article in *Goldberg v. Kelly.* On the expansion of the "new property" through administrative law doctrines and statutory interpretation, see R. Shep Melnick, "Courts, Congress, and Programmatic Rights," in Sidney Milkis and Richard Harris, eds., *Remaking American Politics* (Boulder, Colo.: Westview, 1989) and Jeremy Rabkin, *Judicial Compulsions: How Public Law Distorts Public Policy* (New York: Basic Books, 1989), esp. chap. 2.

32. Ronald Brickman, Sheila Jasanoff, and Thomas Ilgen, *Controlling Chemicals: The Politics of Regulation in Europe and the United States* (Ithaca, N.Y.: Cornell University Press, 1985), 45–46.

33. Robert Kagan, "Adversarial Legalism," in Landy and Levin, *The New Politics of Public Policy;* and Patrick Atiyah, "Judicial-Legislative Relations in England," in Robert Katzmann, ed., *Judges and Legislators: Toward Institutional Comity* (Washington, D.C.: Brookings Institution Press, 1988).

34. Mary Ann Glendon, *Rights Talk: The Impoverishment of Political Discourse* (New York: Free Press, 1991).

35. *The Politics of the Administrative Process,* 182–83.

36. *A Government of Strangers: Executive Politics in Washington* (Washington, D.C.: The Brookings Institution, 1977), chap. 3.

37. Joel D. Aberbach, Robert D. Putnam, and Bert A. Rockman, *Bureaucrats and Politicians in Western Democracies* (Cambridge, Mass.: Harvard University Press, 1981), 95–96.

38. *The End of Liberalism: Ideology, Policy, and the Crisis of Public Authority* (New York: Norton, 1969), 292.

39. See John M. Mendeloff, *The Dilemma of Toxic Substances Regulation: How Overregulation Causes Underregulation at OSHA* (Cambridge, Mass.: MIT Press, 1988).

40. Robert Kagan, "Adversarial Legalism and American Government," in Landy and Levin, *New Politics of Public Policy,* 98–104.

41. Melnick, *Regulation and the Courts,* chap. 9.

42. *Bureaucracy,* 299–300.

43. *Bureaucracy,* 95.

44. For compelling examples, see Jameson W. Doig and Erwin C. Hargrove, eds., *Leadership and Innovation* (Baltimore: Johns Hopkins University Press, 1987).

45. Martha Derthick, *Policymaking for Social Security* (Washington: The Brookings Institution, 1976), 21.

46. Arthur Altmeyer, quoted in *Policymaking for Social Security,* 31.

47. Quoted in Arthur M. Schlesinger Jr., *The Coming of the New Deal* (Boston: Houghton Mifflin, 1958), 308–9.

48. *The President and the Parties: The Transformation of the American Party System since the New Deal* (Oxford: Oxford University Press, 1993), chaps. 3–6.

49. "Commonwealth Club Address," in *Public Papers and Addresses of Franklin D. Roosevelt* (New York: Random House, 1938), 1:752, 753, and 756.

50. "State of the Union Address," 1944, in *Public Papers and Addresses of Franklin D. Roosevelt,* 13:41.

18

Separation of Powers and Contemporary Politics: The Case of the Telecommunications Act of 1996

Jessica Korn

One of the most familiar strains of the conventional twentieth-century attack on the American system of separation of powers is that it sinks attempts at national policymaking with inevitable gridlocks, deadlocks, and stalemates.[1] With regard to the Clinton Administration's push to enact comprehensive health-care reform in 1994, for example, one recent article screamed: "It's the Institutions, Stupid! Why Comprehensive National Health Insurance Always Fails in America."[2]

One might reasonably have expected the usual grumbling about structurally induced gridlock to cease in the face of the Telecommunications Act of 1996, one of the most comprehensive regulatory policy statutes enacted in decades. It reflects precisely the sort of legislative resolution of extensive, divergent, and strongly held views for which critics of the separation of powers clamor. President Clinton, former Speaker Newt Gingrich, and former Senate Majority Leader Bob Dole were not the only ones who expressed great pride that a bill that had "been in the works for over a decade" was about to become law.[3] Senator Ted Stevens observed that simply by looking at the "scope of the definitions" in the new statute—"dialing parity, exchange access, information service, interLATA services, local exchange carriers, network elements, number portability"—one could see how profoundly the Communications Act of 1934, which had succeeded in bringing the nation's "fledgling communications system into the age of telecommunications," needed a facelift. As one of the nation's longest-serving senators (since 1968), Stevens stated that the day of the statute's passage was "one of the most significant days" he had seen during his tenure as a senator.[4]

Congress's true achievement in enacting the Telecommunications Act of 1996 was in codifying—simply and clearly—the broad-based consensus for allowing competition in all segments of the telecommunications industry. Since the affected players include myriad, fast-changing, and technologically complex industries within the jurisdiction of a myriad of federal, state, and municipal regulatory commissions and zoning boards, there has been nothing simple or clear, naturally, about the implementation of the statute—except, perhaps, the expectation that the transition to competition would be messy and time consuming.

Despite this achievement, the frustration inherent in much of the conventional wisdom about telecommunications policy today suggests that resolving complex regulatory details should have been much easier than it has been. The conventional wisdom concludes that the statute is an out and out failure since "we all know, of course, that the Telecommunications Act of 1996 . . . hasn't exactly worked as planned."[5]

From this point of view, had the Telecommunications Act "worked as planned," competition among providers of local telephone service would already be in place. The classic political scientist's critique of the constitutional separation of powers, in other words, holds true yet again in the case of contemporary telecommunications policy.[6] That classic view is embodied in the political science of Theodore Lowi.

In *The End of Liberalism,* Lowi explains that the American separation of powers undermines the government's capacity for effective administration by separating direct legislative authority from the exercise of delegated administrative powers. Without detailed guidance on how to exercise the administrative authorities associated with new statutes, Lowi claims, Congress creates an "imposition of impotence" on the government because administrators are forced to respond piecemeal to the demands of the variety of interested groups affected by the new policy authority. The Telecommunications Act provides sorry evidence to support this claim, supposedly, because it allows so many important details to be worked out as part of the process of implementation.

Harvey Mansfield's classic review of Lowi's book cuts directly to the mischaracterization of representative democracy animating Lowi's critique.[7] Lowi's complaint about the formal separation of administration from legislative authority is rooted in his objection, curiously, to the representative flavor of the administrative process that the separation of powers fosters. Lowi believes, as Mansfield explains, that "laws enacted democratically need to be 'implemented absolutely' or 'carried to absolute finality.'"[8]

But if it is really the effective implementation of laws that Lowi's view aims to foster, he would have paid more careful attention to the powerful point about administration articulated in *The Federalist:* the "requisite stability" in governmental authority that makes competent administration possible itself relies on the people's ongoing "confidence in the public councils."[9] Or, to put it in Mansfield's words, good administration "is so far from being essentially opposed to representation as to require it and further it."[10] In this regard, the Telecommunications Act of 1996 represents a profound achievement indeed when viewed from the perspective of how the framers hoped the separation of powers would work.

For most of this century, the nation's telecommunications industry has consisted of a regulated monopoly, AT&T, which promised universal service to hard-to-get-to areas, such as the tops of mountains and ninety-person towns far away from anywhere, in exchange for guaranteed rates of return on capital investments, and freedom from competitors. But the easy justification for a special compact between the government and one firm began to falter as technological innovation in telecommunications exploded soon after WWII. As defense-related research-and-development projects in microwave, radar, electronic circuitry, and materials science became focused on commercial applications, AT&T lost more and more of its monopoly status as provider of technological innovations relevant to consumers of telecommunications services. As new companies came up with better, cheaper, and faster ways to do what AT&T was doing, they put pressure on the FCC to let them into the telecommunications business.

The FCC's most famous case of chipping away at AT&T's monopoly status was in 1969, when the agency allowed a new company, Microwave Communications, Incorporated, to offer private-line long-distance telephone service at a deeply discounted rate. MCI quickly expanded this service, which it called Execunet, to make it possible for anyone with a touch-tone phone to connect to MCI's long-distance network simply by dialing a few extra numbers. MCI's expansion of its Execunet service meant it was reaching into the residential market for long-distance service. In other words, MCI had become a direct competitor to AT&T's long-distance service. By 1978, when Execunet was in the clear from regulatory and court battles, MCI succeeded in opening the long-distance market to competition, putting AT&T on the road to divestiture, and putting the concept of regulated monopoly on the road to extinction.

Soon after MCI began slinging its shots as David did to Goliath, AT&T drafted the Consumer Communications Reform Act of 1976, supported by the Communications Workers of America and the National Association of Regulatory Utility Commissioners, to "eliminate the emerging competition in private line services and terminal equipment." It aimed to put MCI out of business by stating that "the authorization of lines, facilities, or services of specialized carriers which duplicate the lines, facilities or services of other telecommunications carriers . . . is . . . contrary to the public interest."[11]

But stomping its feet around Capitol Hill had exactly the wrong effect for AT&T. It might have been otherwise had it been operating in a parliamentary system in which the powerful group of the moment finds it relatively easy to ram new statutes down the throats of its weaker opponents. But in a separation-of-powers system, the wheels of the representative process, though exceedingly well oiled, grind exceedingly slowly. So, AT&T's proposed reform of telecommunications policy taught the proponents of competition to make use of Congress as a forum in which to voice their opinions.

By introducing a bill that threatened to prohibit the FCC from authorizing any further exceptions to monopoly control of the telecommunications industry, AT&T initiated the political mobilization of all those whose interests were aligned with competition. This included not only the growing universe of entrepreneurs who had new telecommunications technologies to sell, but also the large users of telecommunications services, like banks, automobile manufacturers, and oil companies, who were looking forward to seeing their long-distance telephone bills drop.

Once the growing group of procompetitive interests were drawn into the legislative arena to insure that AT&T's bill went nowhere, they decided to stay. AT&T's bill did indeed go nowhere, and from 1978 to 1996, every single bill introduced to reform the Communications Act of 1934 "accepted competition as desirable."[12] Before the divestiture of AT&T in 1982, Communications Act reform bills sought to restrict monopoly power from spreading into areas of the industry witnessing fast-paced technological innovation. Then the divestiture itself, codified in Judge Harold Greene's Modified Final Judgement (MFJ), which became effective in 1984, formally eliminated the system of regulated monopoly from the long-distance market. But it preserved the regulated monopoly status of the local phone companies from which AT&T had been divested.

Restructuring the regulatory system around the new demands of the MFJ—opening the long-distance market to competition, while preserving the monopoly status of phone companies at the local level—was not easy. The complexity of the regulatory apparatus that had grown up to govern AT&T's monopoly included cross-subsidies from the local to the long-distance market and back again in all areas of the business. Prices for easy-to-serve, high-population areas were inflated to cover the cost of hard-to-serve rural areas. Prices for business customers were jacked up to keep residential rates artificially low. So, creating a level playing field for competitive providers of long-distance telephone service meant teasing those long-established cross-subsidies out of each other. Doing so took over a decade of policymaking pushing, pulling, proposing, and reacting among affected players, including large users, small users, and new entrants as well as the incumbent AT&T, through as many courts, commissions, and agencies as were available.

This process of rearranging the regulatory structure in the long-distance market around the competitive pursuit of new customers and delivery of new services led the local phone companies, over time, to desire the advantages of shedding their regulatory monopoly status too.[13] In other words, the very participation during the 1980s of the local phone companies in the messy regulatory processes that opened up the long-distance market to competition is precisely what led them to support the elimination of their own monopoly power. Quite the accomplishment, from the point of view of those who believe that laws should be based on a broad-based consensus of interests.

Nonetheless, many telecommunications policy analysts miss the significance of the statute. They take for granted the representative legitimacy in the formulation of policy that our constitutional democracy makes possible.[14]

For example, Scott Cleland, a well-known Washington, D.C.–based telecommunications guru, complains that the Telecommunications Act of 1996 is a statute whose procompetition stance is nothing more than "a lot of ambitious over-promising." The statute's celebration of marketplace competition is a whole lot of hogwash, according to Cleland, because "competition will take a lot longer than people expected."[15]

But whose expectations is Cleland referring to, exactly, when he makes reference to the amount of time "people expected" the dismantling of regulated monopolies to take? Cleland claims that his policy views carry a unique neutrality because, unlike the "traditional Wall Street sell-side analyst who analyzes companies or recommends the purchase of stocks," Cleland's clients "expect my best unbiased assessment of 'what is and what will be' rather than the common 'what should be' analysis of company advocates and those involved in the political or regulatory process."

Cleland is undoubtedly agnostic with regard to picking winning firms. But as a "policy analyst for the investment community who tracks regulatory, technological, and competitive developments in the communications sector for large institutional investors," Cleland represents clients who have a powerful bias in favor of minimizing uncertainties in the marketplace. In other words, Cleland's clients do not have much patience for politics. Cleland believes that Congress did not know what it was doing when it enacted a procompetitive statute. He argues that legislators "overestimated the advancement of technology" and "underestimated the economic efficiencies of a regulated natural monopoly."[16] So, he argues, it is no surprise that Congress was unable to give the FCC clear and absolute guidelines for dismantling the remaining regulated monopolies in the telecommunications industry. Implicit in this view is the Lowi-esque dismissal of the representative process at work: the emergence of a broad consensus favoring a particular policy is not enough to justify enactment of statutes. The separation-of-powers system, it seems, makes it too easy for Congress to enact new policy convictions.

More to the point: attacks on constitutional structure remain an easy target for those who look to cloak in high principles their attempt to get their way out of public policy without having to waste time or money negotiating with potentially opposing interests. Mansfield's illumination of the connection between constitutional principle and constitutional structure enables us to recognize—and appreciate—the way in which sound policy emerges from the representative legitimacy of our political institutions.

NOTES

1. See, for example, James L. Sundquist, ed., *Beyond Gridlock? Prospects for Governance in the Clinton Years—And After* (Washington: The Brookings Institution, 1993).

2. Sven Steinmo and Jon Watts, "It's the Institutions, Stupid! Why Comprehensive National Health Insurance Always Fails in America," *Journal of Health Politics, Policy and Law* 20 (Summer 1995): 329–72.

3. *Congressional Record,* 104th Cong., 2d sess., vol. 142, daily ed. (1 February 1996): S718 (Sen. Bob Dole, R-KS).

4. *Congressional Record,* 104th Cong., 2d sess., vol. 142, daily ed. (1 February 1996): S691 (Sen. Ted Stevens, R-AL).

5. Allan Sloan, "Remember How the Mighty AT&T Stumbled as SBC Acquisition of Ameritech Unfolds," *Washington Post,* May 19, 1998.

6. Theodore Lowi, *The End of Liberalism: Ideology, Policy, and the Crisis of Public Authority* (New York: Norton, 1969).

7. Harvey Mansfield, "Disguised Liberalism," in *The Spirit of Liberalism* (Cambridge, Mass.: Harvard University Press, 1978).

8. Mansfield, 41.

9. Alexander Hamilton, James Madison, and John Jay, *The Federalist Papers,* ed. Clinton Rossiter (New York: Mentor, 1961), no. 37, 226; no. 62, 381.

10. Mansfield, 41.

11. Gerald Brock, *Telecommunication Policy for the Information Age: From Monopoly to Competition* (Cambridge, Mass.: Harvard University Press, 1994), 151.

12. Brock, 152.

13. See Richard Vietor, "AT&T," in *Contrived Competition: Regulation and Deregulation in America* (Cambridge, Mass.: Harvard University Press, 1994).

14. Mansfield, 40.

15. Scott Cleland, quoted in Carolyn Hirschman, "A Look Back: The Telecommunications Act of 1996," *Telephony* (February 10, 1997), 7.

16. Senate Judiciary Committee, *Consolidation in the Telecommunications Sector: Hearings before the Subcommittee on Antitrust, Business Rights and Competition,* May 19, 1998 (Scott Cleland, Legg Mason Wood Walker, Inc.).

19

The Care of Souls in a Constitutional Democracy: Some Lessons from Harvey Mansfield and Alexander Solzhenitsyn

Robert P. Kraynak

Americans often call their form of government a democracy because it derives its just powers from the consent of the people. But the people rarely exercise those powers directly and cannot do whatever they please because the Constitution restricts them, which means America is a constitutional democracy or what the founders called a republic. In a constitutional democracy, the people govern through representatives, and the state is restrained by checks and balances to protect the rights and liberties of everyone. Constitutional democracy in this sense is a type of limited government that arises from the theory of natural or human rights.

Although the natural-rights understanding of constitutional democracy is the most common one, it does not exhaust all the possibilities of constitutionalism and may even obscure a more important one. As Harvey Mansfield has argued, constitutionalism is not only about limiting the powers of government to protect natural rights; it is also about the *soul*. Every constitutional system, whether it acknowledges the fact or not, is a "regime" in the classical sense: a comprehensive social order imposed by the ruling group that reflects its view of the good life. As a regime, the constitution shapes the souls of its citizens in accordance with its ruling principle, which means a democratic constitution tends to produce the opinions and tastes of the majority in everyone, creating a popular culture or mass society. In Plato's words, the regime in the city imposes a regime in the soul, making politics the art whose business it is to care for souls. In this view, constitutionalism cannot avoid the issue of steering souls to virtue and away from vice because "statecraft is soulcraft."[1]

Yet if it is true that constitutionalism is concerned not only with limiting power to protect natural rights but also with ordering the soul to virtue, then defenders of constitutional democracy face a serious difficulty, if not a fatal contradiction. They must be defenders of both limited and unlimited government. They must defend a conception of the constitution that limits the state in order to prevent arbitrary power, overzealous interference with private lives, and especially the totalitarian temptation to transform human nature; but they must also include in that conception a means for imposing on people for their own good and shaping their minds, hearts, and souls in accordance with virtue. Is it possible to combine the seemingly inconsistent ends of protecting freedom and inculcating virtue in a coherent theory of constitutional democracy?

I think it is possible, though difficult. Many statesmen and political philosophers concerned with the fate of modern democracy have struggled to combine the two ideals. The classic case is Tocqueville, who combines a vigorous defense of democratic liberty with sustained attention to institutions and *mores* that inculcate virtue.[2] In our times, a defense has been undertaken by numerous thinkers, among whom Harvey Mansfield and Alexander Solzhenitsyn deserve special consideration for the depth and originality of their thought on this matter.

Examining these two authors together as defenders of constitutional democracy may seem unusual because their works appear to have few affinities, and many think Solzhenitsyn is unsympathetic to democracy. Yet, as I shall argue, they are surprisingly similar in their conviction that the primary purpose of politics is not the protection of rights (which they see as morally neutral) but to defend the dignity and perfection of the human soul. And both maintain that constitutional democracy is the best means for defending the soul in modern times where the all-powerful centralized state threatens the soul's integrity with ideological lies and degraded dependency. This makes their approach "prudential" in the classic sense of viewing constitutional government as a means for realizing the higher ends of virtue and spiritual development. Yet it does not reduce the case to expedience, because their prudence is based on an understanding of the permanent ends and limits of human nature. For Mansfield and Solzhenitsyn, political freedom is necessary for realizing virtue and spiritual development because the human soul cannot flourish without a sense of responsibility for its actions, and virtue is most noble when it is voluntarily chosen. In this light, constitutional government is prudentially wise in all times and places, while democratic constitutionalism is a prudent concession to the spirit of the modern age.

In the analysis that follows, I argue that Mansfield arrives at this view by using the classical prudence of Aristotle, while Solzhenitsyn uses the Christian prudence of St. Augustine. I conclude by suggesting that their prudential wisdom permits greater hope for reconciling the care of souls with constitutional democracy than is commonly thought to be possible.

THE DIGNITY OF THE HUMAN SOUL

It is disturbing to modern ears to hear defenders of constitutional government speak about the human soul rather than about human rights. As Mansfield observes in *America's Constitutional Soul,* "modern democracy is unhappy with the word *soul"* because it sounds too religious or moralistic to inject into politics. The reason, he tells us, is that modern political philosophers specifically intended to take the soul out of politics because they believed the concern with perfecting the soul through virtue or saving the immortal soul led to theocratic politics, religious wars, and oppression by moral zealots. Instead of talking about the soul, modern political philosophers prefer to talk about empirical things, like economic interests, power, and rights. And Mansfield concedes that they have a point: the quantitative measurement of rights is a more exact way of judging nations than trying to determine if the "common good" in the classical sense has been realized. For the latter involves judging not only concrete factors, such as the existence of political prisoners or political corruption, but also intangible notions of moral health and good character, spiritual and cultural development, friendship, and harmony of the diverse parts of society. Nevertheless, Mansfield insists, the intangibles are the ultimate standard for judging a nation because they indicate the health or sickness of its soul.[3]

Solzhenitsyn not only agrees, he deliberately tries to restore moral discourse about the soul to politics and social science. His writings abound with many striking examples: "beyond upholding *rights,* mankind must defend its *soul,* freeing it for reflection and feeling"; "the greatness of a people is to be sought not in the blare of trumpets . . . but in the level of its inner development, in its breadth of soul . . . in healing its soul"; because of modern progress "we had forgotten . . . the human soul"; and "the destruction of our souls over three-quarters of a century is the most terrifying thing of all."[4]

Why do these thinkers put such an emphasis on the soul in politics? Is it merely nostalgia for the Greek polis in Mansfield's case or for the Christian Middle Ages by Solzhenitsyn?

I do not think so. They believe that "soul," though an old-fashioned idea, is an indispensable concept for all ages because it is the foundation of the dignity of man. The soul is what makes us human, the cause of our essential difference from the animals that makes us rational and responsible beings with capacities for moral and spiritual development. Without the soul and the dignity it conveys, there is no basis for justice in politics—no real reason why we should treat others fairly and decently rather than as animals or subhumans. The soul is the intangible basis of ethical standards in politics that keeps us from being lost in a sea of relativism where anything goes and only material outcomes are counted.

But how do we know that men have souls, rather than being mere bundles of instincts or expressive selves? For Mansfield and Solzhenitsyn, the primary evidence for the existence of the soul is the pride that human beings take in their integrity beyond all calculations of material interest. Such integrity reflects a kind of "natural conscience" that says to people, sometimes in the most appalling circumstances, that certain actions are beneath one's dignity as a human being to do even at the cost of survival and personal gratification.[5] According to Mansfield, the motivation for such acts is not explicable as the Kantian rational will asserted against the determinism of nature. Rather, it is the pride or spiritedness or "manliness" of men asserting their nature as rational beings in the given hierarchy of nature, as Plato and Aristotle understood it. Mansfield describes this motivation in *The Spirit of Liberalism* as "a certain spirit in the soul of a human being that gives him the pride to defend his humanity."[6] This is virtue in the classical sense: an ordered soul in which reason rules the lower passions with the help of pride.

For Solzhenitsyn, the order of the soul arises partly from natural pride and stubbornness; but ultimately it comes from a sense of the divine spark in human beings—of our creation in the image and likeness of God—which includes rationality but also more mysteriously points to our spiritual and religious nature. Beyond possessing natural souls, men have "divine souls" that resist degradation to the subhuman or even acceptance of the merely human desire for earthly happiness and everyday contentment.[7] While Solzhenitsyn sometimes describes the longings of the divine soul in Platonic terms—as in the scene from *First Circle* (chap. 48) where prisoners lost in timeless contemplation experience the Platonic pleasures of philosophical friendship, or in *Cancer Ward* (chap. 30) where the old doctor declares the "meaning of existence" to be preserving "the image of eternity" in each person—Solzhenitsyn's highest ethical standards are Christian. He finds the fulfillment of our divine souls in the Christian virtues of "repentance and self-limitation" for the sake of God and other human beings. They transcend the classical moral virtues of courage, magnanimity, and justice (which he also praises explicitly) because Christian virtues are based on the purest motive, sacrificial love.[8] In Solzhenitsyn's view, Christianity is necessary for healing the soul: "It show[s] us the way: *sacrifice.*"[9]

According to Mansfield and Solzhenitsyn, then, the soul is the seat of man's rational and spiritual essence, the defining trait of humanity in the natural hierarchy of beings or the created hierarchy of the Christian cosmos. Without soul, there would be no basis for human dignity and no conduct worthy of man. The existence of the soul also implies that we can choose to become good or evil and are ultimately responsible for our lives.

For Mansfield, this account of the soul is developed most fully in the works of Aristotle—not, however, in *De Anima,* which is a theoretical account of "soul" as the source of motion and awareness in living beings, but in the *Politics,* where we see citizens making practical choices about who should rule. The implication is that the practical account of the soul is more revealing than the theoretical one because the practical account shows the human soul taking responsibility for itself and asserting its dignity. In Mansfield's reading of Aristotle, the debate about justice in politics is the attempt to define what it means to be human by elevating some quality (such as the physical body or wealth or noble birth) to preeminence and excluding other qualities. Conflicts arise because the attempt to define our humanity requires the ability to see virtue or the well-ordered soul. But as Mansfield says (quoting his favorite line from Aristotle), "the beauty of the soul is not as easy to see as the beauty of the body," which turns politics into a kind of shadowboxing match over the invisible soul. The claims put forward are "partisan because they absolutize [some] quality as the human quality . . . [thus] the establishment of human dignity involves the promotion of some humans over others, one party over others, one country over others."[10] For Mansfield, Aristotle's *Politics* is the best treatise on the human soul because it shows men striving for dignity and responsibility by ruling themselves and others in the name of justice.

In the case of Solzhenitsyn, the best insight into the human soul is found not in classical philosophical texts but in the harsh experience of Soviet prison and labor camps. Yet one could argue that he too discovers the human soul in politics—in the experience of unjust rule or oppression and the radical denial of freedom. Such experiences inspire countless stories of the "ascent of the soul" and the "corruption of the soul" that Solzhenitsyn records in the *Gulag* and in his literary works. The gist of all of them, historical as well as fictional, is that every human being has both good and evil tendencies within himself and that the struggle to resolve the conflict shows that the responsibility for becoming good or evil lies in one's own soul. The majority of people have their souls corrupted by imprisonment and suffering, reducing them to vicious animals; but a significant minority preserves its integrity and is never corrupted (perhaps as many as 20 percent, Solzhenitsyn estimates at one point in the *Gulag*).[11] Some, like the characters Ivan Denisovich and Matryona, preserve their integrity through natural conscience and simple piety. Others, like Solzhenitsyn himself, experience a self-conscious ascent of the soul to God, an affirmation of the existence of God as the creator of the universe and the judge of human souls.[12] For Solzhenitsyn, such reactions to oppression and suffering testify to an inner freedom from animal instinct and environment that has no adequate explanation except the existence of an intangible human soul.

What is unusual about Mansfield and Solzhenitsyn is the practical founda-tion they provide for affirming the existence of the soul. They do not derive their views theoretically or theologically by appealing, for example, to Plato's *Laws* (book 10), where the existence of soul is proven from the or-derly motions of the universe; or to Aristotle's *De Anima,* where soul is in-ferred from the motion, sensation, and rational awareness of living beings; or to Scripture, which asks, "What does it profit a man if he gains the whole world but loses his own soul [*psychen autou*]?" (Matt. 16:26).[13] Despite their appeals to practical experience, Mansfield and Solzhenitsyn do not view the existence of the soul as a postulate of practical reason in the Kantian sense—as a logical presupposition of rational morality that enables one to infer the existence of freedom, immortality of the soul, and God from the possibility of moral action. While resembling Kant in his practical orientation and pas-sion for human dignity, Mansfield and Solzhenitsyn are following the classi-cal and Christian idea of a human essence that is naturally given or mysteri-ously created by God. For them, the dignity of man lies in the intimation of the soul as the image of a higher order of being—an "image of eternity"—that is dimly felt by most human beings while being fully revealed only in the highest examples of virtue.[14]

Without saying so explicitly, they are appealing to classical natural right and Christian natural law—to standards whose premise is the existence of an intangible human soul with natural inclinations to rational and spiritual perfection.

MANSFIELD'S ARISTOTELIAN PRUDENCE

If the perfection of the soul is the end of politics, what form of government is best suited to attain this end? Obviously, one cannot assume that it auto-matically requires democracy, because the direct implications go in the op-posite direction, toward moral authoritarianism by a virtuous elite who im-pose on others to improve their souls. This is precisely what modern democrats fear about soul-talk. Their suspicions might be further aroused by statements of Mansfield and Solzhenitsyn that openly challenge the deepest prejudice of our age—the unexamined assumption that democracy based on human rights is the only legitimate form of government. Mansfield invites all political scientists to question if "democracy is the only regime" so that they can become aware of the merits of other regimes.[15] And, of course, Solzhenitsyn has been accused of having tendencies toward tsarism and theocracy—a charge that Edward Ericson has helped to dispel without explaining satisfactorily Solzhenitsyn's praise of moderate authoritarianism and persistent opposition to rights as the basis of legitimate government (as well as Solzhenitsyn's sometimes harsh criticism of Andrei Sakharov, the human-rights activist).[16]

I think that the only way to clarify this crucial issue is to show that Mansfield and Solzhenitsyn are reviving an old approach to politics that is properly called *prudential*—an approach which seeks the best possible means for attaining perfection of the soul in a world that is inherently imperfect because it is marred by fallible and sinful human nature. In this light, moral authoritarianism by a virtuous elite is fine in theory but misguided in practice, making political freedom indispensable for realizing virtue as well as for personal security. This approach, which Mansfield derives from the classical prudence of Aristotle and Solzhenitsyn from the Christian prudence of St. Augustine, is neither as doctrinaire as one based on natural rights nor as fragile as one based on expedience; it leads to a powerful defense of constitutional democracy based on an understanding of the permanent ends and limitations of human nature.

Let us first examine Mansfield's prudential reasoning, as presented in *Taming the Prince, American's Constitutional Soul,* and the first chapter of *The Spirit of Liberalism,* "Liberal Democracy as a Mixed Regime." The common theme of these works is the comparison of Aristotle with Locke and the American founders. What is original and controversial about Mansfield's interpretation is the claim that all were aiming at the same goals—defending human dignity and creating citizens with virtuous souls—while differing about the best strategy for realizing these ends. In this light, the modern constitutionalism of Locke and Madison is not so much a continuation of Machiavelli's rebellion against the ancients as it is a new way of achieving the goals of Aristotelian political science in modern conditions.

But what is Aristotelian political science? According to Mansfield, it is a rational analysis of political regimes which holds that the theoretically best regime is the rule of perfect virtue while the best regime in practice dilutes or approximates virtue by mixing it with political freedom and the rule of law. To establish this interpretation, Mansfield emphasizes Aristotle's discussion of kingship at the end of book 3 of the *Politics.* It is the culmination of a debate about who should rule (the democrats, the oligarchs, or impersonal law) that has been left unresolved because the claim of perfect virtue has not been considered. To give perfect virtue its due, Aristotle describes the case of an ideal king who is so preeminent in virtue that he is like a god among men and deserves the fitting title of "kingship over all" (*pambasileia*). In judging his claim to rule, Aristotle argues that, despite the many advantages of the rule of law, the only just course would be to give him absolute and unlimited power to do good for himself and others.

Mansfield's interpretation is that Aristotle raises the hypothetical case of a perfectly virtuous ruler (without specifying if he is a philosopher-king or someone more down-to-earth) to show that such rule is not only impossible but also *undesirable*. It is impossible because no one of such stature exists; it is undesirable because the absolute rule of an ideal king would leave his fellow citizens in a condition of moral immaturity, denying them the opportunity to become responsible for themselves. Like a father of perfect virtue whose children never emerge from his shadow, he would be a perfect man but a bad father because his children would never grow up. Thus, the perfectly virtuous king is not merely unrealizable, as Plato taught; he is undesirable in the real world where many decent people need freedom and responsibility to become virtuous on their own.[17]

In this distinction lies the whole difference between Platonic and Aristotelian political science. As Mansfield says, "Aristotle thought that Socrates' philosopher-king was too daunting to the gentlemen" who have some capacity to rule; and "Aristotle was mindful of the danger posed to human freedom by the most excellent soul." Mansfield tilts to Aristotle over Plato because Aristotle allows for political freedom and human responsibility for lesser human beings than the philosopher: "We need a political science capable of discerning responsibility. Such a political science is essentially Aristotelian."[18] It is a tricky business, however, because "responsibility" is not simply accountability for one's action, regardless of the end. Aristotelian responsibility is the free choice of Nature's given end (happiness through virtue) which Nature points to but does not automatically guarantee, leaving people free to complete or to thwart her intentions. To fulfill Nature's intentions, a delicate balance is needed, requiring regimes to point to virtue as the end and even to encourage the right habits during an extended period of tutelage, while giving mature people freedom to develop and to exercise virtue on their own.

From this prudential wisdom, Mansfield draws the conclusion that "Aristotle's kingship . . . is beyond all politics, since there will be many who do not conform to the rule of the one best, who indeed have a legitimate claim against it. . . . [It is simply] a theoretical best regime against which to measure actual regimes. Aristotle's practical preference is for the mixed regime and the rule of law [that] its impartiality makes possible."[19] In other words, after perfect kingship, Aristotle's second choice is an imperfect approximation that is better for most actual people. The second choice is a mixed regime under the constitutional rule of impersonal law—which Mansfield takes to mean the specific mixture of oligarchy and democracy of book 4 that results in a middle-class regime or "polity" where the majority rules for the common good as modest property owners and citizen-soldiers. One might object that Aristotle's second choice after perfect kingship is not the middle-class polity of book 4 but the aristocratic republic described in books 7–8 (a small city-state of liberally educated gentlemen who live the good life of leisure devoted to politics, war, and liberal learning, like the aristocratic senators of the Roman republic). Yet even if the correct ranking of

Aristotle's regimes is (1) perfect kingship, (2) aristocratic republic, and (3) middle-class polity, Mansfield's main point is sound: the prudential wisdom of Aristotle leads to a criticism of the rule of perfect virtue in favor of mixing diluted virtue with political freedom under the constitutional rule of law.[20] This brings Aristotle only one or two steps away from Locke and the American republic.

To close the gap even further, Mansfield treats Locke and Madison as modern Aristotelians who faced a new situation created by Christianity that required them to promote virtue indirectly, as "disguised virtue." This reading of modern political philosophy is heavily influenced by Marsilius of Padua, the fourteenth-century Latin Aristotelian or Averroist who sought to free the development of the soul from the influence of the church by lowering the goal of politics from virtue to the minimal conditions of peace and order found in all societies while locating legitimacy in the consent of the people. Mansfield sees Locke and Madison backtracking from Machiavelli and Hobbes to carry out the Aristotelian project of Marsilius: "Locke and his friends . . . desired passionately to defend the dignity of man, which they saw endangered by the enslavement of men to priests and priestly education. To counter this menace, their defense of human dignity took the form of a denial of the superiority of soul, because it was soul and its invisible virtue which gave the priests their handle. . . . They accepted the equality of man because it was a necessary consequence of the primacy of the body, and they left human dignity at human liberty out of the same necessity."[21]

In other words, Locke and the American framers, who founded modern constitutionalism by limiting the state to protecting property rights and personal liberty, were not hostile to virtue and human dignity; they merely feared the exploitation of higher ends by religious leaders seeking power over others. Their strategy was to take the soul out of politics and to focus on preserving the body and material interests under the name of natural rights. But they did not, Mansfield insists, have a debased view of man. They sought to promote perfection of the soul indirectly—through the constitutional forms and formalities of liberty and through concepts such as "interest," "ambition," and "energy" that sound morally neutral but in practice promote moral virtue. *The Federalist,* especially, must not be seen as reducing constitutional government to mechanical checks and balances but as establishing formal procedures for offices that would encourage or "call forth" virtue. Thus, federalism and the separation of powers are not merely divisions of power that protect private rights; they are designed to encourage voluntary virtue in local self-government and virtuous leaders in national offices. In Mansfield's formulation: "Interest in the office is a republican concealment of virtue" and "energy [in the executive] is another term" for the virtue demanded by great political enterprises, such as the New Deal or the Reagan Revolution.[22]

The implication is that the moderns were every bit as concerned with virtue as the ancients. In fact, Mansfield suggests, the American founders may be superior to the ancients because they sought *voluntary* virtue—a nobler conception than one that makes virtue required, habituated, or automatic.[23] American constitutional democracy can be seen, therefore, as a mixed regime that approximates the classical mixed regime while differing in one crucial respect. The classical model mixes democracy with oligarchy to produce polity by requiring both parties to consciously improve their souls by accepting some of the other's claim—a real lesson in justice, moderation, and friendship that turns a mixture of two unjust regimes into a single just regime. By contrast, America mixes democracy with *liberty,* rather than with oligarchy or aristocracy or some elitist principle. The American expectation is that liberty itself will produce excellence by encouraging the elites (among intellectuals, businessmen, and politicians) to excel in the virtues of their callings without being forced by the regime to do so.

The weakness of this voluntary system, Mansfield painfully admits as he surveys the decline of America, is that liberty may be used not to cultivate virtue or human excellence but to promote permissive freedom ("expressive selves") and equality of result ("affirmative action"). The soul of America is not healthy today, he says, because it suffers from the degraded dependency of the welfare state, and this is chiefly due to the intellectual elites who have betrayed their call to excellence by losing their spirit or manliness and embracing radical equality and sensitivity.[24] Nevertheless, the American Constitution "is an Aristotelian regime formalized in writing." Its formal procedures not only protect freedom but also channel freedom to the higher end of Aristotelian moral virtue, forming souls by promoting the pride and self-restraint of a self-governing people: "The sovereign people, having chosen to ratify and live by the Constitution, becomes the constitutional people."[25] Though America has strayed from the original design, its unhealthy soul is one of the risks of freedom and still may be cured, Mansfield hopes, by dismantling the welfare state and reinvigorating the manly spirit of voluntary virtue.

SOLZHENITSYN'S CHRISTIAN PRUDENCE

If we turn from Mansfield to Solzhenitsyn, we can observe a similar pattern of thought. Both are guided by a hierarchy of being that creates a sharp distinction between what is theoretically best and what is practically possible—between an idea of perfection that is impossible as well as undesirable in politics and various kinds of imperfection that create opportunities for prudence to operate. Both Mansfield and Solzhenitsyn, it could be said, are guided by the proverb that "the perfect is the enemy of the good."

For practitioners of Aristotelian prudence like Mansfield, the wisest course in politics is to approximate the perfect virtue of ideal kingship by establishing mixed regimes that permit freedom and responsibility. For practitioners of Christian prudence like Solzhenitsyn, it means accepting a more clear-cut distinction between "two kingdoms" or "two cities": the spiritual realm of God, whose end is otherworldly salvation achieved through the church and an order of charity and grace; and the temporal realm of Caesar, whose end is the more modest notion of earthly happiness achieved through the state, the economy, the military, and social relations. My contention is that the doctrine of the "two cities," originally formulated by Christ in the Gospels and later by St. Augustine in *The City of God,* is the basic intellectual framework of Solzhenitsyn's political thinking. It is clearly adopted in his early works and offers the best explanation for his distinctive political views, which consistently oppose totalitarianism and favor limited government while rejecting modern Western theories of human rights.

The Augustinian framework first appears in an early collection of essays, *From under the Rubble* (1974). There, Solzhenitsyn praises "the Blessed Augustine" for asserting that a state without justice is no better than a band of robbers. He also develops Augustine's argument that most states never achieve justice but still must be obeyed, although there is a point beyond which injustice becomes unbearable. To determine that point, Solzhenitsyn appeals to the doctrine of the two cities:

> In relation to the true ends of human beings here on earth . . . the state structure is of secondary significance. That this is so, Christ himself teaches us. 'Render unto Caesar what is Caesar's'—not because every Caesar deserves it, but because Caesar's concern is not with the most important thing in our lives. . . . The state system which exists in our country is terrible not because it is undemocratic, authoritarian, based on physical constraint—a man can live in such conditions without harm to his spiritual essence. Our present system is unique because over and above its physical and economic constraints, it demands total surrender of our souls . . . [to] the conscious lie. To this putrefaction of the soul, this spiritual enslavement, human beings who wish to be human cannot consent. When Caesar, having exacted what is Caesar's, demands still more insistently that we render unto him what is God's—that is a sacrifice that we dare not make! The most important part of our freedom, inner freedom, is always subject to our will. If we surrender it to corruption, we do not deserve to be called human.[26]

At first glance, this appeal to God over Caesar seems to imply indifference to political freedom and political regimes, an error commonly attributed to St. Augustine himself. But Solzhenitsyn is not indifferent to politics (and neither is Augustine). What they believe, in precise terms, is that the "state structure is of secondary significance" compared to the spiritual realm. This is not indifference, because it means the state has a definite but limited purpose that it may not legitimately exceed and that justifies resistance if it is exceeded. Yet the standard of legitimacy is confusing to modern Western intellectuals because it is not set by an inviolable sphere of private rights in which one is free to do as one pleases. Rather, it is set by a permanent hierarchy of ends ordained by God, which makes the spiritual things of the soul and its "inner freedom" primary and relegates the material things of earthly happiness, including the "external freedom" controlled by the state, to secondary status. Herein lies a criterion for distinguishing legitimate and illegitimate regimes that is derived from the Christian doctrine of the two cities rather than the Enlightenment doctrine of natural or human rights.

According to the Christian doctrine, a regime is legitimate if it respects the distinction between the two cities and confines the state to the limited ends of the temporal realm, even while recognizing that political leaders and nations are accountable to God for their actions. In contrast, a regime is illegitimate if it violates the distinction between the two cities by unifying sovereignty under one head—either in totalitarian fashion (where the state tries to absorb the church and the rest of social life), or in theocratic fashion (where the church tries to absorb the state by direct clerical rule or indirectly by making the emperor or king the head of the church).

Solzhenitsyn opposes all forms of unified sovereignty because his Christian-Augustinian approach requires a distinction of the two realms with recognition of the primacy of the spiritual. He is most vehemently opposed to totalitarian Communism, because it raises the state to primary significance and attempts to crush the church and spiritual life with state-imposed atheism. He views totalitarianism as radically evil because it makes an idol of the secular state, allowing Caesar to usurp God's realm and corrupting the soul by destroying its inner freedom. Such tyranny causes spiritual enslavement to materialistic ideologies and must be resisted or overthrown.

But Solzhenitsyn is almost as strongly opposed to theocracy, because it too violates the distinction of the two cities. He says in *The Mortal Danger,*

> I have been repeatedly charged with being an advocate of a theocratic state, a system in which the government would be under the direct control of religious leaders. This is a flagrant misrepresentation. . . . The day-to-day activity of governing in no sense belongs to the sphere of religion. What I do believe is that the state should not persecute religion and that religion should make an appropriate contribution to the spiritual life of the nation. Such a situation obtains in Poland and Israel and no one condemns it; I cannot understand why the same thing should be forbidden in Russia.[27]

While this position may sound "theocratic" to Western liberals who favor a completely secular society, it is actually a consistent application of the two-cities doctrine, which requires distinct spheres and distinct personnel (civil vs. religious leaders) but not the elimination of religion from national life.

In Solzhenitsyn's view, the failure to maintain a proper distinction is precisely what has misled the Russian Orthodox Church over the years. In his *Lenten Letter to Patriarch Pimen* (1973), he rebukes church leaders for surrendering the independence of the church to the tsars over "the last centuries" and to the present Communist authorities. Without spelling out the details, this seems to put Solzhenitsyn on the side of the Old Believers who, at the middle and end of the seventeenth century, resisted the church reforms of Patriarch Nikon that led to theocratic unification of church and state; their demise enabled modern tsars to build a centralized state supported by religious nationalism.[28] While Solzhenitsyn's critique of the church's servility toward tsars and commissars seems antimodern, it is consistent with views expressed in *Rebuilding Russia* that look forward to the post-Communist age: "The Church will be helpful to our social recovery only when it . . . frees itself completely from the yoke of the state and restores a living bond with the people." The implication is that the premodern relation of church and state is a model for the postmodern relation in recognizing a proper balance of the two cities—resisting state absolutism and secular totalitarianism as well as theocratic and messianic pretensions of the state, while preserving a vital role for spirituality in Russian national life.[29]

From this perspective on church and state, Solzhenitsyn is prepared to be flexible about forms of government. As long as the state is limited, in the general sense of avoiding the unified sovereignty of totalitarianism or theocracy, and confines itself to the modest ends of the temporal realm while permitting the spiritual realm to flourish, it has a basic legitimacy. Under this generic notion of limited government, however, Solzhenitsyn recognizes a crucial difference between regimes that are restrained solely by the limited ideological ends they pursue and "constitutional" regimes that limit power by law, institutions, and moral self-restraint. This leads him to a prudential ranking of three legitimate regimes that may be chosen as circumstances permit: (1) the least desirable choice (a "liveable or bearable" regime) is the moderate authoritarianism of traditional tsarism; (2) the most desirable choice is the constitutional monarchy of the early twentieth century under Nicholas II and Prime Minister Stolypin; and (3) a reasonable second choice is the constitutional democracy proposed in *Rebuilding Russia*. Let me comment briefly on each of these choices in Solzhenitsyn's writings.

In the early works, *Letter to the Soviet Leaders* (1973), *From under the Rubble* (1974), and *Mortal Danger* (1980), Solzhenitsyn advocates moderate authoritarianism as a transitional regime for Russia from totalitarianism to a new society. As Ericson points out, this is prudential in the sense of being tactically wise or expedient: it is a way of getting the existing authorities to renounce Communism without having to give up their power. What Ericson overlooks, however, is the rather favorable view of traditional authoritarianism as well as the severe criticism of modern democracy that Solzhenitsyn offers to justify this transitional government—reflecting an Augustinian pessimism about politics than few Western liberals would express. The only comparable view is Jeane Kirkpatrick's distinction between "authoritarian" and "totalitarian" regimes. She regards the former as legitimate because they are limited in scope, confining themselves to security and order (even if they sometimes use repressive measures) and leaving alone the religion, customs, property relations, family structures, and cultural life of the nation. By contrast, totalitarianism is unlimited in scope, using repressive measures systematically to transform human nature according to an ideological blueprint that inevitably leads to mass murder and concentration camps.[30] Like Kirkpatrick, Solzhenitsyn views traditional Russian tsarism as liveable or bearable because even its worst rulers had limits imposed by religion, rival elites, and local councils: "If such systems have functioned for centuries on end in many states, we are entitled to believe that, *provided certain limits are not exceeded,* they too can offer people a tolerable life, as much as any democratic republic can"; and "the majority of governments in human history have been authoritarian, but they have yet to give birth to a totalitarian regime" as did the weak democracies of Russia, Italy, Germany, and China. Simply put, centuries of tsarism never destroyed the soul of the Russian people, while seventy years of totalitarian Communism nearly succeeded in doing so.[31]

Yet in subsequent writings, Solzhenitsyn indicates that traditional authoritarianism is a minimal standard and that constitutionally limited governments are preferable, as long as the true meaning of freedom is understood. This point is often missed because Solzhenitsyn is so critical of Western societies for establishing legal rights without preserving a religious basis for moral self-restraint. Indeed, Solzhenitsyn rejects the modern theory of rights as the basis of constitutional government because it has no inherent principle of self-limitation or self-sacrifice: "'Human rights' are a fine thing, but how can we be sure that our rights do not expand at the expense of the rights of others? . . . Most people in a position to enhance their rights and seize more will do precisely that. . . . Human freedom, in contrast, includes voluntary self-limitation for the sake of others." And, as Solzhenitsyn emphasizes, this is precisely "the true Christian definition of freedom."[32] The dilemma for Solzhenitsyn is that constitutional government requires legal limits to protect freedom, but it is endangered by legalistic rights and requires a Christian basis that places restrictions on freedom.

The reason for the dilemma is that political freedom is not an absolute good or an end in itself but a conditional good whose value is determined by the ends it serves. If it merely serves material well-being, it loses its value and becomes illegitimate. If it serves higher spiritual goods (the goods of the soul), its value and legitimacy are enhanced. But the goods of the soul that justify freedom often contradict freedom or are nurtured by severe forms of unfreedom—including imprisonment, war, suffering, and spiritual discipline that cultivate inner strength by suppressing external freedom or develop the soul by repressing the body ("Bless you, prison, for nourishing my soul," Solzhenitsyn says at the end of *Gulag* volume 2). The same paradox is expressed in Solzhenitsyn's powerful statement that "freedom of action and prosperity are necessary if man is to stand up to his full height on this earth; but spiritual greatness dwells in eternal subordination, in awareness of oneself as an insignificant particle." Political freedom, then, is necessary as a first step toward higher ends because it gives man the pride and dignity to stand on his own and to be responsible for himself; but attaining the higher ends demands subordination of the self to a permanent hierarchy of being in which one is merely "an insignificant particle."[33]

Obviously, there is no perfect political solution to the paradoxical demands of freedom and higher obligation. They are as different as pride and humility and can be perfectly reconciled only in an ideal world where freedom is used solely for self-limitation in service to the highest good—a condition that Solzhenitsyn compares to a new historical or anthropological stage that would be like the change from the Middle Ages to the modern Renaissance and Enlightenment, a postmodern age of voluntary religious obligation.[34] Meanwhile, in the imperfect world of late modernity, political freedom must be granted with strict conditions, giving people responsibility while surrounding them with controls that encourage moral and spiritual development. Solzhenitsyn describes two constitutional regimes that establish the proper kind of controlled political freedom.

The best example is the constitutional monarchy of Russia's Duma period, nominally under Tsar Nicholas II but actually governed by Prime Minister Pyotr Stolypin until he was assassinated (1906–11). Solzhenitsyn analyzes this regime in a long chapter of *August 1914: The Red Wheel* devoted to Stolypin, who is clearly Solzhenitsyn's ideal of a heroic man and a great statesman. The greatness of Stolypin was his courageous effort to "persuade Russia that the epoch of constitutional government was here to stay," even while resorting on occasion to extralegal action to achieve this goal.[35] His program was a balancing act that sought to preserve the traditional basis of Russian authority in tsarism and Orthodoxy while implementing modern reforms—above all, land reform that would create a new peasant class of bourgeois-citizens, who would own and cultivate their own land and participate in local councils (*zemstvoi*). This difficult combination of old and new—of tsarism and Jeffersonian democracy, as it were—required a fearless crackdown on revolutionary terrorists that put Stolypin and his family at great risk (eventually costing him his life) as well as astute political maneuvering to persuade the emperor of his plans and have them approved by right- and left-wing factions of the Duma.

Solzhenitsyn's case for Stolypin is an exercise in revisionist history that reads like a chapter from Plutarch or like Aristotle's account of perfect kingship. He praises Stolypin for his "invincible strength of character" and describes him in the grandest terms: "his qualities were, in truth, kingly; a second Peter ruled Russia—as energetic as the first . . . as radical a reformer but with an idea that distinguished him from Peter the Great: 'To reform our way of life without damage to the vital foundations of our state and the soul of the people.'" His assassination, Solzhenitsyn concludes, was a tragedy "for the whole twentieth century" because only Stolypin could have saved Russia from Communist revolution.[36]

The Stolypin regime obviously depended on chance—on the survival of a single great man as well as the peculiar circumstances of a liberalizing autocracy—and could not serve as a durable model for Russia. Thus, when Solzhenitsyn finally published his concrete proposals for the post-Communist age in *Rebuilding Russia* (1991), he recommended neither moderate authoritarianism nor constitutional monarchy but constitutional democracy. His frank admission that "the future Russian Union . . . will need democracy very much" indicates a change in practical judgment but not a break with his fundamental principles.[37] For he justifies democracy on prudential grounds, as a realistic approximation of Stolypin's vision in new and different circumstances.

Solzhenitsyn's prudential approach is evident in the denial that democracy or any regime is "the ultimate form of government." Why, then, choose democracy? In the first place, he says, "we cannot be said to have much of a choice: the whole flow of modern history will unquestionably predispose us to choose democracy"—meaning it is an inevitable fact of the modern age; there is no going back to monarchy. But he warns against glorifying democracy, as some do by elevating it from a "particular state structure into a sort of universal principle of human existence, almost a cult." To make himself absolutely clear, Solzhenitsyn says we must choose democracy "as a means, not as an end in itself . . . not because it abounds in virtues, but only in order to avoid tyranny."[38] Its purpose, like all government for Solzhenitsyn, is to defend the dignity of the human soul, in the first place by protecting against tyrannies that crush the soul and then by encouraging moral and spiritual development, while recognizing that the noblest examples of virtue will be voluntary.

Accordingly, he says, in an echo of the two cities, that the Orthodox church should be independent of the state so it will not glorify the state and make politics primary. For "the more energetic the political activity in a country, the greater the loss to spiritual life. Politics must not swallow up all of a people's spiritual and creative energies." The same goes for economics: "neither a market economy nor general abundance constitutes the crowning achievement of human life."[39] These arguments are the most sober endorsement of democracy that I have ever read. They do not appeal to the collective wisdom of the people nor to the sovereignty of the people nor to the rights of man but suggest that a constitutional democracy in which politics and economics remain secondary to spiritual activity—to faith, family, and artistic life—can care for the soul almost as well as other regimes. To enhance that possibility, Solzhenitsyn sketches a constitutional order with three basic elements.

The first two are derived from Stolypin, whom Solzhenitsyn cites approvingly in *Rebuilding Russia:* "Stolypin believed that it is impossible to create a state governed by laws without first having independent citizens," meaning landowners who were also self-governing citizens. Thus, in the post-Communist age, the first task is to restore private ownership of land and houses. Solzhenitsyn strongly defends private property and free enterprise in "modest amounts . . . which [do] not oppress others" because they are "an integral component of personality": they nurture mystic ties to the Russian land; they strengthen the family (especially when men make an adequate salary so "women have the opportunity to return to their families to take care of the children"); and they contribute to stability and a sense of fairness among people.[40] The second element of the Stolypin plan that Solzhenitsyn promotes is local government, beginning with the long task of re-creating the Russian village through local councils and face-to-face moral leadership. His models are the conservative Swiss cantons and the *zemstvoi* of nineteenth-century Russia applied to the village level. The whole scheme depends on these two elements, because "democracy must be built from the bottom up."[41]

The third element is the national government, which resembles a mixed regime rather than a purely democratic structure. The national legislative body will be a people's assembly chosen indirectly by the tiers of the *zemstvoi* system, each of which chooses the next higher level. It will be balanced by a quasi-aristocratic upper chamber consisting of "highly respected individuals of lofty moral character, wisdom, and rich experience" whose mission is to provide moral wisdom about legislation and to represent the different "estates" of society—a purely advisory body that sounds like Sparta's *gerousia* of venerable elders. A strong presidency will also be needed to assure national cohesion; the selection process will begin with nominations of candidates from the national assembly and end with popular election while avoiding parties and divisive campaigns. The general vision is that of a Russian nation organized as a corporate hierarchy from the bottom up with participatory bodies for different kinds of people at all levels. Unlike most Western models, this is constitutional democracy of a corporatist character that seeks to establish "a moral order among the people."[42]

CONCLUSION

The lessons of Mansfield and Solzhenitsyn are extremely valuable because they show us bold and novel ways of thinking about constitutional democracy. Instead of beginning with natural or human rights, as liberal philosophers do, and then arguing for limitations on government to protect an inviolable sphere of private rights, they begin with the dignity of the human soul. Their highest priority is the perfection of the soul through classical and Christian virtues. This makes them "monarchists" in theory, because the claim of perfect virtue and the primacy of the city of God are hierarchical principles that imply deference to rulers with moral and spiritual perfection. Yet prudence dictates a different course because moral and spiritual perfection is so rare, so difficult to recognize, and so daunting to many decent people who are capable of mature and responsible behavior. In the fallen world of politics, "the perfect is the enemy of the good"—which implies that constitutional government and its principles of political freedom and rule of law are not merely expedient but required by the permanent ends and limitations of human nature. This puts rights in proper perspective, as means to higher ends rather than as ends in themselves, which helps to control their dangerous tendency to subvert traditional moral authorities and to create a culture dominated by the one-dimensional pursuit of material well-being.

Thus, through the recovery of classical and Christian prudence, Mansfield and Solzhenitsyn have developed an approach to political freedom that might be characterized as Constitutionalism without Liberalism—an achievement that offers greater hope for reconciling the care of souls with modern democracy than would be possible within liberalism alone.

NOTES

1. This elegant phrase is borrowed from George Will's book *Statecraft as Soulcraft*, which argues that the American founders were insufficiently concerned with soulcraft, a point disputed by Mansfield. George F. Will *Statecraft as Soulcraft: What Government Does* (New York: Simon and Schuster, 1983).

2. In "Tocqueville's Constitutionalism," I argue that Tocqueville is able to combine the two concerns by carefully blending together ancient and modern conceptions of constitutionalism. Robert P. Kraynak, "Tocqueville's Constitutionalism," *American Political Science Review* 81 (1987): 1175–95.

3. Harvey C. Mansfield Jr., *America's Constitutional Soul* (Baltimore: Johns Hopkins University Press, 1991), 206, 209–19.

4. Alexander Solzhenitsyn, *Rebuilding Russia: Reflections and Tentative Proposals* (New York: Farrar, Straus, and Giroux, 1991), 49–50; "Repentance and Self-Limitation," in Alexander Solzhenitsyn and others, *From under the Rubble,* trans. under the direction of Michael Scammell (Boston: Little, Brown and Co., 1974), 120, 140; "Liechtenstein Address" (1993) in Alexander Solzhenitsyn, *The Russian Question at the End of the Century* (New York: Farrar, Straus, and Giroux, 1994), 118.

5. The phrase "natural conscience" does not appear in Solzhenitsyn but has been aptly applied by Mahoney to describe an enduring sense of good and evil that mod-

ern ideologies have been unable to destroy; see Daniel J. Mahoney, "The Experience of Totalitarianism and the Recovery of Nature: Reflections on Philosophy and Community in the Thought of Solzhenitsyn, Havel, and Strauss," in *Community and Political Thought Today*, ed. Peter A. Lawler (Westport, Conn.: Praeger, 1998), 211–12.

6. Harvey C. Mansfield, Jr., *The Spirit of Liberalism* (Cambridge, Mass.: Harvard University Press, 1978), Preface, xi.

7. Ronald Berman, ed. *Solzhenitsyn at Harvard : The Address, Responses, and Reflections* (Washington, D.C.: Ethics and Public Policy Center, 1976), 10; Mansfield, *Soul*, 165; see the sensitive discussion of Solzhenitsyn's portrayal of man's spiritual nature in Olivier Clement, *The Spirit of Solzhenitsyn* (New York: Harper and Row, 1977), 99–158.

8. "Repentance and Self-Limitation," in *Rubble*, 106–7, 136–37.

9. Solzhenitsyn, "Lenten Letter to Patriarch Pimen," in John B. Dunlop, ed., *Alexander Solzhenitsyn: Critical Essays and Documentary Materials* (New York: Collier, 1973), 555, emphasis in text. The debate about the predominance of classical Greek or Christian elements in Solzhenitsyn's thought is a complex one.

It can be developed by comparing Schmemann's influential article "On Solzhenitsyn" in Dunlop (28–44), which argues for "the Christian inspiration of his writing," with Delba Winthrop's article, which argues for the predominance of a classical Greek (Platonic-Aristotelian) view of the moral and intellectual virtues. See Delba Winthrop, "Solzhenitsyn: Emerging from under the Rubble," *Independent Journal of Philosophy* 4 (1983): 91–101. Solzhenitsyn replied to Schmemann's article by saying, "it explained me to myself" (Dunlop, 44). Solzhenitsyn, then, accepts the description of his writings as Christian.

Yet it is also true that whenever Solzhenitsyn has been asked directly about his religious beliefs, he has given cautious and evasive replies. As Pontuso records, when Solzhenitsyn was asked, "Are you a Christian?" he replied cautiously, saying he was not a socialist and the answer should be clear from his books. James F. Pontuso, *Solzhenitsyn's Political Thought* (Charlottesville: University Press of Virginia, 1990), 253–55, n. 47.

His biographer Scammel says, "Solzhenitsyn certainly believes in God though it is not always clear whether it is a Christian God. . . . He is a deist and does not understand mysticism and the life of the church." Michael Scammel, *Solzhenitsyn: A Biography* (New York: Norton, 1984), 992.

Against this hard line, Walsh argues more persuasively that Solzhenitsyn's ascent to God lacks the "rational self-sufficiency of deism" and that Solzhenitsyn is "a man feeling his way toward Christianity." David Walsh, *After Ideology: Recovering the Spiritual Foundations of Freedom* (San Francisco: Harper, 1990), 151.

I would agree with Walsh by suggesting that Solzhenitsyn adopts Christian ethics and anthropology and that his politics are Augustinian; but as far as his ultimate beliefs are concerned he is a Christian seeker rather than a full believer—he has accepted God the Father but not yet God the Son. He therefore incorporates elements of classical Greek rationalism and approaches religion from practical-moral viewpoints like Deism, but he thinks that life is not complete without Christian redemption (healing or repentance) and knows that this is Christ's mission. Yet he has not embraced the supernatural miracle of divine redemption and Christ's resurrection, although he is searching and aspiring to such faith.

10. Mansfield, *Spirit,* 3–5.

11. Alexander Solzhenitsyn, *The Gulag Archipelago* (New York: Harper and Row) vol. 1, trans. Thomas P. Whitney (1973); vol. 2, trans. Thomas P. Whitney (1974); vol. 3, trans. Harry Willetts (1976), 3:630.

12. Solzhenitsyn, *The Gulag Archipelago,* 3: 614–15.

13. The Greek is from *The Precise Parallel New Testament: The Greek Text and Seven Translations,* ed. John R. Kohlenberger III (New York and Oxford: Oxford University Press, 1987), 94.

14. Winthrop, "Solzhenitsyn Emerging," 99.

15. Harvey C. Mansfield, Jr., *Taming the Prince: The Ambivalence of Modern Executive Power* (New York: Free Press, 1989), 296.

16. Solzhenitsyn criticizes Sakharov in *Rubble* (15–25) and praises moderate authoritarianism in Alexander Solzhenitsyn, *The Mortal Danger,* trans. Michael Nicholson and Alexis Klimoff (New York: Harper and Row, 1980), 59–64. In correcting false impressions about Solzhenitsyn, Ericson tends to overstate Solzhenitsyn's democratic sympathies while Walsh offers a more realistic appraisal in *After Ideology* (228–33). Edward E. Ericson Jr., *Solzhenitsyn and the Modern World* (Washington, D.C.: Regnery Gateway, 1993), 155–75. I argue below that Solzhenitsyn offers a prudential argument for democracy.

17. Mansfield, *Taming,* 39–44, 70–71.

18. Mansfield, *Taming,* 52, 291–92.

19. Mansfield, *Taming,* 70.

20. I think Mansfield tends to conflate the mixed regime of book 4 with the aristocratic republic in books 7–8 in order to bring Aristotle's prudential teaching closer to America (see *Taming,* 46). An alternative reading can be found in Behnegar's article, "The Liberal Politics of Leo Strauss." According to Nasser Behnegar, Strauss interpreted the classical philosophers to be saying that "the practically best regime is an aristocracy," and Strauss endorsed that view. In addition, Strauss states that "liberal or constitutional democracy comes closer to what the classics demanded than any alternative that is viable in our age." See Nasser Behnegar, "The Liberal Politics of Leo Strauss," in *Political Philosophy and the Human Soul: Essays in Memory of Allan Bloom* (Lanham, Md.: Rowman and Littlefield, 1995), 260–61.

21. Mansfield, *Spirit,* 9.

22. Mansfield, *Soul,* 215–16; *Taming,* 257, 294.

23. Mansfield, *Soul,* 216; Harvey C. Mansfield, Jr., "The Revival of Constitutionalism," in *The Revival of Constitutionalism,* ed. James W. Muller (Lincoln: University of Nebraska Press, 1988), 226–27.

24. Mansfield, *Soul,* 84–100, 209–20; *Spirit,* 9–15.

25. Mansfield, *Taming,* 276, 290.

26. Solzhenitsyn, *Rubble,* 105, 24–25.

27. Solzhenitsyn, *Mortal Danger,* 63–64.

28. Solzhenitsyn, "Lenten Letter," in Dunlop, 552; see *Rubble,* 116, 136; *Russian Question,* 108.

29. Solzhenitsyn, *Rebuilding,* 53; see Ericson, 182–85.

30. Jeane J. Kirkpatrick, *Dictatorships and Double Standards: Rationalism and Reason in Politics* (New York: American Enterprise Institute, 1982), 23–52, 96–140.

31. Solzhenitsyn, *Rubble,* 23–24, emphasis added; *Mortal Danger,* 60; *Russian Question,* 106–8.

32. Solzhenitsyn, *Rebuilding,* 54–55; *Rubble,* 136–37.

33. Alexander Solzhenitsyn, *August 1914: The Red Wheel, Knot I,* trans. H. T. Willetts (New York: Farrar, Straus, and Giroux, 1989), 530; see also Solzhenitsyn's criticism of Tolstoy for not seeing political freedom as the first step toward spiritual development in *Gulag* vol. 3, 189, and Mahoney's elaboration, 220.

34. Solzhenitsyn points to this new stage at the end of his "Harvard Address" and elaborates it in *Rubble,* 137; see Pontuso, 192–217.

35. Solzhenitsyn, *August,* 530.

36. Solzhenitsyn, *August,* 568–69, 582, 606.

37. Solzhenitsyn, *Rebuilding,* 82.

38. Solzhenitsyn, *Rebuilding,* 61–63.

39. Solzhenitsyn, *Rebuilding,* 49, 53.

40. Solzhenitsyn, *Rebuilding,* 34–42.

41. Solzhenitsyn, *Rebuilding,* 82–90.

42. Solzhenitsyn, *Rebuilding,* 96–104.

20

Churchill's Understanding of Politics

James W. Muller

> Politics is almost as exciting as war and quite as dangerous. In war you can
> only be killed once, but in politics many times.
>
> —Winston S. Churchill

In 1930, in his twelfth luster, Winston Churchill published his autobiography, *My Early Life,* tracing his life from his earliest recollections of boyhood in Ireland to his marriage in 1908.[1] Seven decades later, after more than a dozen editions and translations into a like number of languages,[2] *My Early Life* remains one of the finest books of the twentieth century. It is Churchill's most approachable, most widely read, and most charming work.

When his autobiography appeared, Churchill was a senior statesman who had held every major cabinet office in the British government except the foreign ministry and the prime ministry, but seemed to be nearing retirement. His political career, meteoric at the start and lately crowned by four and a half years as chancellor of the exchequer, had been shattered in between by his resignation as first lord of the admiralty during the Dardanelles campaign of 1915. Pondering his father's fortunes in *My Early Life,* Churchill makes an observation that might as well be applied to his own: "It is never possible for a man to recover his lost position. He may recover another position in the fifties or sixties, but not the one he lost in the thirties or forties" (61). Having changed parties twice, Churchill had no claim to be a loyal party man and was mistrusted by Tory regulars. In an interwar Britain still suffering from losses in the Great War and turning her back on the larger world to focus on domestic matters, he was a man out of season in his concern for strategy, diplomacy, and empire.

This difference between the spirit of the Victorian era and the mood of the
1930s is the theme of Churchill's preface to *My Early Life:*

> When I survey this work as a whole I find I have drawn a picture of a vanished
> age. The character of society, the foundations of politics, the methods of war,
> the outlook of youth, the scale of values, are all changed, and changed to an ex-
> tent I should not have believed possible in so short a space without any violent
> domestic revolution. I cannot pretend to feel that they are in all respects
> changed for the better. I was a child of the Victorian era, when the structure of
> our country seemed firmly set, when its position in trade and on the seas was
> unrivalled, and when the realization of the greatness of our Empire and of our
> duty to preserve it was ever growing stronger. In those days the dominant forces
> in Great Britain were very sure of themselves and of their doctrines. They
> thought they could teach the world the art of government, and the science of
> economics. They were sure they were supreme at sea and consequently safe at
> home. They rested therefore sedately under the convictions of power and se-
> curity. Very different is the aspect of these anxious and dubious times. Full al-
> lowance for such changes should be made by friendly readers. (9)

Churchill paints this "picture of a vanished age" in his autobiography to contrast it with the 1930s, showing the reader his reservations about the disappearance of that older world. In telling his tale he offers opinions that "conflict with those now generally accepted"; some merely represent "a phase" in
his early life, but others are "modern pronouncements" (9). The understanding of politics that Churchill presents in this book diverges from the fashion
of the 1930s—or of the turn of the millennium—yet it still engenders in the
reader a lively regret that something good has been lost. Our author, at any
rate, considers his "story of youthful endeavour" more than a reminiscence
of bygone days: for he ends the preface by suggesting that "it might be of interest to the new generation" (10) and dedicates *My Early Life* to them (7).[3]

THE CHARACTER OF SOCIETY

In the passage I have quoted from his preface, Churchill names five elements
of the transformed world. First among them is a change in "the character of
society." As late as 1896, in an idle half-year before his regiment was sent to
India, Churchill experienced "the amusements of the London Season":

> In those days English Society still existed in its old form. It was a brilliant and
> powerful body, with standards of conduct and methods of enforcing them now
> altogether forgotten. In a very large degree every one knew every one else and
> who they were. The few hundred great families who had governed England for
> so many generations and had seen her rise to the pinnacle of her glory, were in-
> terrelated to an enormous extent by marriage. Everywhere one met friends and

kinsfolk. The leading figures of Society were in many cases the leading statesmen in Parliament, and also the leading sportsmen on the Turf. Lord Salisbury
was accustomed scrupulously to avoid calling a Cabinet when there was racing
at Newmarket, and the House of Commons made a practice of adjourning for
the Derby. In those days the glittering parties at Lansdowne House, Devonshire
House or Stafford House comprised all the elements which made a gay and
splendid social circle in close relation to the business of Parliament, the hierar-
chies of the Army and Navy, and the policy of the State. (103–4)

By 1930, many of the young men who would have taken their places in society had perished in the Great War. Their places in Parliament and in the
armed forces had fallen to men of new families, less brilliant and powerful,
unknown and unrelated to those who had governed England for genera-
tions, and not bred up as sportsmen.

The importance of the last point should not be overlooked. André Maurois,
a wartime interpreter to Churchill's regiment in Flanders, afterward wrote a
novel called *The Silences of Colonel Bramble* exploring differences between
the British and the French. On the first page, Major Parker tells the French interpreter Aurelle that "to interest a Frenchman in a boxing match, you have to
tell him that his national honor is involved; to interest an Englishman in a war,
you need only suggest to him that it resembles a boxing match." The standards of conduct unknown to the new men had traditionally been learnt at
public schools, whither the sons of old families had resorted to "soak up the
prejudices of our class, without which we should be dangerous and unhappy," as the major explains to Aurelle.[4] Not coincidentally, the early chapters of *My Early Life* describe Churchill's experiences at school, from the
"cruel flogging" he received at St. George's School, which he tactfully disguises as St. James's (26), to a lesson in how officers looked out for one another at the military academy at Sandhurst (63–64). But his longest stretch of
schooling was at public school at Harrow, where he discovered the standard
of conduct at the swimming pond when he pushed in an older boy by mistake. Making a quick recovery, Churchill apologized to his mark, later a cabinet colleague (31–32). More comprehensively, he took his cue from the "in-
comparable" Harrow songs, which he judged "the greatest treasure" that the
school possessed (55). So when later in the long Indian afternoons he won-
dered what ethics might be, he supposed "they must mean 'the public school
spirit,' 'playing the game,' *'esprit de corps,'* 'honourable behaviour,' 'patriotism,' and the like" (123).[5]

Before Churchill's regiment went to India, he experienced, "if only for a
few months," a world that was soon to vanish. He spent long weekends "in
those beautiful places and palaces which were then linked by their actual
owners with the long triumphant history of the United Kingdom." Among
these memories, he singles out "the Duchess of Devonshire's Fancy Dress
Ball in 1897," which "reproduced the scenes upon which Disraeli dilated in

his novels."[6] The crowd in Green Park watched the duchess's guests as they arrived, and between dancers and gawkers on a summer night there gaped "the gulf which in those days separated the rulers and the ruled" (104). A few years later, Paul Cambon arrived at the Court of St. James's to begin his mission as French ambassador. When he retired in 1920, he told Churchill that in the intervening years he had "witnessed an English Revolution more profound and searching than the French Revolution itself": gently and peaceably "the governing class have been almost entirely deprived of political power and to a very large extent of their property and estates" (105). Churchill laments that many of England's great houses "have been turned into hotels, flats and restaurants"—one of them even into a museum in which "Socialist Governments drearily dispense the public hospitality" (104). He is sorry to see the brilliancy of aristocratic society dissolve into ugliness and mediocrity with the coming of democracy.

As a descendant of John Churchill, who became the Duke of Marlborough when he led the armies of Britain and her allies against Louis XIV in the War of the Spanish Succession, Churchill belonged to one of England's leading families and was well placed to meet others bred up in a tradition of public service. The officer corps was full of such men. Through friends he met Sir Bindon Blood, "one of the most trusted and experienced commanders on the Indian frontier," and was able to extract from him "a promise that if ever he commanded another expedition on the Indian frontier, he would let me come with him" (106–7). Churchill's "young, beautiful and fascinating" mother served as his ally in his ongoing efforts to get to the scene of battle, leaving "no wire unpulled, no stone unturned, no cutlet uncooked" (76, 167). When the British commander in Egypt tried to exclude him, even the prime minister had a hand in allowing the young subaltern of horse to ride in one of the last cavalry charges in British history at the Battle of Omdurman in 1898 (178–82). While Churchill was first looking for a parliamentary seat, one of his "more remote connexions" introduced him to the party manager, who encouraged the young man until he discovered that he had little money for his campaign; but even then he admitted that Churchill's "was an exceptional case" because of his father, Lord Randolph Churchill, who had been chancellor of the exchequer and leader of the House of Commons (217).

THE FOUNDATIONS OF POLITICS

Like his son after him, Lord Randolph spent his whole adult life as a member of Parliament. Churchill called the House of Commons his father's house and himself a child of the House of Commons; but he studied politics in his father's speeches and at his father's table long before he began to frequent the Distinguished Strangers' Gallery. As a Harrow boy he "had read every word" that

Lord Randolph spoke, for "everything he said even at the tiniest bazaar was reported verbatim in all the newspapers, and every phrase was scrutinized and weighed" (46). The second element of the transformed world described by Churchill in the preface was a change in "the foundations of politics"; after the Second World War he had a telling dream about how he would explain to his father the changes since Lord Randolph died in 1895.[7] But after he left Harrow School he "was well circumstanced" to gain political intelligence:

> Politics seemed very important and vivid to my eyes in those days. They were directed by statesmen of commanding intellect and personality. The upper classes in their various stations took part in them as a habit and as a duty. The working men whether they had votes or not followed them as a sport. They took as much interest in national affairs and were as good judges of form in public men, as is now the case about cricket or football. The newspapers catered obediently for what was at once an educated and a popular taste. (47)

Churchill had ample opportunity to learn the politics of the old world before it disappeared. He breaks off a description of his successful campaign in the Khaki Election of 1900, called by the Conservatives to profit from the victory in South Africa, to remark that "in those days we had a real political democracy led by a hierarchy of statesmen, and not a fluid mass distracted by newspapers. There was a structure in which statesmen, electors and the press all played their part" (372).

Churchill took his stand with the "Tory Democracy" championed by his father. What he admired in the older democratic constitution was its ability to conduct a debate outside Parliament in which statesmen were the orators, electors the judges, and newspapers the conduit for bringing the debate to those who did not hear it in person. "In those days," he writes,

> our wise and prudent law spread a general election over nearly six weeks. Instead of all the electors voting blindly on one day, and only learning next morning what they had done, national issues were really fought out. A rough but earnest and searching national discussion took place in which leading men on both sides played a part. The electorate of a constituency was not unmanageable in numbers. A candidate could address all his supporters who wished to hear him. A great speech by an eminent personage would often turn a constituency or even a city. Speeches of well-known and experienced statesmen were fully reported in all the newspapers and studied by wide political classes. Thus by a process of rugged argument the national decision was reached in measured steps. (370–71)

Churchill points to the candor and high-toned reasoning of an orator like Joseph Chamberlain, who spoke on his behalf for more than an hour in the Khaki Election; he pleased his audience most by carefully correcting a mistake he had made "to the prejudice of his opponents," lest he be unfair (372).

But "all this," Churchill observes, "was before the liquefaction of the British political system had set in" (373).

What is this "liquefaction"? Our author does not tell us in so many words, but leaves it to be deduced from elements of the political system of the 1930s that contrast with the solider edifice of his youth. The old structure required an electorate that was more than "a fluid mass distracted by newspapers." The people had a "taste" for politics, following with interest the fortunes of their champions in person and in the press, hearing or reading with appreciation sustained arguments in Parliament or out of doors. This was the convergence between "an educated and a popular taste." But when the people lost interest in public affairs and were drawn to political controversy only by titillation, newspapers gave up printing speeches, serving up slogans and allegations instead of arguments and evidence. Rather than being an engrossing game, politics became only an occasional diversion, a distraction forced to compete with easier entertainments for popular favor. At the same time, the old structure depended on "a hierarchy of statesmen," lest the nation take its political cues at hazard from a "fluid mass." What Churchill calls "a real democracy" therefore depends on public acknowledgment of an aristocratic element in the regime. When "the gulf" separating rulers from ruled was filled in by familiarity and equal pretensions, rhetorical abilities declined along with the adherence to standards that made rhetoric a fair arbiter of political fortune. Talented men forsook the habit and duty of public service. Common deliberation and the practical wisdom of statesmen declined in favor of public-opinion polls, and politics was understood more as a clash of interests or passions than of arguments. The extreme democracy that came to dominate free countries in the twentieth century now goes further than it had by 1930, but in *My Early Life* Churchill already rued changes that would give us sound bites, instant analysis, and image politics.

In the old structure, speeches out of doors set before a wider audience the debate on the floor of the House of Commons, where British politics were made. Churchill first met the leaders of Parliament at his father's table: "It seemed a very great world in which these men lived; a world where high rules reigned and every trifle in public conduct counted: a duelling-ground where although the business might be ruthless, and the weapons loaded with ball, there was ceremonious personal courtesy and mutual respect." The young man was struck by the way that political opponents met socially for amicable conversation, and the contrast between the "incredibly fierce," "blunt or even savage things" that Lord Randolph said to his fellow parliamentarians in politics, where frankness was required for free debate, and the hospitality of the welcome he gave them at home (48). Similarly, Churchill marked wonderingly how some "rough interchanges" between his father and Sir William Harcourt in the House of Commons were immediately followed by Sir William's cordial greeting to his opponent's son in the gallery

(49).[8] Lord Randolph "said what he thought" in politics (62). He seemed to his son "to own the key to everything or almost everything worth having" (60). Aspiration to carry on his father's work certainly played its part in Churchill's study while his regiment was in India, when he asked his mother to send him the last hundred years of the *Annual Register,* a report of the proceedings of Parliament, so that he could study their debates, take notes, and form his own conclusions on past controversies in preparation for taking his place there.[9] Nor did this diligence cease after he became a member of Parliament. Churchill's official biography of his father, researched and written during his first term in the House of Commons, was not just a work of filial piety, but a sympathetic and searching investigation into British parliamentary government, preparing him for a place in the cabinet.[10]

The voters are susceptible to moments and moods. Churchill writes ruefully that "democracy does not favour continuity," and "the Englishman will not, except on great occasions, be denied the indulgence of kicking out the Ministers of the Crown whoever they are and of reversing their policy whatever it is" (235). He concludes that his father's career as a minister came to an end because England preferred repose to Lord Randolph's accustomed turbulence (60–62). He dismisses elections as "wearing clatter" (235). But when he took his seat in the House, "it was an honour to take part in the deliberations of this famous assembly which for centuries had guided England through numberless perils forward on the path of empire" (377). Churchill is more impressed with the opinion of the House of Commons. Britain's old constitution arranged her statesmen in a hierarchy, assigning to each a place according to the judgment of his fellow parliamentarians. "In those days," he writes, "the proceedings in the House of Commons were fully reported in the Press and closely followed by the electors. Crucial questions were often argued with sustained animation in three-day debates. During their course all the principal orators contended, and at their close the parties took decisive trials of strength" (377). Churchill lost no time in preparing his first speech, on the South African situation, which he knew well from recent experience in the war. He was advised by Henry Chaplin, "Don't be hurried; unfold your case. If you have anything to say, the House will listen" (378), and so it proved. Churchill concludes that the House of Commons "is always indulgent to those who are proud to be its servants" (380). The great respect he had for British parliamentary government arose from its ability to set the nation's course through free, full, and frank deliberation.

THE METHODS OF WAR

When Churchill was a boy, his father paid him "a formal visit of inspection" as he played with his toy soldiers, which numbered almost fifteen hundred.

Afterward Lord Randolph asked his son if he wanted to go into the army. Churchill said yes, and thenceforth it was decided. He passed the preliminary examination for the army class at Harrow School, which entailed drawing a map of a country, by picking New Zealand at random and learning its geography before the examination. It happened to be the country he had to draw; Churchill likens his luck to an *en plein* at Monte Carlo (33). For the entrance examination to Sandhurst, however, he needed more than luck. He finally had recourse to a "crammer" named Captain James, who gave his students "far more than a sporting chance." The captain trained them to answer the kind of questions the civil service commissioners were likely to ask:

> Captain James—if he had known it—was really the ingenious forerunner of the inventors of the artillery barrages of the Great War. He fired from carefully selected positions upon the areas which he knew must be tenanted by large bodies of enemy troops. He had only to fire a given number of shells per acre per hour to get his bag. He did not need to see the enemy soldiers. Drill was all he had to teach his gunners. Thus year by year for at least two decades he held the Blue Ribbon among the Crammers. He was like one of those people who have a sure system for breaking the Bank at Monte Carlo, with the important difference that in a great majority of cases his system produced success. (43)

But this method, as Churchill suggests, was ahead of its time. The methods of war current in his youth were more like his lucky hunch about New Zealand than the "system of intensive poultry-farming" perfected by Captain James (43). A change in "the methods of war" was the third element in the transformation described by Churchill in his preface.

At Sandhurst in the 1890s he learnt the "thrill and charm" of cavalry drill, leading up to the "joyous excitement" of the charge. Soon afterward, however, war flung cavalry aside "in its greedy, base, opportunist march" (78):

> War, which used to be cruel and magnificent, has now become cruel and squalid. In fact it has been completely spoilt. It is all the fault of Democracy and Science. From the moment that either of these meddlers and muddlers was allowed to take part in actual fighting, the doom of War was sealed. Instead of a small number of well-trained professionals championing their country's cause with ancient weapons and a beautiful intricacy of archaic manœuvre, sustained at every moment by the applause of their nation, we now have entire populations, including even women and children, pitted against one another in brutish mutual extermination, and only a set of blear-eyed clerks left to add up the butcher's bill. From the moment Democracy was admitted to, or rather forced itself upon the battlefield, War ceased to be a gentleman's game. (79)

Though none of these horrors had yet "broken upon mankind" when Churchill had his cavalry training with the Fourth Hussars at Aldershot (78), and war was still a gentleman's sport, he and his brother officers used to wonder what would happen to cavalry "if a half a dozen spoil-sports got themselves into a hole with a Maxim gun and kept their heads" (79). Churchill imagines that the honor of warfare might have been saved by a convention establishing equal national teams on the model of the Olympic games. But in the twentieth century war passed from "the hands of the experts and properly-trained persons who knew all about it" and became "a mere disgusting matter of Men, Money and Machinery." The result, Churchill recalls, was a "demoralisation" that caused military men to think "that the British Army would never again take part in a European conflict" (80). Officers at the Staff College were convinced that the world had become "so sensible and pacific—and so democratic too"—that future wars would be only against "savages and barbarous peoples"—or at best "the poor Indians" (58–59). Churchill remembers conversing with Sir William Beresford about the prospects for a renewal of war in Europe; the old sportsman and cavalry officer, who had served with distinction in several wars, declared "that there would never be another war between civilized peoples" (106). It was the usual Victorian expectation, ruefully shared by young officers who despaired of seeing "active service" (88–89). Yet a time would come, Churchill writes, "when the world got into far deeper waters" (106), for "the age of Peace had ended. There was to be no lack of war. There was to be enough for all. Aye, enough and to spare" (89).

What is missing from modern warfare is nobility, which comes from the old-fashioned prowess and bravery of fighting men. New technology is irresistible in its application to war, because a statesman has a responsibility to preserve his country. But when modern science can take the place of courage, success in war owes more to ingenuity than to virtue. Our author was acutely aware of this change when the Anglo-Egyptian armies fought the Dervishes in the Sudan in 1898: the Dervishes, he wrote, "were as brave men as ever walked the earth," but their spears had no chance against British machine guns.[11] In the scientific war between civilized countries in the twentieth century, the chances were more nearly equal, but the scope and reward for courage just as doubtful. Churchill recoiled from the wholesale mechanical slaughter of trench warfare in the First World War. Similarly, the man who had charged at Omdurman lamented the disappearance of horses from the battlefield. He considered horsemanship "one of the most important things in the world." No one who has read *My Early Life* can forget Churchill's paean to the equestrian art:

And here I say to parents, especially to wealthy parents, "Don't give your son money. As far as you can afford it, give him horses." No one ever came to grief—except honourable grief—through riding horses. No hour of life is lost that is spent in the saddle. Young men have often been ruined through owning horses, or through backing horses, but never through riding them; unless of course they break their necks, which, taken at a gallop, is a very good death to die. (59)

A twentieth-century cavalryman may feel a sort of affection for his tank, but that can hardly replace the close attachment between a mounted man and his horse. For a man who loved animals as much as Churchill did, the banishment of elephants from military life in India was also heart-rending. Elephants used to draw the cannon, saluting with their trunks as they passed on parade. Now they have been given way, he reports, to "clattering tractors drawing far larger and more destructive guns. Thus civilization advances. But I mourn the elephants and their salutations" (134).

THE OUTLOOK OF YOUTH

The young Churchill was encouraged by the favor and example of many older men. Later, by writing *My Early Life* and dedicating it "to a new generation," the seasoned adventurer was clearly seeking to pass on some of his own spirit to the young.[12] Churchill excelled in the spirited part of the soul. His teachers found him intractable at school: he tells us that "where my reason, imagination or interest were not engaged, I would not or I could not learn" (27). He and his friend Jack Milbanke discomfited their masters by resuscitating "an old custom" waiving required football during trial week, insisting on their right to study even if they did not carry it to ungentlemanly excess (54). When the eighteen-year-old Churchill was cornered on a bridge in a game of tag, with pursuers closing in from both ends, he confounded them by leaping twenty-nine feet into a chine, hoping to break his fall by embracing a fir tree on the way down; he sustained such serious injuries that "for a year [he] looked at life round a corner" (44). His decision to go into the army owed much to a youthful view "that it must be a thrilling and immense experience to hear the whistle of bullets all around and to play at hazard from moment to moment with death and wounds" (90). With his vivid imagination, the young Churchill often reflected on the risk of death, which figures in many of his earliest memories in the first chapter of *My Early Life*. As the story unfolds, he takes care to warn his reader against courting death unwittingly, remembering a misadventure far from shore on the lake by Lausanne, when the boat from which he and a friend were swimming was almost carried away by a strong breeze (51–52).

The fourth element in the transformation outlined by Churchill in his preface is the change in "the outlook of youth." Having embarked upon a military career, our author soon took the trouble of seeking out one of the rare places where peace did not obtain, hoping to make "a private rehearsal" of courage. So it was that in 1895 he and "a brother subaltern" climbed ashore in Cuba, where the Spaniards were trying to put down a rebellion (90). Churchill realizes that his readers may be hard put to appreciate his antici-pation of this adventure, but he tries to explain what he felt:

> The minds of this generation, exhausted, brutalised, mutilated and bored by War, may not understand the delicious yet tremulous sensation with which a young British Officer bred in the long peace approached for the first time an ac-tual theatre of operations. When first in the dim light of early morning I saw the shores of Cuba rise and define themselves from dark-blue horizons, I felt as if I sailed with Captain Silver and first gazed on Treasure Island. Here was a place where real things were going on. Here was a scene of vital action. Here was a place where anything might happen. Here was a place where something would certainly happen. Here I might leave my bones. (91)

A few days later, the young British officers rode into the jungle early in the morning with a Spanish column, expecting to make contact with the enemy at any moment. Churchill recalls their thoughts in *My Early Life:*

> We think that something is going to happen; we hope devoutly that something will happen; yet at the same time we do not want to be hurt or killed. What is it then that we do want? It is that lure of youth—adventure, and adventure for ad-venture's sake. You might call it tomfoolery. To travel thousands of miles with money one could ill afford, and get up at four o'clock in the morning in the hope of getting into a scrape in the company of perfect strangers, is certainly hardly a rational proceeding. Yet we knew there were very few subalterns in the British Army who would not have given a month's pay to sit in our saddles. (94)

Churchill was rewarded only a few days later by coming under hot fire: it happened to be on his twenty-first birthday. He came safely home from Cuba, but in the next few years saw active service on two more continents. Much the greatest part of his autobiography is given over to recounting these military adventures: in the Malakand country on the northwest Indian fron-tier he learnt to drink whisky and was mentioned in dispatches, on the upper Nile in the Sudan he quaffed champagne and charged with the cavalry at Omdurman, and in the South African veldt he became the toast of Britain by escaping from a Boer prison in Pretoria and making his way back to safety. Readers reared in peace and unaccustomed to danger may measure them-selves uncomfortably against the larger-than-life protagonist of this tale, wondering how it would be to live like Churchill.

No doubt our author meant to foster dissatisfaction with a humdrum life. He did not intend to be reckless: having suffered an injury to his shoulder, Churchill substituted a pistol for his sword in hand-to-hand fighting in the Sudan (204), and, when a Boer horseman demanded his surrender at gun-point after the wreck of his armored train, submitted because he had lost his pistol (266). Nor, despite doubts in quiet moments about the truth of Christ-

ian religion, was he unwilling to pray for divine help in adversity, or un-
grateful to receive it (129–30). But his autobiography ingeminates the excitement of an adventurous life: as he says of his adventures with the
Malakand Field Force, "it was all very exciting and, for those who did not get
killed or hurt, very jolly" (147). Churchill likens the world that opened to him
after he left Sandhurst to "Aladdin's cave" (73) and then, in his most memorable passage, reflects on those years of active service:

> When I look back upon them I cannot but return my sincere thanks to the high
> gods for the gift of existence. All the days were good and each day better than
> the other. Ups and downs, risks and journeys, but always the sense of motion,
> and the illusion of hope. Come on now all you young men, all over the world.
> You are needed more than ever now to fill the gap of a generation shorn by the
> War. You have not an hour to lose. You must take your places in life's fighting
> line. Twenty to twenty-five! These are the years! Don't be content with things as
> they are. "The earth is yours and the fulness thereof." Enter upon your inheri-
> tance, accept your responsibilities. Raise the glorious flags again, advance them
> upon the new enemies, who constantly gather upon the front of the human
> army, and have only to be assaulted to be overthrown. Don't take No for an an-
> swer. Never submit to failure. Do not be fobbed off with mere personal success
> or acceptance. You will make all kinds of mistakes; but as long as you are gen-
> erous and true, and also fierce, you cannot hurt the world or even seriously dis-
> tress her. She was made to be wooed and won by youth. She has lived and
> thrived only by repeated subjugations. (74)

If, in its last lines, Churchill's exhortation seems to resemble Machiavelli's advice on how to handle fortune,[13] what precedes them distinguishes his viewpoint from that of the insinuating Florentine—particularly his gratitude at the
beginning and his warning against "mere personal success." Churchill endeavors to encourage in a new generation a public-spirited devotion to Britain
and her empire, a great inheritance that will be theirs "to keep or cast away."[14]

THE SCALE OF VALUES

The final element on Churchill's list of changes that transformed the world is
the one whose meaning is least obvious: he calls it "the scale of values."
Some intelligence of his meaning may be gathered from the way he describes the outlook of British soldiers on the eve of the Battle of Omdurman:

> This kind of war was full of fascinating thrills. It was not like the Great War. No-
> body expected to be killed. Here and there in every regiment or battalion, half
> a dozen, a score, at the worst thirty or forty, would pay the forfeit; but to the
> great mass of those who took part in the little wars of Britain in those vanished
> light-hearted days, this was only a sporting element in a splendid game. . . .

Everything depends upon the scale of events. We young men who lay down to sleep that night within three miles of 60,000 well-armed fanatical Dervishes, expecting every moment their violent onset or inrush and sure of fighting at latest with the dawn—we may perhaps be pardoned if we thought we were at grips with real war. (195–96)

But the twentieth century brought "war where the hazards were reversed, where death was the general expectation and severe wounds were counted as lucky escapes, where whole brigades were shorn away under the steel flail of artillery and machine-guns, where the survivors of one tornado knew that they would certainly be consumed in the next or the next after that" (195). The effect of this change may be judged from Churchill's own experience: of his "many friends" at Sandhurst, no more than "three or four" survive: "The South African War accounted for a large proportion not only of my friends but of my company; and the Great War killed almost all the others" (73). This contrast of scale has its effect on opinions of our ability, by our choices and actions, to affect events. Victorian Britons, as described in Churchill's preface, were "very sure of themselves and of their doctrines," whereas the postwar generation reflected more "anxious and dubious times." The retreat of eminent leaders from twentieth-century democracy discouraged the idea that men could be found on the same scale as the problems they had to confront. At the same time, the experience of the Great War made men unsure whether the growing power of science would benefit or destroy them.

Churchill takes up these questions most thoroughly in *Thoughts and Adventures,* a book published in 1932;[15] but they also figure in his autobiography. In studying the understanding of politics that he offers there, one is constantly brought back to the contrast between the old world and the new that he makes the theme of the preface. "I wonder often," Churchill writes,

whether any other generation has seen such astounding revolutions of data and values as those through which we have lived. Scarcely anything material or established which I was brought up to believe was permanent and vital, has lasted. Everything I was sure or taught to be sure was impossible, has happened. (81)

The changes wrought by democracy and science might make men think that nothing in the world is fixed. Yet Churchill shows us that this is an exaggeration. He finds in human nature both the permanence and vitality to allow men happiness. He has "been happier every year since I became a man" (52), and he concludes his autobiography by telling us that in 1908 he "married and lived happily ever afterwards" (385).[16] Through striking portraits of men and women who helped him shape his own early life,[17] our author reminds readers that human beings can face the circumstances of their world with confidence, humor, and goodwill.

NOTES

1. Churchill writes in the preface, however, that "this tale lies" in a "quarter-century." He was born in 1874 and his earliest recollection is from 1878, so he means the last quarter of the nineteenth century. Later he calls 1895 to 1900 "the staple of this story": after four chapters on his schooling, the next two dozen chapters treat his adventures in those years. Although *My Early Life* concludes with his marriage as the proper end of his early life, only its concluding chapter takes up events after 1900, recounting the beginnings of his parliamentary career in 1901 and 1902 but leaping over the years before his wedding in September 1908. Thus Frederick Woods, editor of the Centenary Limited Edition of Churchill's writings in the 1970s, was almost right to claim that "the book covers his early years up to the moment when he was first elected to Parliament." To Winston S. Churchill, *My Early Life: A Roving Commission* (London: Thornton Butterworth Limited, 1930), 9, 15, 74, 384–85, hereinafter cited parenthetically by page number in the text, cf. Winston S. Churchill, *My Early Life,* ed. Frederick Woods (London: Library of Imperial History, 1973), 1.

2. For details of editions and translations, see Frederick Woods, *A Bibliography of the Works of Sir Winston Churchill,* 2d rev. ed. (Godalming, Surrey: St. Paul's Bibliographies, 1979), 60–64, and Richard M. Langworth, *A Connoisseur's Guide to the Books of Sir Winston Churchill* (London: Brassey's, 1998), 129–47. The current American edition is Winston Churchill, *My Early Life, 1874–1904* (New York: Simon & Schuster, 1996), with an introduction by William Manchester that reflects changes in public opinion since the book was written. The span of years newly attached to the title of this edition correctly places Churchill's birth in 1874, though he was born November 30, ten days later than Manchester has it (x), but there is no textual justification for a closing date of 1904.

3. Among other faults, the latest American edition of *My Early Life,* cited in the previous note, omits Churchill's dedication "to a new generation."

4. André Maurois, *Les Silences du Colonel Bramble* (Cambridge: Cambridge University Press, 1937), 1, 4 (my translation). Harvey Mansfield told me about this book. Compare Churchill's remark on the 1945 British general election in his war memoirs:

> Owing to the fact that the soldiers' votes must come home to be counted, a further twenty-one days had to elapse between the polling in the United Kingdom and the counting of votes and declaration of results. . . . In several Continental countries, when it was known that the ballot-boxes would be in charge of the British government for three weeks, astonishment was expressed that there could be any doubt about the result. However, in our country these matters are treated exactly as if they were a cricket match, or other sporting event. Long may it so continue.

Winston S. Churchill, *The Second World War,* 6 vols. (Boston: Houghton Mifflin, 1948–53), 6:519.

5. For a fuller account of Churchill's schooling, see my "'Backward and Precocious': Winston Churchill at School," *The World & I* 12.12 (December 1997): 290–317.

6. Churchill refers to "one of his most celebrated descriptions" (104), presumably that of the festival at "Deloraine House": see B[enjamin] Disraeli, *Sybil; or, The Two Nations,* 3 vols. (London: Henry Colburn, 1845), 3:86–98 [bk. V, chap. 7].

7. Churchill's dream in November 1947, first described to several of his children at dinner, was recorded with their encouragement in a "Private Article" found among his papers after his death and published as Winston S. Churchill, "The Dream," *Sunday Telegraph* (London), 30 Jan. 1966. It has been reprinted in Randolph S. Churchill and Martin Gilbert, *Winston S. Churchill,* 8 vols. and 15 companion vols. to date (London: Heinemann, 1966–), 8:364–72, and also published as a book, Winston S. Churchill, *The Dream* (United States: Churchill Literary Foundation, 1987).

8. How well Churchill learnt this lesson may be gathered, for instance, from Britain's declaration of war upon Japan on December 8, 1941. Criticized afterward for his "ceremonial style," he rejoined that "after all when you have to kill a man it costs nothing to be polite." See Churchill, *The Second World War,* 3:542–43.

9. Lady Randolph actually sent her son only twenty-seven volumes, which were still in the library of his family at Squerryes Lodge, with Churchill's handwritten notes, when Mrs. Minnie S. Churchill, Sir Winston's granddaughter-in-law, kindly arranged for me to see them in May 1998. In this, as in other things, Churchill's efforts were prodigious: imagine an aspiring American politician today resolving to read and annotate the last hundred years of the *Congressional Record* in anticipation of becoming a member of Congress!

10. Winston S. Churchill, *Lord Randolph Churchill,* 2 vols. (McMillan and Co.).

11. Winston Spencer Churchill, *The River War: An Historical Account of the Reconquest of the Soudan,* 2 vols. (London: Longmans, Green, and Co., 1899), 2:221.

12. Speculation about Churchill's intention in writing books, including *My Early Life,* has been dampened by many biographers' hasty attribution of his literary efforts to financial need, or by scholarly prejudice against books so well written by a man who never went to college. Though Churchill lived like a lord without inherited wealth and was able to support his family by his writing (which makes some writers envious), his remarkable shelfful of books owes more than has been recognized to his own curiosity, and to a generous wish to share with readers what he had learnt. See my "Churchill the Writer," *The Wilson Quarterly* 18.1 (winter 1994): 38–48, reprinted in a supplement entitled "Essays in Biography: The Best of the *WQ*" (1995): 23–33.

13. In *The Prince,* chap. 25.

14. Churchill pointed to the importance of this choice at the end of a new introduction to *The River War* penned in 1932. See Winston Churchill, *The River War: An Account of the Reconquest of the Soudan* (London: Eyre & Spottiswoode, 1933), ix–xi.

15. Winston S. Churchill, *Thoughts and Adventures* (London: Thornton Butterworth Limited, 1932), esp. 243–80; see also my "'A Kind of Dignity and Even Nobility': Winston Churchill's *Thoughts and Adventures,*" *The Political Science Reviewer* 16 (1986): 281–315.

16. See especially the biography of his marriage by Churchill's youngest daughter, Mary Soames, *Clementine Churchill* (London: Cassell, 1979), recently supplemented by Mary Soames, ed., *Speaking for Themselves: The Personal Letters of Winston and Clementine Churchill* (London: Doubleday, 1998).

17. He uses the same approach on a larger canvas in a book of brief lives published later in the decade: Winston S. Churchill, *Great Contemporaries* (London: Thornton Butterworth Ltd., 1937).

Publications by
Harvey C. Mansfield

BOOKS

Statesmanship and Party Government: A Study of Burke and Bolingbroke. Chicago: University of Chicago Press, 1965.

The Spirit of Liberalism. Cambridge, Mass.: Harvard University Press, 1978.

Machiavelli's New Modes and Orders: A Study of the Discourses on Livy. Ithaca, N.Y.: Cornell University Press, 1979.

Thomas Jefferson: Selected Writings. Editor, with introduction. Wheeling, Ill.: H. Davidson, 1979.

Selected Letters of Edmund Burke. Editor, with an introduction, "Burke's Theory of Political Practice." Chicago: University of Chicago Press, 1984.

The Prince, by Niccolò Machiavelli. Translator, with introduction. Chicago: University of Chicago Press, 1985. Second edition, with corrections and a glossary, 1998.

With Laura F. Banfield. *Florentine Histories,* by Niccolò Machiavelli. Translator, with introduction. Princeton, N.J.: Princeton University Press, 1988.

Taming the Prince: The Ambivalence of Modern Executive Power. New York: Free Press, 1989.

America's Constitutional Soul. Baltimore: Johns Hopkins University Press, 1991.

Machiavelli's Virtue. Chicago: University of Chicago Press, 1996.

With Nathan Tarcov. *Discourses on Livy,* by Niccolò Machiavelli. Translator, with introduction. Chicago: University of Chicago Press, 1996.

With Delba Winthrop. *Democracy in America,* by Alexis de Tocqueville. Translator, with introduction. Chicago: University of Chicago Press (forthcoming).

ACADEMIC ARTICLES AND REVIEWS

"Sir Lewis Namier Considered." *Journal of British Studies* 2 (1962): 28–55.

Review of *Dimensions of Freedom,* by Felix E. Oppenheim. *Journal of Politics* 24 (1962): 597–98.

"Party Government and the Settlement of 1688." *American Political Science Review* 58 (1964): 933–46.

"Rationality and Representation in Burke's 'Bristol Speech.'" In *Rational Decision,* edited by C. J. Friedrich, 197–216. *Nomos* 7. New York: Atherton Press, 1964.

"Sir Lewis Namier Again Considered." *Journal of British Studies* 3 (1964): 109–19.

Review of *Burke, Paine and the Rights of Man: A Difference of Political Opinion,* by R. R. Fennessy. *The Burke Newsletter* 6 (Spring 1965): 443–45.

"Whether Party Government Is Inevitable." *Political Science Quarterly* 80 (1965): 517–42.

Review of *The Tradition of Natural Law: A Philosopher's Reflections,* by Yves Simon. *The Burke Newsletter* 7 (Spring 1966): 598–601.

Review of *The Correspondence of Edmund Burke, Volume V: July 1782–June 1789,* edited by H. Furber. *Political Science Quarterly* 81 (1966): 673–74.

"Burke and Machiavelli on Principles in Politics." In *Edmund Burke: The Enlightenment and the Modern World,* edited by P. H. Stanlis, 49–79. Detroit, Mich.: University of Detroit Press, 1967.

Review of *Political Representation in England and the Origins of the American Republic,* by J. R. Pole. *Studies in Burke and His Time* 8 (1967): 793–99.

"Burke on Christianity." *Studies in Burke and His Time* 9 (1968): 864–65.

"Comment on Mr. Plumb's Paper." In *Man versus Society in Eighteenth–Century Britain,* edited by James Clifford, 135–38. London: Cambridge University Press, 1968.

"Impartial Representation." In *Representation and Misrepresentation,* edited by R. A. Goldwin, 91–114. Chicago: Rand McNally, 1968.

"Modern and Medieval Representation." In *Representation,* edited by J. R. Pennock and J. Chapman, 55–82. *Nomos* 11. New York: Atherton Press, 1968

Review of *Coleridge and the Idea of the Modern State,* by David P. Calleo. *Journal of Modern History* 40 (1968): 431–33.

Review of *The Growth of the British Party System,* by Ivor Bulmer–Thomas. *Political Science Quarterly* 83 (1968): 473–74.

"Bolingbroke, 1st Viscount," and "Burke, Edmund." In *Encyclopedia Americana* 4: 160, 793–95. New York: Americana Corporation, 1969.

Review of *The Concept of Representation,* by Hanna Pitkin. *Political Science Quarterly* 84 (1969): 678–80.

Review of *Politics and Experience,* edited by Preston King and B. C. Parekh. *Studies in Burke and His Time* 10 (1969): 1284–87.

"Disguised Liberalism." *Public Policy* 18 (1970): 605–19.

"Machiavelli's New Regime." *Italian Quarterly* 13 (1970): 63–95.

"Hobbes and the Science of Indirect Government." *American Political Science Review* 65 (1971): 97–110.

"Thomas Jefferson." In *American Political Thought,* edited by M. Frisch and R. Stevens, 23–50. New York: Scribner, 1971.

"Necessity in the Beginning of Cities." In *The Political Calculus: Essays in Machiavelli's Philosophy*, edited by A. Parel, 101–26. Toronto: University of Toronto Press, 1972.

"Party and Sect in Machiavelli's Florentine Histories." In *Machiavelli and the Nature of Political Thought*, edited by Martin Fleisher, 209–66. New York: Athenaeum, 1972.

"Sound Advice from Yale." *Polity* 5 (1972): 95–111.

Review of *Thomas Jefferson as Social Scientist*, by C. Randolph Benson, and *Thomas Jefferson: A Well-Tempered Mind*, by Carl Binger. *American Political Science Review* 67 (1973): 982–84.

Review of *Tribunato e resistenza*, by Pierangelo Catalano. *Journal of Modern History* 46 (March 1974): 129–31.

Review of *Studies on Machiavelli*, edited by M. Gilmore. *Renaissance Quarterly* 27, no. 3 (1974): 321–22.

Review of *Corruption, Conflict and Power in the Works and Times of Niccolò Machiavelli*, by Alfredo Bonadeo, and *Machiavelli and the Art of Renaissance History*, by Peter Bondanella. *Renaissance Quarterly* 28, no. 1 (1975): 68–70.

Review of *Polybius*, by F. W. Walbank. *Political Theory* 3 (1975): 232–34.

"Strauss's Machiavelli." *Political Theory* 3 (1975): 372–84.

"Reply to Pocock: An Exchange on Strauss's Machiavelli." *Political Theory* 3 (1975): 402–5.

"The Prestige of Public Employment." In *Public Employee Unions*, edited by A. L. Chickering, 35–50. San Francisco: Institute for Contemporary Studies, 1976.

"The Right of Revolution." *Daedalus* 105 (Fall 1976): 151–62.

Review of *The Social Thought of Rousseau and Burke: A Comparative Study*, by David Cameron. *Studies in Burke and His Time* 17 (Winter 1976): 64–68.

Review of *Thomas Hobbes in His Time*, edited by Ralph Ross, Herbert W. Schneider, and Theodore Waldman. *American Political Science Review* 71 (1977): 660–61.

Review of *The Machiavellian Moment: Florentine Political Thought and the Atlantic Republican Tradition*, by J. G. A. Pocock. *American Political Science Review* 71 (1977): 1151–52.

Review of *History: Choice and Commitment*, by Felix Gilbert. *Journal of Interdisciplinary History* 9 (Summer 1978): 156–58.

With Robert Scigliano. "Representation: The Perennial Issues." Pamphlet published by the American Political Science Association, 1978.

"The Media World and Democratic Representation." *Government and Opposition* 14 (1979): 318–34.

"On the Political Character of Property in Locke." In *Powers, Possessions and Freedom: Essays in Honour of C. B. MacPherson*, edited by A. Kontos, 23–38. Toronto: University of Toronto Press, 1979.

Review of *John Locke and the Theory of Sovereignty: Mixed Monarchy and the Right of Resistance in the Political Thought of the English Revolution*, by J. H. Franklin. *Review of Metaphysics* 32 (June 1979): 752–54.

Review of *Liberalism and the Modern Polity: Essays in Contemporary Political Theory*, edited by Michael J. Gargas McGrath. *American Political Science Review* 74 (1980): 172–73.

"Marx on Aristotle: Freedom, Money and Politics." *Review of Metaphysics* 34 (1980): 351–67.

Review of *Liberty and Property: Political Ideology in Eighteenth–Century Britain,* by H. T. Dickinson. *William and Mary Quarterly,* series 3, 37 (October 1980): 671–73.

Review of *The Idea of Historical Recurrence in Western Thought: From Antiquity to the Reformation,* by G. W. Trompf. *Review of Metaphysics* 34 (December 1980): 400–2.

"The Ambivalence of Executive Power." In *The Presidency in the Constitutional Order,* edited by J. Bessette and J. Tulis, 314–34. Baton Rouge: Louisiana State University Press, 1981.

"A Medley of 'Mediology.'" Review of *Le pouvoir intellectuel en France,* by Regis Debray. *Government and Opposition* 16 (1981): 254–57.

"Machiavelli's Political Science." *American Political Science Review* 75 (1981): 293–305.

Review of *The Quattrocento Dialogue: Classical Tradition and Humanist Innovation,* by D. Marsh. *Review of Metaphysics* 34 (June 1981): 794–95.

Preface to *Essays in Political Philosophy,* by J. E. Parsons Jr, vii–x. Washington, D.C.: University Press of America, 1982.

"The Anti–Power Ethic." Review of *American Politics: The Promise of Disharmony,* by Samuel P. Huntington. *Government and Opposition* 17 (1982): 362–69.

Review of *Dissidence et philosophie au moyen age: Dante et ses antecedents,* by Ernest L. Fortin. *American Political Science Review* 77 (1983): 270–1.

"On the Impersonality of the Modern State: A Comment on Machiavelli's Use of *Stato.*" *American Political Science Review* 77 (1983): 849–57.

Review of *The Practice of Political Authority,* by Richard Flathman. *Independent Journal of Philosophy* 4 (1983): 180–81.

Review of *Moral Philosophy at Seventeenth-Century Harvard: A Discipline in Transition,* by N. Fiering. *Review of Metaphysics* 37 (September 1983): 116–18.

"The Absent Executive in Aristotle's *Politics.*" In *Natural Right and Political Right,* edited by P. Schramm and T. Silver, 169–96. Durham: Carolina Academic Press, 1984.

"The Teaching of Citizenship." *PS: Political Science and Politics* 17 (Spring 1984): 211–15.

"Constitutionalism and the Rule of Law." *Harvard Journal of Law & Public Policy* 8 (1985): 323–26.

"How Dangerous Is Machiavelli?" Review of *Citizen Machiavelli,* by Mark Hulliung. *Review of Politics* 47 (1985): 298–300.

Preface to *The Government of Poland,* by Jean–Jacques Rousseau, translated by Willmoore Kendall, vii–viii. Indianapolis: Hackett, 1985.

"The Forms of Liberty." In *Democratic Capitalism? Essays in Search of a Concept,* edited by Fred E. Baumann, 1–21. Charlottesville: University Press of Virginia, 1986.

"The Constitution and Modern Social Science." *The Center Magazine* (September/October 1986): 42–53.

"Choice and Consent in the American Experiment." *The Intercollegiate Review* 2 (Spring 1987): 19–23.

"The Modern Doctrine of Executive Power." *Presidential Studies Quarterly* (Spring 1987): 237–52.

Comment on "Aristotle's *Polis:* A Community of the Virtuous," by Lloyd Gerson. In *Proceedings of the Boston Area Colloquium in Ancient Philosophy,* edited by J. Cleary, 226–28. Washington, D.C.: University Press of America, 1987.

"Edmund Burke." In *History of Political Philosophy*, edited by Leo Strauss and Joseph Cropsey, 3rd ed., 687–709. Chicago: University of Chicago Press, 1987.

"Hobbes on Liberty and Executive Power." In *Lives, Liberties and the Public Good*, edited by G. Feaver and F. Rosen, 27–43. London: Macmillan Press, 1987.

"The Religious Issue and the Origin of Modern Constitutionalism." In *How Does the Constitution Protect Religious Freedom?*, edited by Robert A. Goldwin and Art Kaufman, 1–14. Washington, D.C.: American Enterprise Institute, 1987.

"Republicanizing the Executive." In *Saving the Revolution: The Federalist Papers and the American Founding*, edited by Charles R. Kesler, 168–84. New York: Free Press, 1987.

"Constitutional Fideism." Review of *Constitutional Faith*, by Sanford Levinson. *Yale Journal of Law and the Humanities* 1 (1988): 181–86.

"Machiavelli and the Modern Executive." In *Understanding the Political Spirit*, edited by Catherine H. Zuckert, 88–110. New Haven, Conn.: Yale University Press, 1988.

"Representative Government and Executive Power." In *Economy, Diplomacy and Statecraft: Three Lectures on the Bicentennial of the United States Constitution. Colorado College Studies* 27 (1988): 25–36.

"The Revival of Constitutionalism." In *The Revival of Constitutionalism*, edited by James W. Muller, 214–27. Lincoln: University of Nebraska Press, 1989.

"Social Science and the Constitution." In *Confronting the Constitution*, edited by Allan Bloom, 411–36. Washington, D.C.: American Enterprise Institute Press, 1990.

"Between the New Deal and the Reagan Revolution." Review of *Congress, the President, and Public Policy*, by Michael Mezey. *Government and Opposition* 24 (1991): 278–80.

Introduction to *Machiavel, L'art de la guerre*. Paris: Flammarion, 1991.

Review of *The Counter-Reformation Prince: Anti-Machiavellianism or Catholic Statecraft in Early Modern Europe*, by Robert Bireley. *American Historical Review* 97 (February 1992): 182.

Review of *Equality Transformed: A Quarter-Century of Affirmative Action*, by Herman Belz. *Journal of Interdisciplinary History* 23 (1992): 423–25.

"Executive Power and the Passion for Virtue." In *Studies in American Political Development* 6 (1992): 217–22.

"Human Rights in Emergencies." *Critical Review* 6, no. 4 (1992): 575–85.

"Political Parties and American Constitutionalism." In *American Political Parties and Constitutional Politics*, edited by Peter W. Schramm and Bradford P. Wilson, 1–16. Lanham, Md.: Rowman and Littlefield, 1992.

Foreword to *Priests as Physicians of Souls in Marsilius of Padua's "Defensor Pacis,"* by Stephen F. Torraco. San Francisco: Mellen Research University Press, 1992.

"Tough Times for the President." Review of *The Beleaguered Presidency*, by Aaron Wildavsky. *Review of Politics* 54 (1992): 680–82.

"The Great Edmund Burke." Review of *The Great Melody*, by Conor Cruise O'Brien. *The New Criterion* 10 (November 1992): 8–11.

Review of *Machiavelli in Hell*, by Sebastian de Grazia, and *The Machiavellian Cosmos*, by Anthony J. Parel. *American Political Science Review* 87 (1993): 764–65.

"Professional Education and the Examined Life: Defining Terms." In *Technology and Responsibility*, edited by Athanasios Moulakis, 1–9. Boulder, Colo.: College of Engineering and Applied Science, 1993.

"Returning to the Founders: The Debate on the Constitution." Review of *The Debate on the Constitution,* edited by Bernard Bailyn. *The New Criterion* 11 (Sept. 1993): 48–54.

"The Silence of a Mechanism." Review of *The Silence of Constitutions; Laws, Men, and Machines;* and *American Political Ideas,* all by Michael Foley. *Government and Opposition* 28 (1993): 126–29.

"Responsibility and Its Perversions." In *Individualism and Social Responsibility,* edited by W. Lawson Taitte, 79–99. Austin: University of Texas Press, 1994. Also published in French in *Démocraties, l'identité incertaine,* edited by Chantal Millon-Delsol and Jean Roy, 112–20. Bourg-en-Bresse: Musnier-Gilbert, 1994.

"Responsible Citizenship Ancient and Modern." A pamphlet containing the 1994 Kritikos lecture. Eugene: University of Oregon Press, 1994.

"The Unfinished Revolution." In *Three Beginnings: Revolution, Rights, and the Liberal State,* edited by Stephen F. Englehart and John Allphin Moore Jr., 9–30. New York: Peter Lang, 1994. Reprinted in *The Legacy of the French Revolution,* edited by Ralph C. Hancock and L. Gary Lambert, 19–41. Lanham, Md.: Rowman & Littlefield, 1996.

"Friends and Founders." Review of *The Republic of Letters: The Correspondence between Thomas Jefferson and James Madison,* edited by James Morton Smith. *The New Criterion* 13 (May 1995): 69–72.

"Democracy and Populism." *Society* 32 (July/August 1995): 30–32. Reprinted in *A New Moment in the Americas,* edited by Robert S. Leiken, 27–30. New Brunswick, N.J.: Transaction Publishers, 1995.

"Machiavelli and the Idea of Progress." In *History and the Idea of Progress,* edited by Arthur Melzer, Jerry Weinberger and Richard Zinman, 61–74. Ithaca, N.Y.: Cornell University Press, 1995.

"Political Theory as Historical Artifact." Review of *The Descent of Political Theory,* by John G. Gunnell. *Review of Politics* 57 (1995): 372–74.

"Self–Interest Rightly Understood." *Political Theory* 23 (1995): 48–66.

"The Twofold Meaning of *Unum.*" In *Reinventing the American People,* edited by Robert Royal, 103–13. Grand Rapids, Mich.: William B. Eerdmans, 1995.

"Passions et intérêts." In *Dictionnaire de Philosophie Politique,* edited by Philippe Raynaud and Stéphane Rials, 453–57. Paris: Presses Universitaires de France, 1996.

Foreword to *Tocqueville and the Nature of Democracy,* by Pierre Manent. English translation. Lanham, Md.: Rowman & Littlefield, 1996.

"The Formal Constitution: A Comment on Sotorios A. Barber." *The American Journal of Jurisprudence* 42 (1997): 187–89.

"The Legacy of the Late Sixties." In *Reassessing the Sixties,* edited by Stephen Macedo, 21–45. New York: W. W. Norton, 1997.

Foreword to *No Liberty for License,* by David Lowenthal. Dallas: Spence Pub., 1997.

Foreword to *Piety and Humanity,* edited by Douglas Kries. Lanham, Md.: Rowman & Littlefield, 1997.

"Some Doubts about Feminism." *Government and Opposition* 32 (1997): 291–300.

"Virilité et libéralisme." *Archives de philosophie du droit* 41 (1997): 25–42.

Review of *Athenian Democracy: Modern Mythmakers and Ancient Theorists,* by Arlene Saxonhouse. *American Political Science Review* 92 (1998): 449–50.

With Delba Winthrop. "Liberalism and Big Government: Tocqueville's Analysis." In *Tyranny and Liberty*, 1–31. London: Institute of United States Studies, 1999.
Review of *Machiavelli*, by Maurizio Viroli. *American Political Science Review* 93 (1999): 964–65.
Introduction to *The Opium of the Intellectuals*, by Raymond Aron. New Brunswick, N.J.: Transaction Publishers, 2000.

POLITICAL WRITINGS

"Defending Liberalism." *The Alternative: An American Spectator* 7 (April 1974): 5–9.
"Liberal Democracy as a Mixed Regime." *The Alternative: An American Spectator* 8 (June 1975): 8–12.
"The American Election: Towards Constitutional Democracy?" *Government and Opposition* 16 (1981): 3–18.
"The American Congressional Election." *Government and Opposition* 18 (1983): 144–56.
"The Forms and Formalities of Liberty." *The Public Interest*, no. 70 (Winter 1983): 121–31.
"The Underhandedness of Affirmative Action." *National Review*, 4 May 1984, 26–34.
"The American Election: Entitlements versus Opportunity." *Government and Opposition* 20 (1985): 3–17.
With Delba Winthrop. "A Summer Seminar on 'The American Experiment.'" *This Constitution*, no. 9 (1985): 34–37.
"Affirmative Action versus the Constitution." In *A Melting Pot or a Nation of Minorities*, edited by W. Lawson Taitte, 91–110. Richardson, Tex.: University of Texas at Dallas, 1986.
"Gouvernement représentatif et pouvoir exécutif." *Commentaire* 9 (Winter 1986–87): 664–72.
"The Partisan Historian." Review of *The Cycles of American History*, by Arthur Schlesinger. *The American Spectator*, February 1987: 38–39.
"Pride versus Interest in American Conservatism Today." *Government and Opposition* 22 (1987): 194–205.
"Debating Liberal Education." *The Harvard Salient*, Commencement 1987, 10.
"Beauty and the Beast." Review of *Men and Marriage*, by George Gilder. *Policy Review*, Winter 1987, 76–78.
"Constitutional Government: The Soul of Modern Democracy." *Public Interest*, no. 86 (Winter 1987): 53–64.
"Straussianism, Democracy and Allan Bloom, II: Democracy and the Great Books." *The New Republic*, 4 April 1988: 33–37. Also published in French as "La Démocratie et les Grands Livres." *Commentaire* 11 (Summer 1988): 492–96.
"Harrington's Long Road Is, at Last, Not a Lonely One." Review of *The Long-Distance Runner: An Autobiography*, by Michael Harrington. *Washington Times*, 29 August 1988: D7.
"The American Election: Another Reagan Triumph." *Government and Opposition* 24 (1989): 28–38.
"Le libéralisme et la vertu." *Commentaire* 12 (Winter 1989–90): 682–83.

"The State of Harvard." Review of *The University: An Owner's Manual,* by Henry Rosovsky. *Public Interest,* no. 101 (Fall 1990): 113–23.

"Dewey, All-Out Democrat." Review of *John Dewey and American Democracy,* by Robert B. Westbrook. *Times Literary Supplement,* 24 January 1992: 26.

"The Vision Thing." *Times Literary Supplement,* 7 February 1992: 3–4.

"When the People Have Spoken." Review of *We the People,* by Bruce Ackerman. *Times Literary Supplement,* 24 April 1992: 8.

"Is America on the Way Down?" A symposium. *Commentary,* May 1992: 23–24.

"Only Amend." *The New Republic,* 6 July 1992: 13–14.

"Change and Bill Clinton." *Times Literary Supplement,* 13 November 1992: 14–15.

"Harvey C. Mansfield, Jr., The Question of Conservatism." Interview in *The Harvard Review of Philosophy* 3 (Spring 1993): 30–47.

"A Debatable Fusion." Review of *The Shaping of American Liberalism,* by David F. Ericson. *Times Literary Supplement,* 23 July 1993: 26.

"Teaching in the Age of Sensitive Speech." In *Confidential Guide to Courses at Harvard-Radcliffe 1993–94,* 178. Cambridge, Mass.: Harvard Crimson, 1993.

"Liberalism in the Emperor's New Clothes." Review of *Sexy Dressing, Etc.,* by Duncan Kennedy. *The Boston Book Review* (Spring 1994): 9.

"Equality and Comfort." Review of *Liberty, Justice, Order,* by John Morton Blum. *Times Literary Supplement,* 10 June 1994: 13.

"Why Equality Is Ridiculous." Review of *In Defense of Elitism,* by William A. Henry III. *Wall Street Journal,* 6 September 1994: A10.

"Foolish Cosmopolitanism." Reply to Martha Nussbaum. *Boston Review,* October/November 1994: 10.

"Newt, Take Note: Populism Poses Its Own Dangers." *Wall Street Journal,* 1 November 1994: A20.

"Toward Liberalism, Capitalism—and Sanity." Review of *New French Thought: Political Philosophy,* edited by Mark Lilla. *Wall Street Journal,* 21 December 1994: A12.

"Hero or Anti-Hero: In the Ring with Professor Harvey Mansfield." Interview in *Boston Impact* (Spring 1995): 21–22.

"Un entretien avec Harvey C. Mansfield." *Le Monde,* 10 April 1995: 12.

"Real Change in the USA." *Government and Opposition* 30 (1995): 35–47.

"Veritas." In *The National Endowments: A Critical Symposium,* edited by L. Jarvik, H. London, and J. Cooper, 13–15. Los Angeles: The Center for the Study of Popular Culture, 1995.

"A Gay Makes His Case." Review of *Virtually Normal,* by Andrew Sullivan. *Wall Street Journal,* 31 August 1995: A7.

"Look, No Tocqueville!" Review of *The Next American Nation,* by Michael Lind. *The National Interest,* no. 41 (Fall 1995): 99–102.

"The National Prospect." A Symposium. *Commentary,* November 1995: 85–86.

"Enlightenment Supporter Sees a Dark Future for Democracy." Review of *On the Eve of the Millennium: The Future of Democracy through an Age of Unreason,* by Conor Cruise O'Brien. *Washington Times,* 10 December 1995: B8.

"Was It Really a Myth? The Persistence of Individualism in America." *Times Literary Supplement,* 9 February 1996: 7.

"Less Means Less: The Second Coming of American Conservatism." Review of *Dead Right,* by David Frum. *Times Literary Supplement,* 10 February 1996: 7.

"An Idea and Its Consequences." Review of *Neoconservatism: The Autobiography of an Idea,* by Irving Kristol. *National Review,* 12 February 1996: 27–28.

"A Powerful Friend." *Reader's Digest,* February 1996, 6.

"Paterfamilias." Review of *Founding Father: Rediscovering George Washington,* by Richard Brookhiser. *The New Criterion* 14 (March 1996): 62–65.

"A Great-Books Junior College." In a symposium titled "Nineteen Great Ideas for Repairing Civic Life." *Policy Review,* March/April 1996: 23.

"Harvard Loves Diversity." *The Weekly Standard,* 25 March 1996: 27–29.

"Re–politicizing American Politics." *The Weekly Standard,* 29 July 1996: 24–26.

"Bring Back Respectability." In a symposium titled "What One Thing Could We Do Now to Improve the Livability of Our Cities, Towns and Suburbs?" *The American Enterprise,* November/December 1996: 67–68.

"The Unprincipled Majority." Review of *Freedom's Law,* by Ronald Dworkin, *Times Literary Supplement,* 6 December 1996: 8.

"The Tragedy of Max Weber." Review of *Max Weber: Politics and the Spirit of Tragedy,* by John Patrick Diggins. *The Weekly Standard,* 9 December 1996: 33–37.

"The Election of 1996." *The American Enterprise,* January/February 1997: 28–31.

"Karl Popper." *Panorama,* 16 January 1997: 91.

"Platonici e Reaganiani: Lobby con Filosofia." *Panorama,* 27 March 1997: 121.

"Ancient or Modern." Review of *Machiavelli's Three Romes,* by Vickie Sullivan. *Times Literary Supplement,* 11 April 1997: 30.

"Backlash: The Trouble with Feminism." Review of *Women and the Common Life,* by Christopher Lasch. *The Weekly Standard,* 14 April 1997, 31–33.

"Loveless Liberation." *The American Enterprise,* May/June 1997: 13–14.

"Gentlemen's Gentlemen: Edmund Burke's Critique of Theory." *Times Literary Supplement,* 11 July 1997: 15.

"The Virtues of C–SPAN." *The American Enterprise,* September/October 1997: 46.

"Men of Principle." Review of *Vindicating the Founders,* by Thomas West. *Wall Street Journal,* 31 October 1997: A20.

"Why a Woman Can't Be More Like a Man." *Wall Street Journal,* 3 November 1997: A22.

"The City of Manent." Review of *The City of Man,* by Pierre Manent. *The Weekly Standard,* 15 June 1998: 31–33.

"The Partial Eclipse of Manliness." *Times Literary Supplement,* 17 July 1998: 14–15.

"Politiquement Correct," *Commentaire* 21 (Fall 1998): 617–28.

"Why a Good Man Is Hard to Find." *The Women's Quarterly,* no. 17 (Autumn 1998): 4–6.

"A Nation of Consenting Adults." *The Weekly Standard,* 16 November 1998: 35–37.

"Defending Propriety." In a symposium titled "Acquitted." *The Weekly Standard,* 22 February 1999: 24–26.

"Whatever Happened to Skepticism?" Review of *New Federalist Papers,* by Alan Brinkley, Nelson W. Polsby, and Kathleen M. Sullivan, and *The Reopening of the American Mind,* by James W. Vice. *Times Literary Supplement,* 26 February 1999: 11–12.

"Consulting Old Nick." Review of *Machiavelli on Modern Leadership,* by Michael Ledeen, and *The New Prince,* by Dick Morris. *Wall Street Journal,* 10 June 1999: A24.

Response to Francis Fukuyama's "Second Thoughts." *The National Interest,* no. 56 (Summer 1999): 34–35.

"Naturally Proud." Review of *The Great Disruption,* by Francis Fukuyama. *Times Literary Supplement,* 16 July 1999: 12.

"The Trouble with Stanley." Review of *The Trouble with Principle,* by Stanley Fish. National Review, 7 February 2000: 46–48.

Name Index

Adair, Douglas, 220
Adams, Henry, 191n10
Adams, John, 221
Altmeyer, Arthur, 258
Aristophanes, 72n10
Aristotle, xi, 3, 17, 20–24, 28nn4–6, 29n12, 51, 63–64, 67, 102, 110n2, 119, 131, 142–75, 210, 217n17, 233, 271, 273–80, 284, 288n9
Augustine, 271, 276, 280, 288n7

Bacon, Francis, 62–73, 165
Bailyn, Bernard, 197
Ball, Robert, 258
Bayle, Pierre, 91–99
Bazelon, David, 255
Beresford, William, 299
Blackstone, William, 203
Bonaparte, Napoleon, 112, 186
Brennan, William, 254
Brierly, J. L., 182
Burke, Edmund, 197, 246, 250
Bush, George, 138

Cambon, Paul, 294
Carter, Jimmy, 242, 243
Chamberlain, Joseph, 295
Chaplin, Henry, 297

Churchill, John (Duke of Marlborough), 294
Churchill, Randolph, 294–98
Churchill, Winston, 291–305
Cicero, 165
Cleland, Scott, 268
Clinton, Bill, xii, 219, 243, 264
Cohen, Wilbur, 258
Coke, Edward, 195
Conklin, James C., 237
Constantine, 36

Davis, Jefferson, 234
Declaration of Independence, 137, 179–81, 184, 185, 188, 189–90, 192–93, 197–202, 206–7, 209, 238–40, 259
Democritus, 50
Derthick, Martha, 258
Descartes, 165
Diderot, Denis, 101
Dole, Robert, 219, 264
Duane, James, 220

Epicurus, 95
Erasmus, 74
Ericson, Edward, 275, 282
Essex, Earl of, 75

317

Subject Index

republican government, xi–xii, 121–23,
    131–40, 142–75, 186, 188–90,
    197–200, 205–18, 219–32, 270–90.
    See constitutionalism
responsibility, xi, xii, 3, 9–10, 11–15,
    136, 212, 215, 219–32, 249,
    251–53, 270, 271, 274, 277, 280,
    284

separation of powers, 121, 156–58, 210,
    219–32, 235, 249, 255, 264–69

spiritedness, xii, 14, 18–29, 135, 138,
    150, 151, 153, 207, 210, 213, 233–45,
    250, 293, 299, 300, 302
statesmanship, xi, xii, 15, 100–110, 153,
    186, 230, 233–45, 249, 259, 260,
    261n13, 291–305

Virtue, xi, xii, 3–17, 21, 23–27, 36–37,
    81–85, 108–9, 130, 142–75, 210,
    211–14, 224, 227–28, 230, 238–44,
    260

About the Contributors

Mark Blitz is Fletcher Jones Professor of Political Philosophy, chair of the Department of Government, and director of research at Claremont McKenna College. He has taught at Harvard University and the University of Pennsylvania and has served as associate director of the United States Information Agency and as a senior professional staff member of the Senate Committee on Foreign Relations. He is the author of *Heidegger's* Being and Time *and the Possibility of Political Philosophy* and of numerous articles on political philosophy and public affairs.

Paul A. Cantor is professor of English at the University of Virginia. He is the author of several books on Shakespeare, as well as of *Creature and Creator: Myth-Making and English Romanticism*. He has taught at Harvard University and has served on the National Council on the Humanities.

David F. Epstein is deputy director of net assessment, U.S. Department of Defense. He is the author of *The Political Theory of* The Federalist and of other works in political philosophy.

John P. Gibbons, since completing undergraduate and graduate work at Harvard, where he wrote his Ph.D. thesis on Marsilius of Padua, has worked in a variety of financial services firms, serving most recently as chief financial officer at Freddie Mac.

Ralph C. Hancock is professor of political science at Brigham Young University. He is the author of *Calvin and the Foundations of Modern Politics* and editor of *The Legacy of the French Revolution* and *America, the West, and Liberal Education*. He is currently working on the problem of theory and practice in Leo Strauss, ethical postmodernism, and Tocqueville.

Charles R. Kesler is professor of government and director of the Henry Salvatori Center at Claremont McKenna College. He has written extensively on American politics and political thought. His new edition of *The Federalist Papers* is published by Penguin Putnam, Inc.

Jessica Korn is the founding editor in chief of the *Gallup Management Journal*. Prior to teaching as an adjunct professor at Columbia Business School, she worked on the Telecommunications Act of 1996 as the lead telecommunications policy analyst in the office of Senator Pete V. Domenici (R-N.M.).

Robert P. Kraynak is professor of political science at Colgate University. He is the author of *History and Modernity in the Thought of Thomas Hobbes* and of the forthcoming *Christian Faith and Modern Democracy*

William Kristol is editor and publisher of *The Weekly Standard*. He served as chief of staff to Vice President Dan Quayle during the Bush administration, and to Secretary of Education William Bennett under President Reagan. He taught politics at the University of Pennsylvania and Harvard, and coedited *The Neoconservative Imagination: Essays in Honor of Irving Kristol.*

R. Shep Melnick is Thomas P. O'Neill Jr. Professor of American Politics at Boston College and cochair of the Harvard Program on Constitutional Government. He is the author of *Regulation and the Courts: The Case of the Clean Air Act* and *Between the Lines: Interpreting Welfare Rights* and coeditor of *Taking Stock: American Government in the Twentieth Century.*

Arthur Melzer is professor of political science at Michigan State University and codirector of the university's Symposium on Science, Reason, and Modern Democracy. He is the author of *The Natural Goodness of Man: On the System of Rousseau's Thought* and coeditor of *Multiculturalism and American Democracy* and *The Problem of Technology in the Western Tradition.*

Peter Minowitz is associate professor at Santa Clara University in California, where he served as chair of the Political Science Department and is codirector of the Environmental Studies Institute. In addition to his book on Adam Smith (*Profits, Priests, & Princes*), he has published articles on Machiavelli, Marx, Leo Strauss, Frank Herbert, and Woody Allen. He is currently writing a book about diversity, multiculturalism, and affirmative action in Jesuit universities.

James W. Muller is professor of political science at the University of Alaska, Anchorage, and academic chairman of the Churchill Center, Washington, D.C. He is editor of *The Revival of Constitutionalism; Churchill as Peacemaker, Churchill's "Iron Curtain" Speech Fifty Years Later,* and a forthcoming new edition of Winston S. Churchill, *The River War: An Historical Account of the Reconquest of the Soudan.*

Clifford Orwin is professor of political science at the University of Toronto. His major work to date is *The Humanity of Thucydides.* His current projects include a series of articles on Rousseau, a study of the political thought of Flavius Josephus, and a book on the politics of compassion.

Jeremy Rabkin teaches constitutional law and international law in the Department of Government at Cornell University. His most recent book is *Why Sovereignty Matters.*

Susan Meld Shell is a professor of political science at Boston College. She is the author of *The Rights of Reason: A Study of Kant's Philosophy and Politics, The Embodiment of Reason: Kant on Spirit, Generation and Community,* and articles on Machiavelli, Rousseau, German Idealism, and American political thought.

James R. Stoner Jr. is associate professor and director of graduate studies in political science at Louisiana State University. He is the author of *Common Law and Liberal Theory: Coke, Hobbes, and the Origins of American Constitutionalism* and of several essays on the common-law dimension of American constitutional law.

Nathan Tarcov is a professor in the Committee on Social Thought, the Department of Political Science, and the College at the University of Chicago. He has also taught at Harvard University and has served on the policy planning staff of the Department of State. He is the author of *Locke's Education for Liberty,* editor and translator with Harvey C. Mansfield of *Machiavelli's Discourses on Livy,* and editor with Clifford Orwin of *The Legacy of Rousseau.*

Glen E. Thurow is provost and professor of government at the University of Dallas. He is the author of *Abraham Lincoln and the American Political Religion* and of other works in political philosophy and public affairs.

Jerry Weinberger is professor and chair of the Department of Political Science at Michigan State University. He has published books on the political philosophy of Francis Bacon and is currently at work on separate studies of Benjamin Franklin and Martin Heidegger.

Kenneth R. Weinstein is senior fellow and director of the Washington office of the Hudson Institute. His wrote his Ph.D. thesis on Pierre Bayle and has published articles on topics in political philosophy and public affairs.